THE LITERACY SPECIALIST

Also Available

Best Practices of Literacy Leaders,
Second Edition: Keys to School Improvement
*Edited by Allison Swan Dagen
and Rita M. Bean*

The Literacy Specialist

LEADERSHIP AND COACHING FOR THE CLASSROOM, SCHOOL, AND COMMUNITY

FOURTH EDITION

Rita M. Bean
Virginia J. Goatley

THE GUILFORD PRESS
New York   London

Copyright © 2021 The Guilford Press
A Division of Guilford Publications, Inc.
370 Seventh Avenue, Suite 1200, New York, NY 10001
www.guilford.com

Printed in the United States of America

This book is printed on acid-free paper.

Last digit is print number: 9   8   7   6   5   4   3   2

Library of Congress Cataloging-in-Publication Data

Names: Bean, Rita M., author. | Goatley, Virginia J., author.
Title: The literacy specialist : leadership and coaching for the classroom,
    school, and community / Rita M. Bean, Virginia J. Goatley.
Other titles: Reading specialist
Description: Fourth edition. | New York : The Guilford Press, [2021] |
    Revised edition of: The reading specialist, c2015. | Includes
    bibliographical references and index. |
Identifiers: LCCN 2020040891 | ISBN 9781462544608 (hardcover) | ISBN
    9781462544554 (paperback)
Subjects: LCSH: Reading teachers—United States. | Reading—Remedial
    teaching—United States.
Classification: LCC LB2844.1.R4 B43 2021 | DDC 428.4071/2—dc23
LC record available at *https://lccn.loc.gov/2020040891*

About the Authors

Rita M. Bean, PhD, is Professor Emerita in the School of Education at the University of Pittsburgh, where she served as director of the Reading Center for 25 years. Prior to joining the university, she taught at the elementary school level and also served as a reading supervisor for grades K–12. Dr. Bean has developed elementary and middle school reading curriculum materials and has published numerous articles and book chapters on reading curriculum, assessment and instruction in reading, professional learning, and the role of reading specialists and literacy coaches. She served as a researcher on several large grants, including Reading First in Pennsylvania and Pennsylvania's Striving Readers Comprehensive Literacy Grant. She is a member of the Reading Hall of Fame and a former board member of the International Literacy Association (ILA), and served as chair of the ILA's Commission on the Role of the Reading Specialist. Dr. Bean also served as co-chair of the ILA committee that developed the *Standards for the Preparation of Literacy Professionals 2017.* She is a recipient of the University of Pittsburgh's Chancellor's Distinguished Teaching Award and Distinguished Service Award for her community and outreach efforts in improving literacy. Dr. Bean has also received awards from the Keystone State Reading Association, the Association of Literacy Educators and Researchers, the ILA, and the Pennsylvania branch of the International Dyslexia Association.

Virginia J. Goatley, PhD, is Interim Dean of the School of Education and Professor in the Department of Literacy Teaching and Learning at the University at Albany, State University of New York. A former elementary teacher, she has collaborated on several federal research grants focusing on teacher preparation and professional development that supports effective literacy classroom practice. Dr. Goatley is a regular participant in national and statewide efforts for teacher education and preparation of literacy professionals. She served as coeditor of the *Journal of Literacy Research*, a board member for the Association for Advancing Quality in Educator Preparation, co-chair of the New York State Professional Standards and Practices Board for Teaching, and lead writer for the ILA committee that developed the *Standards for the Preparation of Literacy Professionals 2017*. Dr. Goatley is a recipient of the Albert J. Kingston Service Award from the Literacy Research Association, the President's Excellence in Faculty Academic Service Award from the University at Albany, and the Council Service Award from the New York State Reading Association.

Preface

The Literacy Specialist is written for the many literacy specialists, literacy coaches, and other educational leaders working in schools to improve both the literacy performance of individual students and the effectiveness of literacy programs for all students. It is also written for those individuals who are enrolled in programs preparing them to become literacy specialists or literacy coaches.

In this fourth edition of the book, there are two significant changes that contribute some new and unique perspectives about the role of the literacy specialist. First, Virginia (Ginny) Goatley, a new coauthor, brings her expertise in teaching candidates in literacy specialist programs and her research findings to this new edition. Second, the revised title—from *The Reading Specialist* to *The Literacy Specialist*—acknowledges what we have learned about how to improve the reading and writing of students, especially those experiencing difficulty with literacy. Although reading instruction is a clear responsibility for literacy specialists, they also have "responsibilities for oral language development, writing, digital and multiple literacies, visual literacy, and the power of literacy learning to change lives" (International Literacy Association [ILA], 2018a, p. xi).

The two of us have enjoyed our writing partnership and believe that our various perspectives have made this fourth edition a special one. As indicated in the book's subtitle, we have three primary goals:

1. To provide information and ideas that inform prospective and current literacy professionals about leadership and its importance to their success in schools.
2. To provide insights into leadership roles and responsibilities, from

teaching students to collaborating with teachers to addressing larger systemic issues, such as designing curriculum or developing a community partnership program.

3. To provide practical ideas and resources that help literacy professionals effectively perform their roles at the student, teacher, and system levels.

We build on the framework established in the first three editions, using current research and knowledge in the field to address important educational issues. The book identifies and describes the many roles that administrators ask literacy specialists (in grades PreK–12) to fulfill. We believe literacy specialists will be able to use this book as a quick resource when a question or issue arises. The book can also be used as a textbook for those enrolled in literacy specialist or literacy coaching programs. Likewise, those involved in professional learning experiences designed to build leadership skills will find the book helpful, as will coaches involved in working with teachers, individually or in groups.

The book continues to focus on the many important responsibilities of literacy specialists. The major changes and additions to the fourth edition include the following:

- *A new framework.* In Chapter 1, we introduce a new framework for thinking about the role of the literacy specialist. Using the ILA *Standards for the Preparation of Literacy Professionals 2017* (ILA, 2018a), we highlight the instructional role. At the same time, literacy specialists will also have responsibilities for working to some extent with teachers and also for addressing systemic or organizational issues. Regardless of the focus (student, teacher, or system), literacy specialists will need the leadership, interpersonal, and communication skills to collaborate effectively with other educators. As a result of ongoing research about the ways that literacy specialists and coaches function in schools, and related research about shared and teacher leadership in schools, we emphasize the importance of leadership across all roles and responsibilities. Those responsible for supporting the work of teachers have leadership responsibilities, as do those who deliver instruction to students. When developing family or community involvement programs, leadership is necessary. Developing curriculum or facilitating school change also requires leadership.

- *An emphasis on standards.* Given the state-level adoptions of more rigorous high-level standards for students that emphasize the importance of preparing students to be future-ready, we use examples throughout the book to discuss ways literacy specialists can collaborate with teachers to develop and implement instruction aligned with the demands of these literacy standards. In Chapter 8, there is an extensive section in which we present a framework for developing a comprehensive literacy program.

• *Pam, a case example.* We introduce Pam, a literacy specialist, in each chapter to provide a case example of one literacy specialist, from the time she accepts a position in a school to the completion of her first year. We hope readers will be able to identify with Pam, the dilemmas she faces, and the ways in which she addresses those challenges.

• *Multi-tiered systems of support/response to intervention (MTSS/ RTI).* Although the third edition addressed RTI, in this fourth edition, we describe the broader notion of MTSS/RTI and update information about its importance to literacy specialists. This federal initiative has affected the role of literacy specialists, not only in how they teach students but also in how specialists support and collaborate with teachers, helping them to differentiate their instruction. In this edition, there is more information about MTSS/RTI, defining it and describing what literacy specialists can do to assist in the implementation of programs and procedures that help school personnel differentiate instruction for students. We also discuss in more depth how classroom data can be used for instructional decision making.

• *Diversity, equity, and the need for culturally relevant instruction.* Given the changing populations in our schools, we provide additional research and ideas to help readers think about how to effectively teach and reach all students and to address the "opportunity gap" (Darling-Hammond, 2013, 2014–2015) that exists for many (e.g., English learners, students with special needs). We expand on the opportunities for educators to collaborate with families and community members to increase understandings of and practices for culturally relevant and responsive teaching.

• *Technological issues.* We also include more updated information about how technology has influenced the learning of both students and teachers. Drawing on updated research and instructional information, we share ideas about using technology in the classroom for literacy practices and to improve communication across schools and community. Given the effects of the COVID-19 pandemic, many teachers have become facilitators of remote education. In this book, we highlight ways that literacy specialists and coaches can enhance teachers' capacity with such teaching.

While we have made changes as indicated above, we have also kept some features from previous editions. These include:

• *Key Questions and Additional Readings.* We updated the key questions at the beginning of each chapter to help the reader think about the focus of the chapter. At the end of each chapter, we suggest additional readings, briefly summarized, that extend the information in the chapter, including a brief summary of each resource. We have typically referred to those articles in the chapter, and follow-up reading can assist in developing a deeper understanding of the concepts. Instructors may wish to use the suggested readings for out-of-class assignments.

• *An emphasis on middle and high school literacy programs.* In this edition, there is even more emphasis on adolescent literacy and how literacy specialists working at middle and high school levels can function effectively. In several chapters, there are specific sections that address adolescent literacy. Often these sections focus on supporting content-area teaching and disciplinary literacy. In Chapter 3, there is a description of the instructional role of the literacy specialist at the middle and high school levels, and in Chapter 9 we discuss assessment at those levels. In Chapter 8, we present information about secondary-level literacy programs. Further, there are several vignettes that provide descriptive information about how literacy specialists and literacy coaches function in their schools.

• *Literacy coaching.* Current information about literacy coaching is included in Chapters 6 and 7. We provide a framework for thinking about coaching and discuss important aspects of each of the elements of that framework. We describe ideas for "getting started," as well as suggestions for coaching individual and groups of teachers. This edition also includes specific forms or tools that coaches can use as they visit classrooms.

Certain other features of the previous editions also remain, given feedback from readers:

• *"Think about This"*—a set of questions in each chapter to stimulate thinking about the various issues discussed.

• *Reflections*—a set of questions at the conclusion of each chapter to provide opportunities for self-reflection or group discussion.

• *Follow-up activities*—suggested activities, listed at the end of each chapter, to use in a study group setting or in a course.

• *Ideas for course or workshop instructors.* There are activities in Appendix F for use with graduate students or with practitioners in professional learning workshops. We hope those who use the text for teaching a course or a series of workshops will find this section helpful.

• *Vignettes.* Written by practicing literacy specialists who represent the high caliber of exemplary specialists working in schools, the vignettes bring to life the excitement, passion, and commitment of these dedicated professionals. Throughout the book, we refer to these vignettes in sections titled "Voices from the Field," identifying specific ways that these professionals address the topic being discussed (e.g., Celia discusses how she leads efforts to develop a new integrated literacy program for the schools in her district). With the exception of the Voices from the Field authors, we use pseudonyms for all teachers and students.

From the early days of our careers, we have been interested and involved in areas of research and teaching that relate to the role of the literacy specialist. This book is based on our experiences as literacy professionals, critically invested in practices to meet the needs of students and teachers (PreK–12). In addition, it is based on our many interactions through the years with others faced with similar challenges. Many of the recommendations and ideas in this book come from our research and from the interactions we have had with our graduate students, literacy specialists, and literacy coaches in the field.

As mentioned previously, we have had the opportunity to prepare reading specialists, now literacy specialists, for many years. These literacy specialists have taught us a great deal. They have shared their experiences in schools working with readers and writers experiencing difficulties and with teachers to improve the literacy program. We have endeavored to make their voices heard in this book.

The field is a dynamic one; the work of literacy specialists has never been more important, given the emphasis on literacy as a key to future success. It is our hope that this book will serve as a resource for literacy specialists, enabling them to provide the leadership essential for developing effective literacy programs and addressing key questions or issues as they strive to improve student literacy learning in schools.

Acknowledgments

We have been fortunate to work with colleagues in schools and universities across the country who are also committed to improving literacy instruction for students in grades PreK–12. These colleagues have influenced our thinking about the role of the literacy specialist and coach.

Rita: I mention only a few here, acknowledging that there are many more who have profoundly influenced my work. Naomi Zigmond, a friend and colleague at the University of Pittsburgh, with whom I have conducted research for many years, has challenged my thinking and helped me to think more broadly about students experiencing difficulties with reading and writing and how to help them succeed. Likewise, I have been fortunate to work with and learn from Isabel Beck, who has conducted cutting-edge research on reading instruction. Many thanks to my mentor, Robert Wilson, Professor Emeritus, University of Maryland, with whom I coauthored a text highlighting the importance of the leadership and resource role of reading specialists, *Effecting Change in School Reading Programs: The Resource Role* (Bean & Wilson, 1981). Certainly, we have learned a great deal about the leadership role since then, but many of the ideas in that text have withstood the test of time.

Members of the International Literacy Association (ILA; formerly the International Reading Association [IRA]) committees on which I have served have influenced my thinking about the roles of the reading specialist: the IRA Commission established in the late 1990s; IRA's Specialized Literacy Professionals Special Interest Group that conducted a national survey of specialized literacy professionals in 2015; and the ILA Standards 2017 Committee. During meetings, committee members raised important issues, alternative views, and ideas for how the role of the reading specialist/literacy coach might be defined and prepared.

I am especially grateful to my family for their support and encouragement. Thank you, Erin Eichelberger; Derek and Barbie Eichelberger; and my grandchildren, Ethan, Ava, and Dylan, who share their school experiences with me and keep me grounded! And finally, many thanks to Tony Eichelberger, my husband and best friend, for his encouragement, critical reading, and constant reminder that there is a need for the messages that this book conveys.

Ginny: There are many colleagues from my Michigan State University doctoral program and my 25 years at the University at Albany, State University of New York, who have influenced my thinking about literacy instruction and teaching preparation. With my current faculty colleagues, the professional conversations, debates, and plans that advocate for change are always important to me and to our programs/research. I focus on a small group of colleagues who have helped me think directly about literacy specialists and coaches. With her dedication and commitment to teacher preparation, Cheryl Dozier continually influences my thinking about the role of elementary-level literacy professionals in connection to families, school systems, and responsive coaching. In our grant and policy work together, Donna Scanlon helps push my thinking and understanding about the content of literacy instruction and how to best prepare teachers to have the core knowledge they need for teaching young children. Many thanks to Taffy Raphael, my advisor (and coach!) at Michigan State, for encouraging me to enter the doctoral program and then supporting my navigation through many wonderful opportunities throughout my career.

I am fortunate to be involved with many committees, panels, and organizations that continually engage me and the field in conversations about literacy teaching and coaching. These include the many literacy professional colleagues associated with the Albany City Area Reading Council, New York State Reading Association, Literacy Research Association, and International Literacy Association, who are always striving to use and improve best literacy practices with children. I am especially appreciative of the ILA 2017 Standards Committee and the Association for Advancing Quality in Educator Preparation and the many critical conversations involved in revising the standards for literacy and teacher preparation.

Finally, I thank my family and friends for their support and encouragement. I have learned much about literacy instruction from my many nieces and nephews living in states across the country and the world, including the practices and policies of various schools, writing examples, and reading progress. A special "thank you" to Anne House for always making literacy a part of my life from an early age to the present—with much appreciation for the books, book discussions, text messages, and many other models of literacy on an ongoing basis.

The students in our graduate programs and our literacy specialist/coach colleagues had a profound impact on the contents of this book. We have learned much from these individuals, not only about what they do in order to be successful in their role, but also about the questions and concerns that they have about their positions and how to best serve the students, teachers, and administrators in their schools. Their passion for and commitment to their work has served as a source of inspiration for us.

We want to thank Celia Banks, Mark Beck, Katy Carroll, Mike Henry, Katie Regner, and Joy Stephens for their important contributions in writing the vignettes. Also, many thanks to Christina Glance, a reading specialist in West Virginia and a doctoral student at West Virginia University, for permitting us to include her work. Much appreciation to Erin Faeth and Allison Gentle, doctoral students at the University at Albany, who provided assistance with references. At The Guilford Press, we are thankful for Chris Jennison, who initiated the need for this book, and Craig Thomas, who continues to guide and support subsequent editions.

Contents

CHAPTER ONE

The Role of Literacy Professionals in Schools, Classrooms, and Communities

KEY QUESTIONS •

- Why and how has the role of the literacy specialist evolved in recent years? In what ways has it remained the same? What policies and practices influenced this change?

- What are the multiple roles and responsibilities of literacy specialists in today's schools and how are they enacted?

- Why has there been a shift from the term *reading specialist* to *literacy specialist*?

- What contextual factors are currently affecting the role of the literacy specialist?

Much has been learned about how to teach literacy to all students, yet the evidence is clear: There continue to be students in schools at all levels (PreK–12) who are not learning to read or write effectively or who are reading or writing below grade-level expectations. Indeed, the results of the 2019 National Assessment of Educational Progress (Nation's Report Card, 2019) revealed that only 35% of fourth graders and 34% of eighth graders were proficient in reading, indicating that we must continue our efforts to improve student literacy learning. Across the United States, legislators and policymakers, those in the business community, parents, and educators alike have searched for ways to address this dilemma. The federal government has invested in large-scale programs such as Head Start, Reading

First (a professional development initiative of No Child Left Behind [U.S. Department of Education, 2002]), Race to the Top (American Recovery and Reinvestment Act, 2009), the Every Student Succeeds Act (ESSA; U.S. Department of Education, 2015), and other school improvement programs to support literacy instruction. These federal initiatives as well as others developed by states or local districts require that teachers have an in-depth understanding of how to teach literacy.

In order to reach the goals of these various initiatives, schools required literacy specialists to have dual roles: to teach students who have difficulty with literacy and to provide mentoring support to classroom teachers so that all students are successful. The instructional role of the literacy specialist is an important one given it increases the opportunity for students to receive appropriate and differentiated instruction. The leadership role in which literacy specialists work with classroom teachers has been evolving, especially since the early 2000s, with many schools hiring literacy or reading coaches to partner with teachers as a means of improving classroom instruction and enhancing student learning.

Yet the dual role of the literacy specialist is not a new one. As cited in Hall (2004), "the concept of literacy coaching dates back to the 1920's—but they are increasingly in demand in 21st century schools" (p. 11). In 1981, Bean and Wilson, in their book *Effecting Change in School Reading Programs: The Resource Role,* wrote about the need for reading specialists to work as partners with teachers, parents, and administrators, and that "this partnership must be based on mutual trust and respect" (p. 7). In 1998, Snow, Burns, and Griffin reinforced this stance, stating, "every school should have access to specialists . . . reading specialists who have specialized training related to addressing reading difficulties and who can give guidance to classroom teachers" (p. 333). Moreover, the position statement of the International Reading Association (IRA, 2000; now the International Literacy Association [ILA]) on the role of the reading specialist called for such a dual role. It is this dual role that is addressed in this book. This role requires literacy specialists to have expertise with literacy assessment and instruction and to possess the leadership skills that enable them to work with other adults, such as classroom teachers, other professionals (e.g., speech and language teachers, special educators), and the community (e.g., parents, volunteers, universities, community agencies).

Throughout this book, we use the case example of Pam during her first year as a literacy specialist to explore the challenges and opportunities for literacy teaching. In this chapter, we start with her job interview.

Pam was excited about her upcoming interview with a curriculum director at a local school. She was applying for a position as a literacy specialist in one of the elementary schools in the district. Pam looked again at the written description of the position: reading specialist certification required; able to administer literacy assessment tests and analyze results with teachers; plan and implement instruction for students identified as needing Tier 2 instruction; serve as a resource for teachers and support their instruction. Well, she had successfully completed her reading specialist certification program and she had a good understanding of how to assess and then to work with students needing supplemental literacy instruction. She had just finished a course on being a literacy leader, but she was still hesitant about this aspect of the position. With only 3 years of teaching experience, she wasn't sure how she would work with more experienced teachers. She was friendly and had a good sense of humor! Would that be enough?

In this case example, Pam, as a new literacy specialist, recognizes that she will need more than a knowledge and understanding of literacy instruction to be effective in her role. She will need the leadership skills that enable her to work collaboratively with and support her colleagues in their efforts to provide excellent literacy instruction for all students. As you read this book, you will learn more about what skills, knowledge, and dispositions Pam needs to be successful in her role as a literacy specialist. As indicated in the preface, we have three goals for this book:

1. To provide information and ideas that inform prospective and current literacy professionals about leadership and its importance to their success in schools.
2. To provide insights into the leadership role and responsibilities, from teaching students to working with teachers, to addressing larger systemic issues, such as designing curriculum or developing a community partnership program.
3. To provide practical ideas and resources that help literacy professionals effectively perform their role at the student, teacher, and system levels.

What makes the position of literacy specialist an exciting, complex, and challenging one are the opportunities to work with multiple stakeholders who have different needs and perspectives about literacy instruction, assessment, and about the role of the literacy specialist itself. We begin our leadership journey by taking a look at the evolution of this role of reading (literacy) specialist. Although in later chapters, we use the term literacy specialist, in this chapter, we use the terms interchangeably, using the term reading specialist when discussing the history of the role or describing research in which researchers used the term reading specialist.

WHERE WE WERE: THE EVOLUTION OF THE ROLE

Those who don't know history are doomed to repeat it.
    —EDMUND BURKE, 18th-century Irish statesman
        and philosopher

We believe that an understanding of how the role has evolved can be useful to those now seeking to serve as literacy specialists. Educators have learned a great deal about what works—and what doesn't work—for literacy instruction and for the various roles of literacy educators. As you read this section, think about what you see in schools today. What similarities are there in how literacy specialists function in today's schools and how they served in the past?

The presence of specialists in schools dates back to the 1930s when they functioned as supervisors who worked with teachers to improve the reading program. In 1940, Dolch called for schools to employ remedial reading specialists to work with students experiencing reading difficulties, but it was after World War II, in response to criticism of the schools and their inability to teach children to read, that remedial reading teachers became fixtures in many schools, public and private, elementary through secondary. The primary responsibility of the specialist was to work with individuals or small groups of children who were experiencing difficulty in learning to read. Briggs and Coulter (1977) stated, "Like Topsy, these remedial reading services just 'growed,' aided and abetted by government at all levels and by private foundations quick to provide grants of funding for such programs" (p. 216). IRA (1968), in its *Guidelines for Reading Specialists,* strongly supported the remedial role: Five of the six functions described for the "special teacher of reading" related directly to instructional responsibilities. However, there were those educators who began to see the difficulty of reading specialists serving only an instructional capacity. Stauffer (1967) described the remedial role as one of working in a "bottomless pit" and supported the notion of reading specialists serving as consultants.

Support for reading specialists serving in multiple roles continued throughout the next several decades. As previously mentioned, Bean and Wilson (1981) emphasized the importance of interpersonal, leadership, and communication skills for those in reading specialist positions. Their book in many ways was a call for professionals who might serve as literacy coaches, although they did not use that term (Hall, 2004). In 1998, Snow, Burns, and Griffin reinforced the stance of a dual role, stating, "every school should have access to specialists . . . reading specialists who have specialized training related to addressing reading difficulties and who can give guidance to classroom teachers" (p. 333). Moreover, the position statement of the IRA (2000) on the role of the reading specialist called for such a dual role. This role requires reading specialists to have expertise with reading assessment and instruction and to possess the leadership skills that enable them to work with other adults, such as classroom teachers, other professionals, and the community. Below we address several factors that have been responsible for defining the role of reading specialists, including the source of funding that provided support for these specialized professionals and research that contributed to new ideas about literacy assessment, instruction, and the roles of reading specialists.

Policy and Its Influence on the Role of Reading/Literacy Specialists

In 1965, Title I of the Elementary and Secondary Education Act (Public Law No. 89-10) provided large-scale funding to provide supplemental support to students identified as economically deprived. In the initial conceptualization of this program, policies and procedures were developed to ensure that only eligible students were receiving support provided by this funding stream. Moreover, they were to be taught by reading specialists who had the necessary credentials to work with them. Materials and other resources purchased with Title 1 funds were to be used by these eligible students only. Such policies led to what is commonly referred to as "pullout" programs; that is, large, separate, and distinct programs for designated students. By separating the Title I program and its resources from the general school program, it was easier for school personnel to maintain fiscal compliance. However, these pullout programs generated many problems. Often, there was little congruence or alignment between the classroom program and the supplemental program, so students with reading difficulties who could least handle this lack of alignment, received two different programs, with no "bridges" to connect them. Some reading specialists were not knowledgeable about the instruction that students were receiving in their classrooms (Allington, 1986; Slavin, 1987), nor did they share what they were doing with the classroom teachers! Moreover, when students who received Title I services returned to their classrooms, they were frequently asked to learn from materials that were too difficult for them or to use strategies or skills different from those they were learning in their pullout program. Another problem was that, too often, students in these supplemental programs spent their time doing workbook-type, skill-related activities. There was little opportunity to read nor was there much direct instruction (Allington & McGill-Franzen, 1989; Bean, Cooley, Eichelberger, Lazar, & Zigmond, 1991). And some classroom teachers seemed to think that the reading specialists had sole responsibility for teaching these students to read, even though the Elementary and Secondary Education Act (1965) identified the instruction provided by the specialists as *supplemental*.

At the same time, teachers resented the "swinging-door" dimension of pullout programs; their instruction was interrupted by students coming into and going out of their classrooms. This feeling is illustrated in an article from a newsletter published by a teachers' organization:

> Over the past few months I've been noticing that my class has been quietly disappearing. They leave one by one, or in small groups. They come late due to dentist appointments and leave early for eye exams. They are being remediated, enriched, guided, weighed, and measured. They are leaving me to learn to speak English, pass the TELLS test, increase sight vocabulary, develop meaningful relationships, and to be PEP'd or BEEP'd.
>
> They slip in and out with such frequency that I rarely have my whole class together for any length of time on any given day. I don't know when to schedule a test anymore. I've considered administering them during lunch when I'm on cafeteria duty—but then again the "packers" aren't sitting with the "buyers"—so we are still not all together.
>
> One day I accidentally had the whole class in my room. As soon as I discovered it, I quickly gave them their language pretest and posttest! If it ever happens again, they're getting their final exam.
>
> When the office calls for one of my students, I try to be fair about it. My policy is—if they can find them, they can have them. I find you can get one small advantage from all this coming and going, if you work it right. You seat your talkative kids in between the frequent remedials and half the time they'll be next to empty desks.
>
> I am learning to deal with the disappearances. I teach in bits and pieces to parts of the whole. But you can help me out, if you will. If you ever run into any of my meandering students, say "hi" for me—and take them over their timetables please. (Shaler Area Education Association, 1986, p. 3)

Another problem was the stigma associated with leaving the classroom; students were viewed by their peers as being dumb or different, creating a lack of self-esteem in these students. Also, Allington (1986) and others were concerned that pullout programs that provided minimal reading instruction (i.e., 35–40 minutes, several times a week) did not address the serious needs of students.

The results of large-scale evaluations of Chapter 1 or Title I were not always positive, although Borman and D'Agostine (2001), in their meta-analysis of Title I program effects, indicated that "there has been a positive trend for the educational effectiveness of Title I across the years of its operation" (p. 49). They contended that, without these services, students would have fallen further behind academically. The evaluation of Title I has been difficult because it is essentially a funding program, not one that requires specific instructional foci, and there are many variations in the ways that it has been implemented in districts across this nation. At the same time, the great expectation for Title I—that it closes the achievement gap between at-risk, poor students and their more advantaged peers—has not been met.

In 1988, new federal legislation (e.g., Hawkins–Stafford Elementary and Secondary School Improvement Act) and research literature recommended many changes. These changes included recommendations for additional collaboration with classroom teachers and special educators and more emphasis on programs in which reading specialists worked in the classrooms with teachers. Further, schools with large numbers of Title 1 students were also eligible to receive schoolwide funding, which meant that reading specialists could work with all students in that school, rather than only with those who were targeted for Title 1 services. These policy changes influenced the role of reading specialists, making it essential that they be able to work well with their teaching colleagues. Although this movement generated more interaction between teachers and reading specialists, it was not always a "marriage made in heaven"; both partners had to learn to work collaboratively in new and different ways (we address this issue further in Chapter 2).

Two other large-scale policy initiatives had a great influence on how reading specialists worked. First was the reauthorization of the Elementary and Secondary Education Act, with the passage of the No Child Left Behind Act (NCLB, 2001) and its programmatic arm, Reading First. Reading First emphasized the importance of increasing teacher knowledge and understanding of reading instruction. Given the focus on providing job-embedded support for teachers, districts employed reading coaches to work directly with teachers. Often reading specialists, who may not have been prepared to handle these coaching responsibilities, were assigned to function in this role, leading to great variation in how these newly assigned coaches functioned in schools. Deussen, Coskie, Robinson, and Autio (2007) found that on average coaches spent only 28% of their time working with teachers, although they had been asked to spend 60–80% of their time with them. During this time period, the major function of many reading specialists shifted from that of teaching to that of coaching.

The second major initiative was response to intervention (RTI), which was created through the reauthorization of the Individuals with Disabilities Education Act (IDEA, 2004); the goal of RTI was to reduce the numbers of students identified for special education by providing early identification of needs and immediate intervention. This initiative called for a multilevel model for differentiation (i.e., a tiered framework) and for additional, specialized instruction beyond that provided by classroom teachers. Teachers known as *interventionists* were to provide these services. Again, this legislation affected the role of reading specialists who were now being asked to develop and implement "Tier 2" instruction and often given a new title, that of interventionist.

In 2015, Congress reauthorized the Elementary and Secondary Education Act of 1965 with passage of the Every Student Succeeds Act (ESSA; U.S. Department of Education, 2015). The ESSA regulations provide states with flexibility in how they structure their Title 1 programs. Each state submitted a plan describing both long-term and interim goals, with a requirement for indicators of the accountability system (e.g., proficiency on tests, English language proficiency, graduation rates). The ILA (2016a) published an overview toolkit featuring an analysis of ESSA's implications for literacy instruction, including changes impacting funding for schools, new requirements, and links to resources.

Changes in Literacy Assessment and Instruction

Although policy initiatives had a great effect on the role of reading special-ists, changes in knowledge and beliefs about assessment and instruction also created shifts in the role. In the early days of Title I programs, read-ing specialists carefully documented the reading achievement and reading expectancy of students who might be eligible for compensatory services. School districts calculated reading expectancy or potential in various ways, from obtaining the intelligence quotients of students to administering lis-tening comprehension tests, or sometimes using teacher judgments. Only those students who were identified as "discrepant"—that is, their literacy test performance revealed a gap between achievement and potential—were assigned to receive reading services. With growing recognition of (1) the limitations inherent in scores achieved on intelligence and standardized tests and (2) possible test bias in identifying students, regulations elimi-nated the use of a discrepancy formula, and students were identified based on their actual reading achievement.

The criticism of standardized testing also led to the identification of new indicators of success for students and Title I programs, with a pri-mary emphasis on how well students performed on "authentic" measures and indicators of success in the classroom such as grades in subject areas. Schools, therefore, found themselves in the position of creating their own measures, identifying what they wanted students to know and be able to do at various grade levels. And, often, reading specialists found themselves in the position of working with classroom teachers to develop such instru-ments.

Likewise, changes in reading instruction influenced the work of read-ing specialists. As mentioned previously, Allington and McGill-Franzen (1989; Bean et al., 1991), who studied Chapter 1 programs, found that reading specialists often spent their time using "skill-and-drill" methods. Students completed worksheets or participated in specialized programs that emphasized skill instruction. Students spent little time reading! Yet research evidence and theorists in the field were advocating the teaching of more explicit reading strategies, authentic experiences that provided increased opportunities for students to engage actively in reading and writ-ing tasks.

These changes as well as the results of Title I evaluations led to a period in the 1990s when school districts eliminated or downsized the number of reading specialists in their schools. One reading specialist summarized the situation as follows:

> Our grant from Title I is substantial; yet rather than use the expertise of reading specialists in the district's reading program, the number of specialists has dropped in the last several years from 14 to 4. Reading specialists have been assigned to classroom teaching positions or have not been replaced from attrition. Blame for dropping reading scores has been laid at the Title I door; reading specialists are an expensive liability. Reading specialists are being replaced with many, many inexpensive aides. (personal communication from an anonymous reading specialist to Rita Bean, May 1991)

Various programs and strategies were implemented to address the problems of students experiencing literacy difficulties: improving classroom teaching practices, reducing class size, using technology in the classrooms, adding after-school and summer programs, and employing volunteers and aides to work with students. None of these strategies, though they can be somewhat beneficial, seemed to produce the desired results.

Role of IRA in Evolution of the Specialist Role

In 1995, the IRA (now the ILA), recognizing that its members had concerns about these multiple interpretations of the role of reading specialists, established a commission to investigate the role and status of reading specialists in schools. The commission was given two tasks: (1) analyze the literature and research about the role of the specialist, and (2) conduct a survey of members to determine the actual responsibilities of reading specialists. That work was reported in two articles found in *The Reading Teacher* (Bean, Cassidy, Grumet, Shelton, & Wallis, 2002; Quatroche, Bean, & Hamilton, 2001). The work resulted in a position statement: *Teaching All Children to Read: The Roles of the Reading Specialist* (IRA, 2000). Because of the many changes in the role of reading specialists in the decade from 2002 to 2012, that national survey was replicated in 2015, although one difference in the 2015 survey was that we were able to differentiate responsibilities of various literacy professionals (reading specialists, interventionist/reading teachers, literacy coaches, and supervisors). Below, we summarize in more depth the findings of the 2015 study and compare it with the earlier study.

Comparison of the National Surveys of Reading Specialists

There is an old expression: "The more things change, the more they remain the same." However, in this instance, although there were some similarities in the roles of reading specialists, there were also differences in responses to the two surveys. Survey results were similar in the following ways. First, in both surveys (Bean, Cassidy, et al., 2002; Bean, Kern, et al., 2015) respondents tended to be white and female; they were also experienced educators, with most having served as classroom teachers before accepting reading specialist positions. Second, respondents to both surveys indicated that they have dual roles: They instruct students and they also support teachers in providing instruction for students. Third, reading specialists continued to work in both classrooms and in pullout settings, with 40% in the 2015 study indicating that they taught exclusively in pullout settings. Fourth, reading specialists have an important role in administering and analyzing assessment results, and in assisting teachers in using those results for instructional decision making. Finally, the percentage of reading specialists overall serving at the secondary level was still small.

However, there were several differences in responses to the two surveys. First, the word *coaching* was never mentioned in the 2002 survey. In the 2002 study, about 84% of respondents indicated that they served as a resource to teachers (e.g., providing materials and ideas for instruction). In the 2015 study, 89% of the reading specialists supported teachers, but that support included more than providing ideas and materials. Rather these specialists were involved in initiatives such as RTI and they were more involved in helping teachers use data to inform classroom instruction. There were also differences between reading specialists and coaches in how they described their roles. The primary foci of coaches were planning and conferring with teachers, observing, conducting workshops, and modeling lessons. Specialists on the other hand, were involved in leadership activities such as serving on RTI teams, planning and conferring with teachers, and co-teaching, but not as frequently as coaches.

Second, there was also more of a focus on collaborative work, not only with teachers but with other reading specialists and with other specialized professionals (e.g., special educators, librarians, counselors, psychologists). In fact, two key findings in the 2015 study were that (1) there tended to be more than one reading specialist in the school, and they generally worked collaboratively with each other, and (2) they were not the sole reading instructor for the students with whom they worked. These two findings strongly suggest that reading specialists must understand how to effectively collaborate with not only teachers, but other allied professionals, and administrators.

Third, although the percentage of respondents in both surveys who worked at the secondary level was similar, a larger percentage of respondents in the 2015 survey who served in secondary schools self-identified as coaches rather than reading specialists. These professionals were responsible for supporting teachers' instructional efforts.

Fourth, most respondents in the 2015 study indicated they had multiple roles; that is, they taught students, supported teachers, led professional learning efforts, and so on. It was clear, also, that their positions were subject to change depending on funding, district initiative, changes in leadership or school demographics, and so forth. Such a finding requires literacy professionals to be nimble and able to adapt quickly and thoughtfully to meet the demands of their new roles and responsibilities. And again, reading specialists must possess the communication, interpersonal, and leadership skills that enable them to work with others to respond to changing environments, culture, and student needs.

Finally, respondents across all groups indicated they would be better prepared if they had more educational experiences enabling them to assume leadership responsibilities in the school. Such leadership included the ability to work effectively with adults, both individually and in groups, and to facilitate and lead the development of the literacy program. These findings from the 2015 survey have implications for the content in this book that focuses on the leadership role of reading specialists—not only with teachers and other specialized personnel in the schools but with administrators, families, community leaders, and agencies.

One of the disturbing findings of both the 2002 and the 2015 surveys was the virtual absence of men and people of color among the reading specialist population, a problematic finding given the importance of role models for the diverse students in schools today. The increased numbers of literacy coaches at the secondary level seems to reflect the growing emphasis on disciplinary literacy as reflected in standards being developed by the states and also as exemplified in the Common Core State Standards (CCSS; National Governors Association Center for Best Practices & Council of Chief State School Officers [NGA & CCSO], 2010).

The Value of Reading Specialists in Schools

To accomplish their charges, the commission established by the IRA chose to investigate whether the role of reading specialist was valued in the school and whether these professionals were making a difference in instructional practices and student literacy learning. Bean, Swan, and Knaub (2003) sent surveys to principals in schools identified as exemplary. The principals in these schools were extremely positive about the importance of the reading specialists to the success of their reading programs, with 97% indicating that specialists were "extremely" or "very important" to its success. In a more recent study, principals who were asked to identify the value or influence of specialized literacy professionals in their schools, also indicated that these professionals had an impact on the school's literacy program; specifically, they helped to improve instructional practice, raise student achievement, and create a culture of collaboration (Bean, Swan Dagen, Ippolito, & Kern, 2018).

Bean et al. (2003) in their study of reading specialists in exemplary schools found them to be experienced teachers; all but one of them worked directly with students, all also served in a leadership role, and all saw the leadership role as an essential part of their work. These specialists identified the following characteristics of the ideal reading specialist:

- Teaching ability
- Knowledge of reading instruction
- Sensitivity to children with reading difficulties
- Knowledge of assessments
- Ability and willingness to fill an advocacy role
- Ability to work with adults
- Knowledge of reading research
- Lifelong learners
- Ability to provide professional development
- Ability to articulate reading philosophy
- Energy

THINK ABOUT THIS

The descriptors mentioned above reflect comments about reading specialists, but with the current emphasis on the role of the literacy specialist, what other characteristics might need to be considered? Which of the above characteristics do you think are most important?

FROM READING SPECIALIST TO LITERACY SPECIALIST

Previous editions of this book were titled *The Reading Specialist: Leadership and Coaching for the Classroom, School, and Community.* This change in title from reading to literacy specialist reflects the shift in how literacy is taught in schools today, that is, schools now recognize that they must move beyond a narrow focus on reading only, to emphasizing the relationships among all the language arts. This move has been the result of research findings and state standards that call for an integrated model of literacy for teaching students.

In 2018, the ILA published its new set of *Standards for the Preparation of Literacy Professionals 2017* (ILA, 2018a); this document also emphasized the importance of preparing literacy educators who understood that they had responsibilities for teaching the many dimensions of literacy instruction (e.g., reading, writing, speaking, listening, viewing, and visually representing) (ILA, 2018a). And so, the shift from "reading" to "literacy." Although ILA uses the term *reading/literacy specialist* in their 2017 standards document and many states continue to award reading specialist certification, we have chosen to use the term literacy specialist in this book. We recognize, however, that educators use many different titles in the field (e.g., reading/literacy specialist, reading interventionist, literacy coach, instructional coach) to identify these skilled professionals who most frequently teach students and/or have responsibilities to support classroom instruction. Also, although many candidates for these positions are enrolled in programs identified as reading specialist certification programs, many programs use the ILA Standards as the foundation for their programs and include content that reflects current research and scholarship about literacy instruction. Many certification programs require candidates to take courses about oral language development and writing, as well as those that emphasize reading instruction.

When we reflect on the past, we see pendulum swings in terms of where instruction occurs (e.g., pullout, in class, both), how students are assessed, and what and how specialists teach their students. What has not changed is that literacy specialists have always had to serve in a dual role that required them to teach students and support teachers. They have had to be able to communicate effectively with their colleagues to be successful in teaching students.

THINK ABOUT THIS

After reading the previous section, you might want to reflect on what you see in schools today: What are the duties and responsibilities of literacy specialists in the schools with which you are familiar? What have we learned from the past?

WHERE WE ARE TODAY: THE MULTIFACETED ROLE OF LITERACY SPECIALISTS

The results of the Bean, Kern, et al. (2015) study of over 2,500 literacy professionals, as described earlier in this chapter, provided a framework for the 2017 ILA Standards (ILA, 2018a). Many colleges and universities use these ILA Standards as a basis for the development of their literacy specialist programs. The 2017 ILA Standards reflect two important outcomes of the 2015 study: (1) the development of a new term, *specialized literacy professionals,* as an umbrella or overarching term to describe the three positions of reading/literacy specialist, literacy coach, and literacy coordinator; and (2) definitions and standards for each position that are distinct, yet include opportunities for productive overlap. Figure 1.1 describes the level of emphases for three roles; there are no distinct lines between any of

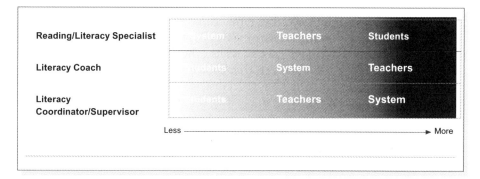

FIGURE 1.1. Levels of emphases. Reprinted with permission from Bean and Kern (2018).

these levels (i.e., student, teacher, system). However, the figure represents an understanding that most often literacy specialists spend most of their time with instruction, and less time working with teachers or the system. Coaches on the other hand, spend more time with teachers, while coordinators tend to focus on responsibilities at the system level. We realize that this may not always be the case, especially when districts are not able to employ more than one specialized literacy professional. These individuals may have both instructional and coaching responsibilities. Also, funding streams may affect how literacy specialists focus their time and work; for example, if a school receives a grant that requires teachers to learn new instructional approaches, literacy specialists may find themselves working more frequently with teachers than with students.

In Figure 1.2, we present a more detailed framework describing the many different tasks of specialized literacy professionals (Bean, 2020). This framework identifies tasks that literacy specialists, coaches, and coordinators may be required to perform. The framework divides responsibilities into three specific areas of focus: student, teacher, and system. Note that there are dotted lines between each of these areas, indicating that literacy specialists will often have roles that require them to have responsibilities beyond their instructional ones, that is, to work to some degree with teachers or to handle systemic issues. Likewise, coaches may find themselves having student-focused responsibilities! In each of the chapters, we describe ways by which literacy specialists and coaches can address these various tasks (e.g., in what ways can you advocate for students, serve as a resource to teachers?).

So, has the world of the reading/literacy specialist changed? We suggest it has. Although the various roles may vary—from instructional through coaching and leadership—all those in literacy specialist roles need leadership, interpersonal, and communication skills that enable them to work

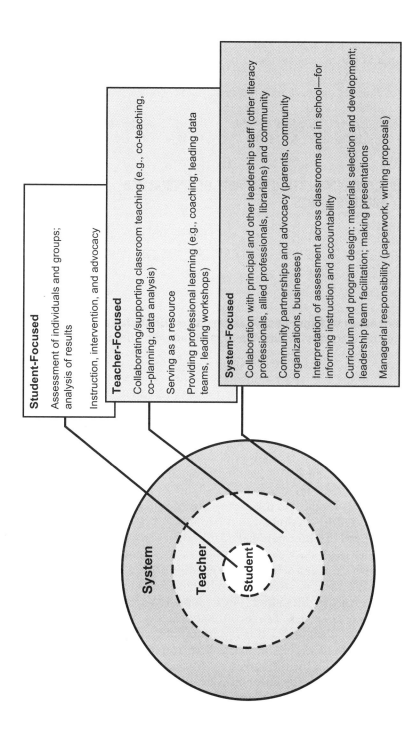

Student-Focused

Assessment of individuals and groups; analysis of results

Instruction, intervention, and advocacy

Teacher-Focused

Collaborating/supporting classroom teaching (e.g., co-teaching, co-planning, data analysis)

Serving as a resource

Providing professional learning (e.g., coaching, leading data teams, leading workshops)

System-Focused

Collaboration with principal and other leadership staff (other literacy professionals, allied professionals, librarians) and community

Community partnerships and advocacy (parents, community organizations, businesses)

Interpretation of assessment across classrooms and in school—for informing instruction and accountability

Curriculum and program design: materials selection and development; leadership team facilitation; making presentations

Managerial responsibility (paperwork, writing proposals)

System

Teacher

Student

FIGURE 1.2. Framework for specialized literacy professionals as literacy leaders: areas of focus. Reprinted with permission from Bean (2020).

effectively in schools as they exist today. Today's schools rely on shared leadership and teacher engagement in developing a common vision, developing expectations for students, and making instructional decisions. These changes in notions about leadership have made schools places of learning for both adults and students. Often, the literacy specialist or coach serves as one of the informal leaders in schools (Bean, 2020; Bean & Lillenstein, 2012; Camburn, Rowan, & Taylor, 2003; Galloway & Lesaux, 2014).

CURRENT FACTORS AFFECTING THE ROLE OF SPECIALIZED LITERACY PROFESSIONALS

In this final section of this chapter, we describe briefly some of the many contextual factors that influence the work of literacy specialists. We encourage readers to think about other factors that, given space, we do not discuss below.

Implementation of Rigorous Standards for English Language Arts and for Literacy in the Various Academic Disciplines

Almost all states have adopted student standards that require rigorous, high-level thinking to prepare students for college and career. Many states have adopted the CCSS developed by the NGA and CCSSO (2010) and others have adapted those standards or developed similar ones. But now the hard work begins: What instructional changes are necessary if these standards are to be used in developing and implementing literacy instruction? The current standards require a new way of teaching that emphasizes the integration of reading with the other language arts, especially writing, and highlight the need for shared responsibility of all teachers in developing literacy skills. Teachers in the content areas, especially at the secondary level, are expected to develop an understanding of how to help their students comprehend the informational texts of their discipline and to support students' ability to produce clear and coherent writing. Literacy specialists and coaches who work in schools implementing these standards will need skills that enable them to work effectively, not just as teachers of students who are experiencing difficulties, but to support and guide content-area teachers who are being asked to incorporate reading, writing, and discussion strategies into their instruction as a means of developing student learning of academic content. The CCSS have been accompanied by an emphasis on literacy instruction for the adolescent learner, given current results on both state and national assessment measures, and the recognition that there is much that can be done to improve instruction at the middle and secondary levels.

Assessment as a Basis for Instructional Decision Making

The use of data to make instructional decisions has influenced what specialists do in schools. Specialists often help teachers administer and analyze test data throughout the year, and most importantly, they are responsible for helping teachers think about how to use these test results to differentiate instruction using different materials, approaches, and/or small-group instruction. However, at times, the emphasis on accountability has led to "teaching to the test," and literacy specialists, as well as classroom teachers, find themselves in the position of providing narrow, focused instruction only. In a more positive vein, the focus on accountability has made it critical that literacy specialists understand how to assess reading growth, interpret results of various assessment measures, and communicate results to others.

The RTI legislation (IDEA, 2004) encouraged schools to use an approach different from the traditional discrepancy approach for identifying students with learning difficulties. RTI also supports early intervention to reduce the number of students qualifying for special education by promoting differentiated instruction as a means of improving success of all students. Currently, RTI and its companion, multi-tiered systems of supports (MTSS) describe academic and behavioral concerns simultaneously. These initiatives require collaboration among classroom teachers, literacy specialists, and special educators with each professional bringing to the table ideas for how to make instructional and behavioral adjustments. Classroom teachers can receive instructional support from specialists; for example, the literacy specialist may be asked to provide supplemental comprehension instruction to a small group of students. The specialist may provide explicit instruction on how to summarize or how to predict to students who seem to have difficulty even after the classroom teacher has presented these lessons to the entire class. Or the specialist may be assigned to deliver specialized or targeted instruction to a small group of readers who seem to be making little or no progress in the classroom, even after modifications have been made by the classroom teacher. Thus, the instructional role of the specialist will continue to be important, but it may require different responsibilities from those expected of them in the past.

Early Childhood Instruction

The research supporting literacy and language activities at the early childhood level as a means of reducing or eliminating future literacy and learning problems has generated a great deal of focus on the instruction that goes on in preschool and day care settings. The federal government has provided funding to assist states in building, developing, and expanding voluntary, high-quality preschool programs in high-need communities. Such programs require early childhood teachers to be well prepared and for better transition programs bridging preschool and kindergarten. Thus, the need for well-prepared literacy specialists and literacy coaches who can work cooperatively with preschool educators to ensure there is a better understanding of what students need to know and do when they arrive in kindergarten—and so that kindergarten teachers have a better sense of what students are learning in preschool settings (see ILA, 2018b, for information on PreK literacy instruction). This movement also calls for more partnering among all individuals and agencies involved in the education of young children: families, teachers, preschools, libraries, and community agencies.

Professional Learning for Teachers

All the initiatives described above have led to an increasing focus on providing effective professional learning experiences for teachers who are being asked by various stakeholders to change the ways they teach. And research evidence about effective professional learning activities suggests that such professional learning be job embedded, ongoing, content-based, and provide for active engagement. Research on professional learning has led to an increased emphasis on coaching in schools, and often a change in the role of many literacy specialists across this country, with some who originally worked only with students now working as partners with teachers to support student learning. This role of coaching requires individuals to have not only an in-depth knowledge of literacy instruction and assessment, but in addition, knowledge of adult learning and excellent interpersonal, communication, and leadership skills. This movement has generated consternation for some literacy specialists whose "first love" is working with students experiencing literacy difficulties, or who feel unqualified to serve as a coach.

The Economic Climate in the United States

Given the economic climate in the United States, educational funding has been reduced not only by the federal government but by states and local districts. Some schools have found it necessary to eliminate coaching positions (Bean, Dole, Nelson, Belecastro, & Zigmond, 2015). As mentioned by Steinbacher-Reed and Powers (2011/2012), often administrators assigned reading specialists to these coaching tasks. They analyzed data with teachers, modeled, and co-taught; their role required them to work with both students and teachers. Again, reading specialists found themselves having multiple responsibilities, ones for which they may not have been prepared, especially in the area of coaching.

WHERE WE ARE GOING: A CRYSTAL BALL?

Although all the issues mentioned above will most likely continue to influence the role of literacy specialists, there are several other current factors that we anticipate will continue to evolve and influence schooling in the coming years.

COVID-19: The Pandemic

In our lifetime, we have not seen anything that has the effect that this pandemic has had on all segments of society. It has created changes in how we socialize, how we do business, and how we educate students. Although many are working to develop contingency plans for addressing remote education (e.g., online, hybrid, or blended learning) what we do know is that there will be long-lasting effects that will influence the roles and responsibilities of school leaders, including coaches and literacy specialists. They will need to learn new ways of reaching and teaching students with learning needs, and creative ways of partnering with teachers and families to enhance student learning.

The Effect of ILA Standards

We suspect that the 2017 ILA Standards (ILA, 2018a) will influence the preparation programs for specialized literacy professionals and for teachers, given the current emphasis on providing high-quality teaching in classrooms across this country. Also, when designing professional learning initiatives, districts can use the ILA Standards in considering what classroom teachers and specialized literacy professionals need to know and be able to do to be effective in their roles. Specific sections in the ILA Standards elaborate on the roles of classroom teachers (i.e., primary, intermediate, and secondary) and those of specialized literacy professionals (i.e., reading/literacy specialists, literacy coaches, literacy coordinators); they provide specific guidance, not only for employing professionals, but for designing appropriate professional learning experiences. There is an emphasis in the standards on ongoing learning and teacher leadership, with peers supporting each other. The revised standards (ILA, 2018a) have the potential to help those preparing literacy professionals to better understand the multiple tasks of assessment, instruction, and leadership and how to work with each other to address individual student, classroom, and organizational challenges.

Technology

Technology has influenced our lives in many ways, from the ways we communicate with each other, to how we gather new information, and how we learn. Nearly 89% of the adults in the United States report that they own or use smartphones, Internet, computers, social media, and tablets (Hitlan, 2018). Over 9 million students in the United States, often in low-income homes or rural communities, lack Internet access at home (USA-Facts, 2020), creating a technological equity issue, further revealed by the COVID-19 pandemic.

Yet, most students in the United States have grown up with technology and are accustomed to using social media, texting, video, and music downloads. Schools then must support students as they learn in this "complex, globally connected, digital world that revolves around digital devices and tools, use of social media, and digital interactions" (ILA, 2018a, p. 16). Technology also has the potential to make literacy more accessible for students, especially those who might experience difficulties with reading and writing. Yet, educators need to be aware of its limitations, including how much time students should spend with their electronic tools, how young children can use digital resources in meaningful ways without diminishing the role of authentic play and communication experiences (ILA, 2019c).

Technology has changed the way in which we define literacy, which has been expanded to address "the multiple ways we read, write, communicate, and collaborate using print and digital technologies" (ILA, 2018a, p. 16). This expansion to digital literacies has had a large impact on the ways we teach and learn in schools. Teachers and specialized literacy professionals now must be knowledgeable about how to "incorporate digital texts, tools, and online resources into learning activities" (ILA, 2018a, p. 17). They must work with learners in ways that enable their students to use digital resources in safe, effective, and appropriate ways. Further, much is available on the Internet and educators must help learners, especially adolescent students, understand how to critically evaluate these various resources. Also, educators must understand how to use the capabilities of electronic texts, mobile applications, and search engines to help students become critical readers.

Moreover, technology will continue to influence the preparation of teachers and specialized literacy professionals and their ongoing professional learning (ILA, 2018a). Many university programs are hybrid in nature in that they provide both face-to-face and online experiences. In light of COVID-19, even more institutions are moving in that direction. Literacy specialists in the field, to improve their knowledge and understandings, may use the electronic resources of professional organizations, participate in blogs, or join webinars. Teachers, too, have become accustomed to gaining information via the Internet rather than attending face-to-face meetings. They regularly participate in conversations via blogs, twitter, and other forms of social media (Affinito, 2018). Specialists who coach may use various technological tools, from video to Zoom or Google Meet, to provide coaching experiences for teachers.

Diversity, Equity, and Inclusivity

Another issue that will continue to affect the role of literacy specialists is that of the increasing diversity of students in classrooms across the country. There has been a steady increase in populations such as students of color, English learners (ELs), transgender students, and students qualifying for special services (e.g., physical and learning differences). By 2027, the National Center for Education Statistics (U.S. Department of Education, 2019a) projects increases of students in the United States in designated categories of Hispanic, Asian/Pacific Islander, and multiracial. Many children in the United States live in poverty in both urban and rural areas, especially those in single-parent households and with parents who did not graduate from high school (see U.S. Department of Education, 2019b). These demographic factors greatly influence the preparation of all educators as well as how they teach in their schools. While there are many definitions and implications of social justice (Banks, 2003; Cochran-Smith, 2010; Comber, 2015; Edelsky, 2006), teacher preparation programs and school districts need to continue to increase efforts toward equal access and opportunities for all students.

A key demographic shift will be students whose primary language is not English. Data from the National Center for Education Statistics (U.S. Department of Education, 2018) indicate that there has been an increase in ELs in schools, from 8.5% identified as ELs in 2000 to 9.5% in 2015. Further, the percentage of ELs has increased in all but eight states, with California, Texas, Nevada, and New Mexico all having more than 15% of their students identified as ELs. According to the National Clearinghouse for English Language Acquisition, by 2025 approximately one of four students will be an EL (*www.ncela.ed.gov*). Further, scholars are raising concerns about policies on immigrant and migrant populations and the implications for the educational system (Patel, 2018; Salas, 2017, 2019). As a group, second-language learners are demonstrating significantly lower levels of academic achievement as compared with native English-speaking students in the United States. Classroom teachers, English language teachers, and literacy professionals need to be able to teach collaboratively in ways that enhance the language and literacy learning of students identifying as monolingual, bilingual, and translingual in learning English literacy skills.

Culture of Collaboration

As we learn more about school change and the need to work with others if we are to improve schooling for all, there is recognition of the importance of collaboration, not only in the school setting but also with external partners (e.g., parents, community agencies, universities). Literacy specialists must have the necessary knowledge and skills to work collaboratively to build those partnerships. This focus on collaboration, and on what is a new wave of school reform (Swan Dagen & Bean, 2014, 2020), will also affect the ways in which literacy specialists work in schools.

Literacy Specialists in Middle and High Schools

Given the increased attention to adolescent literacy, several chapters in this book include a section devoted specifically to literacy specialists serving students and teachers in middle and high schools. In these sections, we provide information about issues especially relevant for those specialists. As mentioned previously, districts are hiring literacy or instructional coaches who have a primary responsibility for working with teachers at the middle and secondary levels. However, at times, these schools will have both a literacy specialist and coach, or they will have a literacy specialist serving dual roles (i.e., teaching students and supporting teachers). Mason and Ippolito (2009) provide an excellent description of four roles of reading specialists in middle and high schools. First, these professionals may administer and analyze assessment tools that they or other teachers can use for instructional decision making. Second, they may support teachers in the disciplines by providing professional learning related to literacy, including co-planning, modeling, or co-teaching with these teachers; in other words, they assume coaching responsibilities. Third, they may work with special educators to assist students with learning differences or difficulties. In other words, they may be involved in working with an RTI team about how best to address the learning needs of students. Finally, they may be involved in creating and evaluating the literacy program at the middle or secondary levels, helping to select or develop programs, materials, or instructional strategies. In other words, they serve multiple roles that differ, depending on the context in which they work, their job descriptions, availability of other personnel, and so on.

Ippolito and Lieberman (2012) describe coaching at the secondary level, highlighting key differences between elementary and secondary contexts. These differences include organizational and cultural differences (e.g., larger numbers of teachers, teacher specialization by discipline, lack of teacher knowledge about literacy) and differences in students' literacy abilities and needs. At the same time, they suggest that these differences between the levels may simply be "differences of degree" (p. 67). The bottom line is literacy professionals at the secondary level have an important role in improving the literacy learning of adolescents and, in order to fulfill that role, they must be able to work collaboratively with their colleagues.

THINK ABOUT THIS

Do you agree or disagree with the contextual factors that have been identi-fied above relative to how literacy specialists might function in schools? Which of the factors have affected you personally? Are there factors that you think should be added?

SUMMARY

The role of the literacy specialist and coach has continued to evolve over the past decades. Currently, we are experiencing a greater emphasis on lead-ership responsibilities, regardless if the professional works with students or teachers. Some changes in roles have occurred in response to research findings about literacy instruction and assessment practices. Other changes have emerged on the heels of criticism about the results of large-scale com-pensatory programs that lacked congruence between classroom and sup-plemental instruction. Other changes have occurred because of influences such as the COVID-19 pandemic. An increased demand for quality teach-ing using evidence-based literacy instruction has created a need for literacy specialists to assume an increased leadership role. Literacy specialists and coaches, however, will continue to fill multiple roles that require them to have an in-depth knowledge of literacy instruction and assessment and the ability to work well with other adults. The increased emphasis on profes-sional learning; improving literacy instruction for all students, PreK–12; and technological capabilities will generate the need for new skill sets and new roles. Moreover, literacy specialists will need to understand how the organization in which they work affects what they do and how they can collaborate with others to create changes that facilitate student learning.

ADDITIONAL READINGS

Bean, R. M., Kern, D., Goatley, V., Ortlieb, E., Shettel, J., Calo, K., . . . Cas-sidy, J. (2015). Specialized literacy professionals as literacy leaders. *Literacy Research and Instruction, 54*(2), 83–114.—This article provides the results of a national survey of specialized literacy professionals; it suggests that these professionals have many leadership responsibilities in schools.

Galloway, E. P., & Lesaux, N. K. (2014). Leader, teacher, diagnostician, colleague, and change agent: A synthesis of the research on the role of the reading spe-cialist in this era of RTI-based literacy reform. *The Reading Teacher, 67*(7), 517–526.—These authors synthesized current research about the work of today's reading specialists and found that these professionals served as both an instructor of students and in a supportive role for teachers.

Ippolito, J., & Lieberman, J. (2012). Reading specialists and literacy coaches in secondary schools. In R. M. Bean & A. Swan Dagen (Eds.), *Best practices of literacy leaders: Keys to school improvement* (pp. 63–85). New York: Guilford Press.—These authors describe ways that reading specialists and coaches at the secondary level can organize their time to work with teachers across multiple content areas and how they can work with their colleagues to create a plan for change in instructional practices.

● REFLECTIONS

1. What skills and abilities do you think are essential for working successfully as a literacy specialist with students? With teachers? With the system? (See Figure 1.2 for a description of various tasks and functions.)

2. With which role are *you* most comfortable (e.g., working with students, teachers, or the system)? What concerns do you have about the other roles?

3. What are the implications of the following issues for literacy specialists and their role: placement in the middle or secondary school; increased emphasis on working with preschool providers; teaching ELs; focus on rigorous, high-level standards; addressing diversity in the classroom and community; use of online or remote learning, digital resources, and tools?

● ACTIVITIES

1. Analyze your own knowledge and skills in relation to the three areas of focus required of literacy specialists: student, teacher, system. Write a summary of your thoughts, indicating your strengths and where you think you may need to gain additional experience or knowledge.

2. Interview a teacher to gain his or her perceptions about the role of the literacy specialist. You may also want to interview a principal (or another literacy specialist), using the same questions.

3. Interview a literacy specialist, asking questions about how he or she fulfills responsibilities in the following areas of focus: student, teacher, system. Possible questions follow:

   a. How do you make decisions about the goals and content of your instruction? (Try to determine *what*—and *who*—determines the instruction.)

   b. Which assessment instruments do you find to be particularly helpful in assessing students' needs?

   c. How do you use assessment results?

   d. In what ways do you serve as a resource to teachers? Do you have any other coaching responsibilities, and if so, what?

   e. If you were able to develop your own assessment program, what would you emphasize or change?

f. What are some of the major literacy difficulties experienced by students in your school?
g. In what ways do you facilitate family involvement or partnerships?
h. What are the major issues or challenges you face as a literacy specialist?
i. How well prepared were you for the position you now hold?

CHAPTER TWO

Teaching Students

AN OVERVIEW OF THE INSTRUCTIONAL ROLE

KEY QUESTIONS ● ● ● ● ● ● ● ● ● ● ● ● ● ● ● ● ● ●

- In what ways does RTI or MTSS affect the work of literacy specialists?
- In what ways can literacy specialists communicate and collaborate with classroom teachers?
- What possible approaches for collaborative teaching between literacy specialists and classroom teachers are available, and what advantages or disadvantages are there to each approach?

Although literacy specialists have multiple responsibilities, one most often associated with the role of the literacy specialist is teaching students, especially those experiencing difficulties with learning to read. To be successful, literacy specialists must be able to work collaboratively and cooperatively with teachers, administrators, families, and community agencies. Therefore, they need the communication and leadership skills that facilitate these efforts. Classroom teachers, who have multiple demands on them, value having literacy specialists provide supplemental support to students with specific needs. Moreover, as mentioned in several studies, literacy specialists themselves value the instructional role (Bean, Cassidy, et al., 2002; Bean, Kern, et al., 2015; Bean et al., 2003). By working with students, literacy specialists can establish credibility with teachers and also get a better understanding of the classroom instruction that their students are receiving. Read about Pam and her initial experiences with instructing students who are experiencing difficulty with reading.

District administrators assigned Pam to work with one school, grades 1–3. She knew that she would be screening students during the first few weeks of school, and she was excited to begin working with students who needed additional support. Several teachers were eager to work closely with Pam and had already talked with her about specific students about whom they were concerned. Both Pam and Jerome, the other literacy specialist assigned to grades 4–5, would serve on the MTSS/RTI team. Decisions would be made by the team about whether to pull out students for Tier 2 instruction or to spend time in classrooms supporting teachers in differentiating their Tier 1 instruction. Although she was confident about the various strategies that would be effective for students experiencing difficulties, she was less certain about just how to plan her week to achieve her goals. Further, she wondered what would be the best ways to work with teachers to accommodate their requests for support. *Oh well,* she thought, *one step at a time.* Luckily, she would be working with a team; she also had the support of Jerome, the other literacy specialist, and could discuss issues or ideas with him.

There is no single model of the instructional role for literacy specialists to follow. Those who work in Title I programs may find themselves in classrooms, in pullout models, or both. Often literacy specialists work with small groups of children; however, there are also times when these specialists work with individual students (e.g., Reading Recovery [Clay, 1985], or Success for All [Slavin, Madden, Dolan, & Wasik, 1996]), or even to provide extensive support to a student experiencing literacy difficulties. Those at middle school and secondary levels often focus on literacy in the disciplines, and although they frequently work in the classroom with content teachers, they may also have responsibility for teaching classes of students needing supplemental literacy support (see Michael Henry's vignette in Chapter 5).

What is essential is that the literacy specialist who is responsible for teaching students experiencing reading difficulties understand the critical elements necessary to promote literacy success for these students. Foorman and Torgeson (2001) provide a summary of the research on effective classroom instruction and on effective instruction for children at risk for literacy failure. They identify three critical components of instruction for students needing supplemental instruction: Such instruction "must be more *explicit and comprehensive,* more *intensive,* and more *supportive* than the instruction required by the majority of children" (p. 206, emphasis in original). They describe the need for both cognitive and emotional support. In other words, these students need instruction that provides more scaffolding to help them complete tasks successfully, and in addition, they need "encouragement, feedback, and positive reinforcement" (p. 209). The importance of emotional support for all students cannot be understated, and such support is especially critical when working with adolescent students whose poor sense of self and feelings of academic inadequacy may limit their willingness to participate in literacy activities.

Because many schools, especially at the elementary level, use some form of the MTSS/RTI framework, we provide a description of that framework before discussing ways that specialists can work collaboratively with classroom teachers, other specialists, coaches, and administrators to address students' instructional needs.

RESPONSE TO INTERVENTION AND MULTI-TIERED SYSTEMS OF SUPPORT

What, Why, and How?

A federal initiative that has had a major impact on how schools differentiate instruction for all students is RTI (sometimes thought of as response to *instruction* rather than *intervention*). This initiative, which emerged from the reauthorization of IDEA (2004) has implications for how schools identify and instruct students who are experiencing learning difficulties. In fact, all 50 states have implemented some sort of RTI framework (Fuchs & Vaughn, 2012). In recent years, RTI has been folded into the framework of MTSS, which addresses academic, social, emotional, and behavior needs of students (see Samuels, 2016, for further definitions). Both RTI and MTSS use a problem-solving model in which (1) the problem is identified, (2) there is an analysis of why the problem is occurring, (3) a plan for intervention and for measuring its effects is developed, (4) the plan is implemented, and (5) the plan is evaluated. The emphasis in these initiatives is on differentiation or meeting individual needs as a means of improving student learning. Below, we focus on RTI, given our focus on literacy interventions for students.

The IRA, in its position statement about RTI, views it as a "comprehensive, systematic approach to teaching and learning designed to address language and literacy problems for all students" (2010, p. 2). RTI is not a program nor does it promote one approach to teaching and learning. Rather, the goal of RTI is to reduce the number of students being identified as needing special education, by providing early identification of needs and immediate intervention (see Johnston, 2010, and Lipson & Wixson, 2010, for literacy specific examples). Mesmer and Mesmer (2009, p. 283) discuss five important steps in the RTI identification process: (1) establish benchmarks for literacy performance and appropriate assessment measures to identify students at risk; (2) implement scientifically based interventions for those who need them; (3) monitor the progress of students receiving interventions;

(4) provide more intensive interventions for students who continue to need help, and continue to monitor their progress; and (5) if a student is not making progress, begin a decision-making process to determine eligibility for special education. Such a program requires involvement of all professionals: classroom teachers, literacy specialists, and special educators. It also requires schools to think differently about how literacy instruction occurs in schools. Moreover, implementation can be more successful when there is a literacy team that leads the effort by discussing assessment results, scheduling, grouping, and instructional decisions (Bean & Lillenstein, 2012). Schools often use a multilevel model for differentiation similar to the three-tiered model developed at the University of Texas at Austin (2005), although there is no requirement that a school use only a three-tiered model (Scanlon, Anderson, & Sweeney, 2017; Scanlon, Goatley, & Spring, 2020). As illustrated in Figure 2.1, such a framework might include the following:

- *Tier 1*—high-quality comprehensive literacy instruction at the classroom level that should meet the needs of most students in that classroom. Most frequently, schools adopt some sort of core program that is used by all students, although some schools have developed their own "homegrown" program. This instruction can include whole-class, small-group, and individual instruction and is generally provided by the classroom teacher. At times, a literacy specialist may assist teachers in differentiating their Tier 1 instruction by co-teaching with them.

- *Tier 2*—supplemental instruction that includes small-group work and often additional time. This instruction is an extension of the Tier 1 instruction; it provides for needs-based, explicit and structured reteaching, and additional practice. Additional time, perhaps 30 minutes a day for 3–5 days a week, is provided for Tier 2 instruction. Schools plan for this instruction in different ways. In some schools, all students participate during Tier 2 time in small-group, differentiated instruction, with some students receiving interventions and others receiving enrichment activities. Students may be regrouped across classrooms based on need (e.g., one group working with fluency, another with comprehension). In other schools, students who need Tier 2 instruction receive it during a nonliteracy period. Often this instruction is provided by a literacy specialist or a tutor prepared to implement such instruction.

- *Tier 3*—intensive instruction that requires additional time, most often individual or in a very small group. This instruction may be provided by the literacy specialist or another professional who has specialized preparation. In some schools, Tier 3 instruction is provided by the special education teacher for students who are not responding to Tier 2 instruction and have been identified as eligible for special education.

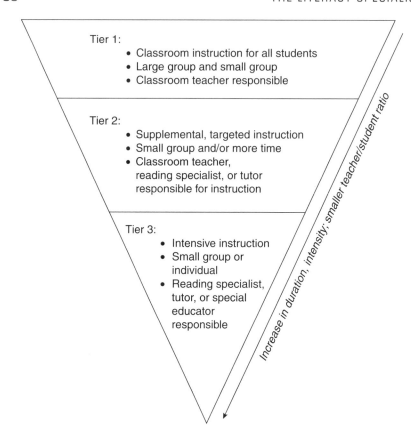

FIGURE 2.1. RTI framework.

All three tiers necessitate careful assessment of skills and progress monitoring to determine students' success and needs. Schools have developed problem-solving or literacy leadership teams to discuss assessment results and their implications for instruction. Assessment is discussed more thoroughly in Chapter 9.

RTI: Its Value, Some Issues and Questions

RTI was originally developed for younger students, especially those in grades K–3; however, it has now become a major force in all 50 states for organizing literacy instruction, especially in elementary schools. Much has been learned about RTI and its potential for improving students' literacy learning; for helping schools identify, at a younger age, students with possible literacy problems and providing the necessary interventions to prevent further difficulties; and ultimately for reducing the number of students identified as needing special education. Further, as based on Fisher, Frey, and Hattie's meta-analyses of thousands of individual research studies (2016), RTI has had a huge impact on student learning.

However, there are still some unknowns and a need for additional research about whether it works for all students as well as questions about the framework itself and how to use it in various contexts.

Willis (2019) in a critique of reading research as it addresses race indicates that "response to intervention has neither improved reading achievement nor curtailed racial disproportionality" (p. 394). She concludes, based on research, that the subjectivity and variability in decisions have resulted in a disproportionate number of students of color, ELs, and students who live in poverty to be identified for special education. Her work acknowledges that all involved in reading education, from policymakers to researchers and those in the field, must be cognizant of the limitations of research and the RTI framework as it relates to providing equitable instruction for all students, and especially for students of color.

Another concern about RTI is in its implementation, specifically, the focus on identifying specific commercial programs for the various tiers as a simple way of differentiating. Such an approach flies in the face of what is known about congruent instruction. Students receiving instruction from more than one teacher or in a different setting suffer when there is a lack of coherence among these programs. They are in fact being asked to learn more than their peers (Scanlon et al., 2020).

Other important questions include: What sorts of Tier 2 instruction are best for students?; How long should students receive Tier 2 instruction before being recommended for Tier 3 instruction?; Does the number of tiers make a difference?; How soon should students be recommended for special education placement? According to Fuchs and Vaughn (2012), some students, with severe literacy difficulties, may need to go directly from Tier 1 to Tier 3. In other words, important support may be denied students if they are required to go through each of the tiers before receiving the intensive instruction they need.

Another important question addresses the use of RTI in middle and high schools. Much less research is available about effectiveness at these higher levels, and questions about the interventions have been raised. However, some secondary schools have attempted to use RTI as a framework for supporting their struggling readers (Duffy, 2009; Samuels, 2009). One key resource for those working at the middle and high school levels is the National Center on Response to Intervention (*www.RTI4success.org*). At that site, there are suggestions and resources for all levels, and there is also a section that provides many resources focused on RTI at the secondary level. Other key resources for all levels include the RTI Action Network (*www.RTInetwork.org*), the ILA (*www.literacyworldwide.org*), and the National Center on Intensive Instruction (*https://intensiveintervention. org/audience/educators*). States generally have websites that provide specific details about the policies and procedures for MTSS/RTI specific to that state.

What should be obvious is that classroom teachers alone—even the very best—would be hard-pressed to meet the expectations of MTSS/RTI. The demands are great in terms of assessment and instruction. Literacy specialists as well as school leadership must become familiar with the goals of RTI so that there is a clear understanding of what it does and does not mean. One of the keys to successful implementation of RTI is for schools to build in additional time and/or more differentiated instruction to improve upon or extend classroom literacy instruction. Moreover, RTI requires experts such as literacy specialists who can "identify just where the reader has gotten off-track and then . . . design instruction that moves the reader back onto an accelerated track of development" (Allington, 2006, p. 20). This practice does not negate the possibility that students may benefit from a special (and different program), especially those at Tier 3, if implementers are aware of what is expected of students across all of their literacy instruction. As stated in the ILA position statement *Children's Rights to Excellent Literacy Instruction* (2019b), students have the right to "integrated support systems" (p. 1). In other words, when schools use various programs, "there should be clear articulation about how such an approach complements or reinforces what is being taught in the classroom" (Bean, 2008, p. 20).

One final question is how RTI "fits" with the current emphasis on CCSS or the high-level college and career standards adopted in many states. Specifically, the standards identify or establish outcomes, that is, the knowledge and skills expectations for all students; they do not, however, provide information about how schools can address the needs of diverse learners (e.g., ELs, special education, high poverty, students of color).

Regardless of the concerns identified, one of the benefits of RTI, in our view, is that it promotes collaborative efforts of many educators, each of whom can bring their knowledge and expertise to the table to discuss students and their strengths and needs. It also emphasizes the importance for ongoing learning of teachers so that they understand how to implement RTI effectively. By using an RTI framework effectively, schools can determine what students have and have not learned, and the instruction and interventions necessary for them to achieve literacy goals and standards. A resource helpful for implementing RTI at the primary grades is the practice guide published by the What Works Clearinghouse, *Assisting Students Struggling with Reading: Response to Intervention (RTI) and Multi-Tier Intervention in the Primary Grades* (Gersten et al., 2009).

RTI at the Middle and Secondary Levels

Reed, Wexler, and Vaughn (2012) noted key differences between RTI at the elementary and the secondary levels. First, at the secondary level there is more of a focus on remediation rather than prevention, given that many of these students have already been identified as needing support. Second, there may not be a need for universal screening, given the available extant data that can be used for making instructional decisions. In other words, more time can be devoted to instruction rather than to assessment. Moreover, students can quickly be assigned to less or more intensive remediation programs. At the same time, these authors indicate the need for ongoing follow-up and progress monitoring.

Below we describe important ways of working in RTI programs at the secondary levels. First, the secondary role may require more of a focus on supporting the instructional efforts of content teachers, that is, co-teaching with teachers of social studies, science, and math, as well as English language arts. This role requires literacy specialists to have a solid understanding of disciplinary literacy and how to work with content-area teachers to teach students "the language and ways of literacy and writing in each of the particular disciplines . . . the history teacher understands the particular ways that language and text 'works' in the field of history" (Anders & Clift, 2012, p. 175). In fact, the focus on disciplinary literacy requires a critical shift that asks literacy specialists to translate the generic literacy practices with which many are familiar (e.g., anticipation guides, graphic organizers) into more discipline-specific variations (Messina, 2013). Several key resources include *Adolescent Literacy* (Ippolito, Steele, & Samson, 2012), *Developing Readers in the Academic Disciplines* (Buehl, 2011), *Best Practices in Adolescent Literacy Instruction* (Hinchman & Sheridan-Thomas, 2014), and *Disciplinary Literacy* (Ippolito, Dobbs, & Charner-Laird, 2019).

Second, literacy specialists may be assigned to teach small groups of students who are experiencing difficulties reading or writing, perhaps using an RTI framework. However, as stated previously, such scheduling is not easy at the upper levels. Secondary schools have been creative in their efforts to develop and implement RTI. Some have adopted intensive programs for students. Other schools have developed tutoring centers or provide after-school support, and some have focused their efforts on providing professional learning experiences, often with coaching, to help content-area teachers provide high-quality instruction. What has been learned is the need for school leadership and professional learning for all involved, and an ongoing commitment to meeting student needs. Again, there is still much to learn about the implementation of RTI at the secondary level, and the extent to which such efforts are effective.

THE INSTRUCTIONAL ROLE OF THE LITERACY SPECIALIST

Collaboration

Regardless of the approach or the location of the instruction, effective literacy specialists must communicate and collaborate with teachers who are providing the "first line" of instruction to students. Only if the literacy specialist knows what the classroom teacher is doing, and vice versa, can the most appropriate instruction be provided for students. It is critically important for the specialist and classroom teacher to be sensitive to expectations and assignments to avoid fragmented instruction. Students who encounter fragmented or additive instruction may show increased confusion—and anxiety. For example, adjustments need to be made so that these students are not asked to do double the assignments required of other students. Having students use their recess time to complete class assignments, or to take their work home because they didn't finish it, can have a negative effect on students' attitude toward literacy and school. In scheduling, specialists should avoid taking students away from subjects such as art or gym, or from participating in special classroom activities (e.g., a movie or community speaker).

Literacy specialists and classroom teachers have been ingenious in finding ways to communicate and collaborate. Often this is done "on the fly," since schools do not always provide the time essential for such planning. Indeed, the challenge of finding time to plan collaboratively with teachers was one of the greatest concerns of literacy specialists who participated in the two national surveys described in Chapter 1 (Bean, Cassidy, et al., 2002; Bean, Kern, et al., 2015). When Ogle and Fogelberg (2001) asked literacy specialists to describe a successful collaboration and the reasons for its success, respondents highlighted the importance of an effective school climate or culture that permits teachers to experiment with new ways of teaching. Literacy specialists, with classroom teachers, have an important role in creating environments that facilitate and reward collaboration. In the following sections, we describe practical ideas for promoting collaboration.

Written Communication

When planning instruction, both teachers and literacy specialists can complete simple planning forms to enable them to determine quickly what is being emphasized by each in a specific week or unit. These forms also serve as a paper trail that can be useful in decision making as well as to provide detailed information to parents and other educators (see Figure 2.2). We suggest that the teacher complete the form and then discuss with the literacy specialist who can plan instruction that aligns with the work of the classroom teacher. There is a place at the bottom of the form for the literacy

Date: Week of _____

Teacher: _____ Grade: _____

Selection/unit being read? _____
_____

Key words being taught? (Attach list, if available.) _____
_____

Emphasis on specific skills or strategies? _____
_____

Any specific request about my role with in-class instruction? _____
_____

What day(s)/time would be best for our in-class sessions? _____
_____

Are there any students about whom you have concerns? _____
_____

Any specific scheduling issues (field trips, assemblies)? _____
_____

Comments:

FIGURE 2.2. Communication form.

specialist to make comments or keep notes about plans for instruction. Some teachers and specialists share or exchange copies of lesson plans. Literacy specialists can then plan their lessons to coincide with those of the teachers (e.g., students are working on distinguishing between fact and opinion, or being asked to verify their responses to questions by doing close reading). The literacy specialist can then plan lessons that address those foci but are more explicit or have more scaffolding for students who need additional support.

Oral Communication

SCHEDULED MEETINGS

School districts have designed many different approaches to providing needed planning time for teachers and literacy specialists. For example, specialists may meet with grade-level or subject-area teachers once a week or bimonthly during a designated planning period. During these meetings, participants can discuss common needs and issues, and they can talk about specific students who may need supplemental help. They can make decisions about who will do what with whom and when! One of the advantages of these meetings is that literacy specialists and teachers learn from each other; such meetings also tend to encourage teamwork. As one literacy specialist said to Rita, "We need to know what is going on. Are teachers planning to show a movie or making a change in what they are teaching? All of this affects my schedule. So, the planning meeting is very helpful." Moreover, these meetings foster the notion that students are the responsibility of all teachers—not only the classroom teacher or the literacy specialist. Too often, in the past, classroom teachers believed that they had little or no responsibility for teaching students experiencing difficulties with reading; rather, it was the literacy specialists' task to teach those students. Another value of these meetings is that literacy specialists can be involved in ways that affect the learning of all students, from those who are excellent readers to those experiencing difficulties. With the advent of RTI, more and more schools are developing creative ways of providing meeting times for teachers.

Common planning time for a grade level and for subject-area teams has become "common" in school districts as a means of making short-term decisions. Some schools provide for planning time during the school day and others incorporate a 30-minute planning time in the morning before students arrive. In one primary school (grades K–3), the school schedule includes a grade-level planning meeting of 45 minutes once every other week with literacy specialists and other specialized personnel; teachers can use that period for their own planning during the other week. To assist with long-range planning, the district may provide time for literacy specialists to meet with individual teachers or groups of teachers to discuss data results several times a year.

Some schools hire substitute teachers to manage classrooms while the literacy specialist meets with teachers. For example, in one school district that is implementing an RTI program, substitutes are hired for 1 day every marking period (four times a year); they teach classes while the literacy specialists and teachers from each of the grade levels meet for 90 minutes to review assessment data and make instructional decisions about content, grouping, and how the literacy specialist will support the teachers at a specific grade level. In another school, grade-level meetings designed to discuss data are held five times a year: the school hired four substitutes and they teach for half a day in the four classrooms at a specific grade level while the specialized literacy professionals and a math coach meet with the teachers. In other words, each grade-level team has half a day to meet with specialized literacy professionals to discuss students' progress and changes in groupings or instruction. Although these approaches may seem costly, they provide the opportunity for in-depth discussions about specific students and how personnel can collaborate to meet student needs. The meetings also provide powerful professional learning opportunities as literacy specialists and teachers share ideas about resources, materials, and various approaches for differentiating instruction.

Literacy specialists may also meet with individual teachers either before or after school, or during a designated time for teacher planning/preparation. However, some teachers may be reluctant to give up their own planning time; school leadership may need to negotiate with teachers' unions or associations so that opportunities for interaction between teachers and specialists are an expected aspect of the school day or week.

INFORMAL CONVERSATIONS

Knaub (2002), in her study of collaborative efforts between specialists and classroom teachers, found that teachers and literacy specialists who worked together became familiar with various types of lessons (e.g., Making Words [Cunningham & Hall, 1994]) and were able to coordinate their teaching effectively and with little planning. Knaub (2002, p. 50) coined the phrase "impromptu partnering" to convey the ease with which literacy specialists and teachers collaborate. There may be opportunities for teachers and literacy specialists to talk briefly when students are working independently. However, this is not an approach that allows for long periods of discussion, since teachers need to be available to teach, assist, or watch as students are engaged in literacy activities. Many times, teachers talk informally during their lunch break or in the halls. We found this same sort of conversation occurring between literacy coaches and teachers; such "opportunistic" discussions provided the basis for later, more intentional work (Bean,

Belcastro, Jackson, Vandermolen, & Zigmond, 2008). Pletcher, Hudson, John, and Scott (2019) in their article about balancing reading/literacy specialist and coaching roles indicate that brief conversations can be as powerful as lengthy ones, if those conversations are focused on a specific point.

Support from Administration

Without administrative support, there is less chance that meaningful collaboration will occur. Research findings indicate that principal leadership is essential for promoting the work of literacy specialists and literacy coaches (Bean, Dole, et al., 2015; Bean et al., 2018; Matsumura, Sartoris, DiPrima Bickel, & Garnier, 2009). Schedules that provide teachers and literacy specialists with opportunities to plan, and policies and procedures that encourage collaboration are necessary for developing effective programs. Likewise, literacy specialists need schedules that enable them to be in specific classrooms during the teaching of appropriate subjects. Even the placement of specific students in classrooms needs to be considered. As noted by Ogle and Fogelberg (2001), in some schools, readers at a specific grade level who are experiencing difficulties are placed in two or three classrooms only so that the literacy specialist has fewer classrooms in which to work. However, this approach can be problematic if a classroom teacher has responsibilities for working with a large number of students experiencing difficulties.

Administrators can also show their support by providing professional learning experiences for all teachers participating in collaborative teaching. It is not sufficient for literacy specialists alone to understand how to work collaboratively; all teachers can benefit from experiences that heighten their own understandings of effective collaboration and teamwork. This notion is especially important as schools attempt to implement programs that meet the recommendations of the RTI initiative, which requires collaboration among classroom teachers and other available specialized personnel (e.g., literacy specialists, special educators). Finally, principals show support by being involved, attending at least some or part of the meetings of literacy specialists and their teacher colleagues, and having an understanding of what the issues and challenges are for literacy specialists in their instructional role.

Clear Procedures and Expectations

Both classroom teachers and literacy specialists must know and understand their roles in the classroom; the lack of explicit procedures can lead to problems. Literacy specialists may feel as though they have no clear instructional responsibility and just "float" around the classroom, trying to anticipate what might be helpful. This type of role seems to generate the feeling in literacy specialists that they are "aides" and that their expertise is not useful or valued. Classroom teachers also experience frustration because they aren't sure what the literacy specialist should do either. Only with the establishment of clear expectations can teachers both recognize and appreciate the benefit of an additional person in their classrooms. However, establishing those clear expectations is not easy, given the culture that tends to exist in schools; that is, teachers are assigned a group of students and are responsible for the academic success of those students only. Teachers have been accustomed to teaching in isolated settings, planning and implementing instruction that they deem best. Figure 2.3 identifies questions that the classroom teacher and literacy specialist can ask each other as they think about how to collaborate and communicate. Given the focus in schools on RTI, there is much more co-teaching in schools and teachers are becoming more accustomed to having other adults in their classrooms.

However, given that literacy specialists are "visitors" in teachers' classrooms, they must respect the experiences, management style, and organizational preferences of individual teachers. In other words, to be effective, literacy specialists should differentiate the ways in which they work in teachers' classrooms. Some teachers may prefer to take a leadership role in making decisions about what the specialist can do and with whom, some will relinquish that role to the specialist, while others will work more collaboratively and want to plan together. Flexibility and communication are key! (More about this topic in Chapter 4, on leadership.)

THINK ABOUT THIS

Would you feel comfortable using the questions in Figure 2.3 in a conversation with teachers? How can you use these questions effectively?

In the following scenario, we describe how Shala, a literacy specialist, and David, a third-grade teacher, planned their lessons for a week, using a framework that builds on the classroom instructional program. We also discuss how Shala works with some of David's students in a pullout setting to provide supplemental instruction for them (see Figure 2.4). The schedule calls for Shala to be in David's classroom 3 days a week—Monday, Wednesday, and Friday—for 30 minutes each day. This week, the class is reading the selection *Marvelous Cornelius* (Bildner, 2015), a story that takes place in New Orleans at the time of Hurricane Katrina and addresses the theme of "doing the best you can do, whatever your job." The story has several vocabulary words specific to the setting (e.g., beignet, gumbo, praline) and important for understanding the story. David and Shala team teach to introduce the selection on Monday, focusing on vocabulary and prior knowledge about New Orleans and hurricanes. Then, to help students who are working in pairs on vocabulary activities, both the literacy

	Yes	No
1. Do we come to class with prepared materials/ideas?	___	___
2. Do we signal our students to come to us when it is time?	___	___
3. Do we follow through on plans made at joint planning sessions?	___	___
4. Do we provide feedback on students' lessons to each other regularly and frequently?	___	___
5. Do we bring materials to joint planning sessions?	___	___
6. Do we share new strategies with the other teachers?	___	___
7. Do we engage in self-reflection after teaching a lesson?	___	___
8. Do classroom teachers try to help the literacy specialist "fit in" with the flow of the classroom?	___	___
9. Do we invite feedback on students/lessons from each other?	___	___
10. Do classroom teachers share expectations for student behavior?	___	___
11. Do we keep to our agreed-upon schedule? (Does the literacy specialist arrive on time? Is the teacher ready for the collaborative lesson?)	___	___
12. Do we discuss our relationships with other classroom teachers/literacy specialists in a professional manner?	___	___
13. Do we have high expectations for students and discuss their strengths and needs in a positive way?	___	___
14. Do we "keep up" on literacy instruction research through our reading of professional journals, attendance at conferences, etc.?	___	___
15. Do we demonstrate respect for each other?	___	___

FIGURE 2.3. Reflective collaboration questions.

Monday	Tuesday	Wednesday	Thursday	Friday
In class (30 minutes)	*Pullout*	*In class (30 minutes)*	*Pullout*	*In class (30 minutes)*
Team teach (introduction to selection). Participate in guided and independent practice (monitor with teacher).	Targeted instruction for several groups of third-grade students (two from David's room).	Targeted, small-group instruction based on student needs.	Targeted instruction for several groups of third-grade students (two from David's room).	Targeted, small-group instruction based on student need; monitor with teacher.

FIGURE 2.4. Shala's weekly schedule with David and his students.

specialist and teacher circulate around the classroom. Shala also takes 5 minutes to talk with a new student about his previous school experience and to listen to him read a grade-level text so that she and the teacher have a better idea of the child's literacy performance.

On Tuesday, the entire class reads the selection together, focusing on the theme of the story and participates in a discussion with the classroom teacher. The classroom teacher assigns students to various learning centers where they complete activities that relate to their specific needs while the teacher monitors their work (Shala had helped David design these centers by providing him with ideas and resources). While the students are working in centers, David provides 20 minutes of supplemental instruction to a small group of three students who need more explicit instruction focused on decoding multisyllabic words. During this center time, Shala works in a pullout setting with two students from David's class and three students from another third-grade classroom who are having decoding difficulties. She is providing instruction that is more explicit, structured, and multisensory to help these students develop stronger decoding skills; these students also do partner reading in each lesson so that they have opportunities to apply what they are learning in authentic reading tasks.

On Wednesday, the goal is fluency practice, using the selection. In the classroom, based on their formative assessment practices, David and Shala formed three groups, with Shala working with a group of students identified as needing additional assistance with fluency, the classroom teacher working with another group on comprehension, and the third group engaging in partner reading. Shala asks students in her group to read and reread a specific section of the selection. First, she models fluent reading (and disfluent reading); she then has various students read the section orally. She also reviews some of the concepts and understandings that the students discussed during the previous day. Students in David's group also read orally, but his group is focused on finding and reading parts of the selection that address specific comprehension issues.

On Thursday, the classroom teacher highlights figures of speech found in the selection and talks with the students about how these make the selection more interesting to read and what they mean. He then gives the students a writing task, asking them to choose a part of the story that they liked best and describe why they liked that part. David again assigns students to centers where he monitors their work. He also spends about 15 minutes providing supplemental instruction to a small group of students who need some reinforcement of the vocabulary taught that week. And again, as she did on Tuesday, Shala meets with the same five students in a pullout setting to work on their decoding skills.

On Friday, students complete their writing assignment and read additional materials that are available in the classroom (Shala and David have gathered materials about New Orleans, hurricanes, and floods). Shala and David hold conferences with students, helping them to think about what they have written and how they might revise or edit their work. For 10 minutes, Shala also pulls aside a small group to review strategies for identifying multisyllabic words because she and David had noted that some students were having difficulty with such words. Finally, the students get to share their written work.

Shala and David use a mutually agreed-upon framework in planning each week's lessons, to avoid extended meetings. On Mondays, Shala knows that she is going to help students with vocabulary; she may also teach a small group to do some review work. On Wednesdays, the focus is on rereading the selection, and Shala often works with the group experiencing the most difficulty. Finally, on Fridays, there is an emphasis on some follow-up activity (e.g., writing, art, or creative dramatics). Keep in mind, Shala and David understand the need for flexibility, should they identify specific needs of the students during instruction (e.g., multisyllabic words). Shala assists with this activity, or she may work with a small group to provide additional literacy practice or review specific strategies or skills. She also helps students in David's classroom, providing the intensive support they need by pulling them from their classroom and working with them in a small group setting. Shala enjoys working with David and getting an opportunity to support instruction for all the students in his classroom. She also appreciates the opportunity to see her pullout students as they work with others in the classroom, as it gives her a greater sense of what challenges they are facing with their classroom work.

This set of procedures is, of course, only one example of how the literacy specialist and teacher may work together. Many different approaches can be used; the approach selected will depend on the curricular demands or the needs of the students.

THINK ABOUT THIS

What do you see as the strengths of the weekly approach that David and Shala have developed? Do you have any questions about it? What skills and abilities do the literacy specialist and classroom teacher need to make this framework effective? What other possibilities might be effective?

APPROACHES TO COLLABORATION

This section describes five approaches to collaboration that are based on the literature (Bean, Trovato, & Hamilton, 1995; Friend & Cook, 2016; Friend, Cook, Hurley-Chamberlain, & Shamberger, 2010) and on observations made of literacy specialist interns and classroom teachers (Bean, Grumet, & Bulazo, 1999). Some of the approaches require in-class teaching, whereas others might occur either in class or away from the classroom; all require collaborative planning. Table 2.1 provides a summary of the approaches and lists the advantages as well as potential problems of each (Bean, 2009).

Station or Center Teaching

Both literacy specialists and teachers can develop stations or centers for teaching, based on the needs of the students and their own expertise or interests. Such stations provide independent activities for some students while the specialist and teacher are teaching others, or a teacher, specialist, or instructional aide can assist students at a center. The classroom teacher might be responsible for leading a station on writing, while the literacy specialist guides a review center for phonics or vocabulary development. This arrangement enables both teachers to work with all students as they rotate through the stations, giving the literacy specialist opportunities to learn more about what readers of all abilities can do, and also preventing students from thinking the literacy specialist works with "struggling" readers only. Stations can be used one or more times a week, thereby facilitating a flexible, heterogeneous grouping of students. Activities provided in the station can be such that students rotate through all of them (writing, listening) or tasks can be differentiated, and students assigned to specific stations (e.g., phonics station for students who need additional practice, fluency station). Throughout the decision-making process, the teachers and specialist maintain flexibility to make sure they are meeting the immediate and changing needs of students.

If the teacher is not guiding the work of the students in the station, activities need to be such that they promote effective independent and/or partner work. In one kindergarten, students collaborate to review sight

TABLE 2.1. Approaches to Collaboration

Model	Advantages	Potential problems/ dilemmas	Location
Station or center teaching	• Students have opportunity to work with both teachers • Attention to individual/ group needs or interests • Small-group work • Teachers have some choice (utilizes teacher strengths and interests) • Teachers share responsibility for developing and teaching	• Time-consuming to develop • Noise level in classroom • Organizational factors • Management factors	In class
Targeted teaching	• Focuses on individual or group needs • Individual or small group • Targeted instruction • Uses strengths of teachers to meet needs of students	• The need to know both classroom reading program and specialized approaches • Rigid grouping	Either in class or pullout
Parallel instruction	• Pacing/approach can vary • Small-group instruction • Same standards/ expectations for all students • Easier to handle class	• May not meet needs of students • Noise level in classroom	Generally in class (can be pullout)
Teach and monitor	• Same standards/ expectations for all students • Immediate reinforcement or help from monitor • Opportunity to do "kidwatching" (assessment) • Teachers can learn from each other (demonstration)	• One teacher may feel reduced to aide status • Lack of attention to specific needs of children	In class
Team teaching	• Same standards/ expectations for all students • Uses strengths of both teachers • Teachers share responsibility • Students have opportunity to work with both teachers • Attention to individual/ group needs or interests • Small-group work	• Lack of common philosophy or approach to instruction	Generally in class

vocabulary. One station can be devoted to computer use, such as working with a particular literacy program, playing a literacy game that provides for extended practice opportunities, writing an original composition, responding to a reading selection, or using the Internet to investigate a specific topic.

One of the advantages of learning stations is that the teachers working together can design activities for areas of literacy in which they have specific expertise or interest. They can also focus their energies, thus reducing preparation time. Although the development of activities for stations is time-consuming, once developed, they can be used at future times or in different classrooms. Moreover, activities can be shared across grade levels. Some key resources for center activities at the elementary levels include the Florida Center for Reading Research (*www.fcrr.org*) and Diller's (2005) *Literacy Workstations for Grades 3–6*. Often, teachers can obtain ideas for stations from blogs on the Internet, though they need to carefully consider the quality of the instructional suggestions. Stations can be useful at the middle and high school levels for promoting student engagement and motivation; they can be used effectively by content-area teachers who want to provide various interactive activities for students. Check *www.readwritethink.org/classroom-resources* for ideas to develop independent activity stations; the website provides resources for grades K–12 classrooms. Rickert (2017) also describes ideas for developing centers at the secondary level, including stations that help students to: (1) open their books, (2) annotate, (3) make a real-world connection, (4) use video, and (5) conference.

A word of caution: Stations should not serve as a substitute for teaching. Students need the direct instruction provided by teachers. Further, stations must be carefully constructed so that they provide meaningful learning experiences for students. To implement stations effectively, teachers need excellent organizational and classroom management skills. Some teachers may have difficulty with the noise level that occurs in their classrooms, hence the need for collaboration in establishing classroom rules for moving through the stations. In the beginning of the year, teachers and specialists may choose to use just one or two stations, helping students to understand how to function in such stations, the rules for moving from one to another, and so on. Such a practice also provides teachers with a better understanding of how to manage station activity effectively.

Targeted Teaching

Classroom teachers who have responsibility for many students may not be able to focus or target instruction to the extent necessary for some students to achieve success. The literacy specialist can address specific needs of individual or small groups of students by selecting supplemental materials that provide for reinforcement of learning. They can adjust the level of material used, practice fluency with material at students' instructional level, or provide more explicit, scaffolded instruction to support student learning. They may use a specific reading program or approach developed for students who are having difficulty learning to read (e.g., materials from Literacy Collaborative (Fountas & Pinnell, 2006) for Tier 2 students (*http:// literacycollaborative.org*). Students who need additional exposure to the vocabulary of a story (perhaps even before the story is introduced) may be grouped for instruction, while other students work on their writing projects or do independent reading.

In one school district, literacy specialists teach selected primary children individually for short 10-minute mini-lessons, asking them to read orally, or work with specific vocabulary words that present difficulty for them. The specialist next provides opportunities for students to compose a sentence that can be read, cut into strips, reordered, reread, and taken home for practice (along with the book that has been read). In another school, in the intermediate grades, literacy specialists work with small groups of students who need additional support with comprehension; their major focus is helping students understand and use specific comprehension strategies such as those described in *Explaining Reading: A Resource for Explicit Teaching of the Common Core Standards* (Duffy, 2014). At the high school level, literacy specialists may teach students who need more help with study skills or with reading their science textbook. They may also be assigned to teach two or three classes of students who have been identified as needing literacy support; these students most often are required to take this class, possibly in lieu of an elective or study hall. Although the literacy specialist generally takes responsibility for targeted lessons, at times the classroom teacher may want to teach some of these lessons while the specialist works with other students.

Parallel Instruction

Parallel instruction provides opportunities for reducing the number of students in one group, thereby providing opportunities for differentiated pacing and feedback based on student needs. Both teachers teach the same lesson and the same content but with a different group of students. For example, both teachers may have students reread the story orally, but there may be much more scaffolding by the teacher working with students who are having difficulties reading that selection (e.g., teacher reads more of the selection while students listen, but offers opportunities for students to read aloud). Or, if there is a focus on comprehension, in one group the teacher may provide more opportunity for group discussion while in another group there might be more explicit instruction about a specific reading strategy (e.g., using prediction before, during, and after reading). Parallel instruction, done in the same classroom, can be difficult because of the noise level, with two direct lessons occurring at the same time. Although students seem to adjust nicely to the noise, teachers tell us they have difficulty adjusting to the simultaneous activities going on around them. There are times that the literacy specialist can take the students to another room, if one is available.

Teach and Monitor

In this approach, one teacher presents the lesson while the other moves around the room, helping and supporting children who need assistance. As mentioned previously, this approach has created frustration for some literacy specialists who feel that they are nothing more than aides in the classroom. When the reverse occurs and the literacy specialist assumes the instructional role, a few classroom teachers may see this as a time for them to complete other tasks—marking papers or calling parents—causing concerns for literacy specialists who now have sole responsibility for the classroom of students. Nevertheless, there are many opportunities and advantages for such teaming in the classroom. For those working with young children, an extra pair of hands and eyes can be beneficial. For example, literacy specialists may teach a lesson requiring first graders to manipulate letter cards as they "build words." The classroom teacher can monitor, making sure children have the right cards in the right places. Likewise, writing and reading workshops may require monitoring (and conferencing) by both teachers. Another advantage of this approach is that classroom teachers can observe the literacy specialist using a specific strategy with which they may not be familiar. If the classroom teacher is teaching, the literacy specialist can observe students with literacy difficulties and note how they behave in a group setting ("kidwatching").

Team Teaching

Team teaching may include aspects of each of the models described above. In this model, both teachers plan how they will conduct instruction, whether for a specific lesson or over time. The previous scenario of the third-grade teacher and the literacy specialist (David and Shala, respectively) describes several approaches to collaboration. Both teachers have specific roles based on their expertise and interests. Each works with the entire group as well as with small groups or individuals within that group. Such collaboration requires time for planning, a good working relationship between the two individuals, and common beliefs/ideas about literacy instruction and classroom management. At the secondary level, team teaching can be especially effective as a result of using the respective "expertise" of the content-area teacher and the literacy specialist.

SUPPORTING CLASSROOM INSTRUCTION AND NEEDS OF INDIVIDUAL STUDENTS

One of the dilemmas faced by literacy specialists is that of determining where to put their focus: on helping students succeed in the classroom, or helping students develop literacy skills/strategies that are areas of need. In fact, the only solution is that of doing *both*. Students who are reading below grade level and struggling with the material in their classrooms deserve to receive the help they need to achieve some degree of success. This is especially important in today's schools, given the diversity in backgrounds, skills, and literacy levels of students. For example, ELs, with some additional support and scaffolding of vocabulary instruction, may be quite successful in a content-area classroom. Further, with the emphasis on rigorous, high-level standards and research indicating that students benefit from reading grade-level text to develop world knowledge, specialists may need to provide more explicit, scaffolded instruction to aid students as they work with this more difficult text.

At the same time, students can benefit from small-group or individual opportunities with the literacy specialist to review and reteach the specific skills with which these students are having difficulty. The What Works Clearinghouse (WWC; *http://ies.ed.gov/ncee/wwc*) reports the effectiveness of various intervention programs (e.g., Reading Recovery [Clay, 1985], Read 180 [Houghton Mifflin Harcourt, 2019], Cooperative Integrated Reading and Composition/Success for All [Slavin et al., 1996]). This website is an important resource for literacy specialists, as it provides research evidence that specialists can share with administrators and teachers. The WWC also publishes practice guides that literacy specialists can share with teachers and use for their own instructional planning; topics include teaching adolescent literacy, teaching writing at the secondary level, and teaching foundational skills, among others.

Focus on Classroom Success: Importance of Congruence

The need for congruence between classroom and literacy specialist instruction is recognized as important when working with readers experiencing difficulties (Allington & Shake, 1986; Walp & Walmsley, 1989). Allington (1986) decried the fact that these readers, who are least able to make accommodations, experience two separate and distinct instructional programs. Literacy specialists can promote congruence by reteaching or reviewing a specific skill or strategy important for classroom performance. They can also provide additional practice with specific vocabulary words needed for a selection, guide students in repeated readings of selections being read in the classroom, and help with specific assignments.

Although this focus on congruence is important in the primary grades, it is especially essential for students at upper levels where they are using reading and writing to learn new concepts in various subject areas. Literacy specialists will need to understand the importance of and differences between content-area and disciplinary instruction. As described by Ippolito, Dobbs, and Charner-Laird (2019), content-area instruction focuses on those general literacy skills, such as questioning, summarizing, visualizing, that can be applied across content areas. Disciplinary literacy, on the other hand, "highlights the specialized ways of reading, writing, and communicating unique to each discipline" (p. 13). As discussed by Ippolito et al. (2019), both aspects of literacy are important and should be part of the instructional program from early grades on. Further, teachers of young children should help them become more effective in reading informational text and understanding the disciplines (Brock, Goatley, Raphael, Trost-Shahata, & Weber, 2014; Duke, 2014; Kucan & Palincsar, 2013).

In making decisions about classroom practices, the subject-area teacher and literacy specialist may engage in collaborative discussions about questions such as: What discipline-specific skills do students need to be successful in learning content in the sciences, humanities, or mathematics? What skills and abilities will help the middle school student read and comprehend his or her social studies textbook more effectively? What note-taking skills and review strategies do students in a biology class need so that they are prepared for the unit test? When literacy specialists address questions such as these, they most likely will work in the classroom with the content teacher to promote successful classroom learning.

Focus on Meeting Specific Needs

Students who have not learned various skills or strategies need to have opportunities to develop them; otherwise, they may always have difficulty with literacy. Thus, for students in the intermediate grades who have weak decoding skills, targeting instruction on those skills can be useful. Likewise, if students are assigned to read from textbooks that are above their reading level, they need other opportunities to read silently and orally in books that are at or slightly below their instructional level. In other words, although students can be provided with the scaffolding they need to read "difficult texts," they also need opportunities to read text at their instructional level as a means of developing fluency and gaining confidence in their ability to read (Allington, 2013; O'Connor et al., 2002). The CCSS components led to multiple conversations on text complexity and the nature of instructional texts (see Hiebert's TextProject [*www.textproject. org*] for further discussion). The bottom line is that readers experiencing difficulties need opportunities to achieve success—to build on what they know and can do. The literacy specialist who designs lessons that address the needs of students, provides them with opportunities to practice what they are learning, and creates a desire, not only to learn to read but to read independently. This can make a difference in the literacy learning of readers experiencing difficulties.

Literacy specialists at the secondary level may wish to organize a specific class in which they work with small groups of students who are struggling with literacy. During that class, they can alleviate some of the difficulties the students are facing by reviewing or reteaching specific strategies or skills. For example, students may benefit greatly from lessons that help them learn various Latin and Greek roots and how to improve their vocabulary with such knowledge. Such lessons should help students see the relationship between what they are learning in this small-group setting and the subjects they are taking. No matter the emphasis of the specialist, students must be helped to see the relevance of what they are learning and how it can help them to read effectively and achieve success in their classrooms.

PULLOUT OR IN-CLASS INSTRUCTION: IS THAT THE QUESTION?

In this section, we discuss an issue that has generated controversy in the past for literacy specialists, that is, whether instruction should be in the classroom of the students or in pullout situations. Given the RTI initiative, having multiple teachers in the classroom has become more accepted, although actual implementation is still problematic. Most frequently, there is a need for both in-class and pullout instruction, and determination of the location of supplemental and intensive instruction—as well as who teaches those students—is dependent on the context of the school, including its human resources and the needs of readers and writers experiencing difficulties.

As you read this section, think about how literacy specialists can organize their instructional work to best address the needs of students experiencing difficulty with reading. In the vignette in this chapter, Mark, an elementary reading specialist whose primary responsibility is teaching students, describes his decisions and strategies for effective instruction. Throughout the vignette, Mark describes how he communicates with teachers as a means of informing them about his instruction, providing them with ideas for their own instruction, and learning more about the students that they both teach. Mark also discusses his own views about RTI and how he uses its tenets to guide his work.

In the recent national survey of literacy specialists (Bean, Kern, et al., 2015), we found that pullout instruction was present to the same extent as it was in the earlier survey (Bean, Cassidy, et al., 2002); that is, about 40% of the literacy specialists delivered instruction outside the classroom. It appears that schools now recognize that both pullout instruction and in-class instruction have their merits, and both are used in schools. In-class instruction is useful because it provides help to students in their own class-rooms, supporting the notion of inclusion. At the same time, the success that has been attributed to various tutoring programs, such as Reading Recovery (Clay, 1985) and the tutoring component of Success for All (Slavin et al., 1996), has led to an increase in programs in which students are tutored individually and away from their classrooms.

In 1995, Bean et al. (1995) surveyed teachers, principals, and reading specialists to determine their perspectives about the bridges and barriers of working in each of these settings. Since then, teachers and specialists have become more accustomed to working collaboratively with each other; yet some of the same issues remain. In Figure 2.5, we provide an updated summary of the benefits and problems associated with each of the settings.

Those responsible for organizing the supplemental instruction and designing the work plan for literacy specialists, must think carefully about how to address the potential problems or limitations of settings,

Setting	Benefits	Potential problems
In class	• More opportunities for collaboration and communication between teachers and specialists; promotes more congruence • Potential of less stigma for students; less labeling of students • Specialists may be able to serve more students	• Literacy specialist may not be using expertise (i.e., functioning as an aide) • Noise level and distractibility; • May be a pull-back model • Teachers' difficulty to work comfortably with another in the classroom (i.e., differences in beliefs about literacy instruction or teaching)
Pullout	• Ability of specialists to use instructional strategies that focus on specific needs of students • Engagement of students in ways that promote self-esteem and self-confidence • Facilitates small-group or individual instruction • Dedicated time to students experiencing reading/writing difficulties	• Space for pullout instruction is inadequate or lacks resources • Lack of congruence between classroom instruction and that provided in pullout setting (little communication between specialists and teachers) • Promotes "labeling" of students • Students may miss important classroom work
Combination	• Provides for flexibility and addresses contextual issues (student needs, scheduling, teachers' attitudes and beliefs; availability of space)	• May be confusing if schedule is changed too frequently

FIGURE 2.5. Instructional setting: Benefits and potential problems.

remembering that context is important. For example, there may be differences in how a program is structured because of numbers of students who need additional support, available space for pullout instruction, or attitudes and beliefs of teachers about in-class work. Think carefully about these questions: What are the advantages for students? What are the advantages for teachers in terms of implementation? How does the choice of setting(s) improve classroom instruction as a whole?

In-Class Settings

Benefits

In-class instruction is much more efficient in that students are not pulled from their classroom, so they lose neither time (for travel to instruction) nor focus (the emphasis is on what is needed in the classroom). Furthermore, there may be less stigma when students are not pulled from their classrooms; in other words, students are not identified as "different" from others. Additionally, students who are not targeted for assistance may benefit from the instruction occurring in those classrooms.

When an in-class program is working effectively, the teacher and specialist often feel that they learn from each other and that the quality of instruction is greater as a result of the sharing of ideas and materials. Some instruction is much more effective with two teachers in the classroom— for example, writing or literacy conferences, monitoring work of young children who are using manipulatives, and content teacher and specialist co-teaching to address the literacy and content needs of students at the secondary level. By working in the classroom, the literacy specialist can observe how the targeted students perform in this setting.

Over time, communication and collaboration between the two teachers occur more naturally, with each having a better understanding of the other's expectations. And importantly, the literacy specialist and teacher accept responsibility for the literacy performance of all students in the classroom. Again, the emphasis during the past several years on the use of data to make instructional decisions has led to even more emphasis on the in-class model, with various educators (e.g., literacy specialist, special educator, paraprofessionals) present in the classroom to support the classroom teacher in differentiating instruction for students.

Potential Problems

Given the benefits discussed above, why have in-class programs in some schools been problematic? As mentioned previously, past traditions and our traditional model of schooling have not promoted such collaboration and shared teaching. We are more accustomed to the traditional model in which teachers are responsible for their own classrooms. As we discuss each of these potential problems, we consider them in relation to students, teachers, and classroom instruction.

Some students may have difficulty learning in a whole-class setting and may need the privacy and quiet afforded by a pullout model. They may also need more intensive work in a one-to-one situation. Likewise, the in-class setting may not afford opportunities to teach the skills/strategies that specific students need; rather, the focus may be on helping the group to achieve in that particular classroom. Moreover, students may still be identified as "different"—especially if *pullout* has simply been changed to *pull aside* or *pull back*!

Probably the greatest difficulty with in-class programs is that of differing and conflicting philosophies of teaching or even classroom management. Some teachers do not appreciate (and cannot tolerate) the noise and activity that an additional teacher brings. Neither teacher may have the knowledge and skills necessary for undertaking such a venture. This problem is especially likely to occur when mandates are issued, and teachers and specialists are thrust into such programs without the necessary professional learning experiences. There are also concerns that literacy specialists are not used appropriately or are assigned to so many classrooms and students that they cannot work efficiently or provide *enough* support to those students who need it.

Finally, some classrooms are too small or contain so many students that the specialist cannot work effectively. In some schools, literacy specialists are not provided with a place to work effectively with students in the classrooms or they find themselves moving from one section of the classroom to another, trying to find a place in which to conduct their lessons.

Critical Factors for a Successful In-Class Program

There are two critical factors for a successful in-class program:

1. Teachers and literacy specialists have consistently stressed the importance of scheduling common planning time so that they can implement a successful in-class program. Although some literacy specialists and teachers, over time, learn to plan effectively via written communication or "on the fly," these approaches are not as effective as two or more teachers sitting down and planning together.
2. Both the literacy specialist and the teacher must be willing to "share" the students. This willingness occurs only when the two have respect for each other and can agree on, and enforce, consistent rules for classroom management and student behavior. The two teachers must also talk openly with each other about their

beliefs and instructional practices. Such conversations can lead to successful compromises regarding how the in-class model operates.

Pullout Settings

Benefits

One of the benefits of pullout instruction is that students, when pulled, get the specific instruction that they need (e.g., strategies for improving their comprehension skills, word-attack skills) in a small-group or individual setting, where they can focus on what they are learning. There is evidence that individual tutoring (Pikulski, 1994; Wasik & Slavin, 1993) and small-group instruction are beneficial to students (Elbaum et al., 2000; Manset-Williamson & Nelson, 2005; Sackor, 2001) and that such instruction, when provided by a well-prepared teacher, can improve students' literacy achievement. Classroom teachers may feel that they can better focus their instruction to address the needs of the remaining students. Literacy specialists can focus their instruction; they do not have to worry about creating a distraction in the classroom and they have the materials they need to implement their lessons.

Potential Problems

One of the criticisms of the pullout model is that students lose time as they move from one room to another. One literacy specialist commented to Rita: "I've had to develop an incentive program to encourage children to arrive at my room on time. It's amazing how they can dawdle as they move through the halls, stopping at the water fountain, the bulletin board, or just wandering along." Another criticism is the stigma that occurs when students leave their classmates to receive special instruction. At times, classroom teachers have been critical of the pullout model, feeling that students are missing important instruction, or disliking the disruption that occurs when students leave or enter the classroom. The anecdote in Chapter 1 (p. 6; Shaler Area Education Association, 1986) speaks to teacher concerns about pullout programs. Literacy specialists, too, may feel that they are less aware of what is going on in the classroom in terms of what content is being presented and how; thus, there may be less alignment or congruence between what the specialist and teacher are presenting. Specialists will lack an understanding of how specific students perform in the classroom. Finally, especially at the secondary level, students may have little success in transferring what they are learning in these pullout classes to the work that they do in the content areas.

Salinger, Zmach, Thomsen, and Lefsky (2008), in discussing the impact of several intervention programs at the ninth-grade level, found limited results and identified several difficulties with such programs, including problems with overreliance on commercial programs. Research about intervention or pullout programs at the secondary level, as well as research about programs in which content teachers work more closely with specialists or literacy coaches, is a definite need.

Critical Factors for Successful Pullout Programs

For pullout models to work, there must be careful planning and collaboration between the literacy specialist and classroom teachers. Literacy specialists should be aware of what is occurring in classrooms, even though they are teaching students away from the classroom. One suggestion is that literacy specialists spend some time in the classroom, observing students and teacher instruction. This experience provides literacy specialists with a better sense of how their students perform and behave when in a large-group or classroom setting. Moreover, it should be clear as to whether the instruction received in the pullout setting is supplemental or serves as the core program for students.

Combination Settings

Generally, the best approach to choosing a setting for supplemental instruction is to think about how one might use both pullout and in-class approaches. What might work best in your specific school—given numbers of students who need support, level of need, and even space restrictions? In this chapter, we described Shala's schedule with one teacher in which she worked in the classroom and in a pullout setting. In Mark's vignette, he also describes his instructional schedule, which includes both pullout and in-class work. In Chapter 3, we describe schedules of other literacy specialists, illustrating the ways they use the strengths of both types of settings to design their instructional programs. Note Katie's schedule (Figure 3.1)—although she provides Tier 3 instruction in a pullout setting to various groups of students, she is also available to work in the classroom with teachers who request that she come to their classrooms to support their instruction.

IDEAS TO FOSTER EFFECTIVE COLLABORATION IN INSTRUCTIONAL ROLES

Regardless of whether the literacy specialist works in a pullout setting or goes into the classroom (or both), the following ideas have been helpful to literacy specialists in fostering effective collaboration.

1. *Time.* Teachers appreciate the fact that the literacy specialist is in their classroom as scheduled (even if the teachers are not quite ready for him or her). In talking with teachers about literacy specialists, one of their primary complaints was that specialists did not arrive in their classroom when expected. Arriving and leaving on time are critical, as is adhering to the schedule when taking students from the classroom.

2. *Be prepared!* Have everything needed to teach a lesson, including magic markers, iPads, dictionaries, books, and so on. If going into the classroom, do not assume that the teacher will have the material needed—or be willing or able to take the time to find it. Literacy specialists who teach in classrooms have developed ingenious systems for organizing and carting materials, from using luggage with wheels to movable carts to milk carton containers.

3. *Discuss and establish responsibility.* The literacy specialist and classroom teacher must decide early in the process who will be responsible for giving grades, writing report cards, and making telephone calls to parents about student performance.

4. *Offer to help.* As the literacy specialist, think of ways to be helpful in the classroom. Perhaps the teacher is covering a special unit in which students need to take notes—this would be a great time to give a mini-lesson on note taking to the entire class. Or the teacher may be doing the midyear assessments with his or her students and need some help with students who have been absent.

5. *Meet your commitments.* Teachers have difficulty when literacy specialists make changes in their plans, even if there are legitimate reasons for such changes (e.g., attend an Instructional Support Team meeting to discuss the needs of a specific student or a meeting requested by the principal). These unforeseeable occasions do happen, but to the degree possible, literacy specialists should alert the teacher and reschedule as soon as possible.

6. *Be flexible!* Although the literacy specialist may be on time and prepared, teachers and their classes may not be ready or even present. Assemblies, fire drills, health examinations, and many other events compel teachers to change or adjust their plans. These occurrences are, of course, frustrating to the literacy specialist but may not be avoidable. *Adjusting* is the only helpful response. If some change needs to be made in the lesson (e.g., the teacher did not complete yesterday's lesson and wants to work with the entire group), the literacy specialist can volunteer to assist by helping the students who may have difficulties completing the task or try to rearrange his or her schedule so that the plans can be implemented at a different time. Or it may be a time that the literacy specialist returns to his

or her office or room to do some additional planning, or to assess a child who is new to the school.

   7. Discuss the progress of the students with whom you are working. This is especially important when working with students in a pullout setting. Let teachers know what students are learning and the success they are having. Such conversations help teachers better understand the needs of these students and may open the door to more extended discussions about what can be done in the classroom to facilitate learning.

SUMMARY

Although most literacy specialists have instructional responsibilities, the ways in which they fulfill them may vary. One key to enacting an effective instructional role is collaboration. Literacy specialists must know how to work collaboratively with their colleagues to ensure effective instruction for students. There are many ways of working collaboratively, some of which are more effective when working in the classroom and others more appropriate in pullout settings. Deciding where to work (in class or pullout) is not the key question about instruction for readers experiencing reading difficulties. Rather, the literacy specialist, with teachers and the principal, must think about and identify instructional goals for students and how best to achieve those goals. Given this information, schedules will need to be developed that enable literacy specialists to best meet the needs of students in the specific context or climate of the schools in which they work. Moreover, the increased emphasis on RTI as a framework for providing differentiated instruction to meet the needs of all students has generated the need for literacy specialists to work even more collaboratively with their colleagues in planning and implementing effective instructional programs for all students. Developing and implementing such a schedule is described more fully in Chapter 3.

ADDITIONAL READINGS

Bean, R. M., & Lillenstein, J. (2012). Response to intervention and the changing roles of schoolwide personnel. *The Reading Teacher, 65*(7), 491–501.—After visiting five schools implementing RTI, Bean and Lillenstein describe ways in which roles of specialized literacy personnel have changed, with much more emphasis on collaborative decision making and shared leadership.

Gersten, R., Compton, D., Connor, C. M., Dimino, J., Santoro, L., Linan-Thompson, S., & Tilly, W. D. (2009). *Assisting students struggling with reading: Response to Intervention and multi-tier intervention for reading in the primary grades. A practice guide* (NCEE 2009-4045). Washington, DC:

National Center for Education Evaluation and Regional Assistance, Institute of Education Sciences, U.S. Department of Education. Retrieved from *https:// ies.ed.gov/ncee/wwc/PracticeGuide/3*.—This practice guide identifies five recommendations for identifying and instructing students who may be in need of evidence-based interventions to promote literacy learning.

Shanahan, T., & Shanahan, C. (2012a). Teaching disciplinary literacy to adolescents: Rethinking content-area literacy. In J. Ippolito, J. I. Steele, & J. F. Samson (Eds.), *Adolescent literacy* (pp. 40–59). Cambridge, MA: Harvard Educational Press.—In this chapter, the authors discuss the importance of content-area teachers helping adolescents move beyond basic and intermediate literacy skills to more discipline-specific literacy skills.

● REFLECTIONS

1. What do you think are the skills and abilities that literacy specialists need if they are to work effectively in the classroom? In pullout settings? Both?

2. What skills and abilities do teachers need to collaborate with literacy specialists? In what ways are the skills and abilities needed by literacy specialists and teachers the same? Different?

3. What types of lessons or instruction would work best with each of the approaches to collaborative teaching?

● ACTIVITIES

1. Observe a literacy specialist in an in-class setting. Write a description of the instructional roles of the literacy specialist and classroom teacher. Which approach or approaches to collaborative teaching do they use? What are your responses to these approaches?

2. Observe a literacy specialist teaching student in a pullout setting. Write a description of what he or she is doing with students. Be sure to ask the specialist how he or she made decisions about the instruction.

3. In small groups, discuss the vignette below, reflecting on what Mark brings to the literacy specialist role; identify three important "take-aways" from that vignette. Share work of small groups with the whole class.

Questions to Consider

What can be learned about the role of the literacy specialist from this vignette?

In what ways does Mark serve as a leader?

What questions come to mind after reading this vignette?

MARK: EDUCATION AS MY SECOND CAREER

Prior to my education career, I worked as an attorney for about 14 years. I largely enjoyed it. After some time, however, I found myself questioning whether the practice of law was the right fit for me long term. Idealistic as it may sound, I wanted to help people. Was practicing law allowing me to do that? And if so, was I helping those most in need? After some soul searching, I decided to "take the plunge," go back to school, and become an elementary-level teacher. As I was in school (at age 41!), I quickly developed an interest in teaching reading.

During my first several years as a teacher, I grew a bit frustrated watching students struggle in reading. As important as their time in the general classroom was, the instruction didn't always seem to be meeting their needs. Some students were called on to read text at levels far too difficult and they never seemed to catch up with their peers. Instruction was geared toward where the students were supposed to be, instead of where they were. As such, it was not very effective. This was my second career, after all. I wanted to make a difference. It mattered to me that I be effective in helping all students, but particularly those students who were experiencing reading difficulties. And so, I became a reading specialist and have worked in a charter school in Pittsburgh for 11 years. Approximately 98% of the students are of color and a majority are from low-income families. There are 12 K–5 classrooms and I work with all of them.

I have a complex job with several separate, yet in some way related, duties. I generally tell people that my primary responsibilities fall under three broad categories: (1) assessment, (2) reading groups, and (3) interventions. Let's explore each one briefly before proceeding to broader ideas.

Assessment

Virtually every decision my paraprofessional assistant and I make is based upon some form of assessment. We use DIBELS and AIMSweb for every K–5 student (generally about 264) at the beginning, middle, and end of the school year. At younger grades, we perform assessments such as letter naming, phoneme segmentation, and nonsense words. Beginning at mid-first grade through fifth, oral reading fluency is the focus, although nonsense words are still used until early second grade. We conduct progress monitoring with those experiencing reading difficulties on a monthly basis only. Although we use various techniques to assess understanding of various phonic patterns, I need to stress a word of caution. Such assessments should be done once a year, maybe with follow-up in rare cases, and at the same time, they should be used only to the extent that they give the teacher or reading specialist information that they do not already have. They are not intended to take inordinate time or be placed in a drawer and never used productively.

Reading Groups

Once DIBELS/AIMSweb assessments are complete (usually the first week or two after Labor Day), I divide all students in eight classrooms (first through fourth) into five groups (four in older grades). I generally simply divide the groups based upon the assessment results, having found that subjective decision making with respect to groupings is usually less helpful. In most cases, the group is led by an adult— either the classroom teacher, classroom aide, my assistant, or me. Even specialty teachers and others have participated based upon availability and need. I do not describe these reading groups as "interventions," because everyone in the class is participating. The vast majority of reading groups take place in the mornings. Interventions take place at other times.

Once the groups are set at the beginning of the year, I may on occasion make modifications during the year, taking into account the teacher's observations, even if they vary from the data, and move a student from one group to another. Students may also be moved for behavior reasons; for example, if two students simply should not be together, I will usually insist, in those cases, on a "trade" to keep the numbers relatively equal in all groups.

Guided oral reading is the core instructional component of these reading groups. Groups are scheduled for 25 minutes, 2–3 days per week depending upon the grade level and schedule issues, some of which are completely beyond my control. I always tell all group leaders to narrow their focus because of the limited time. Fluency and comprehension are generally the main goals. Groups that experience difficulties are generally led by me, and I do a quick review of phonics as an introduction before we read text. Group leaders are instructed that during small-group reading, students must be reading, discussing, or writing in response to what they have read. No worksheets! No catching up on work given during whole-group instruction. Reading groups take up most of my morning schedule.

There are primarily two sets of materials used for these reading groups. First, the reading series provides leveled weekly readers aligned with the week of instruction as well as first- and second-grade decodable readers that focus on one or two specific phonic elements. In general, students who experience difficulty and younger students are more likely to use materials from the series. These materials allow for reading texts different than those read in whole-class instruction and can be easily leveled to better match students' fluency with the readability of the texts.

In addition, we have gradually acquired, over 16 years, many chapter books ranging greatly in subject matter, genre, and readability. Older and more advanced students usually read chapter books appropriate for their abilities and interest. In all cases students are asked questions about what they are reading. As these students tend to be more fluent, the focus shifts more toward comprehension, albeit without letting go of fluency completely. Questions tend to be open-ended to help students develop a coherent understanding of the text. I provide most of the materials to each of the group leaders, except on the occasion when a classroom teacher wants to take on that job.

We read a balance of fiction and nonfiction. For nonfiction, we often read from the Who Is/Who Was series, biographies of individuals and groups. I am a fan of: *Who Were the Beatles* by Geoff Edgers and *Who Is Michele Obama* by Megan Stine, although there are many others. We also read from many different fiction texts. Among my favorites are *Holes* by James Sachar, *Because of Winn-Dixie* by Kate DiCamillo, *The Watson's Go to Birmingham—1963* by Christopher Paul Curtis, and *Danny, the Champion of the World* by Roald Dahl. For second- and even some third-grade students, I am also a fan of the *Weird School Series* by Dan Gutman, involving the protagonist, third grader A. J., and his nemesis, Andrea.

I work very closely with all K–5 teachers and assistants, along with my own assistant and the specialty teachers who help with reading groups. My assistant and I provide and organize almost all of the resources for reading groups. When group leaders are using 1- or 2-day decodable readers or leveled books, I e-mail a weekly schedule to everyone involved. When group leaders are using chapter books, from time to time I check in with them.

Interventions

Our other primary responsibility is interventions for students experiencing reading difficulties, which often take place in the afternoon. My assistant and I implement interventions in kindergarten through fifth grade. Again, we use the results of assessments to make decisions about students with whom to work. Monthly progress-monitoring results occasionally help us "graduate" students from interventions and bring in new students who have slipped. In kindergarten, interventions are generally one-on-one. From first through fifth grades, interventions are usually in groups of two or three, depending on scheduling issues and the number of students per grade needing help in the allotted time. Readers' Theater generally works better with slightly larger groups.

Interventions do vary considerably by grade level. There is a healthy dose of phonics in grades K–2 and we work extensively on fluency and comprehension in all grades. I have a set order in which I teach phonics for K–2. It varies considerably between the three grades, but I only review phonics patterns they have already learned in class, often a week or two prior to my instruction. I do a fair amount of phonics/word-building work with the students in groups of two to three. We spend a great deal of time reading decodable text together. Parents are kept in the loop regularly about what we are doing. Reading passages are sent home and students are rewarded for consistently reading out loud to the parents. Signatures are required! It is probably no surprise to anyone that students who read consistently at home show greater improvement in DIBELS results.

A word about RTI. I largely follow the principles of RTI, and I believe they make a lot of sense. We assess all students at the beginning, middle, and end of the year. We largely use that information to decide who needs interventions. We do progress monitoring with the students receiving interventions. We use consistent data-driven criteria that are the same for all students in the same grade level in making these decisions.

However, we do not use the guidelines of RTI inflexibly. We do not specifically group our students into Tiers 1, 2, and 3. Obviously, there are students we conduct interventions with and those that we do not. We generally try to spend more time with students who have more serious needs. We do not stay confined to 30- and 60-minute sessions. Kindergarten interventions have been conducted one-on-one, but generally are as short as 15–20 minutes. Other interventions (grades 1–5) can be around 15–25 minutes, but we try to keep students to two to three per group. In short, rather than following rigid RTI guidelines, we make flexible decisions, often with smaller groups and sometimes less time. While the number of minutes is generally a little less than RTI suggests, the number of students in each group is generally smaller. Scheduling considerations well outside of my control often make this necessary as well. I fully embrace the idea of RTI, as it guides intervention, yet I believe it is necessary to be flexible as to the implementation in order to be most effective in meeting all learners.

A Little Bit of Coaching

As I mentioned, I consider assessment, intervention, and reading groups to be my three primary roles. I am in my 12th year at the same school. And I have always taken an interest, among all other areas, in phonics. I had been concerned that the phonics portion of our reading series simply did not provide enough encounters with words following the pattern being taught that week (e.g., when the instruction called for sounding out three words, I might think 12–15 more appropriate). Some supplemental material has been clearly needed. And the instruction, while not bad, needed some tightening. So, I approached administration and got permission to coach ("in my spare time," as the saying goes) specifically with respect to the areas of phonics, word building, and decodable text in first grade. I then received permission to include kindergarten the following year. The results have been quite positive with respect to the overall quality of instruction. There is now a small amount of additional juggling to my schedule, but it has been worth it given the benefits. And there is one additional bonus. I believe that, in small ways, spending additional time with the kindergarten and first-grade teachers has improved our lines of communication, resulting in small benefits beyond the specific changes to phonics instruction.

Schedule

My schedule is complicated. Reading groups take place in almost every grade two or three times per week for 25 minutes. There are two classes for each grade. So, there are predetermined times for all classrooms, for Teacher A's first grade as well as Teacher B's third grade. During that time, everything stops in the classroom. Five adults (including me and my assistant) each take a group of four to six students to generally work on fluency and comprehension using materials suited to that group. Groups are generally homogeneously grouped. Coaching takes place when I can make it happen, but it usually displaces a small amount of the time allotted to kindergarten. The amount of time spent coaching gradually reduces over the year, allowing me to spend more time with kindergarten interventions.

Leadership

My role in the school is an interesting one. I'm not exactly a teacher, not exactly an administrator. If I had to approximate, I'd say I spend 10% or less of my time coaching, 15% of my time assessing, and 75% of my time working with students. But I do have leadership responsibilities. I am in regular contact with all the teachers and staff who work with K–5 students and/or lead a reading group (currently 26 people). I send out assessment data to teachers the moment I have compiled it and talk with them about the implications for instruction and groupings. When necessary, I try to find some time at the beginning of the day, during their prep periods, or at the end of the day to touch base. When a significant issue arises, I set meetings with grade levels and promise that no meeting will last more than 15 minutes. I send out supplemental homework in kindergarten and first grade weekly. I consult informally with all teachers on a variety of issues, ranging from parental communication, special education matters, a selection of books with appropriate readability, and some of their instructional practices from time to time. With the grades that I coach, I feel more of a responsibility to help make decisions based on curriculum and pacing, as well as a variety of smaller decisions. I always do so in a collaborative way. I often take it upon myself to have parents whose children are experiencing reading difficulties meet with administration, classroom teacher, and me. I am currently on a committee to choose a new reading series for the 2020–2021 school year. I often conduct professional learning workshops.

I believe that I have had a positive impact in the school. As described above, coaching kindergarten and first grade has had real benefits. With respect to new teachers or those changing grade levels, I can help in a variety of ways. The degree and intensity with which I am sought out by teachers varies. Some teachers feel comfortable talking with me at great length about individual students. Others are comfortable knowing that I am available as a resource to answer questions about instruction in general. I interact with all teachers about the students from their classrooms that I work with directly. Many appear grateful that I have helped to provide clear pathways for their instruction and scheduling. On a few occasions, I go into a general classroom to model a lesson or provide a mini-lesson simply because it's more efficient to do so in a whole class than with a few students at a time. I work well with administration, special education teachers, and others to help our students. But mostly, I believe I have had a positive impact in the day-to-day working with students, not yet where they need to be reading, in very small groups that focus upon their needs.

Success!

I particularly enjoy working with younger students because they usually make tangible progress with intervention. For example, I worked with one student one-on-one the entire kindergarten year, focusing mostly on phonics. Earlier in the year, she had showed some spark and made steady progress, but by the middle of the year, she seemed to reach a plateau for a few months. She was not sounding out words and reading words as successfully as I had hoped. I knew, and formal assessment results started to demonstrate, that she was not progressing as quickly as I had initially expected, or maybe even at all for a short period of time.

We continued with an emphasis on phonics and reading text at her level. I had occasion to be able to work with her a bit over the summer after kindergarten. By then, the spark seemed to have returned. She developed the ability to read words (at least most CVC words) accurately and automatically. A casual observer would likely not see her as experiencing reading difficulties anymore. What I was particularly pleased about was that she recognized there were some words she knew so well she could simply read as units but knew to take the time to sound out other words, when she had to.

What, if anything, did I do right? I think the short answer is that she and I simply stuck with it. I continued the instruction, did not allow frustration to derail her or me, and eventually she began to display the success and confidence that she had lost in the middle of the kindergarten year, showing big improvement in accurate and automatic word recognition with accompanying progress reading text. There really is no magic bullet. It's simply good instruction, ample time on task, a positive attitude, and, perhaps, a dash of luck.

CHILDREN'S LITERATURE REFERENCES

Curtis, P. C. (1995). *The Watsons Go to Birmingham—1963*. New York: Yearling.
Dahl, R. (1975). *Danny, the Champion of the World*. New York: Knopf.
DiCamillo, K. (2000). *Because of Winn-Dixie*. Somerville, MA: Candlewick Press.
Edgers, G. (2006). *Who Were the Beatles?* New York: Penguin.
Gutman, D. (2009). *My Weird School #1: Miss Daisy Is Crazy!* New York: HarperCollins.
Sachar, L. (1998). *Holes*. New York: Farrar, Straus & Giroux.
Stine, M. (2013). *Who Is Michelle Obama?* New York: Penguin.

MARK BECK, MEd
Elementary Reading Specialist
Manchester Academic Charter School
Pittsburgh, Pennsylvania

CHAPTER THREE

The Instructional Role

DEVELOPING, IMPLEMENTING, AND EVALUATING

KEY QUESTIONS ● ● ● ● ● ● ● ● ● ● ● ● ● ● ● ● ● ●

- ● What factors should literacy specialists consider when developing, implementing, or evaluating a supplemental instructional program?
- ● What makes creating an effective schedule a complex task for the literacy specialist?
- ● In what ways do the instructional roles of literacy specialists at the elementary, middle, and high school differ? In what ways do these differences require different knowledge and skill sets?
- ● What are important assumptions about instruction for students experiencing literacy difficulties that have serious impacts for literacy specialists who teach them?

DEVELOPING THE PROGRAM

In most instances, newly hired literacy specialists step into a program that is already developed and most likely understood by faculty at the school. Literacy specialists, in fact, are often funded by Title I funds (U.S. Department of Education, 2015), the largest source of federal funding for elementary and secondary education. Eligibility requirements and information about implementation and evaluation provide schools with program guidelines. However, there are situations in which literacy specialists have responsibilities for changing or modifying the existing program. This responsibility has certainly occurred during the past several years as schools have implemented programs that address MTSS/RTI guidelines. Also, literacy specialists are often involved in developing a schedule for themselves at the beginning of the year—a schedule that allows them to see eligible students in an appropriate context and have time to plan with and support teachers.

Before literacy specialists can establish their schedules, however, they must have access to the schedules of classroom teachers with whom they will work. In many schools, literacy specialists work directly with the principal or Title I coordinator to develop this school schedule; if so, then they may be able to provide input about how the schedule affects their ability to work with students, or at least, have an awareness of what the parameters are in terms of their own scheduling.

Getting the Evidence

Regardless of the type of program under consideration by the school administration, literacy specialists and others associated with the development of the program should understand the research and the requirements of the funding stream for the supplemental or compensatory program. It is also helpful if they share this information with classroom teachers who will be directly affected by the program. The information discussed in Chapter 2 should help literacy specialists think about the student population in their school, the funding sources that influence programming, and the advantages and limitations of various approaches to intervention. To develop these compensatory or supplemental programs, evidence is needed about effective literacy instruction and also about assessment, which measures to use, how to interpret for instructional decision making (see Chapter 9), and how to meet student needs in a specific school context.

Sharing the Evidence

As mentioned, classroom teachers and literacy specialists should collaborate in the decision-making process. Classroom teachers should have opportunities to read the literature and talk with their colleagues and literacy specialists about the instructional support program. Getting teacher input about concerns and being receptive to their suggestions will ensure a greater possibility of teacher buy-in and receptivity. When schools are considering program changes, it is helpful for literacy specialists and teacher leaders to visit programs in other schools. The opportunity to see a program in operation can often alleviate any fears or anxiety that teachers and specialists may have about programmatic changes.

Getting Started

If there are major changes in any program, the best way to start is "slowly." One can begin by recruiting teachers at a specific grade level to work with the literacy specialist in a different way. For example, given the current emphasis on high-level, rigorous standards and assessments, and the need for a curriculum that provides opportunities for inquiry and integration of learning experiences, a team of second-grade teachers might decide to use its core program differently (at least for one unit). They may try to relate the selections in the unit about animals to what students are learning in social studies, science, and math, and to provide more writing, listening, and speaking experiences. They may require additional reading of informational text or ask students to write a short "research report." The literacy specialist may work in a slightly different fashion with this grade-level team than with other teams. Over time, it may be that teachers at additional grade levels, with the leadership of the principal, decide to move in this direction. The pilot with one grade level offers opportunities for teachers and the literacy specialist to identify and solve any problems with the new program design.

In recent years, a combination of in-class and pullout programs has become much more prevalent, and teachers are more accustomed to having another adult in the classroom. Yet, some teachers are still uncomfortable if there is another adult in their classroom, and to be effective, literacy specialists will need to function in different ways in different classrooms. Different strokes for different folks! Some compare working in the classroom to a marriage—there must be give and take, compromise—and the recognition that progress does not occur in a straight line. There will be highs and lows! When working with teachers to implement an in-class program, literacy specialists can establish collegiality by giving teachers choices about how the program will function, what part of the literacy block the literacy specialist will support, and exactly how the literacy specialist will support instruction (e.g., working with a small group of struggling readers during the rereading time; preparing specific activities for use at a learning center and then being responsible for that center during instruction). Also, if working in the classroom is somewhat new to teachers and to the literacy specialist, starting with a few volunteers may be an option. Often, when teachers see that the program is an effective one for students, they become more comfortable with the proposed changes. Notice the way that Katie, in the vignette in this chapter, differentiates the ways that she collaborates with teachers.

Given the focus on accountability and MTSS/RTI, teachers are becoming more accustomed and even receptive to working collaboratively with many different support personnel, not only with the literacy specialist but with special educators, volunteers, and paraprofessionals. Those who are hesitant may just need some time to get accustomed to this model, and literacy specialists can help by seeking the input of these teachers about what might work best for them. It is important for literacy specialists to provide choices for when and how they might work in the classroom (e.g., "When would be the best time and day for working in your classroom?"; "What will you be doing?"; "How can I support your instructional efforts?").

Ongoing Professional Learning

Providing professional learning experiences for classroom teachers and literacy specialists about how to collaborate and to work effectively in the classroom can be especially helpful. The school district may choose to bring an outside consultant who is familiar with the work of literacy specialists and/or the importance of collaboration in providing for the instructional needs of all students. Or a literacy specialist and a classroom teacher who are working together could discuss and share instructional ideas with other teachers in the school. They may also invite other classroom teachers to observe them as they are teaching together in the classroom. Teachers may read pertinent materials, for example, *Response to Intervention: A Position Statement* (IRA, 2010); in this document, which describes important notions about RTI, there is a strong statement about the importance of collaboration. The document also calls for a school-level decision-making team that includes teachers and specialized personnel, such as the literacy specialist. It also indicates the importance of providing adequate time for communication and coordination to ensure the development of a coherent, comprehensive literacy program. For other articles that discuss collaboration between literacy specialists and teachers and provide ideas to help develop a deeper understanding of ways to promote a culture of collaboration, see Kelly and Caprino (2016), Ogle and Fogelberg (2001), and Pletcher et al. (2019).

Regardless of whether specialists are responsible for developing a new program, collaborating with a school administrator who is undertaking such an effort, or teaching in an established program, they must consider the culture of the school and classrooms, the need for congruence between classroom instruction and special literacy programs, and scheduling that maximizes the use of their time. Read about Pam and what she does to get a better sense of teachers' beliefs and practices.

> As a new professional, Pam wanted to gain a better understanding of the materials and approaches to literacy instruction for each of the three tiers. She was also interested in learning more about school routines, discipline, schedules, and so forth. While she was assisting with screening students early in the year, she was able to informally observe classroom instruction at various grade levels and examine instructional materials. She also engaged teachers in conversations about their goals for the year, hoping to gain a better understanding of their beliefs about literacy instruction and how congruent they were with hers. She wondered what

their views were about her role and how receptive they would be to her presence in their classrooms. She knew she could learn a lot from her colleagues about what worked well in the past and what changes they might value. Teachers seemed pleased to share their ideas and concerns about their students, and also were curious about how Pam might partner with them.

THE CULTURE OF THE SCHOOL AND CLASSROOMS

Given that literacy specialists generally work with many different teachers in a school, they need to become familiar with the school culture (i.e., its norms or ways of being). What are the responsibilities of teachers and specialists relative to bus and lunch duty? In what ways do teachers and specialists share materials or resources? What are the beliefs of teachers about literacy instruction? Do teachers seem comfortable talking about their beliefs and knowledge?

Literacy specialists should also develop a working relationship with the principal, given the key leadership role of that position. This connection might involve meeting with the principal on a regular basis, perhaps once a week, or sending him or her a weekly summary of the focus of your activities. It also means communicating with principals about any issues or concerns relative to scheduling, students, assessment results, and so on. A lack of understanding or agreement between the literacy specialist and the principal regarding the specialist's role can create serious problems.

In Reading First in Pennsylvania, literacy specialists serving as reading coaches indicated that they were successful in their roles only if a principal understood and supported them in their efforts (Carroll, 2007; Zigmond & Bean, 2008). For example, the principal who lacks knowledge about the importance of collaboration may not arrange schedules that facilitate planning between specialists and classroom teachers. Or a principal who asks literacy specialists to evaluate or supervise teachers, especially those who are experiencing some teaching difficulties, may generate situations that limit the specialists' effectiveness in working collaboratively with teachers. In a study of schools implementing RTI effectively, we found that strong principal leadership was essential; the principal had to have an understanding of RTI and be involved in implementation efforts. These principals attended and participated in meetings of the leadership team, discussing results of assessment data with literacy leaders, and in general, supporting the efforts to differentiate instruction for all students (Bean & Lillenstein, 2012). Most of all, principals were responsible for setting the tone, that is, establishing a climate that provided opportunities for school personnel to collaborate, one in which they felt safe in making their concerns known, and one in which their views were listened to with respect.

Further, literacy specialists should listen to and respect the views of teachers. Teachers who are not accustomed to an in-class approach may not be receptive initially to the presence of the literacy specialist in their classrooms. Teachers may not understand how they can or should function when there is another adult in the classroom. Some teachers have difficulty "giving up" their students; they are accustomed to providing all the instruction in the classroom. A teacher told Rita how she planned for a specific story (one that she loved), including the "costume" she wore to introduce the story and the dramatic entrance that she made! Lacking an understanding of how an in-class model might work, she was distraught to think that some of her students would not have an opportunity to be part of her planned experience. Teachers who are insecure in their role might be threatened by the presence of another professional in the classroom. On the other hand, most teachers, given professional learning experiences that help them understand the importance of collaborative teaching and how they might teach collaboratively, are willing to try the new procedures. Again, given the current MTSS/RTI models in schools today, more and more teachers are becoming accustomed to partnering with others.

Literacy specialists and their teaching partners need to think carefully about the many different issues related to effective collaboration, especially if co-teaching in the classroom is expected. Friend and Cook (2000) identify seven different topics that literacy specialists and teachers might discuss on a regular basis: instructional beliefs, parity signals (how we signal that we are partners), noise levels, classroom routines (instructional and organizational), discipline, feedback to and from each other, and pet peeves.

THINK ABOUT THIS

What questions would you raise regarding each of Friend and Cook's (2000) topics? What are your beliefs about each of these topics that would affect how you work with teachers? Think about how you might talk with a teacher about each of these issues and what you might learn!

Congruence or Alignment

In the previous chapter, we noted one of the concerns about pullout instruction is the lack of congruence or alignment between the instruction provided by the literacy specialist and that provided by the classroom teacher. Such congruence is important for helping students achieve in their own classrooms, which gives them a sense of self-worth and satisfaction (i.e., "I can do it!").

In a seminal article, Walp and Walmsley (1989) discussed three types of congruence: philosophical, instructional, and procedural. They indicated that the easiest form of congruence to achieve is *procedural*, where teachers decide when and how they are going to work together in the class-room. How many times per week and for how long will the specialist be there? What are the classroom management procedures? Who will teach what section of the lesson? How often will the literacy specialist meet with classroom teachers? How will they share information about students?

Instructional congruence is more difficult to achieve, given the need for both teacher and literacy specialist to think reflectively about the strate-gies and skills needed by students, how the teachers will present them, and what materials they will use. Questions such as the following can be asked: "How will the specialist work with specific students; for example, what materials, approaches, and activities?"; "What data are available to provide information to make decisions?"; and "What will the classroom teacher be doing and with whom?"

Philosophical congruence is most difficult to achieve. When teachers working in the same school have similar goals and objectives for each grade level, many times they are able to compromise or agree on an approach that is best for students. But if a teacher has deep-rooted beliefs about how literacy should be taught and these beliefs are not congruent with those of the literacy specialist, these two educators may have difficulties work-ing together. For example, a classroom teacher who is deeply committed to using a core program in a very structured way, with much whole-class instruction, may have difficulty working with a literacy specialist who is promoting more differentiation of instruction with stations or centers in the classroom, small-group work, and opportunities for students to interact with one another.

Furthermore, in addition to differences in beliefs about instruction, teachers and specialists may have differences of opinion about how stu-dents should be disciplined or in procedures for classroom management. Literacy specialists have indicated concerns about some teachers' low expectations of students with learning problems and the disrespect shown toward these struggling readers and writers. It is difficult for literacy spe-cialists to work in a classroom in which such behavior occurs, given that they have little authority or opportunity to intercede or change teacher behavior.

Walp and Walmsley (1989) make clear that literacy specialists and teachers within a school need to discuss the term *congruence* and what it means. They indicate, for example, that congruence may *not* mean "more of the same," nor does a "different" approach necessarily hinder congru-ence (p. 366). In fact, in some schools implementing RTI programs, stu-dents who are having more serious difficulties (often those identified as needing Tier 3 instruction) are taught using a more explicit approach; for example, the Wilson Literacy System (Wilson, 1996) or the Sonday Lit-eracy System (*www.winsorlearning.com*) that may prioritize one aspect of literacy instruction. The key to effective congruence may be the ability of the teacher and specialist to discuss and share knowledge about their philosophical or theoretical approaches to literacy instruction and why certain approaches to literacy instruction may differ, depending on students' needs and abilities.

THINK ABOUT THIS

In what ways can you address philosophical differences about literacy instruction or classroom management that exist between you and a teacher?

The answers to this question are not easy or definitive. Sometimes the specialist can make a difference just by serving as a model. The fact that the literacy specialist is an advocate for students experiencing reading difficulties may also make a difference. The key is that you can learn from each other once you have developed a relationship of trust, but this takes time. If there is serious concern about how teachers treat students, specialists need to consult with supervisors regarding what can or should be done.

Specialists, too, must have someone with whom they can share their experiences and problems—perhaps another specialized literacy professional in the building or the district. Overall, teachers and specialists alike want to do their best to help students learn; therefore, it is infrequent that specialists find themselves in unworkable situations. Nevertheless, they should be aware that such a situation can occur.

Making a Schedule

There is no easy solution for developing an effective schedule. It depends on the number of students with whom the literacy specialist is required to work, the number of classrooms in which these students are placed, and the type of program the literacy specialist wants or is expected to develop. It also depends on the time allotted to the literacy specialist for instruction. In some schools, literacy specialists are assigned to instruction for every period of the day (except for the usual planning period and lunch). In other schools, literacy specialists teach students for part of a day, and use the remainder for various other activities, such as collaborating with teachers or addressing assessment needs. Developing a schoolwide schedule is a huge undertaking. Literacy specialists generally avoid removing students from recess, physical education, music, or art, for literacy instruction. Nor should students miss content-area instruction, if at all possible. In many schools, literacy instruction—both core and targeted instruction— occur during the language arts block; often, some students receive targeted interventions, perhaps from the literacy specialist or another teacher, while other students are participating in enrichment activities.

An effective schedule requires an effective use of time, space, and resources, both human and material (Canady & Rettig, 1995). At the beginning of the year, think about the overall or big picture. When will assessment be scheduled? Common planning time or data meetings? Time for interventions? Moreover, decisions about schedules have to be made so that personnel function in ways that take advantage of their skill strengths (e.g., the classroom teacher with a background in teaching the gifted may have responsibilities for working with enrichment activities during Tier 2). Again, common planning time is critical as it provides for making changes based on student progress and needs. Useful resources about scheduling include *Elementary School Scheduling: Enhancing Instruction for Student Achievement* (Canady & Rettig, 2008), *Scheduling Strategies for Middle Schools* (Rettig & Canady, 2013), and "The Power of Innovative Scheduling" (Canady & Rettig, 1995). Information is also available at *www. schoolschedulingassociates.com.*

When there is only one literacy specialist in a school, there is limited time available for teaching individual students multiple times a week. In the study of literacy specialists in exemplary schools, the number of students with whom literacy specialists worked varied from 20 to 80, with a mean of 52 (Bean et al., 2003). Certainly, the specialist assigned to 20 students can design a schedule that is different from one responsible for teaching 60 students. Issues include how the literacy specialist can provide the following important aspects of intervention support:

- Intensity (frequency with which he or she meets with students)
- Size of group (individual or small group)
- Specific needs of students

Here are specific questions that literacy specialists can ask themselves:

1. How often in a week can the literacy specialist meet with certain students (how should this vary, given the specific ages or difficulties of students)?
2. Which students can be grouped together because of similar needs?
3. Which students should be taught in a pullout setting?
4. In which classrooms can the literacy specialist function effectively (or for what part of the literacy block can the literacy specialist function within the classroom)?

Below, we describe the schedule of one literacy specialist, Katie, who works in a K–6 school with a literacy support team that includes a literacy specialist intern, a paraprofessional, a math coach, and Katie. The team develops and negotiates a schedule with participating teachers. Figure 3.1 illustrates Katie's weekly schedule for a single month. Katie has major responsibility for working with Tier 3 students, providing pullout instruction for 30 minutes two times a week to groups of fourth-grade students during their ELA or science time. She also provides Tier 3 instruction to a group of kindergarten students. Katie has also scheduled four blocks when K–6 teachers can sign up for "inclusion," that is, work with Katie in their classrooms. Because the school is a Title 1 school and all students are eligible for support, Katie instructs many different students. In fact, Katie works with higher-achieving students in grades 1 and 6 (see Figure 3.1, intervention/enrichment rotation groups), because higher achieving students were not showing as much growth as expected, and Title 1 personnel can provide supplemental instruction. Also, there are several periods in which students can choose to come to her room for help. Sometimes students need a quieter place to work, have a question, or need more help. Katie also has some flexible time for coaching, planning, or assessment. On Wednesdays, Katie has planning time with each grade level. During this time, the grade-level teams discuss topics such as the upcoming calendar to see what events are happening and how they impact support services. They also talk about where teachers are in their Tier 1 instruction, if there are any issues, if there's a need to reteach, and so forth. At times, Katie might take some time to share information about a workshop or distribute a resource. The planning time is an opportunity for making connections and facilitating conversations between grade levels. Finally, once a week, Katie plans with her Title 1 team to discuss their work and whether there is a need for any changes in scheduling, instruction, and so forth. Read Katie's vignette at the end of this chapter to learn more about how she serves as a reading specialist in the school.

What makes this program work effectively are (1) the planning meetings that provide for communication among all involved; and (2) the written information the literacy support team provides to the teachers, informing them each month of the services that they will be receiving during that time. Katie indicated that the ways in which the support team works in the classroom with teachers differs, depending on teacher style and preferences. Some teachers want the literacy specialists to work only with students with the greatest needs, while others want to work with those students themselves (in a smaller group setting). In the second instance, Katie works with students who are reading above grade level to further develop their literacy learning and expose them to more challenging text. Still another teacher likes to use the time to lead centers and have the literacy specialist introduce the phonics skill for that week. Almost always, the literacy specialist team member helps the teacher divide the class into smaller groups.

	Monday	Tuesday	Wednesday	Thursday	Friday
7:50–8:30	Bus Duty	Bus Duty	Plan	Gr. 4–6 ELA Meeting	Bus Duty
8:30–8:45					
8:45–9:15 Gr. 2 IE	Gr. 4 Tier 3 #1 5 students during ELA or Science	ELA Inclusion Sign Up K–6	8:45–9:30 Gr. 5 ELA Planning	Gr. 4 Tier 3 #1 5 students during ELA or Science	Gr. 4 Tier 3 #1 5 students during ELA or Science
9:15–10:45	ELA Inclusion Sign Up K–6		9:30–10:15 Gr. 4 ELA Planning		ELA Inclusion Sign Up K–6
10:45–11:15 K IE	KDG Tier 3 Gr. #3 4 students	KDG Tier 3 Gr. #3 4 students	10:15–11:00 Gr. 6 ELA Planning		K Tier 3 Group #3 4 students
11:15–11:30	Plan/Coach/Assess				Plan/Coach/Assess
11:30–12:00 Gr. 1 IE	Gr. 1 Intervention/Enrichment Rotation Groups	Gr. 1 Intervention/Enrichment Rotation Groups	11:00–11:45 Lunch + Plan	Gr. 1 Intervention/Enrichment Rotation Groups	Gr. 1 Intervention/Enrichment Rotation Groups
12:00–12:30	LUNCH	LUNCH	11:45–12:30 Gr. 2 Team Planning	LUNCH	LUNCH
12:30–1:00	Gr. 4 Tier 3 #2 5 students during ELA or Science	Gr. 4 Tier 3 #2 5 students during ELA or Science	12:30–1:15 Gr. 3 Team Planning	Title I Team Planning (work with interns + paraprofessionals to plan for small group and inclusion)	Gr. 4 Tier 3 #2 5 students during ELA or Science
1:00–1:15	Plan/Coach/Assess	Plan/Coach/Assess	1:15–2:05 Gr. 1 Team Planning		Plan/Coach/Assess
1:15–1:45	ELA Inclusion Sign Up K–6	ELA Inclusion Sign Up K–6			ELA Inclusion Sign Up K–6
1:45–2:30	Plan/Coach/Assess	Plan/Coach/Assess	2:05–2:50 K Team Planning OR ESAP		Plan/Coach/Assess
2:30–2:50 Gr. 3 IE	Gr. 6 Intervention/ Enrichment Rotation	Gr. 6 IE ELA Elective Help Student can choose to come to my room for help with any ELA work		Gr. 6 IE ELA Elective Help Student can choose to come to my room for help with any ELA work	Gr. 6 Intervention/ Enrichment Rotation
2:50–3:15			Bus Duty		

FIGURE 3.1. Katie's schedule—February.

WORKING AT VARIOUS LEVELS

In the following section, we describe the work of three literacy specialists, each working at a different level. It will become obvious that the roles they fill have many similarities, even though there are also differences in how the specialists schedule their time and where they put their emphases. (The vignettes in various chapters also provide other examples of how literacy specialists schedule their responsibilities.)

Yvonne: A Literacy Specialist in the Primary Grades

Yvonne is a certified Reading Recovery teacher and also serves as a literacy specialist for kindergarten and first-grade students in one school in her district. During the afternoon, as part of her Reading Recovery role, she works with four first-grade students whom the school has identified as needing individualized support. She follows the procedures and strategies required as part of the Reading Recovery program, seeing each student for 30 minutes a day.

In the morning, Yvonne schedules her time so that she can work in the classrooms of the three kindergarten and first-grade teachers (see Figure 3.2). She also meets with each grade-level team once every 2 weeks, during which time she and the teachers discuss (1) the specific skills, strategies, and content that teachers will be presenting; (2) any data the teachers have about students; and (3) specific students who are experiencing difficulty and what instruction might help them.

Yvonne works in each of the first-grade classrooms three times a week. On 2 days, she assists the classroom teacher who is presenting an activity-based phonics lesson to the whole class; this activity requires children to manipulate letter cards on their desks. She walks around the classroom helping individual students who are having difficulty. In one of the first-grade classrooms, she conducts the lesson so that the teacher, new to the

Time	M	T	W	Th	Fri
8:30–9:10	Gr. 1-A	Kdg. A	Gr. 1-A	Kdg. A	Gr. 1-A
9:15–9:55	Gr. 1-B	Kdg. B	Gr. 1-B	Kdg. B	Gr. 1-B
10:00–10:40	Gr. 1-C	Kdg. C	Gr. 1-C	Kdg. C	Gr. 1-C
10:45–11:15	Planning Time				
11:20–12:10	Lunch				
12:15–3:30	Reading Recovery/Planning/Preparation Period				

FIGURE 3.2. Yvonne's schedule.

district, can learn the procedure. In this classroom, the teacher monitors the students' work. Often, if there is time after students complete this mini-lesson, Yvonne pulls aside a few students and asks them to read material in which they can apply the skills they are learning. The other students write their new words in a journal or complete assigned work. One day, Yvonne works with a small group that needs additional review of the skills taught that week. While she is teaching that group, the teacher is either holding literacy conferences or teaching another group that may also need additional help with a strategy or skill. The groups change each week, depending on the needs of the students.

In the beginning of the year, in the kindergarten classrooms, Yvonne and the teachers focus on phonemic awareness activities. Either she or the teacher teaches the lesson while the other assists and reinforces the students' work. These lessons last only 15 minutes. Then Yvonne works in one of the centers that has been set up in the classroom, generally assisting students who have been identified as needing help with letter recognition or concepts of print. Yvonne also helps when there is a writing activity, taking dictation as students tell her what they want to say. Yvonne and the kindergarten teachers have also agreed that there is a small number of students in each of the kindergarten classrooms who would benefit from additional small-group or Tier 2 instruction for more focused oral language and vocabulary experiences. Yvonne is revising her schedule so that she can work with these six students for 15 minutes, 2 days a week, using activities that she read about in the Walpole and McKenna (2017) book *How to Plan Differentiated Reading Instruction: Resources for Grades K–3*.

THINK ABOUT THIS

What do you think are the strengths of this plan for the literacy specialist? What do you see as potential problems with Yvonne's schedule? In what ways is Yvonne supporting the professional growth of teachers? How can Yvonne change her schedule to make room for this small-group instruction with kindergarten students?

Greg: A Literacy Specialist at the Intermediate Level

Greg works in a setting where the intermediate teachers, grades 4–6, teach either the language arts block or math, science, and social studies. His major role is to provide instruction for students experiencing reading and writing difficulties. At the same time, the principal has asked Greg to serve as a resource to teachers and has allowed him to develop a schedule that provides him with that opportunity (see Figure 3.3). Greg works in the classrooms two times a week with the six teachers responsible for teaching the language arts block. This schedule necessitates careful planning so that

Schedule	M	T	W	Th	F
Period 1	Gr. 4-A	Gr. 4-B	Gr. 4-A	Gr. 4-B	float
Period 2	Gr. 5-A	Gr. 5-B	Gr. 5-A	Gr. 5-B	float
Period 3	Gr. 6-A	Gr. 6-B	Gr. 6-A	Gr. 6-B	float
Lunch					
Period 5	Work with math/science/social studies teachers, assessment/planning with teachers				
Period 6	Same as period 5				
Period 7	Planning				

FIGURE 3.3. Greg's schedule.

when he is in the classroom, he can work productively. During his time in the classrooms, Greg teaches small groups needing additional support with vocabulary or comprehension skills. He may also assist by holding conferences with students about their writing. On Fridays, Greg's schedule allows him to work where needed. He may work with students who have special needs or with teachers who are addressing a specific issue or topic (e.g., outlining). He also uses this time to assess students about whom the teachers are concerned.

Greg works with the content-area teachers to help them incorporate literacy instruction in their content teaching. He has gone into classrooms to work with students on study skills or to conduct mini-lessons requested by the teachers. He did a lesson on writing a research report (how to organize it) for the sixth graders who were given this assignment in social studies. He also did a demonstration lesson, introducing the students and the teacher to the "know, want to know, learn" (K-W-L) strategy (Ogle, 1986) as a means of activating prior knowledge, and creating enthusiasm and an organizational framework for the unit on machines and how they work (for the fifth-grade science teacher). At times, Greg plans with the various content teachers during his afternoon periods. He is now planning to work with Kelly and Russell, the sixth-grade social studies teachers who, after attending workshops about state standards, decided that they wanted to improve students' learning by giving them opportunities to talk in small groups about what they have read. Greg shared the chapter "Discussion in Practice: Sharing Our Learning" (Erdmann & Metzger, 2014) and after reading and discussing it, the three of them developed plans for next steps. Together they planned lessons that the two teachers would implement in their individual classrooms. On Day 1, students would read the chapter and see an accompanying video about the contributions of the Romans to

Western civilization. On the following day, students would be randomly divided into groups of five. They would then engage in a 15-minute discussion, using several open-ended questions their teachers developed. Afterward, students would present a summary of their discussion to the entire class. Greg would be there on the second day, so that there would be two teachers in the classroom, moving around, encouraging, and monitoring the work of students. They agreed that they would meet after the lessons were taught to debrief and decide what did and did not work. They would then continue their planning, focusing on ways that they could improve students' discussion behaviors and student understanding of the content.

THINK ABOUT THIS

What skills do you think are essential if Greg is to be successful in this situation? What problems does Greg face with this schedule? What are your responses to the work that Greg is planning to do with Kelly and Russell? (Who is taking the lead?) Why is the work that Greg is doing likely to succeed? Any possible pitfalls?

Brenda: A High School Literacy Specialist

Brenda is the *only* literacy specialist in a large high school, making her job a difficult one. She has a flexible schedule, except for three periods each day when she teaches small groups of ninth graders who scored at a low level on a literacy assessment measure given at the beginning of the school year, or those recommended by teachers as needing help to pass the state competency test given in the spring. During the other periods, Brenda makes arrangements to partner with a small number of teachers while they are teaching a specific unit. She believes that spending more time in a particular classroom (perhaps almost every day while the unit is being taught) gives her the opportunity to become better acquainted with the students and their needs, and with the teaching style and goals of the classroom teacher. Recently, content-area teachers had attended several workshops about the CCSS, and following those sessions, Leon, one of the history teachers, asked Brenda to work with him when he taught the 4-week unit about American democracy. Brenda and Leon reviewed the unit in the textbook, discussed Leon's goals for the unit, and then decided that they would work together to help students become more familiar with the structure of their textbook as a means of learning how it contributes to a deeper understanding of the content. Students would also participate in close reading and find information in the textbook to validate or justify their answers to teacher questions.

After talking with Leon about the history textbook and its components, Brenda taught a mini-lesson, highlighting various organizational aspects of the textbook, ways in which the author identified important information, and how students might take annotated notes that would improve their understanding of the content. The two teachers then team taught a lesson on voting rights and responsibilities; Leon identified several key questions and students worked in groups of three to discuss the questions and then locate and identify the pages on which the answers to those questions were found. After the small-group session, Brenda and Leon held a discussion with the entire class in which students discussed their answers, going back into the textbook to justify their responses. They asked the students to read an article about the ways in which African Americans in the South in the early 1960s were prevented from voting and the efforts of college students to register individuals to vote. Brenda and Leon planned to ask students, after a class discussion, to write a summary of what they learned, using information from the textbook and from the article that they had read. For this unit, Brenda and Leon focused on several of the standards from the CCSS for literacy in history/social studies (grades 9–12), especially those related to integrating and evaluating multiple sources of information read, and writing summaries based on relevant and sufficient evidence (NGA & CCSSO, 2010).

Brenda's other responsibilities include assessing students at the request of teachers and working informally with teachers who want to talk with her about specific students or instruction that facilitates students' understanding of text material. Brenda also shoulders the major responsibility for making presentations to faculty that help them understand how integrating literacy strategies specific to their discipline can improve student learning of content. Next month, she will give a short presentation to the science department teachers about how to make better use of the diagrams and data in their textbook. She will also meet with science and social studies teachers together to discuss the ways in which they could help students gain a better understanding of the vocabulary specific to those disciplines.

Brenda is a member of the school's leadership team and, just this past week, the team discussed the importance of literacy across the curriculum as a means of improving student learning overall. The school has the opportunity to participate in a funded project in which volunteer teachers and members of the leadership team can attend workshops on literacy to learn how to improve their content-area teaching. Brenda is excited about this opportunity and the chance to work more closely with teachers from the various academic disciplines, but she wonders how she will be able to manage this work, given her teaching responsibilities.

THINK ABOUT THIS

What skills and abilities do you think Brenda needs to be successful in her position? One of Brenda's difficulties is finding the time to work with all the teachers who have requested her assistance. What suggestions or recommendations would you make to Brenda? What are some possibilities that Brenda can consider that may enable her to work more closely with teachers as they begin to implement this new approach to content-area teaching?

LITERACY SPECIALISTS AT THE MIDDLE AND HIGH SCHOOL LEVELS

What should be obvious from the schedules of the literacy specialists described above is that most specialists, from primary through high school, have some instructional responsibility. All specialists need to know how to work with students experiencing reading difficulties either individually, in small groups, or as a whole class. And all need to know how to work collaboratively with the classroom teacher to identify student needs regarding what is required in the classroom curriculum and which strategies or skills the students might need to become successful readers and writers. Furthermore, those specialists working at the middle and high school levels need to have a deep understanding of adolescent literacy and adolescent learners.

In the vignette in Chapter 5 (pp. 149–152), Michael Henry, a high school literacy specialist, describes both his instructional and coaching responsibilities. He introduces his weekly schedule, describing the framework he has developed, which provides students with choice and opportunities for authentic reading and writing activities. Other teachers in the school responsible for intervention also use this framework. Michael highlights the importance of helping content-area teachers understand how they can use some of the same tenets in their own instructional planning.

The 2019 ILA position statement on engagement and adolescent literacy (ILA, 2019d) suggests adolescents need the "opportunity to use literacy in meaningful ways, interact with a variety of texts, participate in assessment for and as learning, and experience a community of learners in and out of school" (p. 1). The 2012 IRA position statement on adolescent literacy (IRA, 2012) also highlights the importance of literacy specialists or coaches who can work both with readers who need additional support and collaboratively with the content-area teacher to improve disciplinary-specific literacy instruction. In the position statement, the literacy/reading specialist or coach is seen as possessing knowledge about general literacy strategies; at the same time, it is expected that content teachers, familiar with their discipline, will be better able to identify the information to be learned, the questions to be asked, and "how texts specific to the discipline are structured, and how to evaluate the accuracy, credibility, and quality of an author's ideas" (p. 6). In other words, the IRA recommends the need for collaboration between the literacy specialist and the content-area teachers. In order to fulfill their roles, literacy specialists at the high school level serve more in a resource capacity or as a coach for teachers than in a direct instructional role (Bean, Kern, et al., 2015; Henwood, 1999–2000). Henwood, a high school literacy specialist, defined her role as a collegial one, indicating that she did not want colleagues to regard her as an expert giving advice: "Instead, I needed to be considered a partner in improving the learning of all students, one who complemented the teacher's knowledge of content with knowledge of the learning process that I possessed as a literacy specialist" (1999–2000, p. 317). Chapter 4 provides additional information about serving as a resource to teachers.

Too often, however, there are no literacy specialists in middle and high schools. However, multiple factors call for specialized literacy professionals who have the expertise to work at these higher levels with teachers and their students: the high expectations for students that require them to be college and career ready; the increasing complexity and availability of multiple forms of literacy, including traditional print materials and digital text; and the diversity and variability of students in schools today (i.e., ELs, students from high-poverty backgrounds). Literacy specialists can perform the following tasks at these levels (IRA, 1999, p. 8):

- Provide tutorial or intervention service.
- Collaborate with content area teachers to provide discipline-specific literacy instruction that will enable students to succeed and become self-sufficient learners.
- Assess students' literacy and writing—and teach them to self-assess their literacy and writing.
- Teach general literacy strategies relating to vocabulary, fluency, comprehension, and study skills.
- Relate literacy practices to life-management issues such as exploring careers, examining individuals' roles in society, setting goals, managing time and stress, and resolving conflicts.
- Offer literacy programs that recognize potentially limiting forces such as work schedules, family responsibilities, and peer pressures.

This list of services should be useful to specialists who are working in middle and high schools as they think about their own job descriptions and how they function in the schools.

THINK ABOUT THIS

In what ways does Michael (Chapter 5, pp. 149–152) exemplify the dual role of the middle and high school literacy specialist? How comfortable would you be serving at this level? Why or why not?

GETTING FEEDBACK (EVALUATING THE PROGRAM)

Literacy specialists who are willing to listen to the comments of teachers and who seek regular feedback as a means of improving what they do will be able to make the adjustments that enable them to be more effective in their roles. Although teacher and specialist can discuss informally each week or so, what has worked well, or any changes they want to make in their collaborative work, a more formal, yet simple midyear assessment might be useful for assessing the overall functioning of the supplemental instruction. For example, Figure 3.4 describes questions that the teacher might complete that can then be used as a basis for a conversation between specialist and teacher. The conversations can lead to possible modifications (e.g., spend more time with ELs; change program so that students are not missing important class time). The specialist may also want to discuss the program with a supervisor, the principal, and other specialists. Reflecting on what has been successful and what has not is an important process for program improvement—monitor and adjust! A more formal evaluation might involve analyzing the impact of the program on the students. At the end of the year, literacy specialists can review the achievement data on the students with whom they have worked. How much progress have these students made? Has the program been a successful one for them? If so, in what ways? We recognize the limitations of this sort of assessment, given that students often receive instruction from more than one teacher; nevertheless, it is important to look at these available data. Progress monitoring data that indicate the impact of the program on student learning can also be a valuable source of evaluation data. Chapter 9 provides ideas for assessing student performance.

STUDENTS EXPERIENCING LITERACY DIFFICULTIES: WHO ARE THEY? WHAT ARE KEY ASSUMPTIONS ABOUT TEACHING THEM?

The primary purpose of this book is to highlight the leadership skills and abilities of literacy specialists; thus, we do not elaborate on specific, evidence-based instructional approaches that might be useful for working with readers and writers experiencing literacy difficulties. We expect that literacy specialist certification candidates in their preparation programs will take courses that focus on such instruction. However, in this section, we do discuss the notion of labels (i.e., dyslexia, students at risk for school failure, attention-deficit/hyperactivity disorder, specific learning difficulties) and whether these labels make a difference in how we instruct students. Which students are the responsibility of literacy specialists who have the in-depth knowledge and expertise required to work with them? At what point would students be better served in special education settings? We

Dear Teacher:

I am interested in getting your feedback on the work that we are doing together to help students learn to read and write successfully. Use this form to jot down your thoughts. Then let's plan a time when we can sit together to discuss your responses.

1. Have you seen any improvement in the performance of readers or writers experiencing difficulties?

   None   Some   A lot

   Please elaborate:

2. Have you seen any improvement in the attitudes of readers or writers experiencing difficulties (are they more positive about reading or writing)?

   None   Some   A lot

   Please elaborate:

(continued)

FIGURE 3.4. Getting feedback from teachers.

3. For pullout programs:

   a. Am I pulling students at an appropriate time (they aren't missing key classroom instruction). If no, any suggestions for change?

   b. What improvements do you see in student learning?

   c. What feedback can I give you about my work?

   d. Is there anything you would like to share with me about these students that might help me plan instruction?

4. For in-class programs:

   a. How easy has it been to create a schedule that enables us to work together?

      Easy   Somewhat difficult   Difficult

   b. Any suggestions for making scheduling easier?

   c. What has been the most positive aspect of our collaboration?

5. What has been the most difficult aspect of program implementation?

6. Any overall suggestions for program improvement?

Thank you,

Literacy Specialist

FIGURE 3.4. *(continued)*

follow this overview with two key assumptions about instruction for students identified as experiencing literacy difficulties. Finally, we identify a list of resources (Figure 3.5) that will be useful to those seeking additional information about teaching students who are experiencing difficulties with reading and writing.

Students Experiencing Literacy Difficulties: Who Are They?

Although some literacy specialists have responsibilities for improving literacy achievement of all students in the school, frequently their major instructional responsibilities require them to work with students experiencing difficulties with reading and writing. Given this responsibility, stakeholders (e.g., families, administrators) will often ask them to identify the cause(s) of the difficulties and what solutions might be available. They might also be asked to provide a label for the literacy difficulty (i.e., does my child have dyslexia?). Causation is difficult to determine, and there are many reasons why students may have difficulties. Some students may have been ill and missed important instruction; others may come from backgrounds where "academic vocabulary" has not been the focus; some may have received ineffective literacy instruction; others may have emotional or motivational conditions that limit their willingness to read or write. Some may have been labeled as dyslexic, as a way to identify those with severe language and literacy difficulties.

As the authors of the ILA (2019a) literacy leadership brief on students experiencing reading difficulties point out, there are many labels for students experiencing literacy difficulties, especially to help them qualify for additional support. However, these labels "have not proven helpful in identifying specific learning strengths and needs, nor do they typically indicate exactly what types of support and instruction will lead to successful reading" (ILA, 2019a, p. 3). There are ongoing debates in the field about the nature of literacy difficulties and literacy specialists must keep themselves familiar with the issues as a means of deepening their understandings of the differences in perspectives (for an example of the debate on the identification and instruction associated with the dyslexia label, see ILA, 2016b; International Dyslexia Association, 2016; and ILA, 2016c). In their book, *The Dyslexia Debate*, Elliott and Grigorenko (2014) offer a range of research and perspectives on the term *dyslexia* and suggest that, "achieving a clear, scientific, and consensual understanding of this term has proven elusive" (p. 38). We do not dispute that some students have severe difficulty learning to read. In fact, research using functional magnetic resonance imaging (fMRI), through which the brain is studied, shows measurable differences in brain activity between dyslexic and nondyslexic individuals (Shaywitz, 2003). However, as stated above, the label does not necessarily help educators determine the nature of instruction and support for these

Developing Foundational Skills

Beck, I. L., & Beck, M. E. (2013). *Making sense of phonics* (2nd ed.). New York: Guilford Press.

International Literacy Association. (2019). *Literacy brief: Meeting the challenges of early literacy phonics instruction.* Newark, DE: Author.

Mesmer, H. A. (2019). *Letter lessons and first words: Phonics foundations that work.* Portsmouth, NH: Heinemann.

O'Connor, R. E. (2014). *Teaching word recognition: Effective strategies for students with learning difficulties.* New York: Guilford Press.

Dyslexia

Elliott, J. G., & Grigorenko, E. L. (2014). *The dyslexia debate.* New York: Cambridge University Press.

Gabriel, R. (2018). Preparing literacy professionals: The case of dyslexia. *Journal of Literacy Research, 50*(2), 262–270.

International Dyslexia Association. (2016). *IDA urges ILA to review and clarify key points in dyslexia research advisory.* Baltimore: Author.

International Literacy Association. (2016b). *Research brief: Dyslexia.* Newark, DE: Author.

International Literacy Association. (2016c). *Research advisory addendum.* Newark, DE: Author.

Spear-Swerling, L. (2019). Structured literacy and typical literacy practices: Understanding differences to create instructional opportunities. *Teaching Exceptional Children, 51*(3), 202–211.

Worthy, J., Svrcek, N., Daly-Lesch, A., & Tily, S. (2018). "We know for a fact": Dyslexia interventionists and the power of authoritative discourse. *Journal of Literacy Research, 50*(3), 359–382.

Teaching Students Experiencing Literacy Difficulties

Foorman, B., Beyler, N., Borradaile, K., Coyne, M., Denton, C. A., Dimino, J., . . . Wissel, S. (2016). *Foundational skills to support reading for understanding in kindergarten through 3rd grade* (NCEE 2016-4008). Washington, DC: National Center for Education Evaluation and Regional Assistance (NCEE), Institute of Education Sciences, U.S. Department of Education. Retrieved from *http://whatworks.ed.gov.*

Gelzheiser, L. M., Scanlon, D. M., Hallgren-Flynn, L., & Connors, M. (2019). *Comprehensive reading intervention in grades 3–8: Fostering word learning, comprehension, and motivation.* New York: Guilford Press.

Gersten, R., Compton, D., Connor, C. M., Dimino, J., Santoro, L., Linan-Thompson, S., & Tilly, W. D. (2009). *Assisting students struggling with reading: Response to intervention and multi-tier intervention for reading in the primary grades. A practice guide* (NCEE 2009-4045). Washington, DC: National Center for Education Evaluation and Regional Assistance, Institute of Education Sciences, U.S. Department of Education. Retrieved from *http://ies.ed.gov/ncee/wwc/publications/practiceguides.*

(continued)

FIGURE 3.5. Literacy resources.

Klingner, K., Vaughn, S., & Boardman, A. (2015). *Teaching reading comprehension to students with learning difficulties* (2nd ed.). New York: Guilford Press.

Mesmer, H. A., Mesmer, E., & Jones, J. (2014). *Reading intervention in the primary grades: A common-sense guide to RTI.* New York: Guilford Press.

Scanlon, D. M., Anderson, K. L., & Sweeney, J. M. (2017). *Early intervention for reading difficulties: The Interactive Strategies Approach* (2nd ed.). New York: Guilford Press.

Scanlon, D. M., Goatley, V., & Spring, K. (2020). Literacy leadership in special education In A. Swan Dagen & R. M. Bean (Eds.), *Best practices of literacy leaders: Keys to school improvement* (2nd ed., pp. 281–303). New York: Guilford Press.

Vocabulary and Comprehension

Fisher, D., Frey, N., & Lapp, D. K. (2016). *Text complexity: Stretching readers with texts and tasks* (2nd ed.). Thousand Oaks, CA: Corwin Press.

Kucan, L., & Palinscar, A. M. (2013). *Comprehension instruction through text-based discussion.* Newark, DE: International Literacy Association.

Robb, L. (2014). *Vocabulary is comprehension, grades 4–8.* Thousand Oaks, CA: Corwin Press.

General

Fisher, D., Frey, N., & Hattie, J. (2016). *Visible learning for literacy: Implementing the practices that work best to accelerate student learning.* Thousand Oaks, CA: Corwin Press.

Institute of Education Sciences, What Works Clearinghouse Practice Guides. Retrieved from *https://ies.ed.gov/ncee/wwc/practiceguides.*

National Institute of Child Health and Human Development. (2000). *Report of the National Reading Panel. Teaching children to read: An evidence-based assessment of the scientific research literature on reading and its implications for reading instruction* (NIH Publication No. 00-4769). Washington, DC: U.S. Government Printing Office. Retrieved from *www.nichd.nih.gov/publications/pubs/nrp/Pages/smallbook.aspx.*

Richardson, J. (2016). *The guided reading teachers' companion: Prompts, discussion starters and teaching points.* New York: Scholastic.

FIGURE 3.5. *(continued)*

individuals. We recommend that literacy specialists become knowledgeable about this label of dyslexia as they will be expected to not only interpret results of assessments, but to select and use effective approaches to teaching students experiencing severe literacy difficulties.

THINK ABOUT THIS

Think about the students in your classroom—what they can and cannot do, and what possible factors might contribute to their difficulties with literacy activities.

Assumptions

Reading instruction has always been controversial with debates about best practices (e.g., whole language/phonics, science of reading). Below we identify two assumptions that we believe are important for literacy specialists to consider.

• Assumption 1: *Effective literacy instruction is effective literacy instruction.* A key goal is prevention of literacy difficulties with early access to effective literacy instruction. When the need for intervention arises, regardless of the area(s) where students are experiencing difficulty (e.g., phonemic awareness, phonics, fluency, comprehension, vocabulary, writing), the specific strategies or approaches for addressing these areas are similar. For example, students who have fluency problems, regardless of the factors underlying those problems, will benefit from partner reading, read-alouds, repeated readings, and reading decodable as well as more authentic texts. Moreover, effective instruction includes not only a focus on foundational skills (e.g., phonics, phonemic awareness) but many opportunities for students to apply these skills in authentic reading and writing contexts. In other words, in addition to intentional, engaging, and efficient phonics instruction, students will need opportunities for language and literacy experiences (e.g., understanding the meanings of words, applying their skills to reading connected texts). Phonics instruction is important, and at the same time, students need to have materials and books that are engaging and appropriate to their skills and backgrounds.

• Assumption 2: *Differentiation is important.* Literacy specialists teach students, not programs. They must be able to differentiate for student needs in terms of the focus of their instruction, the degree of explicitness, pacing, group size, and intensity (see Connor & Morrison, 2004; Powell, Aker, & Mesmer, 2020, for more information on differentiated instruction). They must be able to plan and implement instruction in ways that reflect their deep knowledge of literacy. For example, *Meeting the Challenges of Early Literacy Phonics Instruction* (ILA, 2019e) describes major causes of phonics instructional failure: "These range from a lack of application to authentic reading and writing experiences (where the learning "sticks") to a lack of review and repetition resulting in decayed learning" (p. 6).

The literacy specialist should start with a clear understanding of the learning strengths and needs of each individual student to develop differentiated instructional plans. Some students will benefit from individual instruction, while others may do well in small groups. Some students will need more explicit instruction and more repetitions (e.g., phonics instruction will need to be well sequenced and students will need to be given many opportunities to practice the use of the skills they are learning). Given this assumption, we have concerns about the rigid use of scripted programs, often labeled structured literacy programs, that may restrict literacy specialists' ability and opportunity to use their knowledge and understanding of each individual student to make modifications necessary for student learning. Such structured literacy programs may be appropriate for some students, but the pacing or even reinforcement strategies may need to be modified. Often, educators use these scripted programs for initial literacy instruction, either for all students or for those identified as having reading difficulties. However, as Scanlon, Goatley, and Spring (2020, p. 20), emphasized, there is "no scientific evidence" that supports the preferential use of such structured literacy programs (ILA, 2019a).

In Figure 3.5, we identify selected resources that can be useful for literacy specialists who want to know more about teaching students who have reading or writing difficulties. Many of these resources have practical ideas about how to plan and implement instruction for students. A few are more theoretical in nature and provide background information for literacy specialists who may need important information to use as they advocate for effective instruction of students.

SUMMARY

Literacy specialists must be able to initiate new programs and teach effectively in those that are ongoing. Administrators may assign them to teach in an instructional role at various levels in the schools. Regardless of the level at which they teach, specialists need to understand the culture of the schools to which they are assigned and have a good collaborative relationship with school personnel. Likewise, given the need to work collaboratively with teachers, the issue of instructional congruence is an important one; readers and writers need experiences that will help them integrate and apply what they are learning from several teachers or subjects. Literacy specialists at all levels must be experts on literacy curriculum, instruction, and assessment. Literacy specialists at the upper levels need to understand how students use literacy to learn, using texts from many different sources. Getting feedback from those with whom they work can provide a basis for program improvement. Designing instruction for students experiencing difficulties is something that requires literacy specialists to have a deep knowledge and understanding of evidence-based instruction for all areas of literacy and for those at all levels.

ADDITIONAL READINGS

Graham, S., Bollinger, A., Booth Olson, C., D'Auoust, C., MacArthur, C., McCutchen, D., & Olinghouse, N. (2018—Revised). *Teaching elementary school students to be effective writers: A practice guide* (NCEE 2012-4058).

Washington, DC: National Center for Education Evaluation and Regional Assistance, Institute of Education Sciences, U.S. Department of Education.— In this practice guide, the authors provide four recommendations for improving writing of elementary school students. These recommendations include providing daily time for writing, encouraging multiple purposes for writing, creating an engaged community of writers, and teaching students to become fluent with various writing skills.

International Literacy Association. (2019e). *Literacy brief: Meeting the challenges of early literacy phonics instruction.* Newark, DE: Author.—This literacy brief describes key characteristics of effective phonics instruction and discusses common reasons for instructional failure.

Pletcher, B. C., Hudson, A. K., John, L., & Scott, A. (2019). Coaching on borrowed time: Balancing the roles of the literacy professional. *The Reading Teacher, 72*(6), 689–699.—This article describes strategies for balancing the instructional and coaching roles.

REFLECTIONS

1. At what level would you feel most comfortable teaching?
2. What qualifications do you have that made you choose that level?
3. What skills and knowledge would you need to teach at that level?

ACTIVITIES

1. Ask a literacy specialist to share his or her schedule with you. How similar is that schedule to the ones described in this chapter? What are the specialist's views about his or her schedule (e.g., are there any problems, why was the schedule developed in that way, what is helpful about the schedule)?

2. Discuss the following scenario with other literacy specialists or classmates. As a literacy specialist, you have been assigned to work in the classroom with several intermediate-grade literacy teachers. You have heard other teachers talk about one of them, Sylvia, as a tough teacher who makes her students "toe the line." You see yourself as a teacher who "lets kids have some fun." You give students permission to talk informally and share personal stories, believing that students experiencing difficulties with reading need a low-risk environment in which to succeed. You are worried! What do you think you should do? (Remember, there is no right answer in this situation; what might work best as you begin your work with Sylvia?)

Questions to Consider

What lessons can be learned about the role of the literacy specialist in this vignette?

In what ways does Katie serve as a leader?

What questions come to mind after reading this vignette?

KATIE: 17 YEARS OF CHANGES AND CHALLENGES

I feel as though the idea of being a reading specialist found me, instead of me finding the position. Now that I've been working as a reading specialist for 17 years, I know it was the right profession for me. After graduating from college, I was ready for my own classroom and thought I'd find a classroom job through subbing. As I was subbing, a principal told me about the reading specialist internship program at the University of Pittsburgh and asked me to interview to be a reading specialist intern in her district. I've always been an avid reader. Her question guided me to a place where my love of kids and my love of reading met. It also helped me realize my "super power" of being able to see all the pieces that fit together to form the big picture.

After a year as a reading specialist intern, I was hired in a K–3 school to work with another reading specialist. During that year, I often exclaimed "I don't know what I'm doing!?!?!" to my colleague. Being the ultimate mentor and teacher, she was patient, asked what I thought should be done in the situations, and often told me it was exactly what she would do. With every one of those exchanges, my confidence grew. After only 1 year in K–3, I was moved to our 4–6 grades building as the reading specialist for a year, then moved back to the K–3 building for the next 15 years. Many changes happened during those 15 years, including my mentor being moved to the middle/high school and the math coach moving into my room in her place. Last year, our K–3 self-contained building and our 4–6 departmentalized building combined to become one K–6 building (self-contained and departmentalized stayed the same), and we went from three reading specialists in the district to only one, ME!

Through all of the changes and challenges, the main responsibilities of my job have stayed fairly constant; helping students learn to read, and guiding teachers in instructing reading. Not to say those are my only responsibilities, but those are the two I try to prioritize on a weekly basis. What changes is the way I approach each of those tasks based on the climate and culture of the school, the need of students, the teachers I'm working with, the building schedule, requests from administration, and a million other aspects of a school.

I love working with students and seeing those times when they "get it," but I find those "aha" moments can be even more rewarding when it happens with an adult. My approach to coaching has been more unstructured and informal than most due to our building schedule and all of my varied responsibilities. My title is reading specialist, but my job also encompasses that of literacy coach. The math coach and I have biweekly meetings with each grade-level team. During this time, we talk about upcoming instruction and events, student progress, assessments and the data they provide, standards, pacing, and any other relevant topics. These discussions often include subjects other than just school, which has been a great way to build a rapport with each team and individual. It also allows for team building. During these meetings, individual teachers will often bring up a lesson or concept they would like help researching or teaching. I then e-mail and/or meet with that teacher one-on-one during a planning or morning time. I believe this more informal nature has helped build a level of trust, coordination, and respect between the individual teachers and myself, but also has helped the grade-level teams feel like the math coach and I are part of that team. Something that I have found to be particularly true, I learned when in the reading specialist intern program: Every team functions differently and each member of the team plays a role in how the team functions. Observing this has really helped me understand and know how to approach different teams and the individuals within each team. You use different approaches with different teachers. It is important to get the lay of the land before jumping in and trying to make change.

Change . . . one of the biggest lessons I've learned from working with teachers and have witnessed when working with new coaches is that change takes TIME. I think as teachers we are hardwired to jump in and fix it immediately when we see someone struggling or realize that there are more research-based, effective ways to instruct. That need for an immediate fix often backfires. As frustrating as it can be, it isn't unrealistic for bigger changes to take years. Change often happens in little increments, and it is part of my job to help facilitate the incremental change. Patience is key!

I am lucky that I work with two reading specialist interns, two reading/math paraprofessionals, and a math coach in my room. We are the Title I team. This allows for flexibility in scheduling and working with students, as well as freeing up time for me to work with and coach teachers. All of us see small pullout groups of Tier 3 students at points throughout the day. We also participate in inclusion in ELA classrooms. Since we became a K–6 building, the number of students and teachers I work with has grown and I have found that assigning the paraprofessionals and aides to specific classrooms on specific days frees me up to be able to work with more teachers. This is key to team building.

About 2 years ago, I started an inclusion sign-up through Google Drive. Every 2 weeks I send out a template with the times I'm available to push-in to classrooms. I open this up to all teachers, even if they don't teach ELA (students still have to read in science and social studies—vocabulary instruction takes place in ALL content areas!). Teachers sign up on a first-come, first-served basis for times they would like me in their rooms. From there, I e-mail and meet with teachers to identify their goal for that time period and how they'd like me to help. I also collaborate in planning and create materials if needed. The way I'm utilized depends on the content, the teacher, and her teaching style. In all grade levels, I'm often asked to come in during writing instruction to model a lesson, team teach, or to help with small-group/individual writing conferences. First-grade teachers like me to come in during leveled guided reading lessons to lead a small group. Second grade regularly has me introduce the weekly phonics skill to either a group of students needing extra support or a group of students needing enrichment. This also allows teachers to sign up for me to read an assessment to a small group of students. There are so many possibilities!

Not every teacher signs up. Initially that bothered me, but slowly (see section above about change) more and more teachers are taking advantage of the sign-up time. In our biweekly meetings, teachers will talk about what we did when I was in the room for inclusion time. Other teachers have been hearing this and decide to sign up for a time. It used to be that my inclusion time felt more like I was an aide. I'd walk in to the room not always knowing what the lesson was or what materials were being used. I'd walk from student to student assisting the ones I knew needed help or stand in the back of the room waiting for instruction from the teacher. I know it was frustrating for me, but believe it was also frustrating for the classroom teacher. This sign-up system has eliminated that feeling. Now when I'm in a classroom, there is a clear, shared goal, and I feel I am being utilized in a purposeful way. I also see our students benefiting when a classroom teacher and I work closely together. The students are hearing and seeing the same content or lesson, but in multiple ways from two different people.

There are so many nuggets of information I try to pass on to my interns and anyone interested in becoming a reading specialist. Being willing and able to say, "I don't know, let me find out more and come discuss it with you" is powerful because it shows you don't have all the answers, are still learning, and that you are willing to work with others to figure out what is best for students and teachers. I've mentioned that change takes time and that understanding the dynamics of the teams and individuals you are working with is so important. Part of being able to help create change is the ability to see the big picture and how all the teams fit together within your school and district, but I think the most important quality of a reading specialist is the ability to be flexible. From day to day, I never know what will be thrown my way that will change my daily and weekly schedule. The fast-paced changes that need to be made keep me on my toes and excited for each day to begin. One of the things I find most rewarding and like best about my job are the opportunities I have to work on a daily basis with so many stakeholders important in literacy education—students, teachers, administration, and families. All of us have the same goal: capable, confident, independent readers and learners.

KATIE REGNER, MEd
Reading Specialist
Allegheny Valley School District
Allegheny County, Pennsylvania

CHAPTER FOUR

Leadership of the Literacy Specialist

WHAT DOES IT MEAN?

> Ultimately, your leadership in a culture of change will be judged as effective or ineffective not by who you are as a leader but by what leadership you produce in others.
> —FULLAN (2001a, p. 137)

KEY QUESTIONS

- How is leadership defined in the field?
- What communication skills and strategies are essential for literacy leaders?
- In what ways can literacy specialists work with groups of educators to facilitate improvements in teaching practices and student literacy learning?
- In what ways can literacy specialists serve as a resource to teachers?

Words similar to those in Fullan's quote above have often been used to describe or define individuals in leadership positions. The actions of effective leaders can have a major effect on those with whom they work, creating an enthusiasm for learning and empowering colleagues in ways that enable them to grow professionally and personally (Fullan, 2020). The literacy specialist functions as a leader, whether primarily working with students, working with teachers, or coordinating programmatic efforts at the system level. Although the instructional role of the literacy specialist is a given—accepted by administrators, teachers, and literacy specialists themselves—less clear-cut are the leadership responsibilities assumed if the literacy specialist is to have an impact not only on individual students but on the school as a whole. Yet, in today's schools, it is even more urgent that literacy specialists as well as other teachers recognize and accept their role as leaders (Goatley, 2013). Shared leadership and collaboration among teachers are integral to successful schools in today's world. All leaders must understand the culture of their organization and work with others to develop that culture so that it meets the needs of its members (e.g., teachers and students). We'll say more about organizational culture in the chapter about coaching.

As mentioned in Chapter 1, serving as a leader is an essential role for all literacy specialists, regardless of their title, responsibilities, and tasks. In their respective roles, they can exert an influence on the overall literacy program and literacy learning of all students in the school. In fact, as discussed previously, literacy professionals were perceived by their principals as having important leadership roles (Bean et al., 2003, 2018). In Bean et al.'s (2003) study of literacy specialists in exemplary schools, 100% of the principals in those schools indicated that specialists were important to the success of the literacy programs overall; they were leaders in their schools. In follow-up interviews, these literacy specialists described the many ways they served as leaders, performing activities such as serving as a resource to teachers, conducting professional learning workshops, leading curriculum development efforts, and working with other professionals and community members to improve students' learning. All but one of the literacy specialists interviewed had instructional responsibilities; nevertheless, in varying degrees all were very much involved in leadership activities.

In a national study of the role of literacy specialists (Bean, Kern, et al., 2015), leadership was also identified as being an important aspect of their role. Respondents indicated they were expected to serve as leaders and needed much more preparation about how to lead—to inspire and involve others in the school as a means of building capacity. Moreover, those literacy specialists who served as coaches highlighted the importance of possessing excellent leadership, interpersonal, and communication skills. These skills and competencies are described fully in *Standards for the Preparation of Literacy Professionals 2017* (ILA, 2018a), which places an emphasis on this leadership role for all specialized literacy professionals. Although knowledge and understanding of literacy assessment and instruction are important to the success of literacy specialists, the most effective literacy specialists are those who know how to connect with, influence, and inspire others. When making these connections as leaders, literacy specialists can effect changes at the student, teacher, and system levels. Pam, the literacy specialist, found herself thinking about her role as a leader.

One of Pam's responsibilities was to facilitate the grade level meetings during which she and teachers made decisions about which students would need additional supplemental work and be placed in one of her groups. Another aspect of that group work was for her to collaborate with teachers to make decisions about what changes teachers might need to make in their classroom instruction. Although she enjoyed the work with the second-grade teachers, who seemed eager to raise questions and make suggestions, the third-grade teacher group was a different story! This group of teachers had very different ideas about the "best" way to teach reading: Some agreed that they needed to make changes in order to meet students' needs. A few were convinced that there was little that they could do since students didn't come to school "ready to learn." After each meeting of this third-grade group, Pam would sit and reflect about how she facilitated the meeting. Did she give all teachers enough time to present their views? Did she respect their ideas while at the same time making sure that she raised questions and presented information that would help them make good decisions about next steps? Pam asked Ms. Walker, the principal, for some advice. Ms. Walker told her that it would take some time to develop a trusting relationship with these teachers, one where they saw her as a credible colleague. She reminded Pam that some of these experienced teachers, who had seen changes in the student population over time, were uncertain about how they might best teach the students in their classrooms. This uncertainly probably contributed to their comments about students not being ready to learn. Ms. Walker reminded Pam that change is difficult, and that Pam would need to move slowly but steadily to help teachers reflect on current practices and consider new ones.

WHAT IS LEADERSHIP?

Those who write about leadership define it in many ways. Some think of leadership in terms of the position or job title that a person holds (e.g., the principal, literacy coordinator, professional learning director). Others see leadership as synonymous with control or influence, suggesting that anyone who can influence or persuade others to behave in specific ways has leadership qualities. For example, teachers may be influenced by an experienced teacher who is well respected by peers for his or her ability to teach and willingness to support others. That teacher may facilitate the work of colleagues, serve as a mentor for novice or student teachers, and influence efforts to improve literacy instruction at specific grade levels or the school (e.g., read Katy's vignette in this chapter for her thoughts about serving as an informal leader in her school).

Others see leadership as a set of behaviors; an individual can be a leader by exhibiting certain behaviors associated with leadership, such as solving problems creatively, obtaining commitments from others, or resolving conflicts. Certainly, specific traits or characteristics enhance leadership (e.g., ability to communicate well with others, effective interpersonal skills).

Likewise, style (e.g., democratic, laissez-faire, authoritative) can influence the way in which one leads. A specific principal might be characterized as demanding or known as someone who leads in a top-down manner (authoritative); another principal might be seen as having a democratic style (i.e., involves teachers in decision making and aims for consensus of teachers for solving problems). Another might relinquish leadership—perhaps in an area such as literacy, to another individual such as the assistant principal, a teacher leader, or a literacy coach—and be viewed as laissez-faire.

Leadership in this text is defined as any activity or set of activities associated with working with others to reach or accomplish a common goal, that of improving student learning, especially literacy learning. In other words, leadership is seen as a process, not as a set of traits or styles. It is closer to the notion of distributed leadership as defined by Spillane (2005, 2015) who indicated that leadership is more than the action of one individual; rather, it is the interactions that occur between and among individuals. In other words, school professionals who serve as leaders (formal and informal) are influenced by and influence each other. Further, leadership is shared and distributed among personnel in different ways, depending on the context, the situation, and individual competencies. Note the different scenarios below.

- If the principal has little literacy knowledge, the literacy specialist might be asked to assume major leadership responsibilities for the literacy program.
- A principal with a strong literacy background might choose to serve as the leader of a team of literacy specialists and coaches who work collaboratively to make decisions about instruction, grouping, and assessment.
- The principal and literacy coach might ask teachers who have expertise in using technology to lead efforts to enhance teacher knowledge of and and capability to use digital tools, perhaps for project learning, or to assist teachers in designing remote learning experiences useful at specific times (e.g., building closures because of weather, heating issues, COVID-19 teaching situations).

In this last example, teachers with specific expertise are empowered to serve in a leadership role; leadership is distributed and shared. Again, there are multiple ways to distribute leadership in a school; what is important is that leadership *is* distributed or stretched so that all have opportunities to serve in such a role.

In fact, literacy specialists and coaches often lead by influence; they are employed as instructional rather than administrative personnel and do not have the authority to require teachers to make changes. Rather they suggest, recommend, encourage, and even nudge teachers to make instructional changes. And, although some literacy specialists or literacy coaches regret that they do not have the authority to require compliance, most scholars who write about coaching view the coach's role as collegial rather than evaluative, supervisory, or authoritative (Knight, 2007; Toll, 2005, 2018; Tschannen-Moran & Tschannen-Moran, 2011).

Literacy specialists whose major responsibility is instruction of readers experiencing difficulties can and should function as leaders. For example, a literacy specialist may take the lead in helping several new teachers who have questions about the most effective ways to use flexible grouping in their classroom. Another may co-plan with a fourth-grade teacher who asked for help in leading discussion groups to improve comprehension instruction. A literacy specialist at the middle or high school level may work with the principal and department chairs to design a professional learning plan for improving disciplinary literacy instruction at that level. If a school is going to select a new reading program, the literacy specialist with a strong understanding of literacy curriculum and instruction can be an invaluable member of, or lead, the textbook selection committee.

Leaders are those who promote positive change and inspire and empower others to participate in the process. They lead not only by the power of persuasion but by the power of example. As Covey (2004) states, "Leadership is communicating to people their worth and potential so clearly that they come to see it in themselves" (p. 98). In other words, leadership sets into motion leadership in others.

In *Lead Simply: How to Create That Special Team of People,* Sam Parker (2012) discusses three key aspects of leadership helpful to literacy specialists in schools. Think about how you might actualize each of these key aspects of leadership in your work.

- *Model.* Lead by example, be enthusiastic, focus your energies.
- *Connect.* Be an active listener, encourage an open flow of ideas.
- *Involve.* Share responsibility.

CHARACTERISTICS AND QUALIFICATIONS OF EFFECTIVE LEADERS

People define and describe leaders in many different ways. Think about these four statements relative to effective leaders:

- I think everyone can be a leader. The key is for people to see themselves as being someone who can make a difference.
- One of the important things about leadership is being yourself!
- True leaders are loyal to those who are under them.
- You have to be reliable. When you tell someone you are going to do something, you need to do it!

THINK ABOUT THIS

Think of a leader you know and respect. What qualifications or traits does that individual exhibit relative to their leadership role? What impact does/ did that individual have on your behavior? Do you agree with the four statements above about leadership? Why or why not? What traits or characteristics do you associate with effective leadership?

The statements above reflect thoughts about characteristics of effective leaders. What is key however, is that in schools, everyone—teachers, specialists, and administrators—can serve in a leadership role. When a teacher chairs a committee to select a new textbook, she is assuming a leadership role. When literacy specialists sit down with a new teacher to discuss how to teach readers experiencing difficulties, they are serving in a leadership role. So, too, are teachers who work with a group of volunteer tutors or with student teachers assigned to them for their field experiences. For more information on teacher leadership in general, see Bond and Hargreaves (2014); Curtis (2013); Crowther, Ferguson, and Hann (2008); and Killion et al. (2016).

The following five characteristics contribute to effective leadership: ability to communicate, teamwork, empowerment, goal seeking (having a vision or direction), and respect for others.

Communication Skills

Effective communication is a two-way street. It requires excellent listening and speaking skills. Likewise, it requires excellent reading and writing skills (e.g., sending an e-mail, writing a letter to parents). Below we describe ideas for developing effective oral communication skills (listening and speaking) separately but ask you to remember the importance of communication as a two-way process.

Active Listening

Seek first to understand, then to be understood.
                    —COVEY (1989, p. 235)

We have had opportunities to have informal conversations with coaches, and not just literacy coaches, but life coaches, sport coaches, executive coaches, and even a health coach! Invariably, when asked what they believe is the most important attribute of a coach, they respond, "Being a good listener." Covey (1989), in his book *The 7 Habits of Highly Effective People,* presents this notion as one of the important principles designed to help individuals work with each other effectively. Of course, we know how to listen; we do it all the time! However, too often, we listen to reply, rather than to understand. As Covey (2004) indicates, too often, individuals listen from "within their own frame of reference" (p. 192). He describes a listening continuum that includes "ignoring, pretend listening, selective listening, attentive listening, and empathic listening—only the highest, empathic listening, is done within the frame of reference of the other person" (p. 192). Too often, we listen from our own frame of reference because we are busy evaluating, interpreting, or preparing our responses rather than trying to understand what the person is attempting to communicate. Active listening is one of the key skills of an effective leader. It shows respect and creates trust, essential for effective communication. The following behaviors can contribute to active listening.

1. *Focus on the speaker's message, or as The Hedges Company (n.d.) indicates, listen to the whole person, not just the facts.* Listen for both what the speaker is saying and the feelings expressed. Look for cues that indicate how the speaker feels (e.g., facial expression, body language, posture). For example, a teacher who is telling the literacy specialist about the negative classroom behavior of a particular student, in describing the behaviors, may be feeling confused, unhappy, or even angry about the situation. The active listener attempts to understand both the content and the feelings behind the message. An understanding of content and feelings can be helpful to the literacy specialist in making a decision about how to respond.

2. *Listen out of curiosity rather than to judge* (Hedges Company, n.d.). When you listen with an open mind, interested in what the speaker has to say, you are involved in empathetic listening and will gain a better understanding of what the speaker wants to say—rather than just confirm what you think. A curious listener stays away from interrupting the speaker or finishing sentences. In their book *Joining Together: Group Theory and Group Skills,* Johnson and Johnson (2013) emphasize the importance of nonevaluative listening, indicating that one of the barriers to effective communication is the tendency of individuals to make judgments as they are listening to a speaker. Have you ever found yourself thinking about your reply while someone is speaking? Or interrupting speakers before they finished a sentence? Such behavior is not active listening; it not only limits the listener's understanding of the message but the speaker may react negatively to this sort of behavior.

3. *Make certain that you have a clear understanding of what is being said.* You can test your understanding by rephrasing in your own words what you heard the speaker say. In other words, put yourself in the place of the speaker; reiterate her views or perspectives. You may also ask questions, especially when you are not certain that you have understood the message. Covey (1989) suggests that the listener (1) mimic content (i.e., repeat what is said), (2) rephrase content, and (3) rephrase content and reflect feelings

(pp. 248–249). In other words, there is a need to *clarify* and *confirm* what we are hearing as well as acknowledge the perceived feelings. For example, "You want to move Charla from her current group placement because of her negative interactions with one of the other students in that group. You find their behavior to be disruptive to your teaching. Is that right?"

4. *Use nonverbal indicators of active listening.* Effective listeners understand the importance of nonverbal indicators of active listening: They smile and acknowledge that they are listening by nodding in agreement. They sit in ways that show their interest in the subject and in the listener. Some researchers have indicated that much of effective listening has to do with these nonverbal aspects. Think about an experience you've had, perhaps in talking with a salesperson or trying to get information when your airplane flight has been canceled. It's very easy to determine whether that individual is engaged in active listening—and is listening in an empathetic manner! Speakers are much more willing to carry on the conversation when there is evidence of active listening. Further, they are more likely to trust that you have a real interest in what they are trying to say.

5. *Encourage elaboration.* When speakers are asked to "say more," or to expand on what they are saying, they are more likely to share in-depth their thoughts, concerns, or issues. They will also be more likely to trust the individual with whom they are talking. Sometimes speakers need encouragement to provide additional information or assistance in organizing their thoughts so that the message is clear. Miller and Miller (1997, p. 92) provide three examples of how to invite elaboration: requesting more information ("Please say more"), asking an open-ended question ("Anything else?"), and making a statement ("I'd like to hear more"). Regardless of what you say, it should be sincere, not sound like a trite response.

6. Finally, *stay away from multitasking.* Think about the times someone is sharing something with you, but you are engaged in checking your cellphone messages or sneaking a peek at the e-mail messages on your computer. It is difficult to be an active listener when you are engaged in such behavior. Whether a preset meeting time or impromptu conversation, the way in which you are engaged as an active listener, rather than a multitasker, can make a huge difference in how you are perceived and in what can be accomplished.

Clear, Congruent Speaking

Johnson and Johnson (2013, pp. 132–133) provide important insights about sending messages. Their list is adapted below.

1. *Own messages by using first person–singular pronouns.* If you have a particular feeling or opinion about an issue, make certain that you

indicate this directly, for example, by saying, "I really have problems with ability grouping; these are the reasons."

2. *Make your verbal and nonverbal messages congruent.* As mentioned previously, nonverbal communication is important. Even though you may have a positive message to relate to others, a frown on your face or lack of a positive expression may reduce the impact of that message to others. Listeners attend to more than words: They notice the tone and the nonverbal cues. Rita remembers vividly an experience in observing a second-grade teacher. As this teacher led the students through the lesson, she never smiled or expressed any emotion, even when she complimented certain students on their performance. Rita recalls:

> "This behavior confused me because I did not sense any real connection between the students and this teacher. I wondered whether students were receiving mixed messages or even a single message that this teacher had little enthusiasm for the subject she was teaching or a sense of caring for her students. As we talked after the lesson, the teacher mentioned to me that she was not very expressive. Then she said, 'My students understand that I care.' In other words, she was aware of the nonverbal message that she sent, but she also believed that her students saw past that message. I wondered, however, about the impact of this behavior on students, especially those who were experiencing difficulties as learners."

How do you feel when you are with others in a group meeting and when you say something, an individual in the group seems to be frowning? What are your reactions to this type of behavior? Does it make you hesitate to say more?

3. *Ask for feedback about your message.* Taking the time to ask listeners to restate your message or to ask for questions tells you whether you and your listeners are "on the same page" and whether any confusion exists. In any group session, you might end by summarizing what was said and ask for feedback (e.g., "I think we agreed to develop a plan to locate culturally relevant materials by doing the following. Is that correct? Any questions? Additional comments?").

For a list of dos and don'ts of effective communication, see Bean and Ippolito's *Cultivating Coaching Mindsets* (2016, pp. 78–79) or go to *www.learningsciences.com/bookresources* to download a reproducible version.

THINK ABOUT THIS

Think about your own communication skills. What are your personal strengths? Possible trouble spots? What communication qualities do you appreciate in others? Use the questions in Figure 4.1 to help you think about your own communication skills and those of others.

---

1. Am I an active listener? Do I listen to understand both the content of the message and what the speaker might be thinking and feeling?

2. Do I provide nonverbal indicators of active listening (nodding in agreement, smiling, encouraging elaboration)?

3. Do I use strategies to make sure that I "understand" the words of the speaker (rephrasing or paraphrasing, asking speaker to clarify, elaborate)?

4. Do I build on what the speaker is saying (elaborating or responding in a way that indicates I am listening)?

5. Do I facilitate conversations that indicate the teacher and I are co-learners or working together to solve a problem?

6. Do I summarize what I have heard (or ask the speaker to summarize) as a means of facilitating understanding?

7. Do I ask listeners to give me feedback about what I have said?

8. Do I listen more than I speak? (The 80/20 rule—listening for 80% of the time)

9. Do I give listeners opportunities to ask questions or make comments about what I have said?

FIGURE 4.1. Effective communication: Questions to consider. Adapted with permission from Bean (2001).

Teamwork

None of us is as smart as all of us.
—BLANCHARD, BOWLES, CAREW,
    AND PARISE-CAREW (2001, p. 60)

The ability to work as a member of a team is an especially important skill for literacy specialists because they often work with groups or teams of teachers (e.g., committees, grade-level groups, academic-subject groups). As leaders and members of groups or teams, they must be able to influence and inspire others to work together to improve the school literacy program. When working with a group, consider the following as important for shaping effective teamwork:

- The atmosphere is comfortable and relaxed.
- All members feel as though they have an important role in the group, and all participate.
- Group members listen to one another.
- Leadership shifts from individual to individual, depending on experience or expertise.
- The group works effectively as a unit to achieve its tasks.
- Group members are conscious of how the group is functioning (i.e., they are aware of the interpersonal and communication skills between and among group members).

We recommend Aguilar's (2016) *The Art of Coaching Teams* or Johnson and Johnson's (2013) *Joining Together* for those who want to read more about working with groups. Johnson and Johnson discuss in a clear manner the importance of attending to both *task* and *maintenance* responsibilities of a group, as described by Hersey and Blanchard (1977). That is, there is a goal or task to be met, and group members need to work in ways that enable them to focus on that goal. If the group is not staying on *task*, someone in the group must remind members of their goal; often this is the designated leader. At the same time, the leader must also be conscious of the importance of maintaining a *climate* that enhances the members' ability to work comfortably and effectively with one another. Ideas and comments made by members should be received in an open and receptive manner; all members must be encouraged to participate in the conversation. If necessary, the leader needs to offer guidance or redirect the discussion should the climate shift to an uncomfortable or ineffective atmosphere.

Building a sense of team takes time. Some groups will meet over a long period of time—perhaps a year (e.g., grade-level or academic discipline teams, leadership team). Other teams, after meeting their goal, will be disbanded (e.g., selecting a core literacy program; developing a parent partnership program). Regardless, when the group is forming, members will be trying to figure out what and how they can contribute and how they relate to others in the group. Often, leaders become disappointed or disillusioned when, after one or two meetings, it appears as though no progress is being made. However, it takes time for a group to learn to function effectively. Over time, a group will tend to move from divergent to convergent thinking. All groups go through what Kaner, Lind, Toldi, Fisk, and Berger (1996, p. 20) call "a groan zone," as they work together. When a group functions effectively, it is because they have a clear sense of purpose, are dedicated to meeting their goals, work well together, and believe that they can learn from this experience and from each other.

Empowering Others

The most effective schools are those in which teachers feel as though they have a voice in what happens; they feel a sense of ownership or empowerment. There are several ways in which leaders can empower others. First, they can acknowledge the work of others, identifying colleagues as leaders. They can also encourage others to actively participate, thus promoting leadership behaviors. For example, the literacy specialist may ask an individual teacher to lead a workshop session in which he or she discusses classroom management. In a group setting, the literacy specialist as leader may solicit ideas and thoughts of particular group members, especially those who tend to be reticent to speak but who often have great ideas to share. The literacy specialist can also provide opportunities for decision making that require group participation and consensus. For example:

> "We've come up with three different ideas about how we want to pro-mote parent involvement in our schools. Let's talk about each of these, and what they mean in terms of planning and implementation. All of us as a group need to decide whether we will attempt to do all of these or will focus on just one. After listing pros and cons, we should try to come to a consensus as to our future direction."

Achieving Goals: Having a Vision

This characteristic of effective leadership is what some would call "the bot-tom line": the ability of the leader to help others to first decide upon goals or a vision, and then work with the group to reach them. Without a sense of direction, a goal, or a vision, little can be accomplished. When a decision is needed (e.g., about materials or a curriculum issue), the leader must be able to work with others in ways that ensure one is made. First and foremost, it is essential to establish (1) a clear understanding of the goal to be achieved and (2) a commitment of the group to achieving that goal. In addition, leaders must make certain that those with whom they are working have the skills and resources they need to achieve those goals. Finally, there must be recognition and support every time a step is taken that moves the group toward goal achievement.

Respect for Others

Effective leaders respect those with whom they work. They seek and value the ideas of others; they recognize their own limitations. So, although effec-tive leaders have a sense of vision and work energetically to reach that vision, they are also respectful of the views of others. They are honest and fair in their dealings with their colleagues. Leaders who are seen by colleagues as "having all the answers" will soon find themselves without anyone to lead! Moreover, there will always be diverse perspectives when working with others; effective literacy specialists accept these differences and recognize that those with diverse views can help others think more creatively about various problems and solutions. Effective leaders try not to take things personally—rather, they listen to see if they can learn some-thing from others' criticism (Willink, 2019). Remembering that all indi-viduals have different ways of making sense of the world can enable you to react differently to individuals, to practice a new form of compassion and connection (Berger, 2012, 2019). In other words, conflicts are not necessar-ily personal but may be the result of an individual's attempt to make sense of a situation from his or her perspective.

WORKING WITH GROUPS

As mentioned previously, most literacy specialists, regardless of role, will find themselves working with small groups. The specialist may be the leader of the group, and on other occasions a member of the group. In either case, an understanding of basic group dynamics and how to conduct a group meeting are critical for the group to work effectively. By taking into consideration the following steps, meetings can be more productive with less grumbling about them being a waste of time.

Planning and Preparation

Planning includes setting goals for each meeting, preparing the agenda that assists in meeting these goals, and handling logistics for the meeting itself. Any informational items that do not need discussion can be prepared for distribution or sent to participants prior to the meeting. It may be productive to spend the first few minutes of a meeting, especially the initial meeting of any group, on helping the group to become acquainted (or reacquainted) with one another. Group leaders may want members to introduce themselves, share some personal information, or discuss their views about working on the task to which they are assigned. The agenda should be structured so that items of priority are discussed first; a specific amount of time can be designated for each item so that those at the bottom of the agenda are also addressed. Effective leaders also review the agenda and ask members if they have any items to add to that list.

Part of initial planning includes providing for the place in which the meeting will be held. If the meeting is a large one and information is being presented, a classroom setting with rows of desks may serve as the venue. But if group participation is desired, the room should be one in which participants can sit in a circle and see and hear one another. The physical space matters! Often it helps if refreshments are provided, especially if the meeting is an after-school one. All materials needed for the meeting should be at hand (e.g., handouts, flip charts). Planning also includes making decisions about how records are kept and disseminated. For some meetings, it might be important to keep minutes so that there is a permanent record of decisions made.

Establishing Norms for Group Behavior

The time spent in establishing rules or norms for group behavior is well spent; otherwise, the group may flounder as it attempts to make decisions or address difficult issues about which individuals are at odds. Similar to classroom settings, such norms are better established at the beginning of the school year or when a group is being formed. Otherwise, a leader may have to work to redirect the process if the group is working in a dysfunctional manner (e.g., only two of the six teachers do most of the talking and, in fact, make the decisions in terms of scheduling and grouping; the other four leave the meeting "rolling their eyes" and feeling as though their voices are not being heard). Norms for the following may need to be addressed:

- What processes for decision making will the group use (e.g., consensus, voting) and for which decisions?
- What roles are needed for effective group functioning (e.g., Is there a need for a note taker or a facilitator? Will leadership change each meeting)?
- How will conflict be addressed?
- How will the group make certain that all members have opportunities to be heard?

Although a working group tends to develop its own set of rules and behaviors, the leader plays an important role in helping the group to decide on these and then to follow them. It is also wise to post these norms or rules and review them before starting a meeting. It may also be helpful if the principal works with the literacy specialist during initial meetings of the group to establish those norms. Figure 4.2 provides a sample of what a list of norms might include, although the best way to proceed is to ask the group to establish its own norms. The leader can talk with the group members about what they value when they attend meetings, asking members to identify ways of working that make meetings effective (e.g., members arrive on time).

- Have a focused agenda.
- Begin and end the meeting on time. (Everyone arrives on time!)
- All participants have an "equal voice."
- Be civil—agree to disagree.
- Be an active listener.
- Challenge ideas—not people.
- Presume positive intentions of team members.
- Make decisions based on the issue being discussed. Some decisions can be made by majority vote (e.g., best time to meet); key decisions are best if consensus is reached (e.g., "Which of the three reading programs are we going to choose as a basis for our curriculum?").
- Come prepared for the meeting (e.g., documents ready).
- Turn off cellphones and other technology that might distract from conversation.

FIGURE 4.2. Suggested meeting norms.

Attending to Task and Relationship Aspects

Accomplishing goals or tasks is of key importance for both leader and team members. Who has not heard grumbling about useless meetings in which items are discussed, rehashed, and then discussed again at the next meeting? At the same time, members must be sensitive to the way in which the group is working so that all feel valued, participate, and assume responsibility for group achievement. This is not always easy, and some meetings will be better than others. One of the most effective ways to build a sense of "esprit de corps" is to take time at the end of the session to talk about what went well and how the group might modify its behavior to improve its work.

Active Engagement: Using Protocols to Guide Conversations

Often task and relationship aspects of group work can be addressed by using discussion-based protocols, defined as structured processes to guide conversations so that they are focused and productive. Group leaders can use protocols to open or close a meeting or to support groups in their efforts to complete a task. Many different protocols can be found on *www.schoolreforminitiative.org.* Included on the website is the Continuum of Discussion-Based Protocols developed by Ippolito (2013) to help leaders understand that some protocols are better used after educators have developed a greater degree of trust and collegiality, and have worked with each other for an extended period of time. Protocols can be useful to the novice leader who may need ideas for facilitating group action. For example, McDonald, Mohr, Dichter, and McDonald (2007) describe a *Clearing* protocol that might be used to help group members transition from where they were to where they are (e.g., from teaching a class to attending an after-school meeting). The rules are simple: Say what is on your mind, nothing is irrelevant; talk only once; and silence is okay. Such a protocol can help establish a risk-free environment in which participants feel comfortable contributing to the discussion.

We do have a caution about the use of protocols, however. It is important that they provide an authentic task for group members; if they seem contrived, members may become less willing to participate. We encourage you as a leader, therefore, to think about how you can adapt protocols to fit your group, or you might choose to design one that works for you in your context.

Working with Disruptive Group Members

There may be individuals in some groups who are difficult to work with—they do not want to be in the group, they are not accustomed to working with groups, or they antagonize others because they are unwilling to listen to others' ideas. Perhaps individuals such as those described below (adapted from Parrott's [1996] book *High-Maintenance Relationships: How to Handle Impossible People*) have been members of groups with whom you have worked:

- The Critic—constantly complains about whatever is being discussed (e.g., "Why are we talking about changing our schedules again?").
- The Wet Blanket—negative and pessimistic about new ideas or suggestions (e.g., "That will never work!").
- The Control Freak—wants to direct and control the decisions that will be made; tends to talk a great deal and loudly; not inclined to listen to ideas of others; pushes for specific decisions to be made.

There is no simple answer to working with such individuals. Remember that these individuals may have various reasons for behaving as they do: They feel insecure (i.e., they may lack the knowledge or skills to contribute to what is being discussed); they may be dealing with personal issues that are of greater concern to them (e.g., an illness in the family); their values or beliefs may be affecting their responses, and so on. Taking the time to think about the underlying reasons for their behaviors is important.

There are some strategies, however, that may be effective in dealing with, say, George, who tends to be critical of most ideas. First, setting norms for appropriate group behavior as described above is key to changing or at least minimizing the effects of George's disruptive behavior. Second, within a group setting, the leader can often reduce disruptive or hostile behavior by giving George permission to express his frustrations or feelings. For some, having the opportunity to vent reduces or eliminates future negative behavior. Third, if all else fails, the leader may want to talk with George privately and describe the problem, asking at the conclusion, whether there is anything the leader or the group can do to assist George in working more effectively with other members. Finally, we need to remember that each of us can at times be a difficult group member, depending on the topic or our own emotional state at the time.

Planning Again!

A meeting should not end without taking the time to summarize what has been achieved and to make plans for the next meeting. Various members may be asked to take responsibility for handling one or more tasks before the next meeting. It is helpful to send notes or minutes of the meeting to members, highlighting major decisions and reminding them of the tasks that need to be accomplished before the next meeting. And again, taking the time to reflect on what worked well during the meeting provides a starting point for the next meeting. Two key questions to be asked at the end of the meeting are "What have we learned?" and "Where are we now?"

THINK ABOUT THIS

Think about a group of which you are a member (e.g., grade level, developing curriculum). In what ways does that group exemplify the notions identified above about working effectively as a team? In what ways can that group work more effectively? What can you do to facilitate the group work?

The ideas presented above are important for all literacy specialists, and especially those who have major responsibility for leading small groups of teachers, both those who are part of a permanent team (e.g., grade level) or those involved in a goal-driven task (e.g., developing a literacy plan, selecting literacy curriculum). Books that may be useful to those who frequently work with groups include Aguilar's (2016) *The Art of Coaching Teams,* Bean and Ippolito's (2016) *Cultivating Coaching Mindsets: An Action Guide for Literacy Leaders,* Johnson and Johnson's (2013) *Joining Together: Group Theory and Group Skills,* Kaner and colleagues' (1996), *Facilitator's Guide to Participatory Decision-Making,* or Parker's (2012) *Lead Simply: How to Create That Special Team of People.*

THE LITERACY SPECIALIST AS LEADER

Each literacy specialist will handle leadership responsibilities in a slightly different way, depending on (1) job descriptions and opportunities, (2) the degree of fit between his or her personality and a leadership role, (3) his or her leadership skills and abilities, and (4) the school context. Note the different leadership roles that literacy specialists in the vignettes in "Voices from the Field" assume: some have full-time leadership roles (e.g., Celia in Chapter 8), while others, who have more responsibility for working with students, find themselves functioning as leaders less frequently (e.g., Mark in Chapter 2). Literacy specialists who work with students for six periods a day have less opportunity to assume leadership roles but can still serve as leaders as they interact with individual or groups of teachers. The new literacy specialist, with little experience, may not yet be ready to handle complex or large-scale leadership roles but can work with a mentor to gain experience with such tasks. All literacy specialists need to have an awareness of their own leadership skills and strengths and an understanding of how to serve as an effective leader. Certainly, the culture of the school (e.g., opportunity for a leadership role, teachers' receptivity to working collaboratively) will influence the ways in which literacy specialists address the leadership role.

As mentioned previously, Hersey and Blanchard (1977) provide a useful way of thinking about leadership in their discussion of situational leadership. They suggest classifying the actions of leaders into *task* actions (e.g., achieving the goal) or *maintenance* actions (e.g., moving the group along in the discussion or taking into consideration the feelings and competencies of group members). They purport various combinations of leadership can be effective, depending on the makeup of the group: How motivated are members to accomplish this task? How knowledgeable are members? When group members do not have essential knowledge or skills, the leader must engage in high-task behaviors to keep the momentum flowing. Hersey and Blanchard suggest that in these instances, the leader may need to spend more time telling or transmitting information. The leader may also need to convince the members that they can accomplish the job (i.e., selling).

In groups where participants have a great deal of knowledge and are eager to work on the designated task, the leader can work in a different manner, serving as a participant in the group or even delegating responsibility. Imagine the following situation: You are working with a group of experienced teachers who have different views and perspectives about the literacy program they are currently using in their school. Their task is to identify criteria that they can use to select new material. All are eager to get new material, but there are some strong opinions about what constitutes effective literacy instruction and agreement is not imminent. Your role (most likely) is to help the group discuss the salient points in an effective manner while remaining sensitive to the different viewpoints and making certain that all members understand that their thoughts are valued. This group is eager to accomplish the task, and the members have much experiential knowledge. At the same time, they need a leader who can focus them on maintenance or relationship actions that help them to listen, respect different views, and learn from others.

One can also think about task and relationship behaviors when working with individual teachers. For example, if Juan, a third-grade teacher, asks the literacy specialist to help him make modifications in his comprehension instructional practices, he is eager to learn with and from the specialist. Building a relationship will most likely not take much effort; rather, the focus can be on the task of developing ideas with Juan for making changes in his current instructional approaches.

THINK ABOUT THIS

How comfortable would you be in your leadership role in the situation with experienced teachers whose task is to select new materials? What difficulties do you foresee in working with this group? How might you go about preparing for and avoiding those potential difficulties? What essential skills would you need for working with the third-grade teacher who is seeking information about teaching comprehension?

SERVING AS A RESOURCE TO TEACHERS

This section describes ideas for ways in which the literacy specialist can serve as a resource to others. This leadership role is an informal one that can be used by most literacy specialists, regardless of experience or job description.

• *Inform teachers of new ideas and materials.* Such information does not need to be formally presented in a group meeting. Literacy specialists can circulate key journal articles to interested teachers and administrators. They can also summarize articles in interesting ways and place them in faculty mailboxes. For example, after reading several articles about fluency or teaching comprehension strategies, a literacy specialist might develop a flyer summarizing key instructional ideas and send this flyer (electronically or in print) to teachers. For an example of a flyer developed by a reading specialist about possible strategies for developing reading comprehension, see Figure 4.3. A flyer can even include ideas about how the literacy specialist might be available to work with teachers to implement the strategies. Teachers tend to appreciate short summaries that alert them to some possible ways of improving classroom instruction for their students. When new material arrives at the school, literacy specialists can inform teachers that such material is available and volunteer to "try it out" with a selected group of students. They can take new children's books to specific teachers, suggesting that their students might enjoy reading them. The specialist might also ask if she can read the new book to the children—to get a sense of how they respond to it. Sometimes it is helpful to talk about professional issues at lunch or before or after school. For example, the literacy specialist might comment, "So, what do you think about the article in the paper questioning the effect of retention? How does that fit with the policy that we have in our school?"

• *Spread the word about effective teaching: Encourage shared leadership.* As mentioned earlier in this chapter, a major task of a leader is enhancing the capacity of others to lead. So when a novice teacher asks for help with grouping, the literacy specialist may identify one or two teachers who are especially talented in planning for the instructional needs of groups of students. After seeking permission from those teachers, the literacy specialist can suggest the novice teacher observe in those classrooms (with the literacy specialist taking over the class of the visiting teacher) or, if possible, the literacy specialist can observe along with the novice teacher. If so, the literacy specialist can, in a postobservation conference, highlight salient aspects of the grouping in the lesson observed. Literacy specialists generally have a good sense of what teachers are doing in their classrooms and which teachers might be especially effective in using specific approaches or

Strategies for Developing Reading Comprehension
by Christina Glance
Reading Specialist, Morgantown, WV

Comprehension Monitoring: Stop-Think-Paraphrase (STP)[1]
Stop – Student stops reading and covers the text with his/her hand.
Think – Student thinks: "What did I read?"
Paraphrase – Student puts what he/she read in his/her own words.

Main Idea: Very Important Part (V.I.P.)[1]
Students identify and write down the Very Important Parts of literary
and informational texts to demonstrate their understanding.
Fiction:
• *Action* – What was the most important thing the character did?
• *Feeling* – What is the most important feeling the character had?

Non-fiction:
• Students flag an important fact or sentence.
• Then, they write a few key words.
• Last, they use the key words to write a main idea statement.

Retelling: 5 Finger Retell[1]
Students use each finger on their
hand to retell a fictional story.
Thumb – Character
Pointer – Setting
Middle – Problem
Ring – Events
Pinky – Solution

Answering Questions: Question-Answer-Relationships (QAR)[2]
Students color-code and answer questions based on their relationship to the text.
Green – I must go to the text to find the answer. (Who? What? When? Where?)
Yellow – I must slow down and look for the answer. (Compare/Contrast, Cause/Effect)
Red – I must stop and think about the answer. (Why, How, What if?)

Summarizing: Somebody Wanted..But..So..[3]
Students use the phrase to help them summarize the
main idea and key details in the story.
S – Who is the character?
W – What is the main thing he/she wants?
B – Think about the problem(s)
S – How does the character respond to the problem?

> Somebody~Wanted~But~So
>
> _____ wanted _____
> (somebody)   (goal)
>
> but _____
>   (there was a problem)
>
> so _____
>   (this is what happened/how problem was solved)

[1] Richardson, J. (2009). The next step in guided reading: Focused assessments and targeted lessons for helping every student become a better reader. New York: Scholastic Inc.
[2] Raphael, T. (1982). Question-answering strategies for children. *Reading Teacher, November* (36), 86–90.
[3] Beers, K. (2003). When Kids Can't Read; What Teachers Can Do. New Hampshire: Heinemann

FIGURE 4.3. Reading specialist flyer for teachers.

strategies. These specialists are then serving as a resource, and at the same time, sharing and developing leadership capacity in others.

- *Focus on the students.* Teachers want every child in their classroom to be successful readers and writers. Often, teachers have tried many different strategies to help various students—sometimes with little success. Therefore, literacy specialists can serve as a resource by helping teachers implement strategies that may improve literacy performance of one or more students. During a professional learning initiative in which Rita served as a resource to teachers in one school, one of the tasks that she most enjoyed was helping a new teacher learn several effective strategies for improving the decoding abilities of her students. After reviewing assessment data and discussing several strategies, including Cunningham and Hall's (1994) *Making Words* technique, Rita agreed to do a demonstration lesson of that strategy and gave the teacher a copy of the book by Cunningham and Hall. The teacher was very excited about the approach and invited Rita to return and observe her as she taught. The children were learning a great deal— and the teacher was excited about their success—and her own.

- *Be available and follow through on your commitments.* Unless literacy specialists are "seen" in the schools, there may be little chance of serving as a leader. It is easy to find tasks to attend to, such as paperwork or administrative duties, that take specialists away from classrooms. When literacy specialists take the time to stop in and visit teachers, post the days on which they will be at a specific school (if they are assigned to more than one school), or volunteer to help teachers if they see an opening, they are leaders. In one school, Rita noticed a clever sign on the door of the specialist's office on which the specialist indicated where she was at a given time (e.g., in the classroom, in a meeting). Effective literacy specialists also eat with their colleagues or visit the teacher lounge on a regular basis so that they get to know teachers on a more personal level, as well as a professional level.

Often interactions between the literacy specialist and teachers occur informally or "on the fly." Teachers may stop the specialist in the hallway or the lunchroom to ask a question that opens the door to more in-depth conversations later. One literacy coach describes how her interaction with teachers increased when her office was moved from near the principal's office to near the students' bathroom (Bean & DeFord, n.d.). Equally important is providing follow-through on every commitment made. Given their tight schedules, teachers may be unhappy or disappointed about cancellations, even when they appear to be unavoidable (e.g., the principal has asked the literacy specialist to represent him at a district meeting about the literacy program). Certainly, there are times when literacy specialists may need to cancel or make changes in their schedules, but every effort must be made to assure the teacher that the commitment will be honored at a later time. The teachers should also be informed as soon as possible if there is to be a change in the schedule. Also, reschedule as soon as possible. Lack of follow-through will quickly destroy the credibility of the literacy specialist. Teachers may soon decide that there is little they can expect from the literacy specialist and will close the door, literally and figuratively, to future interactions.

• *Be flexible.* Flexibility is an especially critical quality because often creative and effective ideas emerge in the moment, as the literacy specialist works with a specific teacher or teachers, and their implementation usually requires "on-the-spot" adjustments to planned work. These ideas may come from the literacy specialist or the teacher. The most effective literacy specialists quickly think of ways that they can facilitate the development and implementation of these ideas, rather than thinking of reasons why such ideas are impractical. In discussing leadership, Colin Powell said, "You don't know what you can get away with until you try" (Harari, 2002, p. 65). In other words, literacy specialists are most effective when they look for ways to make things happen. Flexibility is also important in terms of working with individual teachers. Consider the following as possible options for working with individual teachers:

○ The literacy specialist may serve as a co-teacher in the classroom to implement guided reading lessons because that teacher is receptive to working with another adult in the classroom.
○ With a different teacher, the literacy specialist may provide materials and suggestions about guided reading to give that teacher an opportunity to think about the approach and how it might be implemented.
○ The literacy specialist and teacher may plan a lesson together, and after the teacher implements the lesson, the two educators meet together to talk about the results and next steps.

• *Be a willing helper!* There are times when teachers are overloaded and can use some additional help from the literacy specialist (e.g., getting ready for the annual parent evening meeting, classroom assessment responsibilities, report card time). Literacy specialists who are willing to assist teachers, even if in a small way (e.g., helping to post student work, assisting with the assessments) will develop better relationships with teachers and ultimately find them to be more willing to listen to ideas that may require some changes on their part.

A RESOURCE FOR SPECIALIZED PROFESSIONALS

Literacy specialists often work with specialized personnel in schools (e.g., special education teachers, speech and language teachers). The focus on data as a source of decision making and the emphasis on differentiating instruction, using RTI, MTSS, or similar models, call for much more collaboration in schools. In a study of schools implementing an RTI approach, there was a greater emphasis on collaboration among school personnel as a means of identifying student needs and making decisions about how to support classroom instruction (Bean & Lillenstein, 2012). Collaborative teams included professionals such as literacy specialists and literacy coaches, special education teachers, speech and language teachers, counselors, and psychologists. The principal also met frequently with these teams but was not always the team leader; frequently the literacy specialist or coach was responsible for leading the team efforts. The group met to make decisions about how to improve literacy instruction for the students in their schools, discussing results of assessment, grouping possibilities, and instructional approaches. All meetings ended with action plans: Who was going to do what, with whom, and when?

Such teams of course may also include teachers of the arts, librarians, and physical education instructors, as well as others. What is important is that those responsible for teaching students receive the same message so they can plan for coherent and coordinated instruction. Although many schools have implemented teams to discuss students with special needs, there should also be informal conversations among these educators. Too often, children with special needs receive multiple and possibly conflicting intervention strategies because of the lack of communication among the educators involved with them. Educators can learn from one another about the various approaches used to improve literacy performance. Note the example in Katy's vignette about teachers across grade levels talking together about the students they have taught or are teaching.

Specialists with various expertise can also support the work of literacy professionals. Speech and language teachers are often well prepared to teach phonemic awareness to young children. Likewise, special educators may appreciate information about the various approaches to teaching reading that the literacy specialist can share with them. Special educators, in turn, often have well-designed behavior management programs or instructional strategies that they can share with others. These issues will of course be addressed in schools using the MTSS/RTI framework.

In addition to working with educators who teach students with special needs, involvement with others—such as art teachers, librarians, technology personnel, and so on—can promote literacy learning for all students in the schools. Music teachers can teach songs that help young children develop their phonemic awareness skills. The arts program can be used in the upper grades as a means of expanding and enhancing students' thematic learning in the various content areas. The librarian can be a source of information about book availability and work with teachers to promote student interest and motivation to read. In collaboration with other organizations, the IRA (2012–2013) released a position statement about the importance of leisure reading and the impact it can have on students' literacy learning. The document highlights the importance of partnering with school librarians. We encourage literacy specialists to work closely with school librarians as a means of improving student literacy learning and enhancing student engagement in and motivation to read.

Interactions with school psychologists may also be an important part of the literacy specialists' role, not only to obtain test information about students but to learn more about the child and to share information that may assist the psychologist in getting a more complete picture of a specific student. Often, the type of assessments that literacy specialists administer help psychologists gain a more specific understanding of the child's literacy instructional needs. Hoffman and Jenkins (2002) conducted interviews with a group of literacy specialists to learn more about their interactions with school psychologists. They found that these literacy specialists had some collaborative experiences with the school psychologists, but that scheduling time for interactions was difficult. They also talked about the importance of establishing good personal relationships and knowing more about how to collaborate effectively.

A RESOURCE FOR ADMINISTRATORS

Principals set the tone and establish the conditions to enhance the work of the literacy specialist; without their support, literacy specialists will have difficulty performing their role effectively (Bean et al., 2018; Bean, Dole, et al., 2015; Matsumura et al., 2009). As stated by Bean and Lillenstein (2012) in their study of five schools, "the principal served as the central person for promoting a risk-free environment, . . . facilitating shared responsibility and accountability" (p. 497). Although many principals, especially those in the elementary school, have an in-depth understanding of literacy instruction, some do not. Given their multiple responsibilities, many do not have adequate time or knowledge to devote to the leadership of the literacy program. They may rely on the literacy specialist in their school for specific information about how the school as a whole is doing (e.g., achievement scores in the literacy areas of decoding, comprehension). Specialists may also need to inform principals as to whether there is a need for additional professional learning about literacy for specific teacher groups (e.g., content-area teachers in the high school want to know more about discipline-specific literacy instruction). Likewise, coaches may need information or advice from the principal about how to better serve the teachers and students in the school. For example, when literacy specialists inform the principal about their activities and solicit support (e.g., changes in scheduling, need for supplemental materials, digital resources), they will be able to do their job more effectively. In other words, a supportive principal can promote the role of literacy specialists and enhance their effectiveness (Ippolito & Bean, 2019).

Cultivating this relationship means that principal and literacy specialists must communicate on a regular basis. Some principals schedule meetings with the specialist once a week; others prefer to receive written updates from the literacy specialist on a regular basis. Because principals are busy with many different responsibilities, literacy specialists may need to initiate interactions, perhaps sending brief e-mail messages summarizing key points about literacy instruction or assessment. Ippolito and Bean (2018), in their book *Unpacking Coaching Mindsets: Collaboration between Principals and Coaches,* provide a series of questions that literacy specialists can use to assess their relationship with the principal. They also encourage principals to complete the same questionnaire. The goal is to help professionals in both roles to think about their perspectives about the school's literacy program and how to develop a trusting and respectful relationship that facilitates effective literacy instruction in the school.

SUMMARY

Literacy specialists all have leadership responsibilities, but these responsibilities differ depending on job opportunities; experience; and the skills, knowledge, and dispositions of the specialist. These dispositions include having the ability to (1) communicate with others, (2) work with teams, (3) achieve goals, (4) empower others, and (5) work in a respectful way with others. The leadership role for literacy specialists is often one that requires leading by influence, and will differ, depending on the context in which one works. Literacy specialists can serve as a resource for teachers, administrators, and other professionals involved with improving literacy instruction for all students, and especially for those students who experience difficulty with reading and writing.

ADDITIONAL READINGS AND RESOURCES

Barth, R. S. (2013). The time is ripe (again). *Educational Leadership, 71*(2), 10–16.—The author discusses why teacher leadership has not been prevalent in schools, the potential for increased teacher leadership, and the rationale for promoting it.

Inspirational leadership video: Lead simply. Retrieved from *www.youtube.com/ watch?v=wb3Zvmae5ks.*—This video describes the three elements Sam Parker (2012) discussed in his book *Lead Simply.*

Williamson, D. (2018, May). Why leadership today is like playing jazz. *The Globe and Mail.* Retrieved from *www.theglobeandmail.com/report-on-business/*

careers/leadership-lab/why-leadership-today-is-like-playing-jazz/article15222682.—Although this short article is about leadership in the business world in Canada, it describes some important ingredients of successful leadership for this complex world in which we live—especially the ability to be flexible and to improvise!

● REFLECTIONS

1. How would you assess your own leadership skills? What do you see as your strengths? Your weaknesses? How might you go about improving the areas you identify as weaknesses or concerns?

2. Why is the leadership role of the literacy specialist an important one? Why do you suppose that some literacy specialists see it as one of their most difficult tasks?

3. Think about a group with which you have been involved recently. What was the leader's style? How did the leader help the group to work effectively?

4. Jot down ideas about how you might actualize the three elements (p. 101) identified by Parker (2012); then discuss your ideas with others.

● ACTIVITIES

1. Interview a literacy specialist to determine what leadership roles he or she assumes. Ask the specialist to identify what skills are needed to perform such tasks and what challenges exist.

2. Attend a group meeting. Think about the leadership style of the leader. How did the group achieve its goals? In what ways did the group exhibit its ability to work together as a team?

3. Discuss the following scenario: What leadership style would be most effective, given the characteristics of the teacher?

   A new first-grade teacher has told you that she is having no difficulties teaching her students, is enjoying her experience, and does not need any specific help from you, the literacy specialist. However, you have been in her classroom and have noticed some classroom practices that indicate that she has very little knowledge of how to teach phonics.

4. In small groups, discuss the following vignette, reflecting on what Katy, as a kindergarten teacher with literacy expertise, brings to her role as a teacher leader. Identify three important "take-aways" from that vignette. Share your work from small groups with the whole class.

Questions to Consider

What lessons can be learned about the role of the teacher leader from this vignette?

In what ways does Katy serve as a leader?

What questions come to mind after reading this vignette?

KATY: TEACHER LEADER

I have been a teacher for 30 years. That's so crazy to write and fathom as a real statement. It is, however, the truth. I've been in Pittsburgh public schools my entire career. I have been a teacher, in mostly primary grades, and a reading coach in a K–8 school. I am currently a kindergarten teacher and my team's leader. My students are all African American. They are curious, intelligent, and constantly make me laugh. I love going to work every day!

One of my favorite parts of every week is time in our school garden. We plant, water, weed, and watch in wonder as things sprout and develop into mature plants. We feel disappointment when something doesn't grow or gets eaten by an unwanted guest. We try new things, like ground cherries and kale, that we aren't sure we will like, but because we have promised to be STAR (safe, teamwork, adventurous, responsible) farmers, we try and often find that we actually like it. We've made tea and hand lotion. We've embraced the smell of the worm bin—yes, it's as bad as it sounds—because it helps us compost food we don't need to throw away.

There are so many similarities between gardening and teaching. Words like growth, patience, problem-solving, and perseverance apply to both. Classes can be seen as gardens with teachers as the master gardeners, knowing what to give each student for maximum growth. Coaches and reading specialists can look at the teachers with whom they work in the same way.

Although I no longer work with teachers in an official capacity as a coach or reading specialist, I am still a teacher leader. I spend a lot of my time, officially or unofficially, trying to help teachers improve their practice.

Some parts of a garden grow without a lot of attention. Provide soil, sun, water, and air and the plant will flourish. Sarah McLachlan has a song from the movie *Charlotte's Web* called "Ordinary Miracle." "The sky knows when it's time to snow, don't need to teach a seed to grow." Mother Nature simply does her thing and we barely notice. Some teachers just need the right conditions to show their brilliance and genius.

Mr. C. had a 6-week placement in my classroom this fall. He is enrolled in a 5-year program at a local university in which students go through a cycle of four 6-week placements throughout their fourth year, to better prepare them for student teaching in their fifth year. He had never been in a kindergarten classroom before. He was very nervous and told me he needed to observe for "the first few days, at least" because he was so unsure of himself and the unknown environment. He didn't need any time at all to show his teaching intelligence. From the very first day he intuitively knew how to interact with the students, when to push, when to step back, when to be silly, when to be rigid.

I first came across the term *with-it-ness* when reading a piece in *The New Yorker* by Malcolm Gladwell. It was actually coined by Jacob Kounin, an educational theorist. Some define it as teachers having "eyes in the back of their heads," but it's more than that. It's a way of communicating with students so they know what the expectations are—eye contact, verbal cues, speaking respectfully to a child who is not behaving appropriately. Mr. C. not only had with-it-ness when dealing with behavior, he had it with content too. He was reflective of his work and mine. Our work together seemed effortless. He was willing to share his reflections of the classroom and my teaching with me. These conversations often included questions about why I did something a certain way or why I responded the way I did. These moments caused me to reflect and have to put into words why I do what I do. We got to a point where we were having what I call "transparent facilitation." We didn't wait until the students went to lunch or the next day for clarification and/or explanation; we had these exchanges in real time. This communication deepened his knowledge and understanding of the many split-second decisions we make as teachers. As a result, he was better able to plan and deliver his lessons. When you provide the right elements, growing seems to be so easy.

Sometimes, however, learning and growing are not that straightforward. One of the ideas I learned this planting season is that it's not always wise to plant the same crop in the same bed two years in a row. If you rotate the beds, you have a better chance of not allowing parasites of a particular crop that live in the soil to potentially destroy what you have planted.

Ms. A. was on my team for three years, her first three years of teaching. She worked so hard every day to get to know her students and understand what they needed to be successful learners. She planned well. She sought help when she felt overwhelmed or didn't understand something. She wanted to learn more about the reading process, so she chose a graduate reading specialist program for her master's degree. She was so excited about what she was learning. I had been through the same program so we had many conversations about professors, course requirements, and electives that might be interesting. She completed some required teaching assignments in my classroom so I could watch and give her feedback.

As an outsider looking in, she seemed to have everything necessary to bloom in her environment. That was not the case. She was struggling on the inside. She was questioning whether teaching was the right career for her. We talked many times about what inspired me to stay in the profession for 30 years, what motivation she had to come to work, and how to work through the anxiety she was feeling about her job. We tried co-teaching, observations, and modeling to see what might spark her enthusiasm. Ultimately, she decided to stay in education but to leave my school. She made a leap of faith and it has worked out wonderfully for her. She has found the joy of teaching again and she is applying her brilliance and dedication in another garden where she is growing effortlessly.

There is a concept in gardening known as "the three sisters," in which you plant corn, beans, and squash together and they thrive by working as partners. The corn grows tall and offers support, the beans pull nitrogen from the air and provide it to the soil, and the squash grows large leaves that cover the soil so it doesn't dry out easily and the prickly vines help keep hungry predators away. This partnership is similar to the type of positive partnerships we can find in schools.

For example, a second-grade teacher had questions about her work. She was trying something new and wasn't sure about what she was seeing in the work and where to go from there. She did not feel completely comfortable taking it to her team, so she assembled her own team of trusted colleagues to help her. She asked two kindergarten teachers and two first-grade teachers to stay after school once a month and talk about the student work her class produced. Because we had taught many of the students in previous years, it was exciting to see how much they had grown. She began each session with an explanation of the assignment. Each teacher looked through the pieces silently, asking clarifying questions, if necessary. We talked about the work as a group: what we saw, how different children approached the task differently—great conversations with teachers talking to teachers about teaching. Finally, we made suggestions for next steps as a whole group and for individual students. We all left feeling refreshed and ready to try things in our own classrooms. It was like a good "sister" talk—one that supports, challenges, and energizes you.

Sometimes gardens produce unwanted, unknown, or unexpected things. No matter how diligent we are about keeping up with gardening chores, something always seems to want to impede the growing process.

I worked with the same team for many years. We weren't always on the same page, but we did a lot of hard work that helped us grow intellectually, educationally, and personally. When changes to the team occurred, they were understandable, but not easy. New colleagues always produce a bit of anxiety, as well as hope for a better team. Sometimes that works out effortlessly and sometimes it does not. I've struggled with the changes this time. Communication is lacking. I thought ideas and the ways we decided to move ahead were clear, only to find out our collective plan was not understood or was ignored. It's been frustrating.

My first inclination is to call these changes, and maybe the people, weeds in my garden. Then I'm reminded of a Ralph Waldo Emerson quote, "What is a weed? A plant whose virtues have never been discovered." So, my hope for my work going forward is to have the patience to discover those virtues. I need to find the fortitude to develop ways to listen and really hear what people are saying to me. I need to take the time to know what each person understands about our work together. As a leader, I have more "growing" of my own to do.

A Chinese Proverb states: "All the flowers of all the tomorrows are in the seeds of today." Patience, responsibility, problem solving, disappointment, understanding, and confidence are all lifelong skills I've learned from gardening. I now apply those skills to my teaching and my work with teachers. Teaching and gardening are hard work, but worth every bit of effort when you see the beautiful results!

REFERENCE

Gladwell, M. (2008, December 15). Most likely to succeed. *The New Yorker.*

KATY CARROLL, EdD
Kindergarten Teacher
Pittsburgh Faison K–5
Pittsburgh, Pennsylvania

CHAPTER FIVE

Professional Learning
THE NEW PROFESSIONAL DEVELOPMENT

Professional development is not about workshops . . .
it is at its heart the development of habits of learning.
                                   —FULLAN (2001b, p. 253)

KEY QUESTIONS ● ● ● ● ● ● ● ● ● ● ● ● ● ● ● ● ● ● ●

● What are the essential differences between the concepts of *professional development* and *professional learning*?

● What are the essential factors in effective professional learning programs and professional learning communities for teachers?

● In what ways can literacy specialists support professional learning initiatives in schools?

Michael Fullan (2001b) in the quotation above identifies an important notion about the professional development (PD) of teachers. Teachers must be internally motivated to learn more about being effective at the craft of teaching, to become lifelong learners. Thus, professional learning (PL), the title of this chapter, is inspired by the *Standards for Professional Learning* (Learning Forward, 2011), which signal the importance of PL based on the day-to-day realities of classrooms and focus on improving student learning. No longer is the emphasis on educators being the recipient of something "done to or for them." Rather, the focus is on teachers being proactive by being involved in collaborative learning, shared leadership, and decision making at the school level. This term does not mean that gaining information through workshops or school meetings is meaningless, but rather teachers have a much different role in what happens in those workshop, meetings, and follow-up activities.

PD in the past tended to be standardized, based on transmission of information, short term, and at times irrelevant to what teachers needed to do to improve their practices. Sessions provided by schools or districts tended to be offered schoolwide, generic, and lacking the intensity and focus to affect teacher practices or student learning. Often, PD was a quick fix or silver bullet; it was based on a "one-size-fits-all mentality." Once teachers had attended a specific workshop or workshops, administrators and other stakeholders expected they would change their teaching practices and student learning would improve. New research about adult learning, school change, and leadership has stimulated new ways of thinking about PL (Breidenstein, Fahey, Glickman, & Hensley, 2012; Kragler, Martin, & Sylvester, 2014; Learning Forward, 2011).

Literacy specialists often have important roles in supporting PL opportunities. They lead workshops to provide information about effective literacy practices (e.g., instruction, assessment) and they facilitate grade-level or departmental team meetings, helping teachers think about instruction for a specific grade, academic subject, or component of literacy. They also assist in the development of curriculum, or they coach, suggesting resources, co-planning and co-teaching, modeling, observing, and providing feedback to individual teachers about their literacy instruction. They serve an important role in facilitating shared decision making and teacher leadership as they work collaboratively with their colleagues. A key to literacy specialists' efforts in providing PL experiences for teachers is their ability to work with school leadership, especially the principal, who establishes the conditions for promoting teacher learning. We follow Pam as she becomes involved in PL efforts in her school.

> Pam and the other literacy specialists in the district met with district leadership to discuss the scores of elementary students on the state achievement test. District administrators were concerned about low scores on the comprehension section of that test and asked the literacy specialists for ideas about what teachers might do to improve their comprehension instruction. The literacy specialists were charged with designing a comprehensive plan for PL that would include large-group workshops, small-group meetings, and follow-up coaching by the literacy specialists. Pam felt comfortable working with the group of teachers at her school but was a little nervous about making large-group presentations to district teachers. Oh well, another learning experience! She knew that she would have the support of her literacy specialist colleagues as they planned this large-group workshop together.

REVITALIZING THE WASTELAND

Too often, teachers have been subjected to and bombarded with, information about new projects or activities that happen to be in fashion at a specific time, even before there was research evidence to establish the innovation as effective. At times, policy changes placed initiatives in schools without attention to the implementation process, that is, the support and resources that teachers needed so that the innovation was implemented as intended. These approaches to PD caused Little (1993) to describe PD in schools as the wasteland of education. Without ongoing support such as coaching and feedback, teachers may have difficulty implementing what they learned in workshop sessions. They may need to practice new approaches and ask questions of their colleagues and more experienced others in order for these new instructional approaches to become an integral part of their classroom practices.

Concern about and interest in literacy instruction from a variety of stakeholders at national, state, and local levels, have led to calls for improving teacher knowledge and performance in teaching literacy. Further, we now have evidence that quality teaching is the single most important variable contributing to student learning (Darling-Hammond, Wei, Andree, Richardson, & Orphanos, 2009; Hanushek, 1992; Rivkin, Hanushek, & Kain, 2005). In fact, having three or four good teachers in succession can be especially important for students and, likewise, having several weak teachers in a row can negatively influence students' learning (Center for American Progress and the Education Trust, 2011).

According to Snow and colleagues (1998), all teachers need support and guidance throughout their careers, including those who have been teaching for extended periods of time, to assist them in updating their knowledge and instructional skills. Given the diversity in our society, teachers must also have a deep understanding of their students—their experiential backgrounds and cultural heritages. Teachers also need to know how to identify student needs and work with others to find solutions that address those needs. Although preparation programs can and should provide foundational knowledge for novice teachers, teachers throughout their careers benefit from ongoing opportunities to learn more about literacy, language, and learning.

THE STATUS OF PROFESSIONAL DEVELOPMENT: WHAT WE KNOW FROM RESEARCH

Previous research on PD indicates that participation in such efforts can change teachers' attitudes and practices and even improve student achievement (Darling-Hammond, Hyler, & Gardner, 2017; Desimone, Porter, Garet, Yoon, & Birman, 2002; National Institute of Child Health and

Human Development, 2000; Sparks & Loucks-Horsley, 1990; Taylor, Pearson, & Rodriguez, 2005). In Taylor and colleagues' (2005) study of PD in schools implementing a school change framework, greater growth was seen in students' literacy achievement in schools that had high implementation, and also, greater effects were seen after two years of implementation. Three important published reports provided key information about the status of PD in the United States: Darling-Hammond et al. (2009); Jaquith, Mindich, Wei, and Darling-Hammond (2010); and Wei, Darling-Hammond, and Adamson (2010). Three key findings included:

- Teachers valued PL experiences, especially those meaningful to them in their daily work. PD not connected to teachers' classroom teaching had little impact on teaching or student learning.
- Teachers had few opportunities for sustained PD experiences, that is, short-term workshops were most common.
- State policies and systems that helped to improve PD for teachers include standards for PD, accountability and monitoring of PD efforts, and agencies in the state that provide PD for districts and resources for schools.

These findings are still relevant today as they provide guidance to districts in planning effective PL experiences. In fact, over the years, evidence about the criteria for quality PD has been growing. Darling-Hammond et al. (2017) reviewed 35 methodologically rigorous studies that demonstrated a positive link between teacher PL, teaching practices, and student outcomes. They identified the following seven critical elements of PL initiatives (pp. v–vi).

1. Content: Teachers need to know *what* is important to learn in respective content field, including literacy.
2. Active learning: The processes or *how* of learning is important.
3. Collaboration: Teachers, working together, can become a collective force for change.
4. Models of effective practice: When teachers develop and review lessons plans, view demonstration lessons, or videos of effective practice, they develop a deeper understanding of what they are learning.
5. Coaching and expert support: Teachers who have support from knowledgeable peers will implement what they are learning more effectively.
6. Feedback and reflection opportunities: Teachers need feedback on what they are doing and opportunities to self-assess and reflect on their performance.
7. Sustained duration: Effective PL initiatives tend to occur over weeks, months, and even years.

The above identified factors are closely related and interrelated (e.g., literacy specialists or coaches [#5] can provide the feedback and reflection opportunities [#6]). At the same time, the ways in which each of the elements is designed, can differ. For example, coaches might work with teachers in different schools via technology, viewing lessons via video platforms such as Zoom or Google Meet, or they might be assigned to a single school. In some PL initiatives, literacy specialists, to support active learning, might use protocols to organize their grade-level meetings. In other instances, teachers might be involved in analyzing student assignments or data from various benchmark measures. Later in this chapter, we describe more completely specific approaches to PL that include the elements described above.

WHAT IS PROFESSIONAL DEVELOPMENT? WHAT IS PROFESSIONAL LEARNING?

In the *Handbook of Professional Development in Education*, Lieberman and Miller (2014) describe two competing models of PD. The prevalent model in schools tends to be the training model of in-service teacher education, in which teachers receive information, often through workshops; these informational sessions are (or should be) followed by some sort of coaching or feedback efforts. Most often, this model is a top-down approach, determined by the district (e.g., we need to improve comprehension) or even the state (e.g., all schools will learn how to implement MTSS/RTI). Although such efforts have merit for providing information, they do little to support transformation of teacher practices. Further, little opportunity occurs in these large workshops to provide for the differences in the specific context in which an initiative is being implemented or address what is known about how adults learn.

The new paradigm, PL as growth in practice, emphasizes the following: a focus on the specific problems of the classroom and school, meaningful collaboration and engagement with ideas, and opportunities for teachers to reflect about their problems and to develop solutions for them (for the 2011 Learning Forward standards, see *www.learningforward.org/standards-for-professional-learning*). In fact, strong PL programs include experiences such as: making practice public; encouraging teachers to take an inquiry stance; and opportunities to network with diverse others, across schools, grade levels, and content areas (Eidman-Aadahl, 2019). This shift from PD to PL emphasizes the importance of developing habits of learning, supporting teachers as lifelong learners. In addition, some states have specific guidelines with policy expectations to guide districts in developing PL goals to include in their comprehensive plans (see New York State example: *www.nysed.gov/common/nysed/files/programs/postsecondary-services/plp-guidance.pdf*).

One approach to this growth-in-practice paradigm is professional learning communities (PLCs). Other approaches similar to PLCs call for schools to function as places of learning, where there are opportunities for teachers to work collaboratively and focus on addressing problems specific to the students in their schools and classrooms. In some cases, teachers may participate in PLCs outside of their school district in order to meet and learn from others who have similar responsibilities. In such cases, it is important to have open discussions about creating and sustaining the communities (Goatley, 2009). Choice is also an important aspect of PLC; in the ILA leadership brief (Hicks, Sailors, & ILA, 2018), PL is described as something done *with* teachers rather than *to* them.

THINK ABOUT THIS

What type of PD or PL have you participated in—school mandated, volunteer, group, or individual effort? Which of the seven elements identified by Darling-Hammond and colleagues (2017) were part of those experiences? In what ways do these elements/activities contribute to your growth as a "lifelong learner"?

IMPROVING PROFESSIONAL LEARNING: SCHOOLS AS PLACES OF LEARNING

By thinking of schools as places of learning for both students and adults, we give credence to the notion that effective educators must be lifelong learners. We also acknowledge that mandating change does not necessarily work. Changes at a deep or transformative level in beliefs, attitudes, and instructional practices can only occur if teachers are given opportunities to participate in inquiry and problem solving to address the specific challenge of their classrooms and schools. Further, school or systemic change is possible only if teachers are involved in collaborative processes that help them develop collective efficacy, that is, a belief that teachers as a group can affect student outcomes. Teachers with strong collective efficacy are willing to take risks and to persist when faced with challenges (Walpole & Vitale, 2020).

There are many kinds of activities that involve teachers in collaborative, problem-solving endeavors. Hicks, Sailors, and the ILA (2018), in their brief, *Democratizing Professional Growth with Teachers: From Development to Learning* describe many different approaches to PL, including literacy coaching; teacher study groups; ongoing opportunities within the school for teacher discussions about classroom-related topics; and unconferences, in which teachers can meet and decide upon the agenda for their PL. We discuss coaching in more depth in Chapters 6 and 7. Below we focus on PLCs as one approach to inquiry learning and the development of collective efficacy in schools.

PLCs can be defined as "groups of teachers who meet regularly for the purpose of increasing their own learning and that of their students" (Lieberman & Miller, 2008, p. 2). Members of a PLC learn from one another in their efforts to improve student learning. Vescio, Ross, and Adams (2008) identified five essential characteristics of PLCs: (1) development of shared values and norms, (2) focus on student learning, (3) reflective dialogue among teachers, (4) making teaching public, and (5) collaboration among educators at the school. However, instituting successful PLCs is not easy. Wood (2007) describes the challenges faced by a district that attempted to implement PLCs: an overemphasis on the process rather than a focus on student learning, resistance by teachers and administrators to the required cultural changes, and lack of time and support. In other words, there is a danger in PLCs that teachers (without leadership) will focus more on the protocol or group activity than they will on what they can learn to facilitate student learning. In order for PLCs to be effective, then, the school must be prepared to begin a journey that requires participants to learn how to hold meaningful conversations that focus on key topics related to instruction and assessment. Teachers need time to talk about and collaborate on important issues related to teaching and assessment; also, there must be leadership that guides them in these collaborative efforts, and support and understanding from school administration. PLCs can be more effective if the principal is a member of the team, working alongside teachers. Early on in the COVID-19 pandemic, many teachers felt a need to become members of a PLC. They had specific questions about remote instruction and about their students that required immediate attention. Teachers were searching for answers and often they were able to get support by holding discussions with their colleagues, specialists and coaches, and their principal. There was an authentic need to be a member of a PLC.

Teachers can also develop as learners when involved in external (beyond the school) PLCs. For example, teachers who have been involved with the National Writing Project are involved in a network of committed educators who communicate with each other on a regular basis. Similarly, National Board–certified teachers may have community-based networks that help teachers extend their learning with colleagues from a range of school districts.

Swan Dagen and Bean (2014) described this emphasis on PL as a means of addressing "the collective ability and capacity of teachers in a school to address challenges and solve problems that enable the organization to become more effective in . . . improving student learning" (p. 44). In other words, to increase overall school performance, more must be done than to improve individual teacher skills and competence; rather, the focus should be on helping teachers work together toward a common vision and participate in decision making and shared leadership as a means of achieving their goals. Regardless of whether a school indicates that it has or does not have formal PLCs, it should establish itself as a place that values both student and adult learning, and where there is an emphasis on teachers working together to analyze data, make decisions about instruction, and participate as leaders in the school. This sense of collective efficacy in which all teachers in the school believe that they have the capability to improve student learning, can have a powerful effect on student learning (Walpole & Vitale, 2020).

STANDARDS FOR PROFESSIONAL LEARNING

One of the sources of information that can drive PL in a school is the standards in the *Standards for Professional Learning* (Learning Forward, 2011), which include seven dimensions: learning communities, leadership, resources, data, learning design, implementation, and outcomes. In an earlier publication, the National Staff Development Council (2001) described three key components of effective PD: context, process, and content. We use these three components to discuss PL as it applies to literacy instruction in schools.

Context

The creation of a successful PL plan must be based on the context in which it is to be implemented. Several questions must be addressed:

- What are the literacy goals and needs of the students in the school? What do teachers need to know and be able to do to address these goals and needs? What are teachers' attitudes about change? What are the experiences, skills, and abilities of the teachers who will implement the plan?
- Is the culture in the school one that is receptive and eager to change? Do teachers work together in a collaborative fashion and focus on the goal of improving student learning?
- Does the leadership in the school support and advocate for PL for teachers?
- What resources are available from the administration and the community?

In one school, faculty may be receptive to new ideas and ready to make changes in how they teach literacy. In other schools, more preliminary work may be needed before the new program can be implemented. Often it is necessary for the leadership team to think about current practices and what may need to be discarded before new practices can be instituted. One of the common complaints of teachers, and rightly so, is that they are always asked to add to what they are doing—in an already filled day!

Other legitimate issues include concerns about various practices that do not seem to fit together, that are incongruent with each other, or that lack support or resources at the school level for a district-mandated practice policy. Key personnel and teachers need to actively discuss these issues if the PL effort is to be successful. Specifically, this area of context focuses on improving teacher quality by establishing conditions in which they can work collaboratively to achieve agreed-upon goals. To learn more about how teachers view the context in which they work, we might ask them to answer questions like the following: What literacy practices do you think parents (students) would like to be different in this school? What would you like to see in this school 5 years from now?

Process

In thinking about processes, school personnel must address the following questions:

● What data are available that will support learning of both teachers and students? Are demographic, perceptual, process, and outcome data used to make decisions? (See Chapter 9 for a description of these types of data.)

● Does the PL plan consider research and theories about adult learners, school change, and PL implementation? The research described in Rohlwing and Spelman (2014) led to the notions about adult learning in Figure 5.1, which literacy specialists can take into consideration when preparing PL experiences for teachers.

- Value meaningful learning—that can be used!
- Value connections—being able to connect new learning to what they already know.
- Appreciate opportunity for active learning and interaction with others.
- Put a high value on self-efficacy (learning must take place in a risk-free environment).
- Appreciate some control over own learning.
- Are responsive to internal motivation.
- Learn in different ways and at different paces.

FIGURE 5.1. What we know about adult learning.

Guskey (2000) identifies seven different models or processes to consider when planning PD experiences: training, observation/assessment, involvement in a development/improvement process, study groups, inquiry/action research, individually guided activities, and mentoring. Some of these models are more effective than others in specific contexts. Often a PL plan is based on a combination of models. For example, in a large-scale, state-funded PD initiative that Rita codirected (Swan Dagen & Bean, 2007), teachers attended workshop sessions throughout the year and developed a focus or action research project, based on their students' literacy needs. Teachers also administered informal assessment tasks to guide their instructional decision making. Further, external coaches consulted with and observed teachers implementing various strategies and gave them feedback about their instruction. In this project, called LEADERS (Literacy Educators Assessing and Developing Early Reading Success), these external coaches were responsible for helping teachers understand various literacy strategies and they assisted in implementation efforts. To generate teacher learning, the following activities were intentionally built into the project: individual choice about a focus project; assisting teachers in interpreting and using the results of student assessment data; introducing teachers to evidence-based literacy strategies to enhance student learning; and supporting teachers with resources, coaching, and feedback. Opportunities for teachers to work collaboratively were an integral part of the project.

In addition to various processes for PL, there are also different sources of PL, including state education departments, districts, or schools. States that receive grants from the federal government or from foundations are often required to offer PL for educators in their schools, including teachers, specialized professionals (e.g., coaches, special educators), and administrators. Districts often offer PL for all schools in their district; for example, if the district decides to use a specific core literacy program, every faculty member responsible for literacy instruction will participate in the PL efforts. In this case, the PL experience may be one developed or provided by "outside consultants."

In other instances, district personnel may develop a literacy program based on standards that they themselves have developed or adopted and then provide the necessary staff development (perhaps using both internal and external experts). These initiatives, whether "homegrown" or based on a commercial program, have the advantage of being focused, given that all teachers participate in the PL activities they need to help them learn how to implement their specific program.

In initiatives in which selected teachers volunteer to participate in a specific program, one of the strengths is the enthusiasm of those who volunteer. On the other hand, such initiatives are likely to spawn several problems. The district and school administrators may not completely understand or support what these teachers are doing; there may be multiple initiatives in the district that cause confusion for volunteer teachers who may be receiving mixed messages. In some instances, volunteers are not certain of what they have agreed to do!

Individual teachers can attend various workshops or conferences and read journals or books that help them make changes in their own instructional practices. These individuals are the "gourmet omnivores" (Joyce & Calhoun, 2010), the 10% of teachers who are always seeking to improve. These teachers are always looking for ways to do a better job of teaching students; they are truly lifelong learners. Still, they may have a difficult time using these newly learned approaches, which may be different from those recommended or required for use in the school, and teachers again may receive little or no support for their efforts.

Process often gets short shrift as teachers receive PL that some call "flavor of the month" or "drive-by" efforts. Successful PL plans generating teacher change have several process-related characteristics in common:

1. *Focus.* Too often, schools have multiple PL efforts going on at one time and teachers have difficulty determining what it is they should emphasize in their teaching. To be effective, however, PL should be aligned with the goals and standards of the district or school. Then with full-speed ahead and laser-like precision, PL activities should be focused on achieving those goals! Smoker (2011) writes about the importance of focus and the key role of three essentials for improving student learning: "coherent curriculum (*what* we teach); sound lessons (*how* we teach); and far more purposeful reading and writing in every discipline" (p. 2). According to Smoker, with a sustained focus on these three elements, we can achieve dramatic results in our schools.

2. *Duration.* Effective programs are long-term or sustained endeavors. They may begin with a workshop in which teachers learn various strategies, but the program continues throughout the year with opportunities for teacher practice, inquiry, and reflection.

3. *Opportunities for feedback.* Teachers need opportunities to participate in inquiry and problem solving, to talk about what they are implementing, what works, and challenges they face. The development plan should include a built-in mechanism to help teachers as they implement new strategies. Peers, literacy specialists, or coaches can visit teachers and help them by demonstrating or observing practices and then taking the time to discuss aspects of the work. Such coaching is supportive rather than evaluative (see discussion of coaching in Chapters 6 and 7).

4. *Embedded into the classroom practices of teachers.* When the PL effort is one closely related to what teachers do every day in teaching and assessing students, there is a much better chance the initiative will succeed.

One of the ways that this "fit" can be accomplished is to have teachers who have been able to implement a strategy effectively present their work to other teachers. Teachers appreciate hearing from those who have actively been able to "do it" in their classrooms, and they value seeing these teachers in action. Also, when teachers collaborate as a group, carefully studying the results of data from assessment measures and the work samples of their own students, powerful changes can occur in instructional practices.

5. *Sense of recognition.* Acknowledge teachers for the work they do. Recognize those who have "expertise"; for example, such teachers can demonstrate for others or assist others in implementation. When teachers feel a sense of accomplishment and empowerment, they contribute significantly to the success of the initiative. They make creative and specific suggestions for how the initiative can work more effectively, and they encourage other teachers to use the new strategies.

All the factors described above are essential if real change is to occur. Jim Collins, who has spent many years studying what makes businesses successful (see *Good to Great,* 2001), found that educators, too, can apply his concepts in creating school change. In his monograph, *Turning the Flywheel* (Collins, 2019), he describes the work of a principal whose change efforts dramatically improved the reading proficiency of students in a turnaround school. Key aspects of this change effort included: hiring teachers who were passionate about their work, building collaborative teams, assessing student progress (early and often), emphasizing learning for all students, enhancing the reputation of the school as a great place to teach, and continuing to employ teachers who were passionate about their work (Molner, 2109).

THINK ABOUT THIS

In what ways does the change effort described in Collins's monograph compare with the learning initiatives in your school? What are your thoughts about what it would take to implement the key aspects of a successful school change described above?

Content

PL must ultimately result in both changes in teacher performance and in student learning; such changes should reflect efforts to achieve specific curriculum goals or standards. So, the question addressed in this text is this: What do teachers need to know and be able to do to provide the most effective literacy instruction for their students? Literacy specialists responsible for PL have multiple resources that they can access to address this question.

Important sources of information about content are the individual state standards for students; some states have adopted the CCSS, and in other states, standards may have been adapted or developed by the states themselves. The ILA standards (2018a) provide up-to-date information about what classroom teachers, literacy specialists, coaches, and coordinators need to know about literacy instruction and assessment. These sources of information are helpful in determining literacy content. Research findings also provide evidence about the effectiveness of approaches to teaching literacy. All literacy specialists should be familiar with the What Works Clearinghouse (*https://ies.ed.gov/ncee/wwc*) as a source of information. This website contains information about various programs and approaches, and a summary of research studies that provide evidence about their effectiveness for students. There are also district student standards aligned closely with state standards; these standards may be written for specific levels (elementary, secondary) or they may be grade specific. They provide important guidance for planning PL for teachers in a specific school or district. A useful resource for helping teachers implement instruction based on standards are *The Common Core Coaching Book: Strategies to Help Teachers Address the K–5 ELA Standards* (Elish-Piper & L'Allier, 2014) and *Collaborative Coaching for Disciplinary Literacy: Strategies to Support Teachers in Grades 6–12* (Elish-Piper, L'Allier, Manderino, & DiDomenico, 2016).

DESIGNING EFFECTIVE PROFESSIONAL LEARNING EXPERIENCES: TIME FOR TEACHERS

During the past several decades, we have been involved in several PL efforts as university faculty members partnering with schools and their teachers in literacy projects. We have also been involved in policy discussions with teachers about developing PL plans and implementing standards. In these endeavors, teachers have been enthusiastic about learning and passionate about their work with students. When they were treated with respect, had some choice about their learning experiences, and saw results for the students with whom they taught, they continued to use what they learned, and most of all, they began thinking of themselves as lifelong learners.

However, in some of these endeavors, especially in large districts, it has been difficult to address the larger issue of overall organizational structure and change (e.g., individual schools may have varied literacy approaches and initiatives and may differ in student and teacher demographics and needs). The partnerships in which we worked may have influenced individual and small groups of teachers and impacted instructional changes, but overall whole-school or districtwide change was more elusive. Also, although we had some impact on principals who were involved with these

PL opportunities, ongoing rotations and retirements of school/district leadership created difficulties in sustaining implementation efforts.

Yet overall change in teacher learning is critical if we are to provide effective education for all students. As described in the Time for Teachers report (National Center on Time and Learning, 2014), three major movements require that we change the ways in which we prepare and provide learning experiences for teachers. They include current emphasis on rigorous, high-level standards such as CCSS; the recent emphasis on evaluation of teachers and teaching; and the fact that the core of teachers in schools today are younger and less experienced. The report discusses five implications for practitioners in schools interested in improving PL of teachers:

1. Assess current PD practices and teacher time use.
2. Consider program models that enable additional time for teacher collaboration.
3. Align benchmark assessments, standards, and curricula, and share relevant, timely data with teachers.
4. Support the development of a cadre of instructional leaders and coaches in schools.
5. Expand opportunities for teachers to develop and share expertise.

In the Time for Teachers report, there are detailed descriptions of 17 schools and the ways in which they were able to successfully implement PL and influence teacher practices and student learning. Schools that were successful spent much more time on both classroom instruction and PL experiences than schools on average. They were committed to creating overall change in their schools by focusing on teacher learning as a major factor in ensuring an effective educational program for all students.

THINK ABOUT THIS

What PL experience has been most useful to you (you have learned a great deal and are able to use what you learned in your teaching)? What process characteristics were part of that PL experience?

GUIDELINES FOR DEVELOPING, LEADING, AND EVALUATING AN EFFECTIVE PROFESSIONAL LEARNING PROGRAM

In this section, we provide more detailed and specific information useful to those involved in PL initiatives, both school- and district-focused.

1. *Know the goals and needs of the school and its teachers.* As indicated previously, an understanding of the context is essential. If literacy

specialists have responsibilities for implementing a long-term PL program in their district, that program should be based on a needs assessment, a plan, and vision (e.g., the district has decided to improve literacy instruction by supporting content-area teachers in their efforts). For additional information, especially when the PL is being offered in a school the literacy specialist is not familiar with, talking with school administrators or teachers, visiting the school, or observing in the classrooms can also be helpful. Lyons and Pinnell (2001) provide an excellent list of characteristics to look for in the school culture (see Figure 5.2).

As you enter the building, what do you see?

1. Is there a welcoming atmosphere?
2. Is the building as a whole clean and attractive?
3. Is the school office a welcoming place where people are acknowledged and helped?
4. Are the classrooms, cafeteria, office, and library clean and attractive?
5. Do staff members speak respectfully to students and do students talk in respectful tones to one another?
6. What is happening in the yard or playground? Are students playing? Are teachers interacting with students?
7. Are the students and their community a visible part of the school? Is student work displayed and valued in the corridors, office, library, and other gathering places?
8. How available are books? Can students find books to read in places besides the library?
9. Is the principal accessible? Does the principal interact in a friendly way with students, staff members, and visitors?
10. Do people in the school talk with one another? What do they talk about? Do they talk about their work?
11. Are professional development books and materials available?
12. Do teachers have a place where they can meet and work together? Is it attractive and welcoming?
13. When asked about the school, what do people say? Are their comments positive?
14. When asked about the students in the school, what do people say? Are their comments positive?
15. When asked about the parents and the community, what do people say? Are their comments positive?

FIGURE 5.2. What to look for in the school culture. Reprinted with permission from Lyons and Pinnell (2001).

2. *Hold sessions in environments that are conducive to learning.* Think about designing the room in which sessions are held to look somewhat like the classrooms of effective teachers: places for small-group work, reading and writing areas, student work on the walls, bulletin boards. Create areas that provide opportunity for group work and discussion. Make the environment a comfortable one, enabling participants to interact as a community of learners. Working in classrooms where desks and chairs are set in rows makes a difference in the interaction and attitude of participants.

Think about the physical needs of the participants. Plan for breaks and refreshments, as needed. Rita's initial work with PL was done with a colleague who always said, "Feed your group!" Although we chuckled about that statement, teachers who come to a Saturday workshop or who attend a PL meeting after school really need—and enjoy—light refreshments. It not only meets an actual physical need but also provides an opportunity for social bonding.

3. *Recognize the learning styles and needs of adults.* As mentioned, teachers, as adult learners, bring to the learning experience a variety of experiences, skills, and knowledge that influence how new ideas are received and the degree to which they acquire and implement new skills. They bring with them their multiple roles and responsibilities, not only as teachers but also as parents, homemakers, and so on. They bring the many experiences they have had in life and work, as well as their feelings or emotions associated with past learning experiences. Teachers participate in PL for monetary incentives on occasion but more often because they hope to gain concrete and practical ideas that will enhance the learning outcomes of their students. Indeed, Guskey (1986) reported evidence that positive change in "learning outcomes of students generally precedes and may be a prerequisite to significant change in the beliefs and attitudes of most teachers" (p. 7). Change is gradual for most teachers and requires a well-developed, long-term effort. Guskey (p. 9) also discussed several characteristics of effective staff development efforts: (a) the new program or approach should be presented in a clear, explicit, and concrete manner; (b) personal concerns of teachers must be addressed; and (c) the person presenting the program should be credible, articulate, and able to describe how the practice can be used by teachers. Even then, some teachers may leave the session not convinced that the new ideas will work for them; at best, they will try them!

Some suggestions for making effective presentations to adults are listed in Figure 5.3. These suggestions come from our own experiences and from *How to Run Seminars and Workshops* (Jolles, 2001), a book useful for those making presentations to groups.

4. *Use a variety of activities and approaches, especially those that require active participation of attendees.* As mentioned previously, active

1. Create an atmosphere conducive to adult learning; it should be relaxed, yet businesslike. Seating should be conducive to discussion and interaction. Plan for breaks and refreshments.

2. Stimulate and maintain interest. Use visuals to reinforce learning; tell stories; ask questions of the group or use small-group activities.

3. Involve participants to engender interest and increase retention. In addition to small-group activities and questioning, the learner can ask participants to perform some tasks.

4. Set goals and inform participants (i.e., What do you expect them to know or do when the session is over?).

5. Show enthusiasm and use your voice effectively.

6. Plan your session so that you know how much time you will give to each segment.

7. Create a strong beginning and ending. This is where you capture the attention of the group and what the group will remember when they leave!

FIGURE 5.3. Making effective presentations.

learning is important: People learn best by "doing," and opportunities for individuals to think about, reflect, and discuss various aspects of literacy will enhance learning. Approaches that have been successful include the following:

• *Study or book groups.* When teachers are involved in activities meaningful to them, they become more engaged in the process and generally more willing to apply what they are learning to their classroom practices. Participation in a study or book group puts teachers in charge of their own learning, providing them with materials they can read, reflect on, write about, and discuss with others. Groups may be formal ones established by the school district, or they may function informally, with several teachers deciding what they will read, and when and how often they will meet. Often there is a designated leader for each meeting, who facilitates the discussion by thinking of questions and activities that may be appropriate for the material to be discussed. Walpole and Beauchat (2008) in their brief, *Facilitating Teacher Study Groups* (*https://files.eric.ed.gov/fulltext/ED530302.pdf*), highlight several important points: Work with participants as co-learners, provide for choice and voice, and facilitate opportunities that enable members to make personal connections. For example, hold discussions about how ideas being discussed might be applied to classroom instruction, the challenges that teachers might face, or the resources they might need. Administrators often ask literacy specialists or coaches to lead such a group, which requires them to facilitate focused and meaningful discussions—not always an easy task. They will need to work with group members to decide upon a schedule for reading assignments, develop key questions to guide the discussion, and support the group in thinking about what they have learned from their reading. Risko and Vogt (2016) provide additional specific ideas for leading book study discussions, including the importance of the leader in guiding the discussion and keeping it focused.

• *Analyzing student assessments or data.* Teachers can collaboratively analyze student assessments to locate student misunderstandings, develop a common understanding of good work, and even make decisions about what instructional strategies have been effective for which students (Darling-Hammond et al., 2017). In the LEADERS initiative, teachers brought samples of their students' work and discussed them with others who taught at the same grade level but in different schools. This activity always generated much discussion and reflection, with teachers able to think about how well their students were doing in comparison with those in other classrooms or schools. More important, teachers discussed which strategies and activities were helpful in promoting successful performance. The analysis of student data also provides opportunities for teachers to make decisions about student needs and strengths. Often, literacy specialists or coaches can follow up with teachers, based on the identification of student curricular or instruction needs.

• *Analyzing student assignments across classrooms.* Often, this activity can complement the analysis of student assessments. Teachers who teach a similar subject at one grade level (e.g., English literature) can share the assignments they ask students to complete to meet a specific standard or objective. Teachers may be surprised when they see the differences in expectations across classrooms. Teachers can discuss various aspects of their assignments (e.g., In what ways does the assignment address a specific standard? What sorts of text are being used? Is extended writing required? Does the assignment provide for student discussion?). The *Checking In Update: More Assignments from Real Classrooms* (Dysarz & Dobrowski, 2016) provides helpful ideas, especially for teachers at the intermediate, middle, and high school levels, for those wishing to delve more deeply into this approach to PL.

• *Lesson study.* This approach to PL was introduced in the United States several decades ago. In this approach, teachers of the same grade level or subject meet on a regular basis to collaborate and plan lessons that then become the focus of inquiry (Collet, 2017). After a lesson is developed, one teacher volunteers to teach the lesson while others observe. After the observation, the teachers discuss the lesson and then it is revised and taught again by another teacher. Lesson study gives teachers opportunities to try new instructional practices; it makes teaching public and teachers learn from each other in a nonthreatening environment.

• *Use of videos (classroom practices).* There is no doubt that "seeing is believing." Although we have often modeled new strategies for teachers in workshops, they always appreciated seeing us demonstrate specific strategies with their students. In the LEADERS initiative, initially we used videos that had been developed for other purposes. As we continued, we were able to show videos made by teachers participating in the project. In one high school participating in a PL initiative, individual teachers agreed to have their lessons recorded and then participated in a group discussion with other teachers, discussing the ways in which the lessons exemplified active engagement of students (the focus of the PD initiative in this school). This was a group of teachers who enjoyed working with one another and were not threatened by making their teaching public! Often, state education departments and professional organizations provide resources on websites. For example, the Georgia Department of Education has modules and videos focusing on various aspects of literacy education, from beginning literacy through instruction for adolescents (*gadoe.org/ Curriculum-Instruction-and-Assessment/Curriculum-and-Instruction/ Pages/Literacy-Reading.aspx*). Videos of classroom instruction are also available from the School Improvement Project in Massachusetts (*www. doe.mass.edu/edeval/resources/calibration/videos.html*). These videos include teaching examples from PreK through grade 12, and teachers can use them for opportunities to learn more about literacy and reflect on their own instruction. Also, they can be useful for providing professional learning support to specialists and coaches. Similarly, the National Board for Professional Teacher Standards (2019) has a range of resources, including videos and information guides, showing case studies of teachers who are National Board certified. Videos are often available on various Internet websites but should be reviewed carefully to determine quality.

- *Technology.* Technology can be used to facilitate professional learning in many different ways: as a communication tool, as a source of valuable information, or to serve as the primary provider of PL. In today's world, teachers can download lesson plans, attend webinars, participate in blogs, and attend classes online. In Striving Readers, a large-scale initiative in Pennsylvania, participating teachers in school districts were released from instruction and attended webinars that had been developed by state content specialists—without leaving their school site! These types of experiences are becoming more and more frequent as technology improves and as school personnel learn to use such technology effectively. In the LEADERS project, we developed a website that participants could access and a private LISTSERV that teachers could use to communicate with others. By using the Internet, teachers can obtain information important to them, receive support and even coaching, and contribute to the learning of others! Several examples of valuable websites include:
  - Alliance for Excellent Education: *alliance@all4ed.org*
  - Education Week: *educationweek.org*
  - ILA: *www.literacyworldwide.org*

- Read, Write, Think: *www.readwritethink.org*
- Reading Rockets: *www.readingrockets.org*
- National Council of Teachers of English: *www.ncte.org*
- Florida Center for Reading Research: *www.fcrr.org*
- Learning Forward: *learningforward.org*

There are also blogs and other social media opportunities that specialists can follow to learn more about literacy (e.g., Shanahan, *https://shanahanonliteracy.com*) and about their own work as specialists or coaches (see Affinito, 2018, for social media ideas). Technology has influenced several large-scale literacy initiatives. In Pennsylvania, teachers and coaches in Reading First participated in a series of online courses on effective primary reading instruction and coaches could also take courses on coaching. Florida also offered a series of online experiences for teachers in grades PreK–12 (Zygouris-Coe, Yao, Tao, Hahs-Vaughn, & Baumbach, 2004). In the Classrooms of the Future initiative in Pennsylvania, whose goals were to improve the ways in which teachers at the secondary level used technology, coaches in the initiative participated in webinars, blogs, and forums to enhance their knowledge and to communicate with others. One of the exciting aspects of this large-scale project was that project leaders could hold regional meetings in different locations and provide information to all participants by using technology. Such efforts, using technology, can provide opportunities for more differentiated, teacher-centered, self-directed models of teacher learning.

  • *Teacher research.* When teachers are given opportunities to identify and then answer their own questions about students' learning, they become the ultimate professionals. They implement various instructional practices and then assess their effectiveness. In LEADERS, we created a simple framework based on four questions for helping teachers think about their teacher research projects:

- What do your students need to become better readers or writers?
- What activities or strategies are you going to use to help students succeed?
- What was the outcome? What effect did your intervention have on students?
- What have you learned about yourself and your teaching?

Teachers summarized what they knew by writing a brief summary and developing a poster that illustrated their responses to each of the questions. Teacher research generates ongoing learning and may facilitate change in classroom practice. Teachers interested in such activities can be encouraged and supported in their efforts. They can discuss their work with other teachers in faculty meetings, write a short column for the school or community newspaper, collaborate with others to investigate a specific issue, or as in LEADERS, develop posters that display evidence of their work and its effect on classroom performance.

   • *Reflection.* Give teachers opportunities to discuss and reflect on what they have done in their classrooms. They can keep logs or be given opportunities to talk informally with their peers about their experiences. One of the greatest opportunities for reflection is after teaching a lesson (discussed further in Chapter 7).

   5. *Provide opportunities for teachers to receive feedback about implementation in the classroom.* In LEADERS, whenever coaches observed teachers, they met with them to discuss the results of the observation (discussed further in Chapter 7). As mentioned in Darling-Hammond et al. (2017), feedback accompanied with opportunities for reflection was one of the critical features of effective PL initiatives.

   6. *Provide for evaluation of the PL initiative.* Both formative and summative approaches evaluating PL are essential (see Chapter 9). *Formative,* or ongoing, evaluation provides opportunities for modification, adaptation, or change. *Summative* evaluation, which addresses impact and results, enables the developer to determine the effect of the PL effort on individuals and on the system as a whole. Guskey (2000) identified five levels of evaluation: participants' reactions, participants' learning, organizational support and change, participants' use of new knowledge and skills, and student learning outcomes.

   In LEADERS, we used the following techniques for addressing each of the levels:

   • *Level 1: Participants' reactions.* Questionnaires at end of each workshop; midyear focus group.
   • *Level 2: Participants' learning.* Teacher content test (pre/post).
   • *Level 3: Organizational support and change.* Interviews/questionnaires with principals and teachers.
   • *Level 4: Participants' use of new knowledge.* Classroom observations.
   • *Level 5: Student learning outcomes.* Pre/posttests developed by project team and administered to students.

Swan Dagen and Bean (2020) in their chapter, "Schools as Places of Learning: The Powerful Role of Literacy Leaders," provide a comprehensive list of activities for developing PL plans and processes.

SUMMARY

In this chapter, we discussed the importance of PD as well as some of the limitations of PD as it has been implemented in schools. Research about effective PL and about PLCs as an approach to improving teacher learning was described. We identified standards for PL followed by a discussion of context, process, and content elements as important considerations in developing any PL initiative. In the final section, we presented guidelines for developing, leading, and evaluating an effective PL initiative in a school or district.

ADDITIONAL READINGS

Collet, V. S. (2017). Lesson study in a turnaround school: Local knowledge as a pressure-balanced valve for improved instruction. *Teachers College Record, 119*(6), 1–58.—The author explores the impact of lesson study as an approach to PL on students' writing and on transformation in teacher practices.

Hicks, T., Sailors, M., & International Literacy Association. (2018). *Democratizing professional growth with teachers: From development to learning* [Literacy leadership brief]. Newark, DE: Author.—In this document, the authors discuss the shift from PD to PL. They describe the notion of PL as a focus on inquiry, critical thinking, and problem solving.

Williams, S. S., & Williams, J. W. (2014). Workplace wisdom: What educators can learn from the business world. *Journal of Staff Development, 35*(3), 10–12, 14–20.—Identifies effective practices common in business and education to promote employee or teacher learning (e.g., mentoring is key; collaboration gets results).

● REFLECTIONS

1. With your colleagues, discuss the PL in which you have participated. What activities did you find to be most useful? What, in your view, was least useful?

● ACTIVITIES

1. Interview an administrator at your school about the PL plan for teachers in the school, especially as it relates to literacy instruction. Think about whether that plan addresses context, process, and content elements.

2. Prepare a PL session for your classmates (or for the teachers in your school) in which you introduce them to one new idea or strategy. Use information from the guidelines in this chapter to develop that presentation. Ask the participants to evaluate the session, using a short questionnaire. Then self-evaluate your performance, reflecting on the ideas presented in this chapter.

3. Read Michael Henry's vignette on the following pages. In what ways is he a source of PL, both for other reading interventionists and for content-area teachers?

Questions to Consider

What lessons can be learned about the role of the literacy specialist from this vignette?

In what ways does Michael serve as a leader?

What questions come to mind after reading this vignette?

MICHAEL: HIGH SCHOOL READING TEACHER AND LITERACY COACH— 12 SMALL WORDS

"You don't really think we read any of this stuff, do you?" These 12 small words completely changed my teaching career.

That weekend, I went home. I revisited a book that I was introduced to during my teacher preparation coursework—*In the Middle* (Atwell, 2005). As a former "remedial reading" student, Atwell's concepts made sense: Let students choose their books, give them time to read in class, check on their progress, and make reading positive—same approach my dad used to help me to become a reader. But could I design this process for the mostly-50-minute-class-high-school-setting?

That Monday, I jumped right in: "I thought a lot about what you said, and we're going to do things a lot differently. You're going to pick out any book you want to read from the library. I'm going to give you time in class each day. You'll write to me each week about your books. You'll talk with each other about your books. You'll read for 20 minutes each night. And when you finish a book, you'll go to the library on your own during class to get another one. That's it."

That day, we took a trip to the library. I'll never forget what happened not long after this change. They read. They wrote thoughtfully and deeply discussed their books. They became readers.

That year, I read. I discussed my reading with them. I shared writing about my books. I checked their reading progress. I responded to their writing. I observed and participated in their discussions. And I read and wrote more and knew my students better than ever before.

That spring, I was hired as our school's first literacy coach. With this role change, I was given sections of ninth-grade reading intervention. I knew what I had to do.

Over summer, I created a weekly framework for my class to follow. That school year, I designed the work protocols that guided students. While the protocols have evolved, now, 10 years later, we still follow the same weekly framework (see Figures 5.4 and 5.5).

What's different now is that we are not only following the framework in my class, students and teachers are also following the framework in all reading intervention classes.

As a literacy coach, I promoted the same concepts across disciplines: (1) Give your students choice, (2) create a predictable framework for your students, (3) design protocols that push your students to produce the kind of work that you want to see, and (d) use the same framework and protocols throughout the entire school year. As it turns out, teachers like this.

- In physics, students research on Mondays, practice math concepts on Tuesdays, seek answers from the teacher and students on Wednesdays, design experiments on Thursdays, and present their design and findings on Fridays.
- In history, students read on Mondays, view historical videos on Tuesdays, and analyze historical images on Wednesdays. They research on Thursdays, and write historical arguments on Fridays.
- In English, students read on Mondays, they plan their own original writing on Tuesdays, they draft on Wednesdays, they draft and revise on Thursdays, and they publish and read on Fridays.

This approach allows the teacher to personalize their teaching. It allows students to produce unique products. And it's been powerfully positive for our entire school learning community.

Our science department now has an annual "Stem Day," where students design original experiments and professionals come in to evaluate and provide feedback. Our history department now has students publish original historical arguments on student-publication websites where real feedback is provided to them in real time. Our English department now has "Lit. Fest," where students read a book as a group and design presentations and videos, and where authors and other professionals come in to discuss how they use literacy in their careers.

It's hard to believe how much influence those 12 small words have had at many levels. Not only did they change so much for me, but they also changed so much for my colleagues, our students, and our school community. Now I can say this: "I know that our students really read a whole lot of stuff." And that's 12 small words I can live with.

Monday (50 minutes)	Tuesday (50 minutes)	Wednesday (35 minutes)	Thursday (50 minutes)	Friday (50 minutes)
• Writing feedback and class samples from previous week (5 minutes) • Written response (45 minutes) • Daily homework/ reading (20 minutes)	• Word work (10 minutes) • Strategic reading mini-lesson (5 minutes) • Self-selected silent reading (20 minutes) • Whole-class audio literacy practice (15 minutes)	• Word work (10 minutes) • Self-selected silent reading (25 minutes) • Daily homework/ reading (20 minutes)	• Word work (10 minutes) • Self-selected silent reading (20 minutes) • Small-group book presentations: face-to-face or blog (15 minutes)	• Word work (10 minutes) • Group reading with comprehension questions and mini-presentation (40 minutes)

FIGURE 5.4. Reading intervention class weekly framework for students.

Monday	Tuesday	Wednesday	Thursday	Friday
• Share whole-class writing feedback • At least 10 individual conferences during writing • Gather common writing feedback samples	• Post-vocabulary work • Question 5–10 students about self-selected reading • Share reading strategy samples • Record reading progress • Model reading • Model active listening and note taking	• Post-vocabulary work • Question 5–10 students about self-selected reading • Model reading	• Post-vocabulary work • Question 5–10 students about self-selected reading • Model reading • Guide and monitor small-group presentations • Gather common discussion feedback samples	• Post-vocabulary work • Question 5–10 students about self-selected reading • Provide small-group texts • Evaluate reading comprehension questions • Evaluate and provide feedback for mini-presentations

FIGURE 5.5. Reading intervention class weekly framework for teachers.

REFERENCE

Atwell, N. (2005). *In the middle: New understandings about writing, reading, and learning* (2nd ed.). Portsmouth, NH: Heinemann.

MICHAEL P. HENRY, EdD
Reading Specialist Certification
Literacy Coach and English Teacher
Reavis High School
District 220
Burbank, Illinois

CHAPTER SIX

Coaching

IMPROVING CLASSROOM
AND SCHOOL LITERACY INSTRUCTION

A good coach will make [his or her] players see
what they can be rather than what they are.
—ARA PARSEGHIAN (former football coach,
    University of Notre Dame)

KEY QUESTIONS

- In what ways can literacy coaching be helpful in supporting teacher and student learning?
- How can the interactive framework of coaching inform the work of coaches?
- What knowledge, skills, and dispositions are essential for coaches to be effective?
- In what ways is coaching at the elementary level similar or different from coaching at the secondary level?

During the past 20 years, much research has been conducted about coaching and coaches related to what they do and their effectiveness. Moreover, educators have developed various models or frameworks for literacy or instructional coaching. Given this increase in knowledge as well as a continuing presence of coaching in schools, we dedicate two chapters to this important PL process. Further, other chapters, including those with discussions about assessment, PL, and leadership, provide useful information about coaching skills and activities.

Although literacy coaching was "very hot" during the years of Reading First with the government's fiscal support for coaching in every school (Cassidy & Cassidy, 2009), it has been somewhat more difficult for schools to employ full-time coaches recently, given reductions in school budgets. Schools have had to become more creative, at times asking literacy specialists or teacher leaders to coach their peers, sometimes on a part-time basis. Steinbacher-Reed and Powers (2011/2012) called this approach coaching without coaches! In addition to budgetary constraints, there has been some hesitation to fund coaching given the lack of substantial evidence about the effectiveness of coaching as a means of improving teacher practices and student learning (i.e., Does coaching make a difference?). Recent research, however, has been more positive about the influence of coaching on teaching practices (Matsumura, Garnier, & Spybrook, 2013; Sailors & Price, 2015; Teemant, 2014) and student learning (Bean, Draper, Hall, Vendermolen, & Zigmond, 2010; Biancarosa, Bryk, & Dexter, 2010; Elish-Piper & L'Allier, 2011; Matsumura et al., 2013). In fact, in a recent meta-analysis of coaching studies, Kraft, Blazar, and Hogan (2018) found that coaching had significant positive effects on instructional practices and student learning. They also found, however, that as the size of the initiative increased, effectiveness declined.

Further, various initiatives that require greater emphasis on teaching quality have increased an interest in and need for coaching (e.g., emphasis on rigorous, high-level standards and assessments, MTSS/RTI and its focus on differentiation of instruction). School personnel recognize that teachers need ongoing PL to make the changes necessary to implement these initiatives effectively. The Time for Teachers report (National Center on Time and Learning, 2014) mentioned in Chapter 5 calls for support of a cadre of instructional leaders and coaches in schools to enhance teacher learning.

At the same time, we suggest the emphasis should be on coach*ing*; not coach*es*. Schools may ask teacher leaders or literacy specialists to coach; they may bring in outside or external coaches. Principals may coach when they visit teachers to provide support and guidance rather than to evaluate their performance. As mentioned previously, there seem to be fewer full-time educators dedicated to coaching. For example, a literacy specialist might spend some of the day teaching readers experiencing difficulties but also assume responsibility for coaching teachers to assist them in providing quality classroom instruction, similar to Joy's responsibilities (see "Voices from the Field" in this chapter). In some schools, administrators have asked literacy specialists to change the way in which they work, moving from primarily an instructional role to a coaching role, perhaps without having the necessary preparation to handle coaching responsibilities successfully. These coaches are then required to learn on the job—sometimes a painful way of gaining essential skills and competencies.

COACHING: WHY AND WHAT?

There is general agreement that educators need ongoing PL experiences to meet the expectations required of them in their various positions. Yet, there is also criticism of many PL activities, given their lack of ongoing support of implementation efforts. Without such support, teachers may have difficulty transferring what they learned in a workshop to actual teaching in the classroom; they may then revert to more familiar and comfortable teaching procedures. For this reason, many schools adopt new approaches and provide follow-up coaching for their teachers. Furthermore, in various federal and state legislation (e.g., Reading First, Striving Readers), there was support for or even requirements for implementation efforts that include a coach in the schools. One state, South Carolina, passed legislation requiring a literacy coach in every elementary school.

Essentially, coaching is an approach to job-embedded, ongoing professional learning focusing on authentic and meaningful learning experiences. L'Allier, Elish-Piper, and Bean (2010), in summarizing research about literacy coaching, identified these seven guiding principles: (1) coaching requires specialized knowledge, (2) time working with teachers should be the focus of coaching, (3) collaborative relationships are essential for coaching, (4) coaching supporting student learning focuses on a set of core activities, (5) coaching must be both intentional and opportunistic, (6) coaches must be literacy leaders, and (7) coaching evolves over time.

As you read this chapter and the following chapter, we discuss each of these guiding principles in more depth. *Coaching* seems to be the right term to use for this supportive work with teachers, especially if we think about the definition of a coach as an individual who provides guidance or feedback that enables someone else to become more proficient. Although educational coaching is not quite the same as sports coaching, we can learn a lot from great sport coaches. These coaches are not only able to teach in the traditional sense but able to inspire and motivate their players to do their very best and to live up to their potential. In Nater and Gallimore's (2006) book about John Wooden, the legendary basketball coach at the University of California, Los Angeles (UCLA), they detail the teaching methods that made him a great coach and teacher: "teacher respect, motivation, self-improvement, deep subject knowledge, preparation, and transferring information" (p. xiv). According to these authors, Wooden thought of himself "first and foremost as a teacher" (p. xiii).

THINK ABOUT THIS

The title of the Nater and Gallimore book is *You Haven't Taught Until They Have Learned: John Wooden's Teaching Principles and Practices* (2006).

What do you think this title means? Do you agree with it? Do you think it
relates in any way to literacy coaching and, if so, how?
    Reread Ara Parseghian's statement at the beginning of the chapter.
Agree? Disagree? How would this statement apply to the work of a literacy
coach in schools?

So it is with literacy coaches: Their role is to work as partners with
teachers in their schools and to support them in facilitating student learning. Teachers may be novices, needing a great deal of feedback or guidance,
or they may be more experienced, having taught for many years. Experienced teachers may benefit from feedback about new approaches, or they
may need reinforcement, reassurance, recognition, or even some motivation that promotes ongoing student learning. Both new and experienced
teachers may have learners in their classrooms whom they are struggling to
teach (e.g., English learners, students with special needs) and would appreciate an opportunity to learn more about how to work with them.

However, those who write about coaching as well as educators in the
field do not always define the word *coach* in a similar fashion. To some,
literacy coaches are teachers who coach children, enabling them to do better. Others see them as teachers with expertise in literacy (often, literacy
specialists) who have multiple responsibilities, from working with paraprofessionals or community agencies to working with teachers in the role
described above—primarily responsible for providing support and guidance—so that classroom instruction for students is effective. Others see
them as individuals who may not have literacy expertise but have the ability
to guide teachers to think more deeply about their teaching practices; these
professionals may be called instructional coaches responsible for supporting teachers across curricular areas.

The coaching role and job title can vary, therefore, depending on the job
requirements of the coach or literacy specialist. Some literacy coaches have
explicit and well-defined job descriptions that describe what they can—and
cannot—do. At the same time, some literacy specialists also coach but in a
less formal way. They serve as a resource to teachers by providing materials
or suggestions for working with readers experiencing difficulty; they attend
or lead study group meetings, conduct professional learning workshops, or
sit and listen to teachers who want to reflect about how to improve their
instructional practices. They also lead meetings in which they and teachers
discuss results of assessment measures and make decisions about instruction. In the vignettes in the "Voices from the Field" sections of this book, all
writers, whose titles differ, have leadership responsibilities and they coach.
Only one is a full-time coach (Dolores); Michael, Katie, Joy, and Mark
have instructional roles and coach teachers informally (e.g., modeling, co-
teaching). Celia, who serves as a literacy coordinator, has a broader role
of overseeing the literacy program, and in addition, provides support for

teachers. Katy is a kindergarten teacher who has an important leadership and coaching role with her peers and with student teachers. Again, these educators exemplify the many different ways in which the literacy specialist role is enacted. And most likely, there are many more variations in how literacy specialists participate in coaching activities! Read about Pam and some of her responsibilities that will require her to coach the second-grade teachers. What skill sets will she need to be effective in this role?

> As Pam and her principal, Ms. Walker, reviewed the 6-week assessment data of the second-grade classrooms, they noticed that fluency scores were problematic. Students seemed to be able to decode words, but they were not fluent in their reading of connected text. Ms. Walker thought it would be worthwhile for Pam to talk with the second-grade teachers about what might be causing these low scores (e.g., too little emphasis on fluency practice, especially with applying their decoding skills to reading both decodable and authentic texts) and then to support teachers in decision making. Both Pam and her principal thought the weekly planning meetings of the second-grade team would provide an opportunity for Pam to work closely with the teachers. But they wondered how Pam might be able to follow up with individual teachers in the classrooms. Pam thought she might be able to make some modifications in what she was doing during the time she was teaching students in these classrooms. Rather than working with small groups of students only, she might do some modeling of appropriate strategies (e.g., paired or buddy reading, repeated readings, Readers' Theater) followed by some co-teaching, after which she and the teacher could reflect on the lesson. A new experience for Pam—she thought she'd check some of her books on coaching! She knew she was treading in uncharted territory; how would teachers respond?

VARIATIONS IN DEFINITIONS OF COACHING

Although we focus on *literacy* coaching in this book, in some schools, coaches have a broader or different role and title. For example, there are instructional, data, academic, and curriculum coaches who are responsible for working with teachers in different subject areas. There are also learning, technology, math, and science coaches who are responsible for supporting teachers' work. There are also individuals with titles such as teacher support specialists, school-based teacher leaders, or learning specialists (see "Voices from the Field" at end of this chapter) whose responsibilities include coaching. And in some schools, principals might ask literacy coaches to focus on some math coaching to prepare students for an upcoming math assessment. Much of what is discussed in this book has relevance to these broader or different coaching roles; however, given the purpose and audience of this book, we focus on literacy coaching. The numbers of books and articles about coaching have increased exponentially in the past several decades—and although there are some similarities across books, there are also some differences. For example, Diane Sweeney (2010) describes what she calls student-centered coaching in which the focus is on setting goals with teachers for student learning and on the importance of coaching cycles to facilitate this process. Toll (2018) describes a problem-solving model to enhance teacher reflection and decision making; she puts less of an emphasis on observing teachers, suggesting that observing can seem like "supervision" and limit the ability of a coach to work as a partner with teachers. Coaching models can differ in the following dimensions:

- Who makes decisions about the focus of coaching? (teacher, coach, student)
- What activities will best address instructional changes? (e.g., critical conversations, observing, modeling, professional learning communities)
- Is the coach considered an expert or a partner?
- Is the model based on a singular view or multiple views of good literacy teaching? (McKenna & Walpole, 2008)
- What is the focus of the model? (e.g., What teachers do; how teachers feel; what teachers think; how teachers collaborate [Toll, 2018])

THINK ABOUT THIS

Think about the dimensions identified above and how coaching might differ, given the variations that can exist. What questions come to your mind about coaching and what it might mean to you as a literacy specialist.

In other words, the nature of coaching is complex. It is no wonder that teachers, administrators, and coaches themselves may have different perspectives of what coaching means! As described in Bean and Ippolito (2016), in their framework for thinking and working like a coach, they indicate that successful coaching requires "thinking about individuals and systems simultaneously, adopting coaching mindsets and roles, differentiating professional learning experiences, and developing a culture conducive to coaching" (p. 6). Below, we describe an interactive framework of instructional coaching that may help those interested in coaching—coaches, teachers, administrators, researchers, and those who prepare literacy specialists—think about the factors that affect how coaching is implemented in a given school.

AN INTERACTIVE FRAMEWORK OF INSTRUCTIONAL COACHING

As shown in Figure 6.1, there are three specific elements—the model, the context, and the coach—that affect how coaching will be defined, implemented, and evaluated within a given school. These elements overlap and interact with one another and each is affected by the other. We discuss each of these below.

Models of Coaching

By thinking about a model or framework, a school or district can identify its major focus or plan for coaching. Will there be a focus on developing teachers' reflective ability? On changing teacher beliefs as well as practices? An emphasis on fidelity of implementation? McKenna and Walpole (2008) describe coaching as a continuum, from soft to hard. They define soft coaching as responsive, invitational, and nonconfrontational. Generally, those who advocate soft coaching focus on coaching as a means of guiding teachers in thinking about their instruction; they are responsive to teachers' needs and goals. Hard coaching is based on the perspective that there are some approaches to teaching that are more effective than others, and it is the coach's role to assist teachers in implementing these approaches effectively. Often, this sort of coaching is directive and considered to be

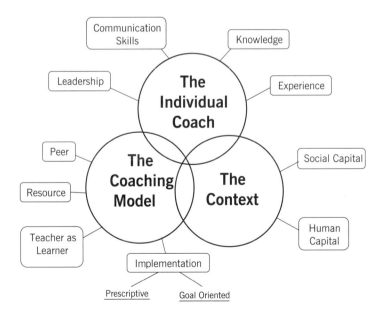

FIGURE 6.1. An interactive framework of literacy coaching.

synonymous with fidelity to implementation (i.e., Is the teacher implementing the program as designed?). Frequently, coaches are focused on developing the technical skills of teachers. However, even in one coaching session, coaches may move between hard and soft coaching, providing what Ippolito (2010) calls a balanced coaching stance. The seesaw in Figure 6.2 provides an appropriate metaphor: in one conversation, coaches may begin by taking a directive stance, and then offer teachers the opportunity to think about and reflect on their work, moving to a more responsive stance.

Coburn and Woulfin (2012) in their longitudinal study on coaching in a large-scale reading reform effort found coaches in this initiative used a balanced approach: They were directive, helping teachers make expected changes in instructional practice; at the same time, they responded to requests that addressed specific needs or those of their students. Because, in our view, there are many informal ways in which specialized literacy professionals can coach, especially informally, we describe below some general models of coaching that professionals may use as they work in schools.

Peer Coaching

In this model, colleagues work with each other to provide feedback and support. This model, proposed by Joyce and Showers (1995), was one of the original approaches to coaching, and emphasized that both coach and teacher were of equal status. In a given school, the language arts teachers in a middle school might decide to implement literature discussion groups, and after attending a workshop and reading resource materials, observe one another as they facilitate these small-group discussions. In 2002, Joyce and Showers revised their procedures for peer coaching by omitting feedback as a coaching component, given that too often, feedback given by peers became evaluative or supervisory in nature rather than supportive, and therefore incongruent with the concept of peer coaching. Also, Joyce and Showers (2002) redefined the meaning of coach. According to them,

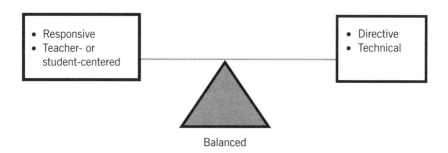

FIGURE 6.2. Coaching stances.

"the one teaching is the 'coach' and the one observing, the 'coached'" (p. 89). In other words, the coach models for the other teacher who then is expected to talk briefly about what he or she observed and then apply the learning in instructional practice. Given the recent emphasis on teacher collaboration and leadership, there has been an increased interest in peers working together, visiting one another's classrooms, and then holding follow-up discussions of what was seen. Such coaching can increase opportunities for developing collective efficacy in the school as it provides teachers with a nonthreatening approach to making their teaching public, sharing and learning from each other.

Resource Model

This model is one in which there is much flexibility. Often, in addition to working with students, the literacy specialist supports teachers in many different ways. Rita's interest in the resource role (and in coaching) began when she became a reading specialist and was told by the assistant superintendent to define her own responsibilities and write her own job description (Bean & Wilson, 1981). If you ever have that opportunity, take it! It's a chance to put all you have learned into practice. Below, we describe the various ways in which Rita assumed coaching responsibilities.

- Supported new teachers who wanted assistance in how to organize their reading groups, teach phonics or comprehension, differentiate instruction, and so on.
- Worked with teachers who had concerns about students who were experiencing difficulties with reading and wanted additional ideas about how to help students succeed.
- Developed approaches with high school teachers to assist them in incorporating literacy into their content teaching. She also worked with a high school reading specialist and together, they started a program in which high school struggling readers tutored elementary students who were having difficulties learning to read.
- Chaired a language arts committee that was charged with developing a comprehensive reading program for the district.
- Served as a member of the leadership committee that addressed concerns about individual students; members included the principal, teachers, a psychologist, and a counselor.

In other words, there were opportunities for working with both individual and groups of teachers and to influence overall school change. The key notion of this role is that the literacy specialist or coach generally responds to requests from teachers or administrators, although there are always opportunities to initiate activities. By being proactive, literacy specialists can seek out possibilities that might exist (e.g., the literacy specialist might note that students in several fourth-grade classrooms are experiencing comprehension difficulties, talk with fourth-grade teachers about what they are noticing, and discuss various options for improving student learning (e.g., model possible strategies for teaching students, co-teach).

Teacher as Learner

In this model, the goal of coaching is to support teachers in achieving their goals and to facilitate teacher learning. This focus on teacher as learner respects the individual goals of teachers, highlights the importance of reflective practice, and provides for individualized coaching. The goal of this model is to enhance teachers' ability to self-manage, self-monitor, and self-modify (Costa & Garmston, 2002, p. 21). Toll's (2006, p. 13) "fresh alternative" model and Costa and Garmston's (2002) cognitive coaching model both emphasize the importance of listening to teachers to understand their concerns, interests, and needs. This model gives a key role to teachers who are expected to identify their own goals and, to the degree possible, be knowledgeable about their own strengths and needs; it supports the notion that teachers are capable of identifying what they need to learn to improve classroom instruction. However, teachers differ in their knowledge and their ability to be self-analytical; moreover, the goals of individual teachers may not be focused on those identified by the school as important for change and improvement.

Implementation Model

We divide this model into two categories: prescriptive and goal oriented. In our view, these two types of implementation are ones that have existed most frequently in schools during the past several decades. They reflect the accountability and standards movements that emphasize the importance of student achievement or learning. Both highlight the importance of implementing selected approaches, strategies, or programs appropriately; both require that coaches have content expertise as well as an understanding of the coaching process. There are differences between the two types, however.

PRESCRIPTIVE

In this type of implementation model, there is little opportunity for teacher choice in strategies, materials, or approaches. The program selected requires teachers to follow certain procedures—at times, scripted—and the coach's role is to make certain that teachers can and do use those approaches in their classrooms (i.e., there is fidelity to implementation). There has been criticism of this type of implementation model because of its focus on teachers as *technicians* rather than as professionals who can make decisions about what the students in their classrooms need and how to provide it. Moreover, teachers may feel these prescriptive programs limit their ability to make necessary instructional changes required when students are experiencing difficulties or not learning. On the other hand, this approach to instruction (and coaching) addresses the need for all students to have equal access to what a school or district has adopted as an "appropriate" approach for teaching reading; coaching can help teachers implement that program or approach as stipulated by the developers. In a paper written for the United States Agency for International Development (2014), Rita acknowledged that in some situations where there are inexperienced staff with minimal understanding of literacy instruction, the reading materials may be scripted in nature, and coaches may need to focus, *initially,* on developing teachers' technical skills. The goal, however, is to move beyond a focus on technical skills to one that helps teachers grow as reflective professionals.

GOAL ORIENTED

In this type of implementation model, there is more opportunity for choice, although the district has adopted a literacy framework with specific goals. For example, at The Professional Institute for Instructional Coaching (*www.tpiic.org*), one of the basic tenets of this model is that coaches will assist teachers in using evidence-based literacy strategies across all content areas. Coaches attend workshops to learn about these strategies, which emphasize the importance of co-constructed learning and active engagement. Teachers can be selective in terms of which strategies might be useful to them in meeting student needs (e.g., active engagement strategies, self-questioning, development of academic vocabulary), and coaches support teachers in achieving *their* individual goals as a means of achieving school goals.

Sweeney's (2010) model of student-centered coaching, described previously, asks coaches and teachers to work as partners, using data, to identify a goal and specific learning targets for students. They design and implement instructional practices that link to the learning targets. The coach will then go into the classroom; they may co-teach or observe the ways in which students are responding to the instructional practices that were designed for them. Teachers and coaches will look at assessment data to determine how well the practices have worked—and the process continues.

The model selected affects how coaches work—which teachers the coaches work with and *how* they work with those teachers. For example, in an implementation model that is prescriptive, the coach will most likely decide whether teachers are implementing a program with fidelity and will work with teachers who are not doing so. The coach might be assigned by the principal to work with a new teacher who doesn't seem to understand what is expected of him or her, and also with an experienced teacher who is having difficulties with implementation. In a resource model, coaches will have much more flexibility, most often relying on requests of individual teachers or encouraging teachers to work with them. In a teacher- or student-centered model, coaches will develop a coaching plan based on goals and needs identified by the teachers or the teachers and coaches together. What is intriguing to consider are the different views that teachers may have of coaching, depending on the model.

THINK ABOUT THIS

Think about Joy (see "Voices from the Field" at the end of this chapter) and her responsibilities. Does she follow a specific model or models? If so, which, and why do you think so?

How might teachers relate to the coaching that they would receive, depending on the model? What do you see as the advantages and potential difficulties with each of the models?

Develop a t-chart with the following headings—Advantages, Difficulties—and discuss with others your views about each of the models described above.

The Context of the School

Recent research highlights several key factors about conditions that must exist in a school if coaching is to be effective. First is the need for support at both the district and school levels; when districts have multiple initiatives that cause confusion among teachers and coaches, or there is a lack of support for the coaching effort, there is little chance that coaching will be effective or sustained. In some districts, there is an individual identified as the coaching coordinator or facilitator, who serves as the coach of coaches, leads PL activities for coaches, and makes certain that problems or issues are addressed. Second, and as important, is the key role of the principal in understanding why coaching is important *and* in supporting the work of the coach (Bean, 2011; Fixsen, Naoom, Blasé, Friedman, & Wallace, 2006; Ippolito & Bean, 2018, 2019; Matsumura et al., 2009; Wanless, Patton, Rimm-Kaufman, & Deutsch, 2013). Literacy specialists/coaches should communicate with principals on a regular basis, seek advice, and provide information about what is needed for effective literacy instruction. The type of communication can differ, depending on the preferences of the principal. There can be set times for meetings, perhaps weekly, or coaches can summarize in writing their weekly activities and highlight issues or topics to be addressed by the principal. For example, a coach may be concerned about dissension in the third-grade team, with several members unhappy about the decision to make changes in student grouping. In this case, the literacy specialist can request a conversation with the principal to discuss the problem in general and talk about ideas about how to resolve this difficulty. Third, literacy specialists/coaches should work with the principal to build teacher support and understanding of the coaching initiative—to develop a sense of trust—so teachers do not see coaches as monitors or evaluators but as individuals who can work with them to improve student learning.

Finally, one of the key factors affecting coaching is the climate or culture in the school. There are two important constructs that underlie context or culture: one is social capital and the other, human capital. Leana and Pil (2006, 2017) discuss two types of social capital: internal and external. *Internal* social capital relates to the interactions and relationships among teachers, administrators, and others that promote a common and shared vision within a school setting. Positive internal social capital includes the following: sense of responsibility for all students, belief that all students in a school can learn, high expectations, and sense of common goals for students. Leana and Pil (2006), in their study of schools in a large urban school district, found significant relationships between what they defined as internal social capital in schools and improved student achievement.

External social capital refers to the links between the school setting and its community. In this case, teachers and administrators work collaboratively with families and with various agencies to promote student learning. This collaboration is exemplified by efforts to inform, seek information, and support families. (This topic is discussed in Chapter 10.)

Human capital refers to the human resources existing in schools: the teachers, their educational experiences and talents, and the additional personnel who support instructional differentiation (e.g., literacy specialists, librarians, literacy coaches, speech and language therapists, school psychologists, special educators). A stable staff, where there is little turnover among teachers, is an aspect of human capital. Literacy coaches can build on the work of the previous year and not have to begin again with many new teachers. Finally, as mentioned above, principals are also an important human resource; their understanding of and support for the literacy coach's role are important to the success of coaches. Principals also have a key role in building external social capital or a sense of community by reinforcing and supporting the work of teachers and literacy specialists/coaches.

The kind of work coaches can do and the outcomes they can achieve are often related to the context or culture of the school in which they work; that is, the norms or ways things get done! Too often, these norms are unspoken and difficult to discern. Listed below are some issues that can create difficulty *or* be a source of support for coaches.

- Work issues related to contract agreements
- Teacher experiences and/or beliefs about students, learning, and teaching
- Leadership issues
- Number of PL initiatives, some of which may not align with others in the schools
- Clarity of and support for the coaching role by administrators and by teachers
- Coach workload and time to work with teachers

There are other issues, of course, and each organization has its own set. In the previous chapter, Figure 5.2 lists questions that help you think about the culture of a school. Described below are two situations that highlight how culture can positively or negatively affect the work of the coach. What is your response to each of these scenarios?

THINK ABOUT THIS

1. In Brown Middle School, the principal and teachers met together to discuss the test scores in the various content areas, including social studies, science, and reading. The content-area teachers were concerned about the test scores and indicated a need to learn more about how to help students with the literacy demands of their discipline. After much discussion, the principal and teachers decided it would be advantageous to change the position of Ms. Smith, the literacy specialist, from one in which she worked with students only to one that provided her with time to work with teachers also. The principal agreed to modify the teaching schedule for the literacy specialist and also to provide common planning time for teachers of a specific discipline. Ms. Smith, who had worked in the school as an English teacher and then as a literacy specialist, had the credibility and respect that enabled her to work collaboratively with teachers in the school.

2. In Green Elementary School, the principal had written a grant to support the work of a literacy coach, whose role would be to support primary-grade teachers in implementing a new systematic phonics program to supplement the core program being used by the district. The teachers were surprised when the principal met with them and told them about the new initiative. He also introduced the coach, who had not worked in the district, but had been a literacy specialist for several years in a neighboring district. The principal explained that the coach's responsibility was to "help them improve their teaching of reading." Although the literacy coach began meeting with teachers on a regular basis, much of what she was asking them to do was unfamiliar to them

and inconsistent with the district reading series. Teachers became frustrated: They weren't sure of the purpose of these new materials and were concerned about the inconsistencies between the district series and the new resources. The literacy coach was even more frustrated because, according to district supervisor, teachers were required to use the district reading series.

What were the differences in the conditions in the schools in terms of their readiness for coaching? Talk with others about those conditions—and about the factors that would promote a successful coaching initiative. What could be changed to promote a better coaching initiative in Green Elementary School?

The Coach

The *Standards for the Preparation of Literacy Professionals 2017* (ILA, 2018a) highlight the need for literacy coaches to have (1) a deep understanding of literacy instruction and assessment, and (2) an understanding of "the processes of coaching, professional learning, organizational leadership and assessment" (2018, p. 43). Previous documents are helpful in understanding the qualifications and qualities needed by effective coaches. The IRA, in its position statement on coaching (IRA, 2004), indicated that the qualified coach is one who has teaching experience at the grade level at which he or she coaches, experience in working with adults, excellent interpersonal and leadership skills, and reading specialist certification. In their brief "Qualifications for Literacy Coaches: Achieving the Gold Standard," Frost and Bean (2006) agreed with those qualifications, but also indicated that such well-qualified individuals may not be available. School districts then often choose the best possible candidate and provide the PL experiences to support that individual. Such on-the-job learning is not the best approach to use but at times it is a reality, and inexperienced coaches may need to begin slowly, learning the content and process of coaching while they are working with and developing relationships with teachers. A helpful approach to on-the-job learning is to have new coaches join a network of coaches so they can learn from the experiences of others. They may also be assigned to work with a mentor coach available to answer questions, provide moral support, and serve as a role model for them. In our conversations with coaches, they indicated that opportunities to meet with other coaches to discuss common problems and possible solutions were the best PL experiences they received.

Even the best-qualified coaches must recognize that their beliefs, styles of teaching, and personalities influence how they work with and perceive others. Kise (2006), in her book *Differentiated Coaching: A Framework for Helping Teachers Change*, explains that all of us have our own preferences for organizing our lives and approaching our work. Some coaches may be extremely well organized and detail oriented; in their classroom teaching, they have explicit rules and regulations for managing their classrooms, believing students need the structure of routines in order to learn effectively. These coaches may find it difficult to walk into classrooms where there is a much more laissez-faire approach to classroom management and organization, even if the teachers in those classrooms are considered to be excellent teachers and students are learning! What is critical is coaches understand their preferences and those of the teacher—and recognize and value the differences. After a presentation that Rita gave about coaching, two coaches came up to her, chuckling. They worked together in the same elementary school and it was clear they enjoyed their work. As one of them told Rita, "I'm like a bulldog; I never give up—I'm tenacious." The other coach said, "And I'm like a gentle, sweet Labrador retriever, nurturing and supporting teachers." They went on to tell Rita it was obvious to them that teachers in the school seemed to prefer working with one or the other, and that was fine with them. In other words, they knew their own strengths and their tendencies, and recognized the same in teachers in the school. Not all schools, however, can offer a choice of coaches to teachers, so it is important for coaches to understand how their personal style, communication skills, and so on, can have an impact on those they coach, and accept that they will be able to work more easily with some teachers than others.

Characteristics of Effective Coaches

Below, we highlight five important qualifications of literacy coaches, based on the coaching literature and research.

1. *Know your stuff.* As one principal put it, it is a given—literacy coaches need to have excellent, up-to-date knowledge of literacy instruction and assessment, and the research that undergirds that knowledge. Coaches need this knowledge in order to analyze the lessons they see and identify the relevant aspects of instruction for discussion with the teacher. Those who have a deep understanding of their field are able to "see" things that novices or those with less understanding may not see. An analogy might be a golf instructor who quickly notices that the student is bending his or her arms (not good), not keeping the lower body stable and balanced, or not following through with her swing. Likewise, the literacy coach can readily observe, for example, (a) when the pacing of the lesson is such that students are having trouble understanding what is being taught, or (b) where the teacher might have stopped to check for understanding or provided scaffolding by showing additional examples, or giving students more opportunities to practice a skill or strategy. Clearly, literacy specialists must be learners themselves, reading the current literature and research, attending

conferences and workshops. These specialists can maintain their own professional libraries and join professional organizations so that they remain knowledgeable (see Chapter 12 for more about the literacy specialist as a lifelong learner).

2. *Experience.* Literacy coaches are more effective if they have had successful experiences as teachers. Although longevity is not an issue, literacy coaches should have experiences that build credibility with classroom teachers and enable them to feel empathy for teachers' many responsibilities. Some can transcend the need for experience, but in the long run, literacy specialists benefit from having worked with classrooms of students with diverse needs and interests.

3. *Ability to work with adults.* When we talk with coaches about how prepared they were to fulfill their roles, many of them tell us they felt comfortable with the content (literacy instruction and assessment), but less comfortable with knowing how to work with adults. Such an understanding requires coaches to develop relationships of trust and how to facilitate activities and experiences that build on what is known about adult learning. As mentioned in Chapter 5, adults come with previous experiences and beliefs that influence new learning, want their learning to be meaningful to them, require multiple exposures to help them see the value of the new initiative or idea, have busy lives, and don't want to waste their time.

4. *Effective interpersonal and communication skills.* To function successfully as a coach who has responsibility for observing and giving feedback to teachers, the literacy specialist must have excellent interpersonal and communication skills. Coaches must be good listeners, able to empathize with the teachers, and provide balanced feedback that reinforces excellent teaching behavior and provides ideas for improvement. They must also be able to develop a trusting relationship with the teachers whom they coach, so that their feedback is valued and viewed as nonthreatening. Essentially, coaches must be able to get their messages across to their colleagues (i.e., the teachers in the classrooms). (See Chapter 4 for more information about interpersonal, communication, and leadership skills.)

5. *Attitudes and beliefs.* Coaches differ in their beliefs and attitudes about literacy, learning, and teaching. The most effective coaches are those who have respect for those with whom they work and enjoy working collaboratively with their colleagues to solve problems. They acknowledge the expertise of their teaching colleagues and what they bring to the table. They are humble about what they know, willing to do their share of the work, and acknowledge and celebrate the contributions of others. They recognize that there is no one right answer to the many complex questions about teaching and learning.

Identified below are principles that should be taken into consideration when one is involved in coaching activities.

1. *Share your plans and ideas with teachers.* Teachers should understand what coaching means and what it does not mean, why they are involved, and how it will benefit their students. Teachers need to understand that the coaching process is not an evaluative one, but rather one that strives to help them be more effective. To the degree possible, invite teachers to participate in the coaching process, as they will be more receptive to the process. Share these ideas over and over again!

2. *Obtain teacher input.* Take time to listen and respond to teachers' concerns. Focusing the coaching on addressing teacher and student needs will make it more likely that the coaching will be received positively by teachers.

3. *Provide opportunities for teacher choice* (e.g., of coaching activity, purpose of coaching, goals).

4. *Provide necessary support.* Once the coaching process begins, provide the resources teachers need to make changes in their classroom instruction. In other words, if a coach or teacher identifies a specific need (e.g., additional learning or supplemental material), resources that address that need should be provided. This may include more or different coaching activities, additional materials, time to work with other teachers, and so forth.

5. *Take time to develop the trust needed to be an effective coach.* Begin with those who are eager and willing to participate. By working with teachers who are receptive, coaches themselves will be more relaxed and can use these initial interactions as opportunities to practice their coaching and communication skills. One builds trust by maintaining confidentiality. Teachers will react negatively if they discover that coaches are talking to other teachers or administrators about them, their teaching, or students. They will avoid working with the coach, if possible, or ignore suggestions made by that coach.

Summary of the Interactive Framework of Instructional Coaching

In sum, coaching does not occur in a vacuum. Successful coaching requires a context in which the conditions are conducive to coaching, a coach who has the dispositions, coaching skills, and knowledge to work within that environment, and an understanding of the model of coaching being implemented. When coaching does not seem to be effective, think about each one of these dimensions:

1. Is the school one in which there is support for, understanding of, and even enthusiasm for coaching?
2. Has "readiness" for coaching been established?
3. Does the coach have the dispositions, skills, knowledge, and abilities that enable him or her to work within that context?
4. Is the model of coaching understood and is it appropriate for the literacy goals and teacher needs in that school?

COMPARISON OF COACHING AT THE ELEMENTARY LEVEL VERSUS THE SECONDARY LEVEL

Ippolito and Lieberman (2012) discuss differences that exist between coaching at the elementary and secondary levels. They suggest that the goals at the secondary level as well as the culture of the school create a different set of challenges for coaches. First, elementary school teachers' focus on instruction is helping students develop the language, literacy, and thinking skills necessary for learning. Teachers at the secondary levels generally have a more laser-like focus on teaching students the content of their disciplines— what students need to know about American history, biology, geometry, and so on. Thus, elementary teachers may be more receptive to coaching that focuses on the improvement of literacy instruction, both in language arts classes and in the content subjects. Teachers at the secondary level may need to be convinced of the importance of such instruction. Second, teachers at the elementary school level because of their preparation experiences, tend to have a deeper understanding of literacy (reading and writing). Teachers at the secondary level are generally subject-area specialists with less knowledge of literacy and its importance to the development of content-area skills.

Third, coaches may find it easier to find time to work with teachers at the elementary level, with more opportunities for flexible scheduling. At the secondary level, the tight schedules and the fact that teachers work with many different students may create a more difficult or at least a different coaching situation. Finally, and probably most difficult, when coaches, who often have elementary school backgrounds, begin their work with secondary content-area teachers, they may need to establish their credibility. Teachers may question what these literacy coaches know about the adolescent learner or about the unique aspects of teaching the disciplines, and rightfully so. Coaches who come to the secondary school with little knowledge of a discipline (e.g., science, social studies) will have to work collaboratively with the content-area teachers, with each contributing to the development of lessons using disciplinary literacy skills appropriate for a specific content area.

At the same time, although these differences exist, there are some similarities. The process of coaching is the same: One must be able to work effectively with groups, hold positive problem-solving conversations with teachers, provide feedback in ways that respect teachers' values and beliefs, and so on. Further, it may be easier for a coach at the secondary level to work in a partnership relationship with teachers. Each has expertise to bring to the partnership, the coach, with knowledge of literacy and coaching, and the content-area teacher, with expertise in the discipline. Indeed, Ippolito and Lieberman (2012) suggest that differences "may be more a matter of degree than of fundamental difference" (p. 69). In fact, in a recent study (Bean et al., 2018), elementary and secondary principals reported few differences in the roles and responsibilities of coaches in their schools.

Given the culture of the secondary school and the focus on working with teachers of the disciplines, school leaders have generated various ideas for implementing coaching initiatives. Some encourage effective disciplinary-area teachers at the secondary level to become certified as literacy specialists or to seek advanced literacy preparation that enables them to serve as coaches for their colleagues. Others have suggested that literacy coaches with elementary school backgrounds focus on working with department chairs or teacher leaders at the secondary level to help them gain a better understanding of literacy; these secondary leaders would then serve as coaches for teachers in their disciplines. What is critical is that school leaders select literacy coaches who have the leadership and interpersonal skills that enable them to work effectively with teachers of the disciplines. There are individuals who can transcend their lack of secondary experience, but they will need the support of administration as well as the ability to work well with adults to be successful. Several resources useful for literacy coaches who work at the secondary level include *Standards for Middle and High School Literacy Coaches* (IRA, 2006), *Developing Readers in the Academic Disciplines* (Buehl, 2011), *Collaborative Coaching for Disciplinary Literacy: Strategies to Support Teachers in Grades 6–12* (Elish-Piper, L'Allier, Manderino, & DiDomenico, 2016), and "Professional Learning as the Key to Linking Content and Literacy Instruction" (Ippolito, 2013).

ACTIVITIES OF COACHING

There are many different coaching activities that can be used to support and guide instructional efforts in schools (see Figure 6.3 for a list). These activities are divided into group and individual activities. Some coaches may also assist teachers by providing direct service to students—that is, assessing students who may have been absent or helping teachers with ongoing progress monitoring, or teaching a group of students for a predetermined amount of time—but the foci in this chapter and in Chapter 7 are on coaching activities.

Group Activities

- Developing, locating, or sharing resources with teachers (written or oral).
- Meeting with grade-level or subject-area teams to discuss assessment, instruction, curriculum, student work, teacher assignments, and so on.
- Leading committee work (developing curriculum, preparing materials).
- Leading or participating in study groups to discuss specific materials read by the group.
- Leading or participating in professional learning.
- Leading or participating in more traditional types of professional learning workshops.
- Participating in lesson study (Stigler & Hiebert, 1999) with groups of teachers.
- Assisting teachers with online PL activities.
- Coaching on the fly (COTF)—unscheduled meetings with groups of teachers (e.g., discuss students, scheduling, family involvement).
- Holding problem-solving conversations with groups of teachers (e.g., grade-level, academic departments, schoolwide).

Individual Activities

- Coplanning lessons.
- Problem-solving conversations with individual teachers (about specific students, assessment, instruction, etc.).
- Modeling.
- Co-teaching.
- Observing and providing feedback.
- Combination—coaches may combine modeling, co-teaching, and observing while working with teachers in the classroom. (Coach is generally in the classroom for an extended period of time.)
- Coaching on the fly (COTF)—impromptu meeting with a teacher to discuss topic of importance to that teacher (a specific student, test scores, etc.).
- Providing resources for the individual teacher.

FIGURE 6.3. Coaching activities.

In an article written in 2004, Rita categorized coaching activities according to three levels of intensity or risk (Bean, 2004; an updated chart can be found in Bean & Ippolito, 2016):

- Level 1: Building relationships.
- Level 2: Analyzing practice.
- Level 3: Transforming practice and making teaching public.

In Level 1, the focus is on informal activities that build a sense of trust and are less anxiety-provoking for teacher and coach (e.g., an informal discussion about a specific student experiencing difficulty). In Level 2, the coach and teacher together might analyze student assessment data and work that informs instruction, and in Level 3, the emphasis is on supporting teachers as they reflect on their classroom practices. Although coaches should begin by establishing a trusting relationship, real change occurs when teachers and coach move on to Levels 2 and 3; that is when teachers begin to analyze their own instructional practices and are willing and excited about making changes that can transform instruction.

THINK ABOUT THIS

In looking at the activities identified in Figure 6.3, which of those would you feel most comfortable doing? Least comfortable? Which do you think would be most comfortable for teachers new to coaching? Least comfortable?

In Chapter 7, we discuss coaching activities that are focused on working with individual teachers. Group activities are discussed in Chapters 4 and 5. Although literacy specialists who have some coaching responsibilities may not be involved in all of the activities described in Figure 6.3, they will, at different times, need the disposition, knowledge, and skills to undertake these responsibilities.

SUMMARY

In this chapter, we discussed the "what and why" of literacy coaching. Then, we presented an interactive framework of literacy coaching consisting of three important components: the coaching model, the context, and the coach. After discussing characteristics of effective coaches, we identified principles of coaching and concluded by identifying the many different activities coaches may use in their interactions with teachers and administrators in their schools.

ADDITIONAL READINGS

Educational Leadership. (2019, November), 77(3).—The entire issue, titled *A Culture of Coaching,* is devoted to coaching and contains articles by coaching experts. This journal issue can serve as an important resource for readers interested in knowing more about effective coaching practices.

Ippolito, J., & Bean, R. M. (2019). A principal's guide to supporting instructional coaching. *Educational Leadership, 77*(3), 69–73.—The authors suggest ideas for how principals can support coaching in their schools by describing some dos and don'ts.

L'Allier, S., Elish-Piper, L., & Bean, R. M. (2010). What matters for elementary literacy coaching: Guiding principles for instructional improvement and student achievement. *The Reading Teacher, 63*(7), 544–554.—The authors present guiding principles about literacy coaching based on research findings and describe examples of how the research findings can be applied to practice.

Skiffington, S., Washburn, S., & Elliott, K. (2011). Instructional coaching: Helping preschool teachers reach their full potential. *Young Children, 66*(3), 12–19.— The authors describe coaching initiatives in several Early Reading First projects, elaborate on their interviews with teachers and coaches, and then present lessons learned about coaching at this level.

● REFLECTIONS

1. Think about a school with which you are familiar and its readiness for coaching, as described in the interactive framework of coaching. What are the conditions that would make coaching easy or difficult?

2. What experiences, knowledge, and skills do you possess to be an effective coach? How comfortable would you be in a coaching role?

● ACTIVITIES

1. Select a book on coaching and read to identify how the author(s) define coaching. Does the definition align with any of the models of coaching described in this chapter?

2. Develop with a group some interview questions that could be asked of a literacy coach. Relate those questions to the interactive framework of coaching.

3. Shadow or follow a literacy coach for a day and then be prepared to discuss what you saw. What coaching activities did you observe?

4. In small groups, discuss the following vignette, reflecting on what Joy brings to her role as a learning specialist. Identify three important "take-aways" from the vignette. Share the work of small groups with the large group.

What lessons can be learned about the role of the literacy specialist in this vignette?

In what ways does Joy serve as a leader?

What questions come to mind after reading this vignette?

JOY: A LITERACY SPECIALIST

When I interviewed for a learning specialist position, the administrator began the conversation with this question, "How flexible are you?" After 6 years in this position, I have an almost daily chuckle as I recall that moment. Broadly, I am responsible for supporting grades K, 1, and 2 (nine classrooms) in a PreK–12 International Baccalaureate private school in an urban city in Tennessee. Of our 850 students, 33% of our students come from countries outside the United States and 46% are students of color. This diversity is what attracts many families to our school.

My responsibilities vary from coaching teachers and leading professional learning activities, to supporting literacy development, supporting and extending math understandings, and collaborating with the counselor on behavior modification plans. Whew! At the end of each day, I hold on to the words I heard from Dan, one of our maintenance staff members, as he picked up strewn papers from a backpack in the hallway . . . "we're here for the kids—whatever they may need."

Contextualizing Experiences

My professional background naturally supported a view of how I work with learners *and* teachers—responding to differences and capitalizing on strengths. Prior to this position, I was a middle and high school science teacher—biology, earth, and physical science. In my third year of teaching, the principal asked me to add a math class to my teaching load, which I did not feel qualified to teach. That year was the year of my most significant growth in understanding the differences among learners. When I did not know how to meet the needs of the vastly skilled math learners in my eighth grade classroom, I sought the help of our district learning specialist. She introduced me to the idea of multiple strategies and approaches to meeting needs. The term *differentiation* became a part of my vernacular. I lived and breathed difference, specificity, unique needs . . . and flexibility!

Mentoring from a learning specialist, as an early-career teacher, was critical to support my growing understandings about (1) learning processes and how they differ from learner to learner, (2) critical conversations with other teachers about what instruction for which students, (3) reflection on my practice—sometimes hourly!—and adjusting, and (4) early theories of brain research.

Flexibility as a Literacy Specialist

Fast-forward to my current position. Although not specified in the official learning specialist job description, the lion's share of my time is spent as a literacy specialist and instructional coach. Each year, the percentage of time allocated between the two responsibilities of supporting reading and writing development and coaching teachers in literacy instruction shifts depending on learner and school needs. Some years, I focus more of my time working with small groups or individuals, providing intervention for developing readers, and in other years I spend more time in classrooms, coaching teachers and supporting instructional strategies. The flexibility of this design is paramount to successful literacy teaching and learning. It is the key to responsiveness. It is the essence of meeting learner needs.

How I come to a schedule to meet the needs of young learners is quite flexible—there's that word again! As school begins, I spend the first 2–3 weeks observing, meeting with kids, reading with them, writing with them, "mathing" with them, learning more about where they are as developing learners. This observational time is unstructured and anecdotal in nature, focusing primarily on practices. Beyond the time with students, the critical time to better understand learners comes from conversations with teachers. We discuss what they are observing. Questions we ask of each other include "What are learner experiences prior to this year?"; "Why are they where they are?"; "What do we need to be focusing on first?"; "What shall we try?" I realize I use the following phrases often: "learn from your learners" or "be students of your learners" or "take a learning stance" when I talk with teachers.

The question "What shall we try?" is not a vain attempt at random solutions. It is our first attempt at a more focused understanding of what strategies and interventions might work to support a student. As teachers meet with their new readers and writers for the year, they are noticing strengths and areas for growth. The powerful conversations I have with teachers as skilled observers, lays the groundwork for my early strategic work with developing learners.

As we come to better understand the learners, we meet in "child study teams" to make a strategic plan for the learners of highest concern. Think on this—studying children! These teams are made up of at least one administrator, a learning special-ist (my partner who serves third and fourth grades), the child's classroom teacher, at least one cocurricular teacher (art, music, science, physical education, Manda-rin, and/or Spanish) and the lower school counselor. Before we meet, we list three to five key anecdotal observations or work evidence. As we go around the table, we share what we are learning about the focus child. This is a generative time of noticing and naming (Johnston, 2004), and it is the beginnings of a structured plan for how to support a child. Once we have a structured plan, I begin adjusting my schedule to meet, support, guide, and intervene.

Responsiveness as a Literacy Coach

Another responsibility of this learning specialist position is to guide professional learning, especially in the areas of reading and writing. Again, there is no official description for this responsibility but more of an understanding that there is a resource in our lower school that teachers can use to guide, formulate, and improve literacy instruction. Sometimes this task is to lead faculty learning. Sometimes this task looks like coaching through grade-level meetings. Most often, this looks like one-to-one questions and wonderings, observations of practice, and coaching through reflective conversations.

For faculty learning, my administrator leaves it to me to decide what needs to be explored and coached. The context of these faculty-wide conversations is based on the concerns, questions, and wonderings of day-to-day conversations with teach-ers. Although it is often a challenge to focus on one specific thing to address, my time in conversation with teachers across grade levels helps me determine growth areas for faculty. Most recently, multiple conversations about our philosophical stance on cursive handwriting instruction lead to several faculty meetings focused on identifying our views and plans for cursive handwriting instruction. This deci-sion is an example of authentic and meaning-based professional development.

More often, however, my role is to guide professional learning on an indi-vidual basis. This part of my journey continues to be the most challenging and most rewarding. Most days, I am conversing with teachers in grades K–2 about learners—the status of the learner per learning goal, what the teacher has tried, what resources have been considered. These conversations are generative and are grounded in a co-learning stance. Along with the teacher, we are figuring things out, based on our expertise and mutual respect as students of the child. I feel quite fortunate about the informal designation of this role.

Most of this coaching occurs in the moment. Recently, I was in a kindergar-ten class during a lesson on building sentences using sight words. As we observed kids forming sentences with sentence strips, we noticed a few of them did not have complete sentences but only segments using sight words they knew. The teacher looked at me and, on the spot, we decided I would pull the three students who needed to better understand the concept of a sentence into a small group. As the teacher worked with the larger group, I revisited the idea of a sentence with the three. We grew our statements into sentences using sticky notes. During the transition to lunch, the teacher and I had a quick conversation. It began with her question, "If you were not in here, how would I have approached the situation of three students needing more work on constructing sentences? Should it be whole group? Or pull them aside later?" Her genuine curiosity for what was best for the kids was a moment of coaching. It took less than 5 minutes—with kid-noise in the background—and we both agreed that working with small groups, helping them co-construct sentences would be good approach to try.

A more structured coaching moment occurred with a seasoned second-grade teacher. She asked me to observe her during a phonics lesson. She wanted feedback on her whole-group design as this is not in her comfort zone. She much prefers small-group instruction. After the lesson, we spent 20 minutes debriefing (over lunch!). I began the conversation with "what did you feel went well?" This set her up as the expert of her practice and opened up windows for me to see what she already sees about herself and places for growth.

In a less-structured coaching moment, I was in a first-grade classroom to observe the teacher conferring with several writers on their small-moments writing pieces. When the teacher focused on others, I checked in with two young writers. As I was conferring with one writer, I saw the opportunity to coach her on developing details about her missing cat. I pulled her to a quieter area of the room as we discussed her next steps. After conferring with this writer, the teacher asked me about what language to use to help another student pull out details in her writing. I suggested that I work with this child during Writing Workshop, to model questioning strategies to support detail development.

Most collaboration/coaching/development occurs during lunch. Generally, I have 20 (mostly) uninterrupted minutes with K–2 teachers. We get to share silly stories of what students have said, discuss a parent e-mail or concern, and primarily say to each other, "This is what I noticed today." I think of Peter Johnston's ideas (2004) around generative language—noticing and naming. Noticing is an essential part of what I do, and I depend on classroom teachers doing the same. Noticing leads to naming leads to asking, which leads to specific support.

Celebrating Successes

This career choice, mostly, is a practice of constant reassessment of where learners and teachers are and what they need from me. Just as importantly, it is a practice of aligning or adjusting what I believe with research of pedagogy. It is not uncommon for my schedule to shift during the year. As time marches on, I am fortunate to be in an environment that both demands and supports flexibility. How my position can be best utilized to support learner growth changes from year to year. I have to be ready for those shifts. For example, I met recently with a second grader I spent many, many intervention hours with last year. He quickly grabbed his current favorite book to read me a section of it. As I listened to his fluent, confident reading followed by earnest conversation about the character, I made a [celebratory] mental note: Stephan is a successful reader. He won't need me so much this year.

REFERENCE

Johnston, P. (2004). *Choice words: How our language affects children's learning.* Portland, ME: Stenhouse.

S. JOY STEPHENS, BA, BS, MS, Certificate in Advanced Studies in Literacy
Learning Specialist
Lausanne Collegiate School
Memphis, Tennessee

CHAPTER SEVEN

Coaching Individual Teachers to Improve Literacy Teaching and Learning

KEY QUESTIONS •

- In what ways can literacy specialists develop a trusting relationship with teachers?
- What ideas are useful for the literacy coach when starting a new school year or a new position?
- What productive coaching activities can be useful for coaching individual teachers?
- What guidelines are useful for facilitating each of these activities?
- What are some guidelines for providing feedback so that it is given and received positively?

Past research indicates that too often coaches do not spend enough time in productive coaching activities, that is, those activities that directly relate to working with teachers, either individually or in groups. For example, Deussen, Coskie, Robinson, and Autio (2007), in a study of Reading First, found that coaches spent only 28% of their time working directly with teachers, although they were expected to spend 60–80% of their time doing so. In later studies, time spent with teachers was found to be influential in improving teaching practices and student learning (Bean et al., 2010; L'Allier et al., 2010). Likewise, beyond *quantity* of time spent with teachers is the *quality* of the coaching that teachers receive: What do coaches see when they enter the classroom, how do they make sense of what they see, and what do they say and do about it (Bryk, Gomez, Grunow, &

LeMahieu, 2015). Further, coaches need to be involved in both individual and group work in order to influence change at the system level (Mangin & Dunsmore, 2015). Bean and Ippolito (2016) suggest that coaches need to maintain a dual focus on the individual and on building the collective capacity of teachers to achieve school goals.

In this chapter, we focus on the ways that coaches interact with individual teachers, while in previous chapters, we described the work of coaches with small groups, such as grade-level teams, disciplinary teams, or interest groups, and also the more traditional, large-group PL sessions to support teacher learning (Chapters 5 and 6). Also, Chapter 4 provided additional information about communication, an important aspect of effective coaching both individuals or groups of teachers.

THE LITERACY SPECIALIST AS COACH: GETTING STARTED

In a study of coaches in Reading First schools in Pennsylvania (Bean et al., 2008), we found some schools employed coaches who were new to the school, while others selected coaches who had been teachers in that school. Both sets of coaches saw advantages and disadvantages to this selection process. Coaches new to a school felt that they came to the position without any previous bias about the school and its staff; teachers likewise had no prior experiences with the coach on which to base judgment. On the other hand, these coaches had no sense of any "land mines." They had to work quickly and effectively to gain an understanding of the culture of the school, including learning about students who attended the school, and teachers' knowledge and beliefs about language, literacy, and learning. Dolores, in the vignette at the end of this chapter, describes coaching experiences in a familiar school and a new school.

Most coaches who were hired from within felt as though they had the credibility and respect necessary to do the job and, in addition, understood the cultural dynamics in the school. They also understood that their prior experiences at the school could be helpful in some ways but detrimental in others. Some experienced resentment because they were no longer classroom teachers or because they had competed for the position with another colleague.

What all coaches new to the position recognized was that they had to begin *quickly* to establish themselves in this role, and at the same time, move *slowly* enough that they could develop a sense of trust between teachers and themselves. Here are several ideas to establish identity in the new role:

1. *Be accessible.* A new coach needs to be seen, walking the halls, or stopping by classrooms to talk with teachers. All coaches and especially

those new to the school should post their schedule and identify their availability; such a schedule can also provide space for teachers to "sign up" for a conversation, request resources, and so on. All teachers should have access to contact information such as an e-mail address or telephone number for the coach. As mentioned in a previous chapter, even the location of the office is important. Bean and DeFord (n.d.) describe the comments of one coach who talked about the importance of location, indicating that she had much more opportunity to talk with teachers when her office was moved from near the principal's office to near the students' bathroom! Coaches who keep their office doors open, who have instructional materials available for teachers to borrow, and who are willing to participate in informal conversations will have an easier time developing that important sense of trust. Some coaches like to keep treats in their offices; teachers who come in to talk often enjoy some candy or a cup of tea or coffee.

   2. Be proactive: Initiate activities and seek responsibilities. New coaches have at times indicated they are not sure what to do or how to start getting involved. In the beginning weeks of school, new coaches can write brief introductory letters describing their backgrounds and then identify some ways that they might work with teachers. Or a new coach can develop a reading room, perhaps in the coach's office, that includes professional and instructional materials, and invite teachers to visit the room to borrow materials. Coaches might also schedule informal conversations with each teacher, suggesting that such a conversation will help the coach get to know the students in each classroom, their abilities and needs, and also how the coach might help teachers address those needs. Figure 7.1 describes ideas for this conversation and suggests possible questions the coach might ask the teacher. Some coaches have asked teachers for permission to teach a mini-lesson in the teachers' classrooms or read to the students to get to know them (since the coach will be visiting or teaching in the classroom throughout the year). And, of course, coaches at the beginning of the year can help teachers as they attempt to conduct the initial assessments often required in schools. Your mantra might be: Be proactive! For example, if a teacher mentions wanting to do more with writing instruction, but is not sure how to begin, schedule a time to talk with the teacher about what she is already doing and her specific goals. In other words, seize any opportunities that are there for the taking. Carpe diem!

   3. Develop a sense of trust. As mentioned in Chapter 6, some activities of coaches are more threatening (e.g., observing and giving feedback) than others. To help teachers understand that coaching is meant to be supportive and nonevaluative, take time to develop a sense of trust between the teacher and yourself. Spending time with teachers in the lounge or eating lunch with them provides opportunities for informal conversations about topics important to them—their hobbies, families, pets, favorite music, and

Schedule a time to meet with each teacher individually in a comfortable space and when it is convenient for the teacher to talk. Below is a suggested framework for the conversation.

1. **Breaking the ice.** Share with the teacher some information about yourself— your goals as a coach, your background (if new to the school). Talk with the teacher about his or her background, interests. Sometimes, there are pictures on the teacher's desk of grandchildren, vacation trips, or pets that can spark a brief conversation.

2. **Setting a goal.** Establish the reason why you are holding these conversations: Get to know the teacher's goals for the students; learn more about the students in the classroom and their strengths and needs; get a sense of how the teacher might want to work with you.

3. **Suggested questions:**
   a. "What are your goals for your students this year (think about broad goals of the reading program)?"
   b. "What are the skills and abilities of students in terms of achieving the goals? Are there specific students that you have some concerns about? How can I help you learn more about your students?"
   c. "What strategies/approaches seem to work for you and help you achieve your goals? What keeps you from achieving your goals?"
   d. "What resources would be helpful to you?"
   e. "In what ways can I be helpful?"

FIGURE 7.1. Questions for an initial conversation with teachers.

so on. Share information about yourself. These informal conversations can help to develop relationships and indicate you care about them as individuals.

Starting the position by serving as a resource to teachers is often helpful (e.g., helping with assessments, developing materials), but so too, is maintaining *confidentiality*. In almost all cases, what coaches see and hear when they talk with teachers or visit their classrooms must remain between teacher and coach, although there may be a few instances when a situation affects the well-being of a child or children, and in that case, confidentiality does not apply. Likewise, administrators may also share concerns with coaches that should not to be shared with teachers. This does put coaches in a difficult spot; as one coach said, "We're in limbo or purgatory. Neither fish nor fowl."

4. *Start with the willing.* Although the job description may require coaches to work with all teachers in a school, if possible, begin with volunteers (i.e., teachers who seem eager for or request coaching support). By working with volunteers, coaches can hone their own skills in a supportive environment. Moreover, the word often spreads . . . "Coaching was very helpful!" Although starting with eager and willing teachers can

be helpful, coaches cannot not stop there. In order to effect school change, they must continue to seek opportunities to work with all teachers in the school, although they will not work with all teachers in the same way nor to the same extent. In fact, one of the reasons that coaching initiatives fail is that coaches are seen as responsible for "fixing teachers," and that they work only with those who are "needy." Teachers tend to stay away from the coach if this is the way that coaching is perceived.

5. *Be a buddy not a bully.* Although coaches may immediately want to demonstrate their expertise by providing explicit feedback to teachers, such feedback may be perceived by teachers as an indication that they are doing something wrong. In the initial stages, coaches should spend more time listening to get a better sense of what teachers are thinking and feeling and what their goals might be in terms of instructional practices. Coaches should be seen as partners, working *with* teachers to improve instruction. They should acknowledge their vulnerability, that is, they don't have all the answers and are pleased to have the opportunity to learn with and from the teachers. In fact, even if districts require that all teachers be "coached," coaching may not result in change. Teachers must have the desire to change as well as the knowledge of how and what to change.

THINK ABOUT THIS

Relate the above ideas to your own context: Which of the above ideas might be most useful to you? Are there other ideas or strategies that might work well? Think about how Dolores in the "Voices from the Field" at the end of the chapter describes the ways in which she develops a trusting relationship with teachers.

In the following box, read about Pam and her initial experience coaching a teacher colleague. Note the ways that Pam draws on the ideas discussed previously to establish a partnership with him.

Now that the principal had asked Pam to coach teachers, she was eager to begin, but not quite sure of just how to start. She remembered some of what she had learned about coaching, especially the notions that coaching should be voluntary and nonevaluative! As she sat at lunch with her teaching colleague, Hank, they began to discuss how he might help his fourth-grade students become better writers. He shook his head and said that "writing was not his strong suit." Pam asked him to say more about what he meant when he said his students weren't good writers. Hank suggested she come to his room to see some writing samples. Pam asked Hank whether he might be interested in partnering with her to investigate some ideas that might be helpful. She indicated that they would need to collaborate in this initiative, because this was not her strong suit either! Hank quickly nodded yes! Pam and Hank settled on a time when they could look at the students' writing samples together. After Pam left the lunchroom, she smiled and thought, "This is a great start—we'll be learning together!"

Pam's potential partnership with Hank is one based on a problem identified by him, about his current teaching. She and Hank will most likely have conversations about his goals for students and identify plans for moving ahead. The two educators may select several coaching activities (e.g., co-planning, co-teaching, modeling), depending on what they think will work best. Most likely, Pam will be working with Hank over an extended period of time, perhaps a 4- to 6-week period, given it takes time to gain the knowledge needed to make changes in one's teaching approach and to practice implementing these new ideas so that they become a part of an instructional repertoire. Fullan (2002, 2011) describes what he calls an implementation dip in performance or confidence that occurs when one is learning new skills or understandings. The coach and teacher need to be cognizant that some difficulties when attempting to change teaching behaviors are to be expected and that improvement will come over time.

In the following section, we describe ideas and activities for working with individual teachers.

COACHING ACTIVITIES WITH INDIVIDUAL TEACHERS

To make good decisions about the what and how of coaching, teachers and coaches will need to talk about student needs, teacher goals, and activities to achieve those goals. Questions to consider include "What would work best to help the teacher achieve his or her goals?" "How would the teacher prefer to work with me?"

In some schools, coaching goals are set by individual teachers who realize that their students are not performing as expected. At times, these goals may be set for specific grade levels or subject areas. A coaching goal may be set by school leadership; for example, teachers may begin to use a new program or set of strategies and therefore all teachers need some help in implementation. Or, for example, if a school has decided that it would like its middle school students to become familiar with Accountable Talk (Michaels, O'Conner, Hall, & Resnick, 2010), an approach for improving classroom discourse, the coach might lead a schoolwide PL activity and then ask teachers in what ways coaches can support their implementation efforts (e.g., modeling, co-teaching, observing peers).

Often, coaches use the following sequence of activities as they work with teachers: I do (model), we do (co-teach), and you do (observations).

To the degree possible, involving the teacher in deciding how to proceed helps the coach establish a more collegial relationship and enhances teacher receptivity to coaching and coaching suggestions. Below we describe each of these activities and some specific ideas to guide a coach's use of them.

Modeling

Too often, the information provided in a workshop or PL activity is not enough for teachers to transfer what they have learned to classroom practice. They need some follow-up that can help them to better understand what is being asked of them. Moreover, that follow-up might require that teachers "see" another teach a specific lesson. Rita remembers how difficult it was to learn to play golf until she watched her instructor show her how to grip the golf club, stand over the ball, and swing from the inside out! She had one of those "a-ha"—I get it!—moments.

One of the most important means of coaching is demonstrating or modeling specific behaviors or strategies. If the goal is to have a teacher learn to use a specific strategy (e.g., Beck & McKeown's [2001] Text Talk) as a means of exposing young children to challenging text, the coach may decide to model that approach while the teacher observes. In the LEADERS project, described in Chapter 5, participating teachers indicated that demonstration lessons were especially helpful. When they observed another individual using a specific approach or strategy, especially in their classrooms with their students, these teachers felt as though they had a much better understanding of how to implement that strategy. Consider the following guidelines for modeling lessons and discussing strategies for change.

1. Establish a purpose with the teacher for the modeled lesson and learn as much as you can about the students and the instruction in that classroom. You will want to know what teachers have already introduced to the students, and what specifically the teacher wants you to focus on in the lesson.

2. Plan with teachers so that collaboratively you have identified the "look-fors." Prior to the modeled lesson, frame questions that the two of you might discuss or reflect on after the lesson (what worked, what didn't seem to work, what questions do you have?). You may model for only part of the lesson and then have the teacher assume responsibility for the lesson. In this way, you can combine the modeling activity with an opportunity for either co-teaching or watching the teacher instruct. This approach provides the teacher with a chance to quickly try out what you modeled.

You might also ask the teacher to assume a role in the lesson, assisting specific students or conducting a small part of the lesson. This active involvement creates more interest and understanding on the part of the teacher—as well as commitment. One effective coach always gave the teacher a role in the modeled lesson (e.g., "I would like you to keep an eye on Roberto and Chelsea while I teach. Generally, they have difficulty following directions. Perhaps if you sat next to them, it would be helpful.").

3. You can provide teachers with a protocol that assists them in focusing their attention on the lesson they are watching. Such a protocol can be quite simple, for example, a T-chart with the following headings: "What I Noticed"/"Questions I Have." Or the chart might have three columns addressing the following: What is the coach doing? What are the students doing? What questions or comments do I have? In some instances, coaches may want to provide protocols that contain information about the specific steps in the instructional strategy being modeled (e.g., procedures for teaching a Text Talk lesson).

4. Discuss the lesson with the teacher as soon as possible after teaching it. Reflect with the teacher on the effectiveness of the lesson. Give them opportunities to ask questions and make comments. "Did you think that I achieved my goals, and if not, why?" "What went well?" "What could have gone better?" Be certain to address those questions that created the need for modeling in the first place! Be honest in sharing with the teacher unexpected aspects of the lesson (e.g., handling of a behavior problem). Few lessons are perfect, and teachers will feel more comfortable working with a coach when they see that the coach, too, is vulnerable and can have difficulty with a disruptive student or elicit little response from students, despite attempts to engage them.

5. Address next steps. There should be some type of follow-up to the modeled lesson. Such follow-up could include observing the teacher presenting the same type of lesson that was modeled, to give the teacher an opportunity to practice the specific strategy or approach. At the same time, there may be teachers who are uncomfortable with this step and the coach may need to do some co-teaching to create a sense of a partnership or co-ownership of the lesson. Likewise, the coach may also co-plan a similar lesson with the teacher, but not observe until the teacher has had an opportunity to teach such a lesson several times. There is more than one way to follow-up with a modeled lesson; often the coach needs to follow the lead of the teacher (i.e., What makes sense for that teacher?).

A few caveats: Some teachers may not require modeling; moreover, they may want the coach to work with them in a different way (e.g., helping them co-plan a lesson). Second, modeling of a specific strategy or approach in all classrooms may not be time efficient. Instead, coaches may want to model in one fifth-grade classroom and find ways to invite the other fifth-grade teachers to observe that lesson (e.g., the principal or other personnel may work with the other fifth graders). Another option is for the coach to produce a video of a modeled lesson in one classroom and then share and reflect on the lesson with a group of teachers during a follow-up group meeting. Finally, the goal for coaching is to move the teacher toward independence; therefore, be cautious when teachers are interested only in having you model for them!

Co-Planning

As mentioned previously, coaches need to understand that individual teachers have varying degrees of openness, willingness, or enthusiasm for coaching. Some teachers may welcome coaches who help them plan (e.g., one lesson, several lessons that focus on developing a specific strategy or skill, or a unit of work). For example, the coach and teacher may want to design lessons that help students understand how to participate in structured discussions to enhance comprehension. Co-planning might include lessons introducing students to key ideas about participating in a discussion and the various roles that they can assume (e.g., leading, facilitating, recording); other lessons may include looking at the materials of instruction and deciding the key questions to ask and where the best "stops" are for asking those questions. The coach and teacher can schedule follow-up meetings where they discuss reactions to and reflections about the lessons. Such co-planning can precede coach observations. These professional conversations can promote teacher learning; they can be conducted with individual teachers or with a group of teachers. For example, a group of second-grade teachers working with the coach might focus on goals for increasing students' ability to understand the theme of the story. Together they can analyze student performance data and decide on learning goals and instructional activities. They may also plan for follow-up coaching differentiated for each teacher. Co-planning can be useful because it builds a collaborative relationship between coach and teacher, and also helps the coach gain a deeper understanding of what teachers know or think about their students, learning goals, and literacy learning.

Problem Solving

Although problem solving is certainly an integral aspect of all coaching activities, we elaborate on it here because of its importance. If the teacher identifies the problem, it tends to be important to them and nonthreatening. Working together to solve problems can help to develop trust between those involved in the process. Toll (2018) describes three phrases of a problem-solving model to coaching: (1) identifying a problem; (2) describing the problem so that it is understood; and (3) deciding on a plan of action. Again, student needs as well as teacher interest can be sources of topics for discussion (see Pam's case example above). Critical issues that teachers are facing at the time can be addressed (e.g., difficulties of one student in the classroom, management issues, working with multiple groups, how to implement a specific strategy, or how to talk with the families of a struggling reader). Collegial problem solving can help the coach and the teacher make key decisions about next steps. Teachers may make changes in grouping of students or try new management strategies. Follow-up coaching activities may be initiated (e.g., the coach may agree to model or to co-teach). Problem solving can be an effective coaching activity for both individual and groups of teachers.

Essentially, this coaching activity is an important approach for developing a relationship of trust; it relies on the teacher to identify and provide important information about the problem, and requires the coach to be an excellent listener who asks questions that lead toward solving the problem. (See Chapter 4 for information about communication skills.) Often, literacy specialists who do not have the formal title of coach are involved in this type of coaching activity—helping teachers think about an issue they are facing and how to solve it.

Classroom Observations or Visits

An effective coaching approach to PD is observing the work of teachers and providing opportunities for reflection and inquiry. By observing, coaches can see what is occurring in the teaching/learning process, provide reassurance, discuss alternative strategies, and in general, work *with* the teacher to improve classroom practices. Often an observation is an effective activity that follows modeling. Going back to Rita's experience with learning to golf, once her instructor showed her the appropriate way to approach the swing, he then asked her to practice it and provided feedback (e.g., good job of gripping the club, keeping your arms straight; you might try standing closer to the ball, following through). Notice that the feedback included some "hurrahs" and some hints.

Observations, however, are too often synonymous with evaluation because too often that has been their primary purpose. In fact, to reduce teacher anxiety, in some initiatives, administrators ask coaches to refrain from using the word *observing*; rather, they use the term *visiting* to describe their work, given that observing too often implies a one-way action. We suggest that coaching observations include opportunities for preplanning and follow-up analysis and reflection that can lead to instructional improvements. In the coaching cycle described below, the focus is on facilitating the teacher's growth and the coach is seen as a resource. Figure 7.2 outlines a cycle for coaching similar to the cycle described in Bean and Ippolito (2016). In the following sections, each of the four steps is described, with examples from several coaching cycles. Appendix A provides a template to

---

Step 1: Planning Conversation
Talk with the teacher, using questions such as the following: What are the goals for the lesson (i.e., What do you want students to learn?)? What do you hope to gain from the coaching experience? What sort of data should I collect and how?

Step 2: Observing
Observe in the classroom, focusing on the aspects that have been jointly agreed on in the planning meeting.

Step 3: Analyzing/Reflecting
Both coach and teacher think about the lesson that has been observed. The coach analyzes data from the observation and identifies topics/issues for discussion. The teacher generates questions and ideas for discussion.

Step 4: Post-Observation Conversation
Coach and teacher meet to discuss the lesson, using data obtained in Steps 2 and 3. Ideas for how the coach might be helpful or follow through should be part of this conversation. The goals of this step are to reflect with the teacher about the lesson.

Were lesson goals accomplished?

In what ways can the lesson be improved to meet student needs?

How might the lesson lead to possible changes or modifications in classroom practices?

FIGURE 7.2. Coaching cycle.

use as a summary sheet for this four-step coaching cycle. By using a summary sheet, coaches can keep track of their work with individual teachers, observe progress, and reflect on next steps.

Planning Conversation

During this conversation, the focus is on planning as an important first step. Walking into the classroom without a focus is like traveling in an unfamiliar city without a map and trying to get from one location to another—there are many different directions to take and many different means of transportation. Likewise, with observation. The planning conversation enables the coach and the teacher to discuss important issues such as those below.

- What are the goals of the lesson? ("I'm teaching a series of lessons that address the standard about comparing and contrasting the structure of two different texts.")
- What is expected of the students during this lesson (i.e., in what activities are they engaged)? What student outcomes are expected?

Is there anything the coach should know about the students? The lesson?
- What does the teacher hope to learn from the observation? What is the focus of the observation?
- What is the best means of obtaining the information needed to address the teacher's goals?
- What are the procedures to follow? (Where should the coach sit? How long will the coach stay?)

The planning conversation provides an opportunity for building trust and promoting reflection. It is an opportunity for the coach and teacher to co-construct the purpose and procedures for the observation. It also allows the coach to gain key information about the class, lesson, and teacher. For example, this may be the first lesson the teacher has taught using a particular strategy, or perhaps there is a student with special needs who just arrived 2 days ago.

One planning meeting between a second-grade teacher and a coach went as follows: Luwanna, a second-grade teacher, had planned a lesson to address standards relative to writing, specifically, informational writing. She wanted Shannell, the coach, to provide her with feedback about the lesson. Luwanna and Shannell agreed that Shannell would observe, noting the procedures that Luwanna used in teaching the lesson. They agreed that Shannell needed to focus on the students to determine whether they understood and were involved in the lesson. Shannell indicated that she would take careful notes of what students were doing and saying; she would also script part of the lesson, to record what Luwanna and the students were saying at significant points in the lesson (i.e., what did Luwanna say to guide students and how did students respond to her questions?). Luwanna reminded Shannell that she would be working with the entire class and that her class was not familiar with informational writing. This would be a lesson introducing a sequential framework to the class. They agreed on a time and place for the observation.

Observing

The classroom is a complex place and a great deal is happening at the same time. Likewise, observing is complex, as each observer comes into the classroom with his or her own biases and perspectives. The principles developed by Gabriel and Woulfin (2017) can be useful in planning for a classroom observation:

- Be sure to focus, as "you can't look for everything at the same time" (p. 73).
- Be aware of the backgrounds and experiences of the specific students

and teachers whom you are observing (not all practices are applicable to all students).

- Be aware of the many influences that affect teacher decision making (the curriculum, PL emphases, resources available). Teachers may be constrained by factors specific to the context.

There are many different frameworks or systems to use for collecting data during observations. There are simple *checklists* that indicate the presence of some behavior or event (e.g., student work is displayed) or *scales* that describe to what extent something is present (e.g., student work is displayed not at all, a little, or a great deal). There are observation systems that are specific to the strategy or skill being taught (e.g., What should be included in a lesson on close reading? On facilitating a discussion about a text?) and there are frameworks that are more general, addressing key elements of effective literacy instruction at a specific level. Observers can also script teacher verbal behavior as a means of obtaining data. Some of these techniques are comprehensive and time consuming, others, less so.

Many states or districts have developed or adopted observation frameworks for teacher performance evaluations. Most frequently, these frameworks are general, that is, not specific to one content area (e.g., importance of active engagement with various grouping arrangements; asking high-level questions). Further, these general observation protocols are often meant to serve as tools to measure or assess what teachers are doing.

However, we suggest that literacy specialists, given their extensive literacy knowledge, consider collaborating with teachers to develop an observation protocol that reflects what is known about effective evidence-based literacy practices (i.e., what do we expect to see in our classrooms?). This protocol could be used to help teachers understand what effective literacy instruction looks like and serve as a tool for instructional improvement. Gabriel and Woulfin (2017, p. 131) provide a pocket version of "look-fors" for key ingredients of effective literacy instruction that provide a good starting point for development of an observational protocol. The observational tools specific to literacy may be helpful to administrators who may not have an in-depth knowledge of effective literacy instruction. These tools can provide for consistency of and a focus on well-defined expectations for classroom literacy instruction. When teachers are aware of observation protocols and are involved in selecting or developing them, there is likely to be more acceptance of their use for making instructional changes.

We want to re-state again, that in our view, coaching should be non-evaluative, that is, a partnership between teachers and coaches. However, coaches should know and understand the evaluative system used in the district and work with teachers in ways that are consistent with the requirements of the evaluation protocol so that there are not any mixed messages about school or district expectations.

EXAMPLES OF OBSERVATION PROTOCOLS

In this section, we describe several observation protocols that may be useful to coaches as a starting point.

Checklists and Scales

Bean, Fulmer, and Zigmond (2009) created an observation protocol for Reading First classrooms K–3 and adapted it for coaches to use while observing literacy instruction in the elementary grades (see Figure 7.3). It provides observers with specific descriptors of what they might expect to see when observing literacy instruction and also a scale to determine the extent to which specific indicators are present in the classroom or seen during the observation period. Because of its comprehensive nature, observers may wish to focus on only one or two dimensions (e.g., instructional practices, classroom environment).

Appendix B describes an observation protocol used for observing in content areas in upper elementary, middle, or high schools. This protocol provides information about how the teacher facilitates learning, the literacy activities of students, and information about grouping and materials used.

Observers can use the observation protocols described above when observing several different aspects of lessons. However, as mentioned, observers who are visiting classrooms to see how well teachers are implementing a specific skill or strategy (e.g., Questioning the Author, Beck & McKeown, 2006) may choose to develop a protocol that describes explicitly what is expected. Or if a school has a literacy framework emphasizing specific strategies, then the literacy coach and teachers may choose to develop an observational protocol focused on those strategies. For example, Thibodeau (2008), a literacy coach, worked with several secondary content-area teachers and taught them several literacy strategies to be used before, during, and after literacy text selections. In that case, an observation protocol can be developed addressing elements of those strategies.

Open-Ended Protocols

There are also open-ended observation systems requiring much skill on the part of the observer, but at the same time, providing meaningful information about what is happening in the classroom. Observers might take notes, using an open-ended but focused template. Figure 7.4 provides an example of such a focused template. The protocol identified broad areas which might be seen to give the observer a structure for the observation and a place to provide comments or even evidence about what is occurring in the lesson (e.g., students are reading to locate specific information in text in response to teachers' question).

Teacher/Coach: _____   Grade/Subject: _____

Date: _____   Time Begin: _____   End: _____

Students Present: _____   Lesson Focus: _____

Materials: (Check all that apply)

Textbook	**Group: (Check all that apply)**	**Adults: (Check all that apply)**	Student Teacher
Board/Chart			Teacher Intern
Computer	Whole Class	Teacher	Other: _____
Worksheet	Small Group	Reading Specialist	
Student Work	Pairs	Reading Coach	
Other: _____	Individual	Instructional Aide	

Protocol to be used as a guide. Scale to be completed after the observation has been completed.

Scale:	Great Extent	Some Extent	Minimal Extent	Not Observed
	(3)	**(2)**	**(1)**	**(0)**
Classroom Environment: Print Rich				
Classroom Library Is Accessible				
Students are able to gain easy access to the library in the classroom. Books are at eye level.	☐	☐	☐	☐
Library Has Wide Variety of Books/Genres				
Library includes informational material, books for pleasure, poetry, language play, reference materials, etc.	☐	☐	☐	☐
Reading and/or Writing Strategies Are Displayed				
Strategies posted are informative tools designed to promote classroom learning.	☐	☐	☐	☐
Reading Spaces Are Inviting	☐ yes ☐ no			
Learning Centers Are Evident	☐ yes ☐ no			
Student Work on Display Inside/Outside	☐ yes ☐ no			

(continued)

FIGURE 7.3. Observation checklist. Adapted with permission from Bean et al. (2009).

Scale:	Great Extent (3)	Some Extent (2)	Minimal Extent (1)	Not Observed (0)
Classroom Management/Climate				
Maintains Positive Learning Environment				
Interactions are respectful and supportive. Tone and atmosphere are encouraging.	☐	☐	☐	☐
Encourages High Level of Student Participation				
Teacher facilitates active engagement of students during lesson.	☐	☐	☐	☐
Maintains Effective Behavioral Routines				
Clear expectations are established by teacher and internalized by students. Minimum time is spent in transitions.	☐	☐	☐	☐
Maintains Robust Literacy Routines				
Teacher facilitates strong literacy routines that are recognized and understood by students.	☐	☐	☐	☐
Preserves Student On-Task Behavior				
Teacher consistently facilitates student engagement during reading instruction.	☐	☐	☐	☐

Scale:	Great Extent (3)	Some Extent (2)	Minimal Extent (1)	Not Observed (0)
Instructional Practices				
Introduces and Reviews Concepts/Skills Clearly				
Teacher develops concept or skill plainly and accurately. The concept or skill introduced is evident.	☐	☐	☐	☐
Differentiates Literacy Instruction				
Teacher appears to use individual student literacy performance in planning instruction. Literacy learning is structured for small groups or individual students.	☐	☐	☐	☐

(continued)

FIGURE 7.3. *(continued)*

Scale:	Great Extent (3)	Some Extent (2)	Minimal Extent (1)	Not Observed (0)
Facilitates Text Comprehension				
Teacher helps students to make connections to targeted concepts; activates student background knowledge; engages students in high-level thinking activities; encourages students to make predictions; summarizes, retells, or makes use of graphic organizers to organize their thinking.	☐	☐	☐	☐
Engages in Coaching/Scaffolding				
Teacher provides corrective feedback by prompting the student in an effort to encourage the student to arrive at the correct answer independently.	☐	☐	☐	☐
Highlights Significance of Reading Process				
Teacher emphasizes the reading and writing process and the use of strategies; "A good reader sees the parts of words to help him or her decode. A good reader/writer does . . ."	☐	☐	☐	☐
*Models Skills/Strategies				
Teacher demonstrates a particular skill or strategy to students.	☐	☐	☐	☐
*Provides Guided Practice				
Teacher supports students in practicing targeted skill or concept. Teacher provides opportunities to practice literacy learning.	☐	☐	☐	☐
*Provides/Monitors Independent Practice				
Teacher has students practice targeted concept/skill individually and monitors by giving feedback when needed.	☐	☐	☐	☐
*Provides Application Activities				
Teacher has students apply targeted concept to new learning for problem solving and independent learning. Students take responsibility for their own literacy learning.	☐	☐	☐	☐

*Gradual release of responsibility model (GRRM; Pearson & Gallagher, 1983).

FIGURE 7.3. *(continued)*

Teacher observed: _____ Grade level: _____ Date: _____

Coach: _____

Time of observation: From _____ to _____

Use this as a guide to write your observations and note areas for discussion with teacher.

Classroom environment (seating arrangements, grouping):

Print environment:

Focus of lesson: What is the goal of this lesson?

Is the purpose clear to students?

Instructional practices	Comments
What is the teacher doing?	
How does the teacher help students if they seem to be having difficulty understanding key ideas or performing specific skills?	
What are the students doing (reading, writing, speaking, listening)? Are they working as a whole class, in small groups, individually?	
Opportunities for student engagement (how are students demonstrating their learning?).	
Other observations: How do the lesson activities help students achieve lesson goal?	

FIGURE 7.4. Open-ended focused observation protocol.

Observers might also choose to describe what is being said and what is happening by scripting exactly what they hear and see. Using paper and pen or a laptop computer, the coach records exactly what is going on in the classroom. The end product provides the coach with "data" to be shared with the classroom teacher (e.g., "Here's the question you used to open the lesson; This is what the students were doing when . . ."). Scripting, however, is intense and should be used when it provides data that addresses the purpose of the observation (e.g., what types of questions is the teacher asking). Specific guidelines are summarized in Figure 7.5. The advantage of this type of scripting is that "actual" behaviors and language are recorded rather than an interpretation or judgment about what is seen (as occurs when the observer makes a judgment, using a scale from 0 to 3). This open-ended scripting can be done selectively, for example, for a 10-minute period when the teacher is interacting verbally with students. So, if the goal of the observation was to focus on student and teacher talk, the scripting during the 10 minutes would provide evidence about the type of question or statement being raised by the teacher, how the teacher responded to student' responses, and the quality of student responses. Teachers are generally intrigued when they see actual evidence of their teacher talk. It does take time to learn to observe using this approach. However, with practice it becomes an effective means of collecting information to share with teachers. See Appendix C for a form for using this approach; this protocol has three columns labeled "Teacher," "Student," and "Observer" comments.

Rather than taking such extensive notes during a lesson, in some schools, with teacher permission, coaches can either audio- or video record a portion of the lesson so that together, coach and teachers can review and reflect on teaching strategies, student activities, student engagement, and so forth.

Consider the following summary points to guide observation practices:

- Focus. Again, it is not possible to observe everything that is going on in a lesson. Therefore, deciding the focus of the observation is essential; if possible, that focus should be determined jointly by both coach and teacher.
- Be objective. While observing, be sure to indicate what you are seeing without being judgmental. As an observer, recognize your own biases and perspectives.
- Be sensitive to the fact that being observed may create anxiety for teachers; students too may behave differently because of the observer in the room.
- When entering a classroom, remain as unobtrusive as possible, finding a spot to sit and observe without interrupting the flow of the lesson. Talk with teachers prior to the lesson about whether they are going to introduce you. Generally, ask teachers to make the

1. Upon entering the room, spend several minutes doing an environmental sweep and collecting information about number of students, literacy environment in the room, and seating arrangements. You may want to draw a picture of the classroom.

2. Using blank sheets of paper, divide the sheet into three columns, identified as "Teacher," "Student," and "Observer" comments.

3. Begin identifying what is occurring in the classroom. If there is classroom discourse (i.e., the teacher is interacting with the students), try to jot down key phrases or words that the teacher and the students are saying. You may also want to identify whether specific students are responding. Remember to note whatever is especially relevant to the focus or goal identified in the planning session. For example, if the teacher wants the coach to attend to levels of questions, then recording the specific questions is important. If the teacher wants the coach to observe whether students are actively involved, then the coach would need to attend to that dimension of instruction.

4. When the teacher is serving as a facilitator (walking around classroom assisting students), the coach can focus on what students are doing, or not doing, as well as what the teacher is doing or saying.

Example of script:

Teacher	Students	Observer
9:00—Walks around helping students; answers their questions.	All are writing in their journals.	
9:05—Helps Margo—asks her to read what she had written.	One student is not writing (has his head down).	Is the task too difficult? Ask the teacher about him.
9:10—Says, "Good work! Who would like to share what they have written with the class?"	Most students raise their hands.	Why "Good work"?

5. Every 5 minutes draw a line under what you have written so that you have some indication of how long various activities have lasted and when they occurred. Sometimes, you may want to draw a line when an activity changes; for example, the teacher has finished reading a story and is now beginning to ask questions about the selection.

6. Use the "Observer Comments" column to write comments when there are events in the lesson about which you want to talk with the teacher or have questions. For example, note the comment above about the student who is not participating in the writing task.

7. Every 5 minutes or so (when it seems appropriate), it is wise to stop writing and just look around the classroom. It is easy to become so immersed in the writing that you miss some of the nonverbal and physical interactions.

FIGURE 7.5. Observation protocol for scripting data.

introduction promptly so that you can quickly and quietly go to a seat where you can observe without causing any disruptions.

- If the teacher asks you to interact with the students and the lesson, you may choose to join in and help teach the lesson. Teachers can learn a great deal by having coaches work with them, and because the coach's goal is to be helpful, this modification may be what is needed at the time. However, the coach may also return at another time to co-teach, asking the teacher to assume full responsibility for teaching this lesson.

- Leave a small sticky note when you leave, thanking the teacher and indicating that you look forward to talking with him or her. Sometimes a positive and specific comment, such as "I enjoyed listening to the students tell what they would do in that situation!" can lessen teacher anxiety about the observation and the follow-up conversation.

Analyzing/Reflecting

Each step of the coaching cycle is an important one; however, the step of analyzing and reflecting is critical, for without it, there is little chance of making an impact on teacher learning and performance. Reflection is the purview of not only the coach but also the teacher. Before meeting for a postobservation conversation, both literacy coach and teacher can think about what occurred in the lesson, and especially how they addressed the questions raised in the pre-observation or planning conversation. Also, teachers can be asked to jot down a few ideas or questions for the postobservation conversation.

It is here, in the analysis phase, that coaches can make good use of the observation checklist, notes, or scripts that they used during the observation. These tools provide excellent information that can be shared with the teacher during the conversation. What levels of questions were asked? What steps did the teacher follow in teaching the strategy? How many students (and who) were not involved during the lesson? Going back through the data and thinking about answers to the following questions enable the coach to think about a strategy for the postobservation conversation to be held with the teacher.

- What are the key points to raise? (Are they related to the goals set by the teacher? How important in terms of possible impact on student learning?) You may choose to summarize some of the key points on a template similar to the one in Appendix B.

- What is the best way to begin the conversation? (Does the coach start with identification of some strengths? Should the coach ask the teacher to discuss his or her views?) Thinking about how to begin a conversation can be helpful in getting the discussion moving in a positive direction. We do not suggest that coaches start by asking teachers to indicate whether they thought the lesson went well! This can lead to some problems, if the coach and teacher are not on the same page! Rather, as suggested by Stanier (2016), the coach might begin by asking a question such as "What comes to your mind about this lesson?" It gives the teacher an opportunity to identify what is important to him or her.

- What changes would best improve the instruction in that classroom? (Are the changes *doable* [e.g., does the teacher have the skills to implement suggested changes]?) Have teachers decide on one or two priority goals. Identify the support needed by the teacher to implement any changes.
- How can the coach be helpful? What approach might be best in working with this teacher (co-teaching, co-planning, etc.)?

Postobservation Conversation

The postobservation conversation should occur as close in time to the observation as possible, not only to allay the teacher's concerns but also because recall and memory of what occurred are much better. However, the analysis and reflection steps are important and should not be eliminated. It's helpful to talk briefly with teachers immediately after an observation, thanking them for the opportunity to work with them, making a positive comment about some aspect of the lesson (e.g., the classroom environment, a student's performance), and identifying a time for the postobservation session.

One goal of the postobservation conversation is to promote teacher reflection to the highest degree possible, focusing on teacher and student behaviors (Who was doing what?), comparing actual and desired behaviors, or considering reasons why these did or did not occur. Another important goal is the development of future action plans: What can the teacher take back from the discussion to improve classroom instruction? Another is to assess the effects of the coaching experience: In what ways was the experience helpful—and what comes next?

Coaches need to be cognizant of the individual strengths, experiences, and learning styles of teachers. Using this knowledge, coaches can think about what stance or stances to take in talking with teachers. Ippolito (2010), for example, writes about a directive, balanced, or responsive approach. Below, we use the descriptors identified by Robbins (1991): coach as mirror, collaborator, or expert.

THE COACH AS MIRROR

In this instance, the teacher is self-reflective and quickly assumes a leadership role during the conversation. The coach then serves to confirm and validate what the teacher articulates. These types of sessions generally move along quite easily because these teachers recognize whether they have achieved their lesson goals, why or why not, and often can suggest possible solutions to any problems. The coach then serves as a mirror by reflecting back to the teacher specific examples that indicate support for or clarification of what the teacher is saying. Both teacher and coach talk about possible next steps. In the example below, the coach is working with an experienced kindergarten teacher who analyzes her own behavior and sets future goals for herself.

> KINDERGARTEN TEACHER: I lost the group after about 15 minutes. They were really with me until I started asking various questions about the main character. I don't think they lost interest in the story; I think they were sitting too long. I wonder if I might have included some sort of movement activity!
>
> COACH: Yes, I think you're right. After about the third question, they started to fidget and seemed somewhat restless. What sort of movement activity might be useful?

THE COACH AS COLLABORATOR

In this case, the coach and teacher work together to determine the strengths and possible weaknesses of the lessons. They are both struggling to identify what was especially effective and what may have been done better. This might also be thought of as a problem-solving stance.

> SEVENTH-GRADE SOCIAL STUDIES TEACHER: It seems to me there has to be a better way to get more students involved in the discussion. The same students are always raising their hands, while the others wait for them to reply.
>
> COACH: Let's talk about this. What do you think might be helpful?
>
> TEACHER: Last week, at our book study, we read an article about holding class discussions. One of the ideas was to have students generate questions for other students. I'm thinking that might work for me. But I have a feeling that I might have to help students learn to do this—if they are to develop good questions!
>
> COACH: I think you have a great point. It might be worthwhile to teach a few lessons that help students think about the kinds of questions that can be asked and answered. For example, the QAR framework gives students a common language to use in generating questions [Carroll, Raphael, & Au, 2011].
>
> TEACHER: That sounds like a great idea. Do you have any written material that can give me a little more background about this? Also, I wonder if we might co-plan this lesson—or perhaps even co-teach it!
>
> COACH: Happy to work with you. I'll get some written material to you about this idea. I think your students will enjoy this challenge.

THE COACH AS EXPERT

In some instances, especially with novice teachers or teachers who are attempting a new approach for the first time, the coach may need to serve as an expert, using directive coaching, and providing information to help teachers understand whether they are implementing various strategies or approaches effectively.

> FIFTH-GRADE TEACHER: So, when I was trying the K-W-L [Ogle, 1986], I wasn't sure what I should do after students identified all they knew about turtles. Exactly how should I move to the W step?
>
> COACH: I think you did a great job! You had the students review what they knew, and then you commented: "Wow, we know a lot, but it appears that there is still much more to learn. For example, I wondered what the differences were between land turtles and sea turtles? What are some things you are wondering about?" You can help to jump-start the students by modeling for them, providing them with one or two examples of what they might want to learn. Often this will help them generate additional ideas.

In any single conversation with a teacher, coaches may find themselves moving from one stance to another, especially as the teacher raises questions or generates ideas. For example, the coach may begin the conversation using a more collaborative stance, but when the teacher asks for explicit guidance, may need to proceed by providing expert advice. The key is language—how we talk with others influences the results of any conversation. In Chapter 4, many ideas about effective communication are described. Just as a reminder here—being a good listener really matters! Remember to listen attentively not only to what is said, but how it is said.

This postobservation session often serves as the planning step for the next cycle! For example, in the planning session described previously in this chapter, Shannell, the coach, talked with Luwanna, the teacher, about her observation of a mini-lesson focused on reading informational text. After observing, the coach and teacher conferred and talked about next steps.

> COACH: Overall, your students seemed to be able to arrange the sentence strips correctly; they really understood the sequence of making a peanut butter sandwich. What do you think the next steps might be; how can you move your students along? [The coach is asking the teacher to generate some ideas to try in the next lesson.]
>
> TEACHER: I think I'd like to have them read some other informational texts that have a focus on sequence. I would also like to ask them to write a set of directions for doing something (e.g., what they do in the morning when they get up).

COACH: Great ideas for the next lesson. Go for it! Let's talk about Juan and Maria, two EL students who seemed to be somewhat puzzled. I agree with you; they seemed to have some difficulty following your directions. I wonder whether it would be good to work with them in a smaller group so that they get more opportunity for support and scaffolding. What do you think?

The coach and teacher agreed that it would be helpful if the coach would teach a similar lesson about sequencing to a smaller group of students, including Juan and Maria, while other students were writing a text that explained what they did in the morning when they got up. The teacher would walk around, helping students as needed. She would also be able to watch and listen as the coach works with the small group. Luwanna felt she could learn a lot by stepping back and "kidwatching."

And back to the beginning! Often planning for next steps has occurred in this final reflective activity. Likewise, subsequent planning sessions can be short, given goals have most likely been established for a teacher. Because of time constraints, planning may have to occur as you are conversing with the teacher before or after school or for a brief time during a teacher planning period. Nevertheless, planning is important; it helps establish a common goal for coach and teacher and focuses the observation!

Below, we identify guidelines for giving feedback so that it is respectful, allows for divergent thinking, and enables teachers to gain both the skill and the will to make changes in their classroom practices.

Giving Feedback

The feedback that coaches provide may suggest that teachers make changes in either what or how they teach. If the teacher and coach together can identify those areas or behaviors in which change is desired (i.e., the coach as mirror or the coach as collaborator), then the feedback session is generally a productive and positive one. On the other hand, there are times when the coach may need to be more directive in working with a teacher. Always, the desire is to provide feedback that is constructive and workable. Nevertheless, some teachers may react defensively and have difficulty accepting feedback. Providing feedback in a carefully balanced and respectful manner can help to alleviate defensive and negative reactions. Here are several suggestions for giving feedback:

1. *Be specific.* Telling the teacher that the lesson was good, fine, or interesting is not constructive—it does not provide information the teacher can use to improve classroom practices. Instead the coach must be as specific as possible. For example, if the coach wants to reinforce the many ways the teacher has made the environment student friendly, he or she can

describe specifically what was seen (e.g., many different kinds of books in places where students could readily access them; student work posted on the walls; a chart labeled "You Made My Day," with students' names on it). Likewise, if the coach has concerns about an instructional aspect of the lesson (e.g., the teacher called only on the few students whose hands were up), the coach can show the teacher the data from the observation showing who was called on and who wasn't. Or if teacher questioning was only at a literal level, even though the emphasis was on inferential thinking, the coach can share data with the teacher, and they can analyze the level of questions together. If a purpose was set for the observation, feedback should address or be aligned with that purpose.

2. *Behave in ways that reduce defensive behavior.* It is natural for all of us to defend what we have done in response to what we perceive as criticism. Coaches can reduce defensive behavior in several ways. First, they can focus on describing what they observed rather than making a judgment about it and, to the degree possible, create a problem-solving situation (e.g., "I noticed that students were less attentive in the discussion part of the lesson than while reading the story. Let's talk about that. What do you think caused their inattention?"). Such an approach promotes collaboration and reduces the tendency for the coach to be perceived as the only one who has the answers. Second, coaches can acknowledge that teachers have unique experiences and knowledge; they know the goals they are trying to achieve and the personalities of the students with whom they work. They have their own perspectives about what occurred in the lesson. They can therefore contribute to the solutions or suggestions in ways the coach cannot. Again, beginning the postobservation conversation with questions that help teachers think about the observed lesson is important. At the same time, these questions should not be ones for which the coach is looking for a specific answer (e.g., "How many students were engaged in this lesson?"). Rather, questions that provide for reflection are important: "In what ways were students engaged in the lesson?"; "In what ways did you accomplish your goals?"; "What might be helpful to you in meeting your goals?"; or as stated above, "What is on your mind in terms of this lesson?"

Although coaches may have a preset agenda that highlights items for discussion, they must be cautious not to ask closed-ended questions to which they already know the answers (e.g., "How many students knew what you meant by 'accountable talk'?"). A more open-ended question or questions might be more productive and generate less teacher defensiveness (e.g., "I'm curious, to what degree do you think students understand the concepts of Accountable Talk? Why do you think so?").

3. *Provide balanced feedback.* Make certain the teacher clearly understands the issue or item under discussion and how it might be resolved. For example, if the teacher is providing opportunities for students to develop

fluency but the students are reading books that are too difficult for them to read fluently, the coach needs to acknowledge what the teacher is doing that is important (e.g., providing fluency practice for students). In addition, however, the coach can help the teacher understand how such practice can be more productive if the students are provided with material that they don't struggle to read. Feedback can be divided into a two-step process, as follows:

- *Discuss the merits of what the teacher is doing* (e.g., the merits of providing fluency practice for students): "We know that in order to be effective readers, students need to have opportunities to practice their reading. Partner reading is certainly an effective strategy, and so is repeated reading. It was great to see that happening in your classroom."
- *Identify the concern or area that needs changing:* "One of the ways that you can increase the effectiveness of the fluency practice you are providing is by changing the difficulty level of the material that students are using. What materials do you have available that might be more appropriate? Or, let's see what is available in the resource room."

In the example above, the coach reassured the teacher that the instructional practices she was using were effective ones, and then suggested a way to increase their effects by working with her to get appropriate materials. Balanced feedback should include specific information as to what is effective and what can be improved. Both the teacher and the coach can explore ideas for how to address the issue being discussed, as most often there is more than one solution to resolving an issue.

4. *Focus the feedback on one or two important possibilities.* Less is more! What is most important for the teacher to consider? How doable is it? Is it something that the teacher can do somewhat easily and achieve success? As a coach, think about what changes or modifications in instruction might make the biggest difference to students—what would make the teaching and learning more effective—and then focus on how and what the teacher needs to know in order to make those changes. Finally, provide the necessary resources, support, and scaffolding.

5. *Celebrate the successes of the teacher.* This suggestion is closely aligned with balanced feedback, but it deserves to be mentioned again. Although the coach is there to help guide improvement, there are most likely aspects of the lesson deserving of celebration (e.g., student work is displayed, there are many different reading materials available for students, the students are engaged). All of us need positive reinforcement and the coach should acknowledge what has been especially effective in the classroom.

6. *Support the teacher in self-reflection efforts.* Even though this suggestion is last, it may be the most important. The old adage, "Give a man a fish and he eats for a day; teach a man to fish and he eats for a lifetime," is appropriate here. If the teacher can identify, address, and think about the lesson—its successes and how to improve it—most likely there will be follow-through in future practices. Such reflective behavior can be facilitated when the coach is a good listener and able to scaffold and build on the thoughts of the teacher.

Coaching can be a valuable approach to improving literacy instruction in a school. It can also be a growth experience for both the coach and the teacher. However, given that schools have not generally focused on this type of supportive coaching, it takes time to build an atmosphere of trust and receptivity. Think about the notions below of effective coaching, made by an individual responsible for working with new teachers (personal communication with coach, 2001).

1. *Confidentiality.* What is seen by the coach and said by the teacher always stays between them. (What happens in the classroom stays in the classroom!) Nothing should ever be repeated, criticized, or made fun of in the teachers' lounge, principal's office, or at a school function. Coaches soon lose their credibility if they share what they have seen or heard with others.

2. *Nonjudgmental.* The coach is present as a colleague, not an evaluator. Bring to the conscious level all the good things that are happening in the classroom and work with the teacher to reflect about possible goals for change. The coach is not there to make a teacher feel incompetent!

3. *Focus.* It is always advantageous to have a mutually agreed-upon target to focus the observation and feedback session. During the conversation, the coach is ready with questions designed to make the teacher think and grow professionally.

One of the most difficult tasks for coaches is providing feedback to teachers because often they have been the peers of their colleagues or recognize they have no evaluative responsibility. Moreover, for many, confrontation or conflict is difficult. Although coaches may have little difficulty discussing the good points in a lesson, often they struggle in raising issues of concern. Learning to do this in a respectful and clear manner takes time. An important point: *Put the focus on what needs to be done to improve student learning and the steps that can be taken to do so.* Learning to be a critical friend takes time and must occur in a risk-free environment where teachers feel comfortable and value making their teaching public.

Remember to start slowly and build a sense of trust, so that you and the teacher feel comfortable talking about instructional improvements.

THE REALITY OF THE SCHOOL

Although many coaches would value the opportunity to work in a systematic way with teachers (e.g., going through the formal observation cycle, from planning through postobservation conversations), school schedules and multiple demands on the coach, as well as differing needs of teachers, create the need for other forms of coaching beyond those discussed previously. One is "on-the-fly" or opportunistic coaching (i.e., coaches make themselves accessible so that they can respond to the needs and requests of teachers). The other is "combination coaching" in which teachers and coaches work together in a somewhat seamless fashion, moving from modeling to co-teaching to observing in the same lesson or literacy block. Coaches may also want to do walk-throughs either by themselves or with other school personnel (e.g., administrator, school curriculum director, special educator). Finally, coaches need to think about how to differentiate their coaching; such efforts will help them to develop a workable schedule and be productive in their work with teachers. Each of these forms of coaching is discussed below.

On-the-Fly Coaching

In a study of coaches in Reading First in Pennsylvania (Bean et al., 2008), we found that frequently coaches spent short amounts of time conversing with teachers, specialists, librarians, and principals in the hallways, between classes, at lunch, or before or after school. Such conversations led to important work with these school personnel, and below we provide some examples of what is meant by on-the-fly coaching.

> Fred, the coach, was stopped by Harry, a third-grade teacher, as they waited for students to get off the bus in the morning. Harry wondered why the district was asking teachers to administer another assessment test, besides the one that was given every 6 weeks. What would be gained by giving this assessment? Fred and Harry spent about 5 minutes talking about the new measure and how it was different from the one that was currently being administered. Fred also told Harry that he would be happy to stop by and show him the informal measure and, if Harry wanted, to model the administration of it with several of his students.
>
> Fred walked with the librarian on their way to the staff meeting that was to be held after school. The librarian told Fred that she was working with the sixth-grade science teacher on a unit about planets.

She wanted to know what she could read that would help her understand this new emphasis on informational text and what she might do in her library classes that would be useful to the students in that science class. Fred indicated that he would e-mail her an article about informational text she might find useful. He also told the librarian he would be happy to spend some time discussing this with her during her planning period.

What is clear is that these on-the-fly meetings generate opportunities for more in-depth coaching and that coaches can take advantage of these quick, spontaneous conversations that come up daily. A meeting held on-the-fly can make a difference!

Combination Coaching

In Rita's work with Reading First coaches (Zigmond & Bean, 2008), we found that some coaches stayed in the classrooms of teachers for an extended period, working with them for an entire reading block of 90 minutes. During this time, they modeled, co-taught, and even observed. Then later that day, or the next day, the coach and teacher discussed their work and planned for the next teaching segment. We saw this sort of coaching when teachers were new to the school or to teaching a specific grade level. Reading First coaches tended to spend extensive amounts of time, within a confined time period, helping these novice teachers learn more about how to provide or differentiate instruction.

Walk-Throughs

Leaders in schools often make frequent, short visits to classrooms to get a better sense of what is occurring across the school. One might describe a single observation as a snapshot or photograph and walk-throughs as a photograph album. Certainly, this description illustrates the advantages of such a coaching approach. If coaches walk through all the classrooms at a grade level (e.g., at least once a week), they will get a sense of the similarities and differences across the classrooms in instruction, environment, and management, which may help coaches as they work with teachers in follow-up meetings. They will get a sense of how a classroom functions over several visits. Also, another advantage is that teachers and students become more comfortable with the coach in the classroom, especially if the walk-through is an informal, friendly event. If the coach is making a walk-through alone, the following suggestions may be helpful:

- Try to get an overall sense of what the classroom looks like (the environment).

- Listen carefully to the teacher to get a sense of what teaching is going on and what instructional strategies are being used.
- Also, when possible, focus on the students to see what they are doing. Take time to stop by the desks of a few children. Ask students to explain what they are being asked to do and why they think it is important for them to complete this task. Do they understand what they are to do? Are they completing a task as expected?

Most often, a simple "thank you" or a wave is enough when leaving the room, especially if coaches have informed teachers that they will be doing these walk-throughs on a regular basis. Teachers also appreciate it if the coach leaves a quick note (sticky notes are terrific!) reinforcing something that occurred during the visit (e.g., "The kids really seemed to be enjoying the story today!"). The note might be addressed to the students: "Dear Students: I especially liked the 'good thinking' when Mrs. Martinez asked you to predict how the story would end! Wow, what clever ideas!"

Walk-throughs with an administrator, such as the principal, can be useful for several reasons: They enable the two observers to establish a common language and focus about the literacy instruction being seen; they may also be instructive for administrators who may have less knowledge and understanding of literacy instruction than the coach. However, coaches need to be careful that these walk-throughs are not seen as evaluative by teachers (i.e., the coach and principal together are making judgments about teachers). When the culture of the school is one in which teachers expect visitors to come into the classroom, and visits occur routinely and as a natural part of the school day, it is less likely teachers will view walk-throughs in a negative manner.

In some schools, walk-throughs are an expected form of PL. Teachers have agreed to make their teaching public and to have their peers visit or walk-through their classrooms. Teachers who have been visited have opportunities to talk with their peers about what they were doing and to respond to questions. While this sort of PL takes time to schedule, it can be a valuable resource.

Digital Tools for Coaching Teachers

There are many ways in which technology can support coaching. Given the time limitations in schools, with both teachers and coaches having difficulty finding time to participate in coaching, technology can serve as an important tool for facilitating the coaching process. In rural areas, distance between schools may also prohibit the frequency of coaching. In a paper that Rita wrote for United States Agency for International Development (2014), one of the difficulties of providing coaching to teachers was the distance between schools and, in addition, the few numbers of available coaches. When coaching time or the presence of coaches is limited, technology can play an important role in supporting coaching initiatives. Further, in times of crisis, for example, extended school closures because of weather or as seen during the COVID-19 pandemic, coaches and teachers need to use digital tools to maintain contact with teachers and as a form of PL. Coaches and teachers in all schools can use e-mail, texting, or phone conversations to arrange schedules or to raise questions that need some thoughtful consideration. Video conferencing platforms, such as Zoom or Google Meet, can be used to facilitate informal conversations, gather large groups for PL, or record teaching video for mentoring purposes. Coaches can watch lessons as they are occurring, or videos of these lessons can be viewed at a convenient time by coaches or teachers and then discussed virtually. Leighton et al. (2018) describe the partnership between a university-based coach and classroom teacher and the ways in which they used multiple digital tools to enhance students' language and literacy skills. The flexibility offered by technological devices created options for these colleagues to participate in a reflective, problem-solving coaching partnership.

In addition to the use of digital tools as a means of enhancing the coaching process, coaches can use the Internet to network with others interested in and wanting to learn more about coaching. Examples include My Coaches' Couch by Vicki Collet (*https://vickicollet.com/my-coaches-couch*), TeachBoost Launch Pad (*https://blog.teachboost.com*), and The Professional Institute for Instructional Coaching (*www.pacoaching.org*).

Differentiating Coaching: Building a Schedule

If coaches are to be productive in their work, they need to consider ways to work effectively with teachers; this means they need to differentiate what they do. Coaches might want to think about the following as they develop schedules. First, group coaching is efficient and effective and may reduce the number of teachers who need follow-up individual coaching. Such meetings may also help coaches identify exactly how they might work with specific teachers. For example, as a result of a fourth-grade-level meeting about improving academic vocabulary, the coach might do the following: provide specific journal articles or Internet sources to all teachers, facilitate a group meeting with teachers responsible for teaching social studies, or model a mini-lesson for a novice teacher who asked for more specific guidance. In other words, group coaching can serve as a source of information about next steps. Grierson and Woloshyn (2013) described a study of PD that involved both semimonthly, small-group PL sessions and weekly individualized coaching. They concluded that small-group meetings were not enough to promote meaningful teacher change; rather, the small-group sessions helped teachers identify goals to be addressed in follow-up coaching. The individualized coaching support helped teachers internalize what they learned during their small-group sessions.

Second, coaches can take into consideration the preferences of teachers as to the coaching approach to be used. When individuals are given choices, they may be more likely to accept and follow through with the ideas provided through such activities. Therefore, if a teacher is hesitant about the coach coming into the classroom, co-planning a lesson might be a first step. Such co-planning can lead to a follow-up conversation between coach and teacher focused on the teacher's reflection about the success of the lesson. The coach does not stop there, however. Next steps might include modeling, co-teaching, or observing. Ultimately, however, the coach may need to make a specific suggestion for a possible next step, especially if students in the classroom are not learning as expected.

SUMMARY

This chapter discussed the importance of coaching as an approach to providing PL for teachers. Ideas for getting started as a coach were identified followed by specific suggestions for modeling, co-planning, problem solving, and co-teaching. We described a four-step coaching cycle: planning conversation, observation, analysis/reflection, and postobservation conversation. Various protocols for data collection were identified, followed by a section on providing feedback to teachers. Finally, we suggested variations on coaching procedures—on-the-fly, combination, walk-throughs, and use of digital tools—followed by ideas for differentiating coaching.

ADDITIONAL READINGS

Blachowicz, C. L. Z., Buhle, R., Ogle, D., Frost, S., Correa, A., & Kinner, J. D. (2010). Hit the ground running: Ten ideas for preparing and supporting urban literacy coaches. *The Reading Teacher, 63*(5), 348–359.—Describes a successful coaching initiative in urban schools and discusses 10 strategies that were essential to its success.

Leighton, C. M., Ford-Connors, E., Robertson, D. A., Wyatt, J., Wagner, C. J., Proctor, C. P., & Paratore, J. R. (2018). "Let's FaceTime tonight": Using digital tools to enhance coaching. *The Reading Teacher 72*(1), 39–49.—Describes the use of digital tools and a problem-solving coaching model to improve students' language and literacy skills.

O'Shell, D. (2109). Using video to showcase great teaching. *Educational Leadership 77*(3), 50–52.—The author identifies tips for developing a process for filming, editing, and uploading lessons to build a gallery of great teaching.

• REFLECTIONS

1. Given your experiences, what are your thoughts about observing in a classroom and then discussing that observation with the teacher? What skills do you think you need to develop more fully?

2. Think about the four steps in the coaching cycle. Which would be the most difficult steps for you to implement? Why? What strategy would you like to develop to increase your confidence in implementing these steps?

• ACTIVITIES

1. Go through a coaching cycle with a colleague. Think about the following after you have completed the cycle. What did you learn from the planning conversation that affected the way in which you observed? In your analysis of the observation, what points did you identify as important to discuss with the colleague? In what ways did you discuss the lesson with the teacher? How successful do you think you were in conducting this coaching cycle? What would you do differently? What feedback did you get from the teacher you observed about your effort?

2. Try providing balanced feedback. Work with a colleague or a member of your class. Here are two scenarios to try. Remember to clarify what has occurred, provide specific feedback about the merits of a situation or behavior, and discuss ways to address any concern.

   Scenario 1: Carlos, a coach, observed Frank, a sixth-grade social studies teacher, as he used an anticipation guide to introduce a new unit on the Civil War. Frank gave the class a sheet on which there were several facts about the war and asked them to indicate whether they agreed or disagreed with the facts. Immediately, hands were raised; students grumbled that they could not read certain words or that they did not know what to do. Frank told them to put the sheet in their desks and to open their books to the first page of the chapter.

   Scenario 2: Laura arrived to observe Greta, a third-grade teacher, who had asked her to watch as she implemented flexible grouping in her classroom. She wanted help from Laura because, at this point, as she stated, "These kids can't work independently." Greta was conducting a guided-reading lesson with a group of six students. On the board was a list indicating what the other students should be doing: read books silently, work on the computer, or complete a worksheet assignment. And some were actually doing those things. However, four or five students were wandering around, talking to others. Two had their heads on the desk and appeared to be sleeping. Every 2 minutes or so, Greta would look around, away from the group with whom she was working, and remind students firmly, "You know what you should be doing. Let's get to it!"

3. Talk with a colleague about the vignette in this chapter. Discuss the multiple ways in which Dolores works with teachers. Compare her approach to working with teachers with those described in this chapter.

Questions to Consider

What lessons can be learned about the role of the literacy specialist in this vignette?

In what ways does Dolores serve as a leader?

What comes to mind after reading this vignette?

DOLORES: THE JOURNEY FROM TEACHING TO COACHING

As a child, all I ever dreamed of was being a teacher. This year I began my 35th year working as an elementary educator. I spent the first 25 years teaching a variety of elementary grades, but the bulk of them were spent teaching first graders. During these years, I had numerous interns and worked with several beginning teachers. I also created district curriculum and often provided professional learning activities for new teachers. I really enjoyed working with teachers. I felt that if I could share with them tips and tools of the trade, it would make things easier for them and positively benefit students. During this time, I also opened my classroom, and became a district demonstration classroom.

Ten years ago, I decided to take a leap of faith and leave the classroom to begin my journey as a literacy coach. I started my journey to a K–5 ELA coach at the same school I was a first-grade teacher. The transition from teacher to coach was easy because I already had a relationship with the many of the teachers. Two years ago, I chose to follow my principal to another school. The new school was struggling with teaching academics and was identified by the state as an "F" school. Providing ELA support to K–5 provided a completely new set of challenges. I had to try to coach teachers and build relationships as the same time. I also had the challenge of working with several teachers new to the profession.

During the past 10 years, I have learned a lot about how to work with teachers. Reflecting back there are several areas that have helped me to be successful.

Planning

First, I have established effective and efficient weekly planning. Teachers have precious little planning time during the day. For them to give up one of these times to plan with a coach, I know that I must make it productive and beneficial. To achieve this goal, I start the year creating norms with the teachers at each grade level. I ask them to work together to generate a list of things that happen when meetings are productive. Oftentimes lists include: be prepared, be on time, limit sidebar conversations, do not take things personally, everyone shares ideas, and stay focused on the topic. Then, we brainstorm what happens when meetings are productive. This list often includes: plans being complete, we are prepared to teach, our students are more successful, and the data will improve. To wrap up this meeting, I make sure that we all agree to hold one-another accountable for our norms. Every year I have done this at least once or twice during the school year; I am able to reference this work to refocus our planning.

To help make our planning time together effective and efficient, I send out a weekly reminder to teams prior to planning. In this e-mail, I remind them of the standard we are going to be focusing on and the text we will be using. I also ask them to begin thinking specifically about strategies we can use to make our teaching clear for our students. Another way I make our planning time productive is to create a uniform planning template for use. The last few years we have used One Drive to store plans and resources. I have organized documents into standard specific folders, which helps keep our materials easily accessible. I have found that by doing this for teams it maximizes the efficiency of our face-to-face time. Teachers are willing to come to planning, because when they leave, they have a clear direction for their daily instruction.

To help with our planning, I have developed a yearlong plan for standards-based instruction. Although we have a basal and a county curriculum, I have found that it has been helpful to focus in on one standard at a time. I like to say we focus on one standard at a time while supporting that standard with all the others. This approach has helped the teachers learn the nuances of each standard. We often talk about the vertical progression between grade levels. This has helped the teachers become more purposeful and intentional with their instruction. With the teachers' involvement, we have created formative assessments for each standard. We have an "A" and "B" test so we can use them to monitor the effectiveness of our daily instruction. These assessments are quick, five-question assessments that match the test specifications of our state test. Because we use these assessments, we do not stop our instruction a few weeks before the test to do test prep; we are doing it all year. We have created these assessments for grades K–5 and collect the data in One Drive. The data are shared with grade levels and students. There is even a little competition going on as to which class can show the most growth. When we share the data with the teachers, we take some time to reflect about what else we could do to help students master the standard.

Coaching: The Work in the Classroom

When I decided to become a reading coach, I started by reading books about coaching and attending professional learning workshops. I found that some of the preparation I had as a cooperating teacher for interns and mentoring new teachers was applicable to my job as a coach. One of the things I love best about coaching is that every day is adventure. My job is to do whatever is needed to support teachers and students. For some teachers I do a formal coaching cycle. This includes me watching them, debriefing the observation with them, setting goals for what the teacher wants to work on, modeling a lesson or two, then moving to co-teaching, and finishing with observing again. This works but is sometimes very time consuming.

I have found there are several other ways that can work just as well. All some teachers need is to watch me model. This works if all the teacher needs is to see an unfamiliar strategy or technique. Once they see it, they are good to go with it. Other teachers benefit by working with me prior to the lesson to talk through the plans before they teach them. If this is the strategy we use, I often have teachers practicing saying it aloud. Then together we can reflect and refine their instructional delivery. Other teachers would rather I just observe and leave some feedback notes with them. This allows the teacher to reflect on my notes before we have a face-to-face conversation. I think the key is to meet the teacher where they are so they can move forward from there. This means that being an active listener is essential. One of the new practices I have tried this year is to videotape teachers during instruction so we can review it together. Even though the teachers have been initially hesitant to be videotaped, the few brave enough to try it have commented on how much it has positively affected their ongoing instruction.

The last few years of being a coach, I have spent at a school with many new teachers struggling to meet the needs of their diverse students. This has pushed me to become an even better coach. These new teachers bring more challenges. They have no bag of tricks to pull from. The challenge for me is to be even more reflective about what they need from me. I find myself asking myself, "What support could I offer to provide the greatest impact?" and "What strength do they have that I can build on?" I also find myself checking in more frequently with the new teachers just to make sure the challenges of teaching are not overwhelming them too much. I have also taken on the role of lead site-based mentor. I am able to meet once a month with all the new teachers. I always start the meeting by asking them to share three things: a celebration, a challenge, and what they are doing to take care of themselves. Gathering them together helps them realize that they are not alone. I make sure the topics of discussion are timely and supportive. We discuss topics such as creating reading groups, holding parent conferences, and completing paperwork. Each of the new teachers do have their own mentor, and I meet with them as well to make sure we are providing as much support as possible.

Alignment with the Principal

I have had the opportunity to coach for two very different principals. One principal's strength was developing procedures. She relied on me greatly to provide content support for all K–5 teachers. After working with her for a few years, she transferred to another school, and I started working with my current principal. My current principal is a true instructional leader. Her former job was ELA county supervisor. She has a deep knowledge of standards and the ability to think outside the box. She is constantly walking through rooms giving teachers feedback and she attends most of our weekly planning sessions. I know in coaching there is supposed to be a data curtain, but with my current principal, this is not an issue at all. When we meet weekly to debrief, we are able to share and brainstorm how we can support our teachers. By working as a team, both our teachers and our students receive the support and encouragement they need to be successful.

DOLORES HUDSON, BA, MA
Reading Coach
Ponce de Leon Elementary
Clearwater, Florida

CHAPTER EIGHT

Developing a School Literacy Program

FACILITATING SCHOOL CHANGE

If knowledge is power, then literacy is the key
to the kingdom.
——IPPOLITO, STEELE, AND SAMSON
(2012, p. 1)

KEY QUESTIONS ● ● ● ● ● ● ● ● ● ● ● ● ● ● ● ● ● ● ●

- What problems or issues do schools face in addressing schoolwide changes in literacy practices?

- How does a focus on high-level, rigorous standards and assessments affect literacy instruction?

- What do literacy specialists need to know about curriculum development and the selection of materials used in a comprehensive literacy program?

- In what ways is technology influencing literacy instruction in schools?

- In what ways do federal and state regulations and guidelines impact school literacy programs?

The previous chapters emphasized the work of literacy specialists at the teacher or classroom level. The goal of this chapter is to provide information and cultivate awareness about the role of literacy specialists in developing and sustaining a comprehensive literacy program in a school or district. Although improvements at the individual teacher or classroom levels are essential, they are not sufficient for overall large-scale program improvement. Literacy specialists have a critical role in facilitating over-all school change efforts, including leading or serving as a member on a literacy leadership committee, working with others to select or develop curriculum or teaching materials, and so on. Read the following to find out how Pam gets involved in activities that affect district-wide change.

> In late spring, Pam attended a meeting with other literacy specialists. Given the newly approved literacy standards at the state level, the school district felt it was time to conduct a needs assessment to determine whether the curriculum and instruction at the school were aligned with these new expectations. This long-term effort would include, in addition to a needs assessment, the development of a plan to make changes in the literacy program for schools (K–12). The district-level curriculum director, Dr. Rivers, who was leading this effort, asked for volunteers, including specialized literacy professionals and teachers, who might work for a 2-week period during the summer. The goal would be to develop a schedule for this ongoing initiative, and tools and approaches to gain perspectives from students, teachers, and families. Pam knew she would learn a great deal by working on this initiative and quickly volunteered. This initiative would require that she work with teachers in different ways, seeking input about both what and how they taught, their challenges, and ideas for change. She wondered whether the teachers in her school would understand the importance of and accept this responsibility. Also, what could she do to prepare herself for the task facing her.

Below we present some ideas to help literacy specialists who serve in important leadership positions think about their role in school change efforts.

BARRIERS TO CREATING LARGE-SCALE CHANGE

There are plenty of books that provide insights for literacy leaders involved in school change and each in some way can contribute to your learning about how to work with others to create deep and sustainable changes in schools (e.g., Bryk, Gomez, Grunow, & LeMahieu, 2015; Fullan & Quinn, 2016; Smoker, 2018). None, however, provides schools with a silver bullet, given the variability that exists in specific contexts. The best advice might be to prepare for the unexpected. We believe it is helpful to think about some of the barriers that create difficulties for those involved in school improvement or reform efforts. Below we describe some of those barriers and relate them to making changes in the literacy program. We find the work of Fullan and Hargreaves (1996) and Berger (2019) helpful in thinking about these barriers.

THINK ABOUT THIS

Which of these barriers may be obstacles to change in your school? In what ways can you and others in your school overcome these barriers in order to move forward with improving your school or district's literacy program?

Too Many Initiatives: Too Much on Their Plates

Teachers are required to do much in today's schools. They need pedagogical knowledge and understanding of their various subjects and grade levels, along with strategies for teaching students with special needs. Some work in schools where the student population is diverse, with large numbers of ELs or students from poverty backgrounds, requiring teachers have skills, knowledge, and dispositions enabling them to work effectively with all students. Moreover, teachers are often asked to learn about and implement many initiatives or programs, some of which are not compatible. These initiatives may be driven by the funding available to school districts, with accompanying regulations and requirements. For example, in one district, a school had obtained funding to implement a math program based on a form of individually prescribed instruction. At the same time, the district was implementing a form of classroom management that recommended whole-class instruction, with provision for individual differences through multilevel tasks. Teachers were confused and legitimately frustrated in the face of administrative refusal to deal with their concerns; administrators contended that there was no problem in a marriage of the two initiatives. If that was not enough to cause problems, one of the schools embarked on a writing initiative that required teachers to attend PL sessions *in addition* to the ones they were attending for the first two initiatives!

Isolation: An Egg-Crate Mentality

A sentiment heard frequently is "It doesn't matter what I hear in school meetings; I just shut my door and do what I believe is best." Often, these statements are made with every good intention by teachers who have seen initiatives come—and go! In the past, schools tended to be organized around an isolationist or egg-crate perspective (Lortie 1975), with teachers assuming major responsibility for the 25 or more students in their classrooms, or at the secondary level, responsibility for the 180 or so students over six periods a day. At the present time, however, given what is known about the importance of shared leadership and collaboration in schools, administrators are asking classroom teachers (K–12) to work with other teachers and specialized professionals to make decisions about how to provide the best possible instruction for students. These decisions require collaboration among grade-level or subject-area teachers and even across grade level or subjects! Teachers are sharing and reviewing student data, both formative and summative, as a means of designing appropriate instruction.

There is evidence such collaboration is important in building a school vision and in creating an environment in which teachers together understand they have an important role in helping students succeed. In fact, results of studies (Goddard, Goddard, Kim, & Miller, 2015; Hord, 2004; Leana & Pil, 2006; Supovitz, Sirinides, & May, 2010) indicate there is a strong relationship between achievement and the extent to which schools exhibit a strong sense of community or a collaborative commitment to effective instruction for all students. Supovitz and colleagues (2010) found that both principal leadership and collaboration among peers in the schools influenced teacher practices and were related to student learning. Goddard et al. (2015) found that strong instructional leadership facilitated greater teacher collaboration and collective efficacy, that is, a belief that together, teachers can increase student learning.

Such a new way of thinking about teaching may be difficult for some teachers who must now share information about their teaching and their students with other educators in the school. For example, teachers might need to discuss with a literacy specialist who provides in-class instruction, ways that students might be grouped, a schedule that would work for both teacher and specialist, classroom management strategies, and specific ideas for instruction. Teacher and specialist must be able to plan, teach, and evaluate what they do on an ongoing basis. Often, there is a need for support and PL experiences to help school personnel collaborate effectively.

Groupthink

Humans have a need to belong to a group, and this need can lead to what is called *groupthink*. Berger (2019) calls this need for agreement a mind trap and indicates that it can be a detriment to creative problem solving. As mentioned above, in today's schools, a great deal of emphasis is placed on developing communities or networks of learners, highlighting the importance of collegiality and collaboration in promoting school change. Although such efforts can be powerful forces for change, there are some downsides. Berger (2019) and Fullan and Hargreaves (1996) highlighted the importance of supporting individual creativity and diversity while, at the same time, enhancing the ability of individuals to work together for change. Once a group establishes a norm or sets a direction, it may be difficult for the creative thinker to be heard. Such an individual may be thought of as reluctant or resistant to change. Yet this individual may be able to bring new perspectives and fresh insights to a specific issue. Those who lead in schools need to be able to "harness conflict rather than pushing it away" (Berger, 2019, p. 19).

Untapped Competence

A barrier closely related to the notion of isolation is that schools are not utilizing the power of teachers. Every educator in the school has the potential to contribute to an effective school literacy program and assume a leadership role in creating school change. When school administration limits the extent to which teachers participate in the change process, they decrease the school's potential for change, ignoring important ideas generated by teachers and creating situations in which there may be minimal teacher ownership of any new initiative. Teachers can provide key information about activities that work or do not work, instructional strategies they have modified so they are more effective for younger or older students, and management techniques that create an atmosphere in which learning can take place. Recognizing the value of teacher knowledge and capability is key to effective literacy coaching! When teacher knowledge and skills are acknowledged and valued, there is an accompanying sense of pride and ownership, enhancing what teachers do in their classrooms. At the same time, school culture must be risk-free; that is, teachers must feel comfortable and confident presenting their ideas for decision making, and they must be supported in learning how to present their ideas. In other words, the school culture must be such that it develops teacher capacity to participate fully in the development of the system as a whole. Think about your school: Do you believe the school culture fully draws upon the competence of all teachers?

Poor Solutions or Failed Reform

The lack of success of many school reform efforts in literacy can be attributed to a variety of reasons: (1) ineffective, overly circumscribed solutions (e.g., a belief that one particular approach or program will create changes in school performance); (2) lackluster or poor implementation (e.g., the selection of effective approaches or programs, but little effort given to helping teachers learn how to implement the program in their classrooms); or (3) lack of sustainability (e.g., too many new initiatives, with little time to learn one well). At times, schools do not stay with an initiative long enough to make a difference. In the evaluation of Reading First in Pennsylvania, Zigmond and Bean (2008) found after 5 years that almost 80% of the Reading First schools had shown increases in the percentage of students reading at proficiency and a reduction in the percentage of students at risk. But for some schools, it took 5 years to reach this goal. In other schools, problems were so complex (e.g., student absenteeism or mobility, weak leadership, teacher turnover) that reform efforts needed to be more comprehensive than a focus on literacy instruction alone.

In a study of the sustainability of Reading First in two states, Bean, Dole, Nelson, Belcastro, and Zigmond (2015) found there was continued use of Reading First components (e.g., progress monitoring, date-informed instruction, dedicated reading block, flexible grouping) when there was teacher, principal, and student stability; buy-in of the program; and funding enabling schools to support personnel such as reading coaches to assist with implementation efforts. Note the ways that Celia, the literacy coordinator in the vignette at the end of this chapter, organized PL activities as a means of facilitating implementation efforts.

WHAT SHOULD WE DO?

Schools that have "beat the odds"—that is, have done better than expected, given the demographics of the school population—provide some direction and inspiration about efforts to make large-scale changes in our schools at both the elementary (Taylor, Pressley, & Pearson, 2002) and secondary levels (Langer, 2001). Wilcox, Lawson, and Angelis (2017) discuss how odds-beating schools implement policy innovations (i.e., CCSS, annual professional performance reviews, data driven instruction) toward school improvement. According to Taylor, Pressley, and Pearson (2002), "Research on effective teachers and schools is surprisingly convergent" (p. 371). These schools employ teachers who have excellent classroom management skills and provide excellent literacy instruction, often involving small-group instruction for students. In these schools, teachers work collaboratively with literacy specialists and other personnel, as well as with the families of students. Bryk, Sebring, Allensworth, Luppescu, and Easton (2010), in their work with the Chicago Public Schools, illustrate the complexity of schools as organizations presenting a framework of essential supports. These include:

- Leadership as the driver of change. Principals have a key role in developing a shared vision and leading schoolwide change efforts.
- Meaningful relationships with families and local community agencies.
- Professional capacity. There is a focus on supporting faculty learning with the school as a place of learning for adults and students.
- A student-centered learning environment where students feel safe and are provided with quality learning experiences.
- Coherent, aligned curriculum and instruction, providing consistency in what students are expected to learn; further, teachers are given the resources and tools they need to succeed.

Bryk et al. (2010) indicate the importance of all these essential supports, comparing school change with baking a cake. Without all the ingredients, it's not a cake (p. 66). In this chapter, we provide guidance to literacy specialists, describing ways that they can help lead efforts to develop a coherent and consistent literacy program. We begin by discussing a needs assessment process as a first step for developing, implementing, and evaluating a comprehensive literacy program.

THINK ABOUT THIS

Think about a school with which you are familiar. To what extent and how does that school address each of the essential supports described above? What strengths does it have? What weaknesses? In what ways can a literacy specialist work in this school to promote school change?

A NEEDS ASSESSMENT AS A FIRST STEP FOR DEVELOPING A COMPREHENSIVE LITERACY PROGRAM

Figure 8.1 describes a framework for developing a comprehensive literacy program, beginning with a needs assessment resulting in a district comprehensive literacy plan document; the other components illustrate important aspects to consider in developing the overall plan. The arrows go in both directions, given districts may initially study their current curriculum as a first step of the needs assessment process. If they have a comprehensive literacy plan, they may be poised to develop the curriculum, using district or state standards. The district comprehensive literacy plan document serves as the basis for reviewing standards, establishing specific goals, and developing a scope and sequence plan (PreK–12). These initial steps provide the basis for decision making about curriculum, instruction, and assessment.

A Needs Assessment as the Basis for a Literacy Plan

The needs assessment provides an opportunity for educators to look at the current curriculum, as well as other aspects of the school literacy program, and determine whether the program addresses the vision and mission of the school or district (Does it take you to where you want to be?). The results of the needs assessment can be used to develop a comprehensive literacy plan that enables educators to see the big picture, that is, how well the district is achieving its goals, the consistency and articulation from level to level, and what needs to be done to improve literacy instruction across the board. In addition, involvement in the process can be an excellent learning experience, increasing knowledge of participants about the literacy emphasis at various levels, establishing a better relationship among teachers at those levels, and in general, helping to create a sense of ownership of the

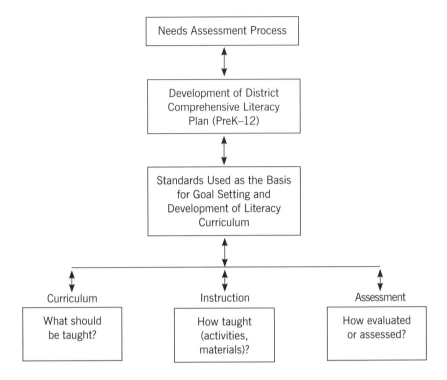

FIGURE 8.1. Framework for developing a comprehensive literacy program (PreK–12).

literacy program. The document also provides a written record to use for curriculum development and selection of resources. Finally, it can be disseminated to the community and other stakeholders as a means of sharing information about literacy in the schools and generating community input, support, and and involvement. Below we identify steps that may be useful to literacy specialists involved in conducting a needs assessment and developing a comprehensive literacy plan for their school or district.

• Establish a literacy leadership team composed of educators from all levels (PreK–12), community members (representing business, community agencies), and families as a means of generating grassroots support and involvement. These stakeholders provide important insights about the culture of the community and how it contributes to school learning. Literacy specialists may lead the effort or serve as members of such teams.

• Use a process to identify the strengths and needs of the district overall and to establish priorities for moving ahead. There are many needs assessment documents available, often provided by states for use by districts; for example, the leaders of a Striving Reading initiative developed the *Pennsylvania Comprehensive Literacy: Local Literacy Needs Assessment* (Pennsylvania Department of Education, 2014) tool for districts to use in submitting grant applications. Districts that did not receive funding also found the completion of the needs assessment to be useful. They learned a great deal about the overall status of literacy in their districts. Team members were surprised at how little they knew about literacy instruction at levels other than where they taught. Any district embarking on a needs assessment process can modify available instruments to meet the needs of their district. Generally, a needs assessment will address the following components: standards and curriculum, assessment, instruction, PL, partnerships with families and communities, and leadership. The questions in Figure 8.2 are important ones to consider when completing a needs assessment. You can use these questions to develop surveys or interview questions to help you obtain necessary information about the literacy program.

 • Obtain the information needed to complete the needs assessment. According to Bernhardt (2013), four different sources of data are essential for thinking about schools and how they can meet the needs of their students. These include *student demographics* (Who are your students and what are their needs?), *perceptions* (including those of teacher, students, and community members), *school processes* (classroom practices, materials), and *student learning* (outcomes based on various assessment measures). In other words, test data are not enough; key information should be obtained from teachers, parents, and students about their perceptions of literacy learning. Constituents may be interviewed, asked to complete surveys or to participate in meetings to discuss their views about the literacy program in their school. Observations in classrooms as well as an analysis of the materials used in schools can provide insights about what is occurring in classrooms. When developing questionnaires for stakeholders to complete, remember that these surveys should not be longer than two to three pages, or individuals may not be willing to complete them. In Figure 8.3 we provide a sample of a survey that can be given to teachers to determine their perceptions of the quality of their PL experiences.

 • The needs assessment process includes getting information from various stakeholders (e.g., teachers, families, students) as well as from available written documents, such as assessment data. Data necessary for completing the needs assessment document must be gathered and analyzed. Previously written documents (curriculum guides or plans) can also be used to determine where the district has been relative to its literacy program. Once data from stakeholders has been analyzed, committee members can work as a group to discuss what they have learned and write their report. In larger

Curriculum

1. Does the school have a vision and mission for its literacy program? Has the school established goals and standards (PreK–12)? Has it considered:
   - The amount of time for literacy instruction at the primary and intermediate levels?
   - The relationship between reading and the other language arts?
   - The role of content-area teachers at all levels, but especially at the middle school/high school levels in helping students address the literacy demands of their classroom?
2. Do standards address the need for a developmental continuum that considers the student at all stages: emergent, beginning, transitional, intermediate, and skilled reading and writing? Do they recognize the needs of learners at the middle school and secondary levels?
3. Are the standards based on what is known about effective literacy instruction and assessment; that is, are they evidence based?
4. Do the standards address the essential elements of effective literacy instruction?
5. Have instructional resources (print and nonprint) been selected that enable teachers to address the goals and standards? Do these resources address the needs of all learners (students experiencing reading and writing difficulties, EL students, etc.)? Do they provide for the varying reading levels of students? Is a variety of materials available (narrative, informational, poetry, etc.)? Do they provide students with opportunities to read about students like themselves and others?
6. Is there a "written framework" or guide that makes the curriculum visible and usable?

Instruction

1. Has consideration been given to how literacy instruction will be organized, including how the differing needs of students will be met? Grouping options? Instructional resources? Additional time? Additional support of specialized professionals?
2. Is there coordination and coherence among the literacy programs in the school (the core, the various tiers of instruction)? Is there support provided to various learners (EL students, students experiencing reading and writing difficulties, etc.)?
3. Are teachers given opportunities to gain knowledge and understanding of the current research and literature about effective, evidence-based literacy instruction?
4. Is there coherence between the written curriculum of the school and actual classroom practices?

(continued)

FIGURE 8.2. Developing a comprehensive literacy program. Adapted with permission from Bean (2014).

Assessment

1. Is there an assessment system (PreK–12) that is coordinated across the grades? Is there provision for outcome measures? Screening measures? Diagnostic measures? Progress monitoring measures?
2. Is there alignment between the standards of the district and the assessment system; that is, is the assessment system measuring what is being taught?
3. Do the assessment measures address high-level cognitive thinking?
4. Do the classroom assessment measures assist teachers in instructional decision making? Do they assist teachers in identifying the needs of the struggling readers, EL students, and high achievers?

Process for Change

1. Is the committee or group assigned the task of developing the comprehensive literacy plan a representative one; that is, does it include constituents at all levels, and so on? To what extent are teachers involved in the curriculum development process? Have they had opportunities to discuss their beliefs and understandings and learn more about how literacy can be taught effectively?
2. Is there leadership support for the development of the comprehensive literacy plan? Is time provided for meeting as a group and are the necessary resources available to members of the group? Do leaders encourage and support the work of the group members?
3. Have teachers been provided with the PL they need to implement the program effectively? Does this PL include opportunities for support and feedback (e.g., literacy coaching)?
4. Do PL activities provide teachers with opportunities to learn from each other, to collaborate? In other words, are teachers working together so that change can occur at the system level?
5. Are administrators supportive and involved in the change effort? Do they understand what is required of their teachers so that they can provide the necessary support?

FIGURE 8.2. *(continued)*

districts, there may be subgroups by grade levels (preschool, elementary, middle school, secondary) responsible for writing sections of the report.

- At times, an individual may be responsible for drafting a specific section that can then be given to committee members for input.
- The report should result in a comprehensive plan that contains the following: mission and vision of the district, identification of goals by priority, and an action plan that indicates who will do what and when.
- Writers should develop a plan that includes both short- and long-term goals. In this way, the district or school can make decisions about which goals are most important and doable!

Dear Teacher: To what degree do you agree with the statements below about the professional learning available to you?

4	Strongly agree
3	Agree
2	Disagree
1	Strongly disagree
0	Haven't experienced; not applicable

Content

Score	Description
	The district has a set of literacy goals and standards across grade levels that are used as a framework to guide professional learning.
	Standards for literacy performance at each grade level have been identified (e.g., what should students know and be able to do?).
	Curriculum and instructional practices are evidence-based.
	Curriculum and instructional practices set high expectations for all students.
	Multiple sources of data are used to determine curriculum and instructional practices.
	The PL resources (e.g., journals, webinars, professional books) available to me help me gain an in-depth understanding of the theory and research underlying practices (why a practice is important).

Collaboration and Sense of Community in the School

Score	Description
	I have a decision-making role in how I learn what is necessary to achieve goals set by the school.
	I am given opportunities to work with my colleagues to learn from them (e.g., grade-level meetings, study groups).
	There is a focus on the value of families and their role as members of the community.
	I am recognized for the work that I do.
	I have opportunities to serve as a leader in planning and implementing PL activities.

(continued)

FIGURE 8.3. Assessing perceptions of teachers about professional learning experiences. Adapted with permission from Bean & Morewood (2007).

Duration and Amount of Time

Score	Description
	PL activities are ongoing (over time) and give me opportunities to develop in-depth understanding of what I am learning.
	I have sufficient contact hours related to the PL topic.

Active Learning

Score	Description
	School makes use of new technologies in helping me achieve my professional goals.
	I use information from my classroom and students in my PL experiences (e.g., student assessments, work samples).
	I am given choices, based on my needs and those of my students.
	I have opportunities to participate in inquiry-based activities that help me reflect and think critically.
	I have opportunities to practice what I am learning with my peers.
	Coaching is useful to me for my own learning.
	I find observation of teaching colleagues to be helpful to my learning.
	My participation in a book study group is helpful to my learning.
	I find outside technology resources (e.g., blogs, videos, podcasts) to be useful for my own learning.

Applying What We Are Learning

Score	Description
	I have opportunities to apply what I am learning in my classroom.
	I have opportunities to try out what I am learning in a risk-free environment.
	Feedback is geared toward supporting and guiding my teaching practices; it is not evaluative.
	I am recognized for what I know and do in my classroom.
	I have opportunities to self-evaluate and reflect on my work.

Additional Comments

FIGURE 8.3. *(continued)*

The time it takes to conduct a needs assessment is not wasted time; it can help school personnel make decisions about priorities and answer questions such as the following:

- What are our immediate or short-term goals? Long-term goals?
- At what level should we begin our work?
- Who should do what and when?

In districts that already have a comprehensive plan based on a needs assessment, literacy specialists and other members of the literacy team may be more involved in the ongoing work of aligning standards with curriculum, instruction, and assessment.

Standards as the Basis for Curriculum and Instruction

State and district standards guide the development of specific curricular goals: the selection of instructional practices, materials, resources, and the assessment measures that determine whether students have met those standards; and if not, what strategies or interventions enable them to do so. Many states across the United States have approved the use of the CCSS (NGA & CCSSO, 2010) that identify outcomes for the English language arts and for literacy in history/social studies, science, and technical subjects. Traditionally, the goals of developing standards were to produce a document that provided for consistency across states in expectations and to increase the rigor of expectations so that graduates would be prepared to function effectively in this ever shrinking and technologically based world (Wixson & Dutro, 1999). According to developers, the CCSS standards identified outcomes but did not mandate or dictate how districts would achieve the goals; in other words, districts were to select or develop their own curriculum, instructional activities, materials, and resources, although as always, they would be guided by state regulations and guidance. Some states have made modifications or adaptations in the CCSS, while maintaining the intent of the standards. Other states have developed their own standards. However, across states, there is recognition of the need for standards with high expectations and the rigor to prepare students who can meet the challenges of living in a complex, global society.

The standards address important issues for literacy specialists and their colleagues to consider:

1. *Use of challenging texts.* Teachers, researchers, and others have raised concerns about the expectation that students read challenging texts that may be above their instructional or independent level. The standards do not expect that all texts must be challenging. At the same time, those students who do not have opportunities to read complex text, are limited

in the access they have to important world knowledge. What is critical is that teachers support students, especially those with reading and writing difficulties, with appropriate scaffolding that assists them as they grapple with this complex content. Students can and should read texts at their instructional or independent reading levels as well as those that are more challenging. Hiebert's Text Project (*textproject.org*) is a helpful resource for understanding text complexity.

2. *Foundational skills.* The basic skills of phonics, phonemic awareness, and so on are not in a place of prominence in the CCSS, but they are in the document and are recognized as a critical aspect of early literacy instruction. The developers of the CCSS wanted to emphasize that these foundational skills were a means to an end rather than an end in themselves. As stated in the ILA research brief about teaching phonics (ILA, 2019e), "The question of whether to include phonics instruction has been resolved. The answer is yes. The discussion now should be how to include phonics instruction as part of an overall literacy plan that is efficient, effective, and timely for all students" (p. 2). This research brief, *Meeting Challenges of Early Literacy Phonics Instruction*, provides practical information about teaching phonics and is a useful reference for literacy specialists.

3. *Vocabulary.* The CCSS call for both teaching of explicit words (in a rich, in-depth manner) and word-solving strategies in all subjects. The standards place vocabulary in the "language" section rather than in the comprehension section.

4. *Writing.* Writing has a strong place in the literacy curriculum and the standards encourage teachers to provide meaningful writing activities for students across the curriculum. Writing should involve a range of opportunities for students to engage in experiences with opinion pieces, information/explanation texts, narratives, and research projects.

5. *Integrated curriculum.* The CCSS or other rigorous standards can best be achieved when the curriculum is integrated and focused on themes making learning meaningful. Many publishers have developed current core literacy programs around themes (e.g., community workers, learning about the weather). These themes list the specific reading, writing, listening, and speaking standards addressed; include various types of texts (narrative, informational); and provide links to the Internet and other digital tools. The core program may also provide suggestions for a research or inquiry project. But rather than adopting a core program with the expectation that it includes such integration, some school districts and teachers have developed their own units, pulling together materials and activities enabling students to meet the standards of their district and state. Celia, in her vignette at the end of this chapter, describes her district's efforts to develop an integrated curriculum for elementary teachers.

A comprehensive literacy plan developed by districts, as well as a review of standards, can enable districts to develop a scope and sequence that illustrates both vertical (grade level to grade level) and horizontal articulation (within grade—what will be taught when).

Guidelines for Curriculum Development: A Process of Change

Curriculum development provides an excellent PL opportunity for teachers to converse with and learn from each other. In their deliberations about curriculum, instruction, and assessment, teachers develop a deeper understanding of what they are planning to implement in their classrooms and a commitment to proposed changes. Several guidelines for developing curriculum follow:

1. *Begin with standards.* Helping teachers become familiar with the CCSS or the standards adopted by their state and how they impact curriculum and instruction is an important task for literacy specialists. We suggest a series of steps below (adapted from McTighe & Wiggins, 2012).

- Have teachers become familiar with the standards by reading the introductory material that explains what the standards are and are not; discuss at grade- or school-level meetings. Talk about how these standards compare with previous ones and discuss the differences (more reading of informational text, close reading).
- Unpack the standards by doing crosswalks. Review a specific standard across several grade levels (e.g., Key Ideas and Details for Literature from K–5) and discuss changes. Initially, a grade-level team may review reading standards for that level. In later meetings, other aspects of the language arts may be reviewed. Teachers can discuss again the implications for curriculum.
- Continue the curriculum development process by unpacking the standards, using four categories: *long-term transfer goals* (what we want students to be able to do), *overarching understandings* (what skilled students will need to transfer learning), *overarching essential* questions that engage students in meaning making, and recurring *cornerstone* tasks that are authentic and relevant (McTighe &Wiggins, 2012).
- Consider how the school will assess student learning. What outcomes are expected and what "cornerstone" tasks can be used to assess those outcomes? Consider various inquiry- or project-based learning opportunities for students.

2. *Importance of teacher involvement.* Literacy specialists in leadership positions can consider the following questions as they move forward in

the curriculum development process: (a) Will all teachers be involved or a representative few?; (b) If not all are involved, how can others be consulted and informed?; (c) What is the time line for the process?; and (d) What are the goals and outcomes of the effort? In developing curriculum, specific teachers can be involved in writing the units or curriculum guide, but they can share their work on an ongoing basis, ask for input, and help all teachers develop an understanding of how the revised curriculum will affect instruction and assessment.

Teachers should be involved in curriculum mapping, perhaps at grade-level meetings facilitated by a literacy specialist or one of the grade-level teachers. They can be provided with copies of the grade-level standards; in one district, the literacy specialist laminated anchor and grade-level standards for each teacher. In another district, the literacy specialist placed the mapping form on a white board so that all teachers could see the previous draft and make comments, changes, or adaptations. Curriculum mapping is a procedure for identifying what has been taught and what will be taught, relative to state or district standards. Jacobs (2004) lists seven steps in the mapping process. In the first step, teachers using an agreed-upon form approved by the district to create a map of the three major elements of their curriculum: (a) content in terms of essential concepts and topics, (b) processes and skills, and (c) products and performances for assessment. Jacobs suggests that teachers use the calendar as a basic guide for compiling the form, recording what they actually do in their classrooms. The remaining steps in her procedure consist of efforts to share what is being taught at the various grade levels and across grade levels, and to make decisions about what needs to be reviewed and revised. Teachers are often surprised by the repetition that occurs across grades or the fact that some topics are not taught at all!

3. *Base work on current research and theory.* Information from books and journal articles can be shared among teachers; study groups can be formed in which teachers discuss what they are learning. Also, administrators may consult outside experts so that teachers can learn more about current knowledge and theory about reading instruction. Often, districts invite an external consultant to address all teachers or a representative committee, to be followed by opportunities for discussion and debate about the issues presented.

4. *Relate teacher beliefs and knowledge about literacy instruction to research.* Any curricular effort will involve teachers with different beliefs and perspectives about literacy instruction and assessment. Having a sense of what teachers believe and know about literacy instruction is important. Literacy specialists can also provide opportunities for teacher reflection and discussion about their beliefs. Teachers bring their own experiences, knowledge, and beliefs to literacy teaching; they interpret research findings

through different lenses. Rita knew a teacher from a secondary background assigned to teach second grade. Although the work in her graduate courses and experiences in primary classrooms convinced her that students needed to learn phonics, her belief was that such lessons needed to be embedded within a meaningful context, and she experienced much difficulty with the core reading program in which phonics instruction was much more explicit and less meaning based. She was also frustrated when listening to other teachers talk about their lessons, which seemed to provide little opportunity for students to read and write. The literacy specialist who understands this teachers' beliefs might be able to help her share her ideas with others so that she and her colleagues can learn from each other.

THINK ABOUT THIS

Think about the individual teacher, described above, whose teaching peers at the primary level believed in a strong and separate decoding program. What problems might arise? How can the beliefs and strengths of this individual be tapped in a way that improves literacy instruction? How can possible misunderstandings be addressed?

To develop a common understanding and terminology, teachers can read current articles about literacy instruction that provide a springboard for discussion. These readings can also provide teachers with up-to-date information enabling them to think more deeply about what they do in their classrooms and how it relates to what research indicates is most effective.

5. *Organize the curriculum guide so that it is usable.* Too often, curriculum plans sit on shelves or in teacher's desks, consulted only infrequently. Those involved in curriculum development should formulate plans that are coherent yet simple to use. Moreover, when plans provide a sequence of literacy instruction for PreK–12, teachers can gain a sense of what students have learned, what they are learning, and what they will learn, providing for better transition and articulation.

6. *Plan for dissemination and for implementation.* Too often, it is the implementation stage that falls short of the goal. Those who have worked on the development of the plan are committed to it—and perhaps use it. Others, if they do not understand the plan and how it works, may just ignore it or implement it halfheartedly. If teachers have been involved during the entire process, they are more likely to accept and use the plan. Keep all teachers informed and seek their input and ownership. PL experiences for faculty are essential if the plan is to become a dynamic, living document. PL can be offered by literacy specialists or coaches in two stages: Initially, general information can be provided to all teachers and subsequently,

literacy specialists or coaches can provide the additional support needed by individual or groups of teachers.

7. *Include evaluation as an integral part of the curriculum framework.* As mentioned above, measurement approaches and tools to assess student outcomes are important components of any curriculum guide. Decisions about assessment instruments, rubrics, and so forth should be an integral part of any curriculum development discussion. (This topic is discussed in depth in Chapter 9.)

Another aspect of evaluation has to do with the content of the curriculum guide itself. Curriculum development, its implementation and modification, should be ongoing; it is a recursive process. Thus, a process for obtaining teacher input about what works and what doesn't work should be developed. Such input can come from grade-level or subject-area meetings, or from the work of a curriculum committee. Evaluation can include reactions of teachers, actual observation of what is occurring in classrooms, and a study of results of various assessment measures used to document student learning. At higher levels, especially middle and secondary, input from students can also inform the evaluation process. Guskey's (2000) five levels of evaluation, described in Chapter 5, is a useful source for evaluating a school's literacy reading program.

Because literacy specialists may have responsibility for leading the development of literacy from the early grades through the middle or secondary levels, below we discuss in more depth critical issues related to these upper levels of schooling.

The Literacy Program for Adolescents

Across the United States, there is an awareness that educators must give special attention to the literacy achievement of students in both middle school and high school. In fact, results of the 2019 NAEP (Nation's Report Card, 2019) indicated that only 34% of eighth graders were proficient in reading, down from 36% in 2017; further, almost all subgroups lost ground in their reading performance. Success at the elementary level does not guarantee success at the upper levels of schooling. A major concern is how to prepare students to meet expectations for citizenship, for college, or for success in most jobs. Achieve and Society for Human Resource Management (2012) conducted a survey that found many graduates lacked the skills to advance beyond entry-level positions. Moreover, many positions now require some type of post-high school preparation, either obtained by technical training or an associate degree, if not college. Soon, there will be a need for even more highly skilled individuals to compete for available positions.

Literacy specialists need to be aware of the special demands required for success in the secondary classrooms. According to the *Time to Act* report (Carnegie Council on Advancing Adolescent Literacy, 2010, p. 12), adolescents face many literacy challenges at the secondary levels, among them, reading more complex texts that require greater conceptual challenge and contain more detailed graphic representations; the ability to synthesize information across texts; and the ability to read texts in various content areas that require different sets of skills. One of the ways in which schools are addressing these disappointing statistics is by aligning their curriculum, instruction, and assessment systems with standards that address college and career success. As indicated by Ippolito and colleagues (2012), there is a "new focus on literacy within the academic disciplines, a more nuanced stance toward comprehension strategy instruction, and an insistence that greater attention needs to be paid to all students reading and writing practices both inside and outside of school" (p. viii). Therefore, at the secondary level, literacy specialists may not only have the task of developing or designing programs for students who are having difficulty with reading, but also work closely with content-area teachers to design approaches that help students process content-specific information. In other words, their work with teachers focuses on helping students understand the ways in which experts in each academic area communicate, that is, help students learn to read and write like historians, scientists, or mathematicians (Ippolito, Dobbs, & Charner-Laird, 2019; Moje, 2007, 2008; Shanahan & Shanahan, 2012b).

A comprehensive literacy program at the secondary levels generally includes several components. There may be a pullout or supplemental program, often based on an RTI model and taught by a literacy specialist, for students experiencing difficulties with reading. The program may also include special study skills classes helping students understand effective study strategies, including how to take tests. To meet the needs of all students, however, decisions will need to be made about how teachers in the disciplines can address the thinking, reading, and writing required of adolescents as they grapple with complex texts. Literacy specialists can have an important role, working as partners with these teachers; both have something to contribute. Literacy specialists provide general knowledge about literacy instruction, and content teachers help identify the literacy skills students need to be successful in specific disciplines. Ippolito, Dobbs, and Charner-Laird (2020) describe the ways in which literacy leaders, such as literacy specialists, can support their content-area colleagues in developing background knowledge about literacy, crafting new instructional strategies and routines that reflect an emphasis on both content-area and disciplinary instruction, and reflecting together about their work. The *Standards for Middle and Secondary School Coaches* (IRA, 2006) can be a useful resource to those working at those levels; in addition to identifying general leadership standards, the document identifies standards for each of four academic disciplines: English, science, social studies, and math.

Other key resources at the secondary level include *Reading Next: A Vision for Action and Research in Middle and High School Literacy* (Biancarosa & Snow, 2004); *Reading and Writing in the Disciplines* (Annenberg Foundation, 2017); *Investigating Disciplinary Literacy: A Framework for Collaborative Professional Learning* (Dobbs, Ippolito, & Charner-Laird, 2017); and *Adolescent Literacy in the Era of the Common Core* (Ippolito, Lawrence, & Zaller, 2013). Elizabeth Moje (2008) raises issues important for those involved in secondary literacy reform: content teachers' knowledge of their own discipline, ways that teachers can encourage students to interact with their content-area texts, role of technology and new media on students' learning, and school structures to facilitate this sort of instruction. She concludes as follows: "The integration of literacy instruction in the secondary schools is a complex change process that will require collaboration, communication, and a commitment to major conceptual, structural, and culture changes" (p. 105).

THINK ABOUT THIS

What are the issues your school, or a school with which you are familiar, needs to consider when developing adolescent literacy programs? What are your thoughts about disciplinary literacy and what it means for literacy specialists in secondary schools?

SELECTION OF MATERIALS

Although schools should identify their curricular goals before selecting materials, too often the reverse is true! Materials frequently equal the curriculum. Although materials must reflect the beliefs and goals identified by school personnel, a strict adherence to the identified materials may lead to a narrow program in which there is little adjustment to meet the needs of the students in the school. In other words, the content and quality of selected materials should reflect the needs and interests of students in the school, as well as the forms of diversity that exist in society (i.e., race, ethnicity, gender, cultural, linguistic, economic). Providing such material in schools is important for increasing both student skills and the motivation to read. Although the need for a wide variety of materials in schools exists at all levels, it is especially critical that adolescents be provided with or self-select materials to which they can relate (Ivey & Johnston, 2013). Brozo and Gaskins (2009, pp. 172–180), in a chapter focusing on adolescent boys, present five principles of engagement that are relevant not only for adolescents but for readers of all ages:

1. Create conditions in classrooms that promote self-efficacy, a belief in one's own capacity to achieve.
2. Promote interest in new reading.
3. Connect out-of-school with inside-school literacies.
4. Make sure there is an abundance of interesting texts available.
5. Provide for choice and options.

Teachers frequently make decisions about classroom instruction based on anthologies or the core reading program. And, given that specific materials, once selected, become a driving force for at least 5 or more years, careful attention must be given to selecting materials, so they align with the objectives, goals, and standards formulated by the district. Too often the selected materials become the curriculum guide or plan for the district.

Guidelines for Selecting a Core Program

Once the district has decided it is going to adopt a specific series as a core reading program, literacy personnel need to think about both process and content issues.

Process

The selection process is extremely important because it often involves more than professional issues. Publishers are eager to obtain adoptions and school districts need to abide by the same guidelines or rules for all materials being considered.

- What selection procedure should be used?
- Will all teachers, or a representative group, serve on the committee?
- What are the rules? If publishers are invited to present their materials, how much time do they get and what can they "give" to or provide for teachers?
- Will the district implement a pilot to help with decision making?

A careful consideration of the process reduces the possibility outcomes will be met by accusations of unfairness or bias in selecting materials. Most districts select a representative group of teachers and administrators to form a committee. All grade levels and, if possible, most of the schools using the materials should be represented. At the same time, parents on the committee can provide a unique perspective and help to generate community support. Students may also be included on the committee, especially if the materials to be selected are for upper levels.

Content

The following guidelines can be useful in thinking about which basal, anthology, or other texts to select:

1. *Review district philosophy and beliefs.* Before proceeding with a review of materials, spend time reviewing or developing the philosophy or guiding principles of the district, especially as they relate to the teaching of reading or literacy. In that way, materials selection can be aligned with the goals of the school, thereby reducing the possibility that the scope and sequence of the core program will become the curriculum of the school.

2. *Conduct a survey of teachers in the district.* A short questionnaire or brief discussions with all teachers can generate a list of priorities. Often, teachers have specific concerns about current materials and their inability to meet the needs of the students. Time spent obtaining ideas about what the group thinks is important and should lessen any later dissension or conflict.

3. *Plan for a research update.* Awareness of current research and theory about literacy instruction is an important component of the process. The district might invite an expert to make a presentation on specific issues; also, the group can read current articles about literacy instruction. Both options should be followed by group discussion. Those committee members involved in reviewing and selecting materials need to be especially cautious in their deliberations and to look closely at the publishers' claims in relation to program effectiveness.

4. *Decide upon the "ideal."* What should the final material look like? What should it include? By selecting or designing a rubric, the group can more efficiently evaluate the materials under consideration. Foorman, Smith, and Kosanovich (2017) designed a rubric for evaluating materials, K–5. The criteria in the rubric are aligned to recommendations from six What Works Clearinghouse practice guides and provide a useful resource for those involved in a materials selection process. When evaluating materials, consider not only the content of the teachers' manual, but the scope and sequence of skills, the supplemental material (including workbooks), and assessment tools or procedures. Although it might be helpful to start with a published rubric, committee members should review it, and make any modifications necessary to address the vision and goals of the district.

5. *Review materials.* The committee can quickly screen and discard those programs that do not meet the identified criteria. Then an in-depth

review must be made of those appearing to be acceptable. The committee can break into smaller groups to review specific texts and present findings to the entire group, or everyone in the group may review all texts. They can consult reviews done by others (e.g., What Works Clearinghouse: *http://ies.ed.gov/ncee/wwc*). The group may decide to track the teaching of a specific strategy or skill through the grades, to determine how the strategy is taught at each level. For example, committee members could focus on how students are taught to summarize from the early grades through grade 8.

Readability of text has always been an important consideration. The CCSS provide a comprehensive framework for assessing text complexity (detailed information is available in Appendix A of the CCSS document, [NGA & CCSSO, 2010]). The three identified factors provide for a more comprehensive view of readability.

- *Qualitative evaluation of the text:* levels of meaning, structure, language conventionality and clarity, knowledge demands.
- *Quantitative evaluation of the text:* readability measures and other scores of text complexity.
- *Matching reader to text and task:* reader variables (motivation, knowledge, and experiences) and task variables (purpose and the complexity generated by the task assigned and questions posed).

6. *Make a final decision.* In addition to using information from in-depth reviews, the committee may talk with teachers in other districts who are using the materials to get their perspectives. They may also consider piloting several programs before making a final decision. Ultimately, the committee should come to a consensus, or if necessary, vote to decide about the text/series selection. It is, of course, much better if the group can agree on the core program to be selected, but this is not always possible. If no clear-cut decision emerges, more time may need to be spent in analyzing available materials.

Materials to Help Students Achieve the Goals Established by the School

Although we focus on the core or basal program above, the same criteria apply to the materials used for supplemental or intensive instruction. Schools have the responsibility of teaching all students; therefore, consideration must be given about how to meet the needs of gifted students, special education students, ELs, and so on. Those leading material selection efforts should be able to justify why they are using specific supplemental materials, how those materials support or enhance the core program, who should use them, and why. Careful attention must be given to how the various materials "fit together."

TECHNOLOGY IN THE LITERACY PROGRAM

We live in a digital world. Many of us routinely order books, clothes, and toys online, pay our bills electronically, search Google or Siri when we have a question, and catch up on our favorite shows via online streaming. We use phones to look at the menu for a new restaurant, learn how others rate the food, see photos of sample food choices—and decide whether we can afford to eat there! Likewise, many children live with multiple forms of technology: They play with games on a smartphone or tablet, interact with their grandparents via FaceTime, and read iBooks that provide for interactivity between reader and text. For some, the computer or tablet has replaced TVs and DVDs, and even regular print books. Young adults use phones for social networking and texting to communicate with their peers, read books, play games, and many daily routines (e.g., homework lists, research searches).

In 2017, children age 8 or younger, on average, "currently spend 48 minutes per day on a mobile device, compared to 15 minutes per day in 2013 and 5 minutes in 2011" (Common Sense Media, 2017). Among teenagers, 62% use more than 4 hours' worth of screen media in a day (Common Sense Media, 2019). Children and young adults are growing up with technology interwoven with activities and expect it to be a part of their lives.

Technology and other forms of information and communication are transforming learning and redefining the way in which we think about literacy. Technology is rapidly becoming an integral part of the school's literacy program. Yet, there is great variability among teachers in what they know about how to use technology effectively and their receptivity to virtual instruction. Indeed, teachers were thrust into the technological world because of the COVID-19 pandemic, requiring them to quickly develop a deeper knowledge and understanding of how to plan and implement remote learning activities. Teachers in today's schools must be competent users of technology, employing it as a tool to enhance the literacy program in their classrooms. They can use technology as an integral part of their repertoire, assigning inquiry projects or group activities, including video projects. They might be involved in using flipped learning (i.e., instructing students online outside the classroom and then having them complete homework in class). There is a need for professional learning that will help them develop a better understanding of how to plan for both synchronous and asynchronous learning experiences for students. And there is a need to help students become comfortable and competent working online.

The development of mobile devices (e.g., iPads) increases the flexibility of technology across locations and activities to increase digital literacy skills (Hutchison, Beschorner, & Schmidt-Crawford, 2012). Beschorner and Woodward (2019) suggest teachers think about long-term plans for developing technology knowledge and integration into classrooms to sustain their efforts. There are growing resources available to help literacy coaches learn about various apps and digital tools to increase personal learning and collaboration with teachers (see Affinito, 2018).

The CCSS (NGA & CCSSO, 2010) highlight the importance of new literacies, indicating that "to be ready for . . . life in a technological society, students need the ability to gather, comprehend, evaluate, synthesize, and report on information and ideas . . . in media forms old and new" (p. 4). Skills and understandings are embedded throughout the CCSS, illustrating specific standards that students are expected to meet (e.g., Anchor Standards for Writing, K–5: "Gather relevant information from multiple print and digital sources, assess the credibility and accuracy of each source, and integrate the information while avoiding plagiarism"; NGA & CCSSO, 2010, p. 18).

Again, teachers do not always feel prepared or comfortable with using these new approaches to learning. Teachers need many skills to use electronic technology effectively: locating resources about literacy on the Internet; communicating with others using technology; entering, accessing, and interpreting data about students and their accomplishments; becoming knowledgeable about the various programs/apps to deliver instruction to students; and integrating technology as part of instructional delivery. Technology requires teachers to assume new and different roles, moving from more teacher- to student-directed instruction (Castek & Gwinn, 2012). PL opportunities, similar to those identified by Coiro (2005), assist teachers in meeting the expectations of these new roles. They include developing learning experiences on a developmental continuum so that teachers can move from novice to expert, differentiating PL so it addresses the differing perspectives of teachers about the value of technology, and providing collaborative learning experiences as a means of enhancing learning. Also, teachers must learn how to guide students in using digital resources wisely as a means of supporting learning (Prensky, 2012).

These new literacies provide new and more complex learning opportunities for students, and technology in the classroom has become much more than adding a software package to the reading program. At the same time, given the availability of such apps, it is important to have criteria for the selection of such programs. McVee and Dickson (2002, p. 639) developed a rubric as a guide for reviewing software for programs designed for use in K–3 classrooms. The rubric identifies the following questions for reviewing software:

1. What observations can we make about overall media presentation?
2. How easy is the software to navigate?
3. Does the software change over time? With each use? With prolonged interactions? Multiple uses?

4. Which types of assessments are built into the program? How important or useful are these for users and teachers?
5. How closely do activities fit classroom needs? Are they interesting? Educational? Fun?
6. How would we rate the overall value of the software? Would this be a good investment for my classroom?
7. How compatible is this software with an emergent literacy approach that integrates reading, writing, listening, and speaking?

These questions can be adapted for use at the upper grade levels. The International Society for Technology in Education (ISTE) Standards (*www. iste.org/standards*) are a resource that schools can use to heighten awareness of what is needed in the area of technology, including information about standards for students, educators, and education leaders.

KNOWLEDGE, UNDERSTANDING, AND THE IMPACT OF STATE AND FEDERAL REQUIREMENTS

Every district, regardless of student demographics, location, or size, is required to comply with state legislation and policy about curriculum, assessment, and instruction (e.g., state standards, state assessment measures). Furthermore, any district eligible for Title I services must apply for funding by writing a proposal addressing requirements (e.g., eligibility, accountability, models for instruction, inclusion of parent involvement programs). Often, literacy specialists have responsibility for writing these proposals. Here, we discuss the role of literacy specialists in relation to various state and federal policies (see Chapter 1 for a description of the policies).

Positions of literacy specialist, literacy coach, and other specialized literacy professionals are often funded by federal or state legislation with specific requirements or regulations affecting the ways in which these professionals work. Therefore, keeping abreast of what is occurring at both the state and federal levels is an important responsibility of literacy specialists. State or federal government agencies send information to school officials and sometimes invite one or more educators from a district to attend informational meetings in which specific initiatives are discussed. Conferences held by the state, local educational support agencies, or professional groups typically offer sessions in which such legislation is described. At the current time, state and federal agencies often sponsor webinars that can be accessed by school personnel at their home site. Information can also be obtained from the state or federal websites on which various legislative actions are described or summarized. The website of the ILA (*www.literacyworldwide.org*) provides useful information, as does the weekly newspaper *Education Week*.

At the present time, as part of the accountability effort, each state must develop a set of standards for what children should know and be able to do in various areas, including reading and writing. Then all students must be tested, in grades 3–8, using assessment measures aligned with the standards. The law also requires districts to administer at least one reading and writing measure at grades 9–12. Results are disaggregated to determine the growth of various groups, including those that are economically disadvantaged, those from racial- or ethnic-minority groups, those with learning disabilities, and those with limited English proficiency. If progress is inadequate, schools are held accountable—that is, low-scoring schools are penalized. The ESSA (U.S. Department of Education, 2015) affects all schools in this country, PreK–12; therefore, literacy specialists at all levels need to be familiar with it and the implications it has for students and their teachers.

SUMMARY

In this chapter, we discussed problems associated with creating change in schools to provide a backdrop to the issue of developing a school literacy program. A discussion about developing a comprehensive literacy program includes information about conducting a needs assessment and using standards as a basis for setting goals and curriculum development. We suggested guidelines for developing curriculum, followed by a discussion of selecting materials, emphasizing the need for establishing criteria for analysis. In one section, we focused specifically on literacy programming for adolescents. We also discussed technology and its impact on literacy education in schools. We concluded with a discussion about the ways in which federal and state regulations and funding affects literacy programming and the role of literacy specialists.

ADDITIONAL READINGS

Bean, R. M., Dole, J. A., Nelson, K. L., Belcastro, E. L., & Zigmond, N. (2015). The sustainability of a national reading reform initiative in two states. *Reading and Writing Quarterly, 31*(1), 30–55.—In this article, the authors describe a study in two states of the sustainability of Reading First components, as perceived by school leaders. The authors discuss factors that affected sustainability.

Fountas, I., & Pinnell, G. S. (2018). Every child, every classroom, every day: From vision to action in literacy learning. *The Reading Teacher, 72*(1), 7–19.— The authors discuss four essential and interrelated elements of a design for a schoolwide system of literacy.

International Literacy Association. (2017b). *Overcoming the digital divide: Four critical steps* (research brief). Newark, DE: Author.—In this brief, key factors that contribute to a digital divide across grade and age levels are described; action steps for overcoming this divide are provided.

● REFLECTIONS

1. Think about the challenges associated with large-scale change described earlier in this chapter as they relate to a school with which you are familiar. Does the school you are thinking about have any of those challenges? Others?

2. Meet with several colleagues to talk about your vision of what an excellent reader (at the end of a specific grade) can do. Discuss your views with each other. How similar are they? Different?

● ACTIVITIES

1. If you are a classroom teacher, try to map your literacy curriculum for the entire year. Use that map to think about whether the curriculum helps you accomplish the goals that you think are important for your students.

2. Select one of the CCSS or one of your state standards for either reading or writing and do a crosswalk across grade levels (e.g., grades 1–5, grades 6–12) to note progression in expectations.

3. Read Celia's vignette and discuss the questions raised in that vignette. Read carefully the section, "Lessons Learned." What are your take-aways from the lessons she describes?

Questions to Consider

What lessons can be learned about the role of the literacy specialist in this vignette?

In what ways does Celia serve as a leader?

What questions come to mind after reading this vignette?

CELIA: MY EDUCATIONAL JOURNEY IN ONE SCHOOL DISTRICT

Although I have been the coordinator of literacy grades K–6 in School District U-46 for the last 5 years, prior to that I served as a district literacy coach for 6 years, and in this vignette, I discuss both roles. District U-46 is the second-largest school district in Illinois, with two early learning sites, 40 elementary schools, eight middle schools, and five high schools. It covers 90 square miles and serves over 40,000 students in grades PreK–12. The population of the district is 54% Hispanic, 26.7% white, 8.3% Asian, 6.5% black, 3.5% two or more races, 0.9% American Indian, 59.1% low income, 31.5% ELs, and 14% special education. I have a long history with this district, which began as a 5-year-old student. I did my student teaching in U-46, then got my first teaching position as a first-grade bilingual teacher. After 8 years as a classroom teacher, I became a Reading Recovery teacher and served in that capacity for 5 years. During a summer professional learning activity I was leading, two administrative interns recruited me to join their ranks as a district literacy coach and after 6 years I was called upon to serve as the coordinator of literacy K–6.

My Role as Coordinator of Literacy K–6

As the coordinator of literacy K–6, bilingual, my primary roles are to facilitate curriculum writing with the selection of materials to support it and provide professional learning activities for over 700 teachers. Last summer, I began the work of facilitating a group of approximately 40 teachers in creating an integrated curriculum. This integration combines literacy, science/social studies, and social emotional standards into units, using an Understanding by Design framework, to guide student learning. Once the group completed the first stage of identifying the desired results (standards), I had to communicate the information to all elementary schools. I planned a half-day overview on the teacher's last required professional learning day in which I also shared the need to attend another full-day session to explore the new curriculum. I worked in collaboration with the curriculum and instruction team to develop professional learning activities for all teachers.

One of the greatest challenges, in a district as large as ours, is sharing information with all 40 elementary schools when there is only one of me. So we decided to hold a Zoom meeting, asking all administrators to follow the directions to log into the meeting at the designated time and then presenting to all remotely, allowing them all to remain in their buildings and still be able to ask questions by typing them in as we presented. Overall, it was a success and we added one more way to engage teachers in learning. It was especially rewarding as we have found that the after-school professional learning opportunities are not well attended, and it is difficult for me to address each teacher's or building's request for support. An added bonus was that all administrators were engaged, as they were the ones facilitating the virtual session.

My Role as Literacy Coach

As a district literacy coach, I provided instructional leadership in several ways. One of my primary responsibilities, with other coaches, was to provide professional learning activities for over 3,500 teachers. We were fortunate, in that we had funds from a grant enabling the district to release teachers for 2 full days, once in the fall/winter and a second time in the winter/spring. Teachers cycled through the professional learning sessions with other teachers from their grade level or content area. So, for example, all first-grade teachers attended the same professional learning activities with their colleagues on 1 of 3 days in a given week. After the full day of professional learning, teams of two coaches visited each school site, where a floating sub was provided so each grade-level team could meet with the coaches to ask and answer questions, as well as have a facilitated work session for about an hour.

The district professional learning program was structured with district guidance about best practice and district needs. Typically, the first half of the day was whole group to ensure all groups received the same information. Small-group activities and cooperative work were always included to engage the participants. During the second half of the day, teachers could choose from a menu of offerings; sessions focusing on ELs and special education student needs were always included as choices.

The district literacy coaches then met with district administration, who gave us guidance for the professional learning activities. The coaches worked cooperatively to determine who would be responsible for presenting each follow-up session and then each person or team planned their professional learning sessions. For the site-based sessions, teams of coaches were assigned to schools in order to provide consistency in support. The goal of these follow-up sessions was to support the needs of each team of teachers as determined by teachers and site administrator.

In addition to this systemic professional learning, district literacy coaches provided one-on-one coaching support by request. Teachers who chose to request support from district literacy coaches submitted a simple form and coaches then followed through with activities that met the needs of the individual teacher (meeting, modeling, observing, and providing feedback). During these sessions we found when we were modeling for teachers, it was best if the teacher had a task to complete while observing (e.g., taking notes and raising questions about what they were observing to guide the follow-up conversation). We created a simple T-chart labeled "What I Noticed"/"Questions I Have." This led to richer and more focused conversations that could truly impact the teacher's understanding.

In my role as a district coach, I didn't have specific instructional responsibilities, that is, I was not assigned to teach students during the day. However, as a coach, by modeling, I had opportunities to provide instruction for students. One of the most frequent requests for modeling was in the area of guided reading. Though it was tricky to plan an effective guided reading lesson for students with whom you have not been working, I first met with teachers, asking questions (e.g., "At which level are the students reading?"; "What reading strategies have you already taught and on which one would you like me to focus the lesson?"; "What resources do you have available for guided reading?"). Once I had a good idea of what the teacher had done and where he or she was headed, I discussed the importance of book selection: The book must not only be at the instructional level of the students, it must lend itself to the strategy being taught (e.g., if I wanted primary students to use picture cues, the book must contain excellent picture cues; if I wanted intermediate students to visualize the piece of text, it must contain language that supported the reader to create a mental image). Once we selected a book, I walked the teacher through the reading and rereading of the text, always keeping in mind, "What will the students do when they reach this challenge and how can I facilitate the use of the reading strategy on which I am focusing?"

After planning and modeling the lesson cooperatively with the teacher, we debriefed the lesson. I asked questions such as "What do you think went well? What do you think I could change?" Referring teachers back to their observation notes, I asked, "What did you notice? What questions do you have about what you saw?" I also shared with the teacher any decisions I may have made that were in response to the students and not planned for in the lesson. However, one thing I was sure to emphasize was the importance of sticking to one focus, ensuring any deviations from the planned lesson continued to support the lesson focus.

Assessment

Our district uses the Fountas and Pinnell Benchmark Assessment System in English and Spanish in order to determine students' text level in kindergarten to sixth grade. In my role as a district literacy coach, I offered staff development in how to administer the assessment, as well as how to use the information to guide instruction. One of the greatest challenges with this assessment is interrater reliability. For years, the district literacy coaches have provided professional learning sessions for administering, scoring, and using the assessment. Yet we still have a great variance between teachers in our district. This is still an ongoing effort for us.

Greatest Challenges

Without a doubt one of the greatest challenges in my role as a district literacy coach and now as a district coordinator is communication. I can't tell you how many times I provided information to a room full of a hundred teachers and it seemed like each one heard something different. I have come to realize the great influence of a person's background knowledge and perspective in shaping the message heard. Of course, how closely they were listening also played a role! To help overcome this challenge, I put key points in writing. With the use of technology, I can do this without sacrificing trees for paper that ended up in file cabinets or garbage cans.

Another challenge I have encountered is teachers who felt they knew everything, and you were wasting their time. Or the teacher who thought your professional learning was another fad and they could just do the same thing they had always done until the fad went away. Cynical and close-minded teachers are one of the great challenges of being a district literacy coach and coordinator. Fortunately, there are only a small number of these teachers in the profession.

Things I Have Learned

- You can't please all of the people all of the time.
- For effective coaching, you must build a trusting relationship.
- Be honest: If you don't know the answer to a question, say so and then go find the answer and return with it.
- If you start with the willing, others will join when they see the student motivation and success.
- Focus on the students; all teachers want their students to succeed.

Take care that you allow some struggle, as that is how people learn and change (I like the story of the little boy that tried to "help" the butterfly out of the cocoon, only to learn that the butterfly couldn't fly because it is the struggle of getting out of the cocoon that strengthens the wings for flight).

CELIA BANKS, MEd
Coordinator of Literacy K–6
School District U-46
Elgin, Illinois

CHAPTER NINE

Assessment of Classroom and School Literacy Programs

Assessment should produce information that
is useful in helping students become better
readers, and assessment should do no harm.
—AFFLERBACH (2016, p. 414)

KEY QUESTIONS

- How do literacy educators use assessment tools and results effectively in schools?

- What are the essential principles underlying effective formative and summative assessment systems?

- How do limitations of standardized assessment measures affect results and interpretation?

Given the current emphasis on testing and more testing (e.g., high-stakes assessment, accountability, teacher performance evaluation), the quotation above serves as an important reminder of the role of assessment measures used to make instructional decisions in schools. The term *assessment* generates much emotion in today's schools, particularly in response to new assessment procedures in the last decade stemming from Race to the Top and ESSA federal mandates. In some cases, the emphasis on assessment is an important means of improving instruction. However, policies may place too much emphasis on assessment, narrowing the curriculum and reducing teacher creativity and flexibility. Some stakeholders are concerned the standardized tests measure only one aspect of student learning and put too much emphasis on the results. There are also concerns about the misuse of limited assessments for decision-making purposes (e.g., retention, graduation decisions, teacher performance evaluation). In reality, systemic assessment can be helpful in making decisions about the total school literacy program, when schools plan and implement assessment as integral with their curriculum and instructional plans. Kapinus (2008) says it well: "The goal of all assessment is to support effective teaching and learning" (p. 145).

Literacy specialists may have many important experiences in their coursework with assessment, but often the emphasis is on assessment of an individual child or a small group of students to inform immediate instructional goals. In this chapter, the focus is on assessment directly related to improving literacy instruction in a classroom or in a school. While literacy specialists have always needed to be well versed in how to use assessment results to help teachers plan instruction, the assessment demands of ESSA (U.S. Department of Education, 2015), the implementation of RTI models in schools, and the current emphasis on rigorous, high-level standards reinforce the need to be proactive in sharing assessment goals. Further, specialists need to be knowledgeable about how to work with teachers and administrators to interpret and use schoolwide results as a means of improving student learning. Read the following scenario to learn about the ways that Pam and her principal collaborate with professionals to make decisions about the assessment plan for the school.

Pam and her principal decided to convene a group of educators in the building—literacy specialists and teachers from each grade level—to take a close look at the schoolwide assessment data. From the big group, they created small groups to look at three different areas: (1) the state test scores, (2) the regular school screening and progress assessments, and (3) portfolios from students receiving extra literacy support. In general, they had a sense of the instruction their students needed most. However, they thought it would be useful to take a close look at the assessment results in a collaborative manner. In doing so, they confirmed what they had suspected. Their students were consistently scoring lower on the writing components of the state tests. Further, they were not seeing the writing scores increase on the school-based writing rubrics they used for assessing writing three times across the year. When they shifted their writing instruction after Common Core standards changes, they focused primarily on informational writing with less time devoted to other types of writing. They raised several questions to consider in next steps, such as further investigation of the match/mismatch between their instructional goals and assessment requirements, the focus of their writing instruction time, and the professional learning needs of teachers in the area of writing. Pam, her principal, and the teachers felt it was a useful learning experience that helped provide a much clearer sense of where to spend instructional time.

DIRECTIONS IN ASSESSMENT

Many states revised their grade-level assessments using funds from the Race to the Top initiative. Some states initially participated in two consortia, Partnership for Assessing Readiness for College and Careers (PARCC) and Smarter Balanced Assessment Consortium (SBAC), to develop new sets of assessment tools that would assess whether students had achieved the rigorous standards, specifically the CCSS, designed to prepare them for college and career. However, given changes in state-level standards and a need for autonomy, most states have withdrawn from these initiatives (see Gerwitz, 2019). Instead, states have decided to buy or develop their own assessment measures to determine overall student learning.

With passage of the Every Student Succeeds Act (U.S. Department of Education, 2015), the federal government continues to require a state level standardized assessment in grades 3–8 and at the high school level. However, the act provided greater flexibility to individual states in the nature of the assessments and created an opportunity for several states to participate in an innovative assessment pilot.

The connections between the CCSS, state-level standards, and new assessments created a shift in assessment goals that reflects the need for balance in how we measure student literacy learning and for what purpose. Afflerbach (2016) calls for coordinated formative and summative assessments in which teachers are able to assess student literacy learning and development on an ongoing basis. Further, assessment should be situated within classroom instruction and learning (Afflerbach, 2017). As students engage with increasing technological options, formal and summative assessments may need to shift to recognize and understand multiple forms of texts and formats for reading/writing (e.g., U.S. Department of Education, 2015; Kervin & Mantei, 2016). Assessments need to reflect the dynamic nature of linguistic and literacy diversity in classrooms with multilingual students (Briceño & Klein, 2018; New York State Education Department, 2017); likewise, stakeholders who interpret them need an understanding of how this diversity impacts assessments and their results. These issues present exciting possibilities as we think about how literacy learning is measured in schools. In the following section, we present information about assessment, what it is, and types of measures.

WHAT AND WHY?

The terms *assessment, tests,* and *evaluation* are often misunderstood. Assessment is the task of gathering data on which to base evaluative or judgment-oriented decisions. Such data are multidimensional, encompassing more than just standardized tests. Assessment can be *summative* in nature, given infrequently (e.g., end of the year or course) and used to evaluate program effectiveness for groups of students. It can also be *formative* or *ongoing*, given at frequent intervals or even during instruction, and educators can use the results to make decisions about instruction for students. Assessment measures can range from standardized tests to observations, checklists, and interviews to performance measures such as writing samples in which students retell or respond to a selection they have read. Even as they are teaching lessons, teachers often modify or adapt what they are doing, based on their informal assessment of whether students are "getting it." Think about the many different measures of student learning available in your school or district. They probably include both summative (end-of-year standardized test) and formative measures (teacher-made tests, student portfolios, writing samples). Then, educators draw on these assessments for *evaluation* purposes such as instructional focus, placement of students (e.g., Tier 1, 2, 3), and small-group interventions.

THINK ABOUT THIS

Read through the writing sample in Figure 9.1. What do you learn about Ruthie as a writer? What do you learn about specific areas of her writing knowledge (e.g., genre)? How could you use the information you learned to help her with next steps in her writing?

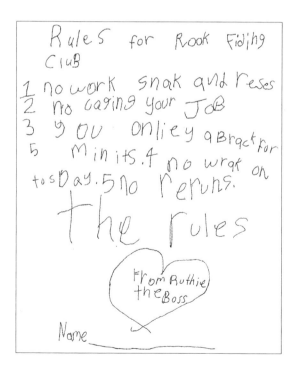

FIGURE 9.1. Ruthie's writing sample.

When Ruthie read her writing to Ginny, here is what she said:

Rules for the Rock Finding Club

1   No work during snack or recess.

2   No changing your job.

3   You only get a break for five minutes.

4   No work on Tuesday.

5   No refunds.

The Rules from Ruthie the Boss

Ruthie developed this contract because she said they needed some rules for their new project to find (and sell) rocks to raise money for a hurricane relief project. In the writing sample, she shows developing knowledge of genre (contract, numbered list, line for signature), content (rules, refunds, breaks, job roles), audience (need for contract, set expectations), and conventions (title, some spelling, capital/small letter). From one writing analysis sample, there is much a teacher can learn about a writer, and multiple writing samples reveal the patterns, growth, and learning needs of each student.

Assessment measures are necessary for a number of reasons, and they are relevant to many different audiences. Below, we identify various types of assessments (e.g., individual assessments, outcome measures, progress monitoring).

Individual Assessments

Screening Tools

Measures that serve as *screening* tools assist teachers in quickly determining whether students are in need of more assistance or more in-depth assessment. According to Mesmer, Mesmer, and Jones (2014), screening tools should have four features: quickly administered, predictive, universal, and objective. In other words, they can be given to all students quickly, they should predict accurately whether students need or do not need help on a specific literacy task, and administration and results should not vary from screener to screener.

Many commercial reading programs provide their own screening measures for teachers and literacy specialists to use at the beginning of the year to coordinate assessment with the literacy program instruction. The assessment may occur before various instructional units to provide baseline information about students and to make initial decisions about which children may need additional support. For example, a screening measure used frequently in schools is the Phonological Awareness Literacy Screening (PALS) for PreK–3 for a comprehensive overview of early literacy skills (see *https://pals.virginia.edu/public/rd-research.html*). DIBELS Next (Kaminski & Good, 2011) assesses the acquisition of early literacy skills K–6; this set of instruments provides information about students' decoding skills, fluency, and comprehension skills. Assessments such as Clay's (2019) Concepts about Print Observation Survey provide a quick set of information on students' awareness of book concepts and basic word knowledge. At the secondary level, literacy specialists may choose to administer a cloze procedure test as a screening measure to determine the readability of a specific textbook, as well as the abilities of students in a specific content class to read that text. Although these initial screening instruments may be useful, they are "screening" instruments and no more. They are meant to provide baseline data and help educators understand which students may need additional support.

Diagnostic Assessments

Diagnostic assessments assist teachers in making decisions about instruction and in pinpointing possible areas to address if a student is experiencing difficulty. If a child has difficulties on a screening measure, the diagnostic measure can provide in-depth information needed to plan instruction. For example, if a child does poorly on an initial screening of decoding, the teacher or literacy specialist may want to administer a more detailed phonics inventory to get a better understanding of what the student can and cannot do. Literacy specialists often use an informal reading inventory to get an in-depth picture of how well students read materials of different genres at various levels. A diagnostic tool, unlike a screening tool, provides information to help literacy specialists and teachers plan the instruction needed by students.

Progress Monitoring

Teachers administer progress monitoring measures throughout the year to help determine whether students have made improvement and to determine the effectiveness of instruction. Progress monitoring measures might include measures of students' recognition of sight words, fluency checks, or skill learning. Other forms of progress monitoring include student work samples or checklists completed by the teacher throughout the year to assess whether students are improving in their ability to perform various tasks (see Figure 9.2 for an example of a checklist for observing the oral reading of primary grade students). Informal and authentic progress monitoring measures are helpful because they are closely related to the instructional practices at a specific grade level (e.g., teachers assess writing samples of

Key

+ = Exhibits this behavior all of the time
✓ = Need for improvement some of the time
0 = Not evident

	Child's Name							
Reads with appropriate phrasing (not word by word)								
Reads with appropriate expression and intonation								
Reads at appropriate rate								
Uses punctuation as a meaning tool								
Uses decoding to figure out unknown words								
Rereads if meaning is problematic								

FIGURE 9.2. Oral reading checklist.

fifth graders three times a year, using a teacher-developed rubric, based on their goals). These measures also provide information that can help teachers decide whether there is a need for additional support, a change in instructional practice, or a need for a more in-depth diagnostic assessment to obtain more information about a child's performance. Literacy specialists can help teachers by talking with them about these data to address two important questions: Are students improving as expected, and, if not, what adjustments in instruction need to be made?

One of the ways to assess progress is through the use of formative assessment, or diagnostic teaching. Teachers can make decisions about instruction by listening to students read orally to see how they self-correct when they experience difficulty, and they can ask students to think aloud to get a better sense of their meaning-making skills. Such formative assessments take advantage of the multiple ways in which students experience reading (e.g., the texts they are reading, the level of thinking required). But using such assessments requires a knowledgeable teacher; again, the literacy specialist can serve in a leadership capacity by helping teachers develop and use these authentic formative assessment tools.

These three types of individual measures—initial screening, diagnostic, and progress monitoring—serve different purposes and require different types of assessment tools. Several key resource books that describe specific measures are *Assessment and Instruction of Reading and Writing Difficulties: An Interactive Approach* (Lipson & Wixson, 2012), *Diagnosis and Correction of Reading Problems* (Morris, 2014), and *Understanding and Using Reading Assessment K–12* (Afflerbach, 2017).

Outcome Measures and Summative Assessment

Many stakeholders, including the school administration, parents, and community members want to know whether their schools are performing satisfactorily. In this case, assessment measures serve as an *outcome* or accountability tool. These summative tools are generally standardized, norm- or criterion-referenced tests. Schools may also use performance measures that assess student learning directly (e.g., writing samples or portfolios) to assess student learning, although cost, design, scoring, and other measurement issues have diminished their use in schools (Lane, 2010). Outcome measures provide for comparison of students from a specific district or school with others like them; they also provide information about the performance of various subgroups (e.g., ELs, special education students, high-poverty students). Most often schools administer these measures to groups of students and use some sort of multiple-choice format. However, test developers are attempting to design tools to better assess high-level, complex thinking skills; they are building assessments that include computer-based task simulations and automated scoring systems, enabling their large-scale use. Likewise, there are attempts to better align curriculum, instruction, and assessment (Goatley, Dozier, & Puccioni, 2020).

Information from outcome measures can be helpful to schools in determining in which areas their program is strong (e.g., students do well in reading vocabulary) and in which they might need to improve (e.g., comprehension scores are low). Results are helpful in determining whether specific groups of students (e.g., ELs, special education students) are experiencing difficulty in learning. At times, administrators also use these measures with other tools, such as teacher observation, to assess teacher performance (i.e., to determine to what degree students have learned while in the classroom of a specific teacher). Such use has its problems, given the many complicated factors that influence student learning.

These measures, however, are not very helpful to teachers for planning daily lessons for the students in their classrooms. They are not diagnostic tools that can be used to inform instruction for individual students. In a study conducted by Buly and Valencia (2002), in which they did additional testing of 108 fifth-grade students who had failed the state reading test given at the end of fourth grade, they found several distinctive and multifaceted patterns of reading abilities that were not discernible in students' performance on the state measure. Their results indicated the state measure was not very useful for making instructional decisions. Yet, these assessments are often known as "high-stakes" measures because state legislation and district guidelines may use these scores for major decisions; for example, student promotion or retention, availability of school funding, or labeling of schools as successful or failing (Afflerbach, 2016; IRA, 2014). Such measures have also been criticized because, given the focus on accountability, some schools have focused on "teaching to the test" by narrowing their curriculum to emphasize only those skills that appear on the test. Further, too often, these tests are limited in their ability to assess complex and high-level reading tasks. It is important, then, to be cautious about how educators use these measures, given their limitations. Research briefs developed by the ILA (2017a, 2017c) highlight the importance of using multiple sources of systematic assessments to make high-stakes decisions about students.

Individual states also use large-scale measures to assess student performance, and often districts rely on those assessment tools as an important indicator of achievement success. In addition, the National Assessment of Educational Process (NAEP), often called the "nation's report card," provides key information about the status of student learning across the United States (see *https://nces.ed.gov/nationsreportcard*).

THINK ABOUT THIS

What are the affordances and concerns about the types of assessments schools use for formative and summative assessment? To what extent do the summative assessment results influence the curriculum in the school—and judgments about the success of the school in educating its students? Do you agree with the concerns raised above about the limitations of these tests?

PRINCIPLES OF ASSESSMENT

The following principles of assessment offer a framework for considering important assessment ideas, often a main responsibility of literacy specialists. Consistent with Standard 3 on assessment and evaluation, in the ILA Standards (2018a), this framework addresses a range of information about implementation of assessment practices.

1. *Facilitate a match between instruction and assessment.* In selecting assessment measures, especially outcome measures over which the school has control, careful attention must be given to the match between the instruction provided in the school and the measure chosen. For formative assessment, Shearer, Carr, and Vogt (2018) use the terms *contextualized instruction* and *contextualized assessment* to help reinforce the need for assessment to match district goals, standards, and benchmarks. For summative assessment, selected tests must align to the curriculum, instruction, and standards of the district. Teachers often bemoan the fact that students are tested on a skill that is not introduced in the curriculum until the following grade level or the month after the test is given! There is strong evidence that the closer the overlap between curriculum and test items, the better students will perform; this just makes sense. This is not to say teachers should be teaching to the test, but it is unwise to ignore the demands of a test students will be taking as a measure of their achievement, especially when the intent is to understand a schoolwide perspective on student learning. At times, this outcome measure is a test developed by the state, based on standards that have been adopted by that state. In such cases, it again makes sense for literacy specialists and their colleagues to work together to decide how and what the schools are teaching so that students can achieve those standards. Only then will the outcome measure be a fair assessment of students' performance.

2. *Develop an efficient systematic approach to assessment.* At all levels (i.e., primary, intermediate, middle, and secondary), literacy specialists and their colleagues make decisions about which components of literacy to assess. In the primary grades, assessment measures should focus on foundational skills, such as phonological awareness, fluency, and phonics, as well as comprehension, vocabulary, and writing. In the upper grades, emphasis should be on general comprehension skills and those related to disciplinary

literacy, academic vocabulary, and writing, including higher-level foundation skills (e.g., structural analysis). At all levels, information about students' writing progress is important for making instructional decisions. The key is for school personnel to select instruments, reflecting a logical and realistic progression from the early grades through high school and across all components of literacy. School personnel can ask themselves: Are we assessing important dimensions of literacy? Is there redundancy—what can we eliminate? In some cases, assessment may take too much time away from instruction and adjustments must be made to reduce the assessment time to maintain instruction and to eliminate "test overkill."

   3. *Develop a system of literacy assessment reflecting district goals.* Too often, there is no agreed-upon system of literacy assessment in the school community. School personnel use many different tools for a range of purposes, some of which are disparate with school goals. Other assessment tools may be so complex to administer or score that classroom teachers tend not to use the results, or as stated above, they may take so much time for administration that valuable instructional time is lost. In other cases, assessment tools differ so much from level to level (e.g., elementary to middle school) it is not possible to determine the ongoing literacy growth of students. Shifts in school/district-level administrators and state policy changes impact the assessment system, such that school educators need to be careful about the broader systemic context to situate assessment changes thoughtfully.

   4. *Select assessment tools that are reliable, valid, unbiased, and practical to administer.* Select instruments that are technically valid and reliable; instruments developed by districts themselves may lack such technical sophistication. For example, if a school decides to assess students' written retelling of a story, careful attention must be given to the rubric used to score this retelling so there is *reliability* or consistency in the scoring of that instrument. Otherwise, little use can be made of the scores. Also, the tools employed must be *valid*—that is, they actually measure what they purport to measure. For example, a spelling test is not a measure of composition skill, although spelling, as part of a convention rubric, could be used as one indicator of performance in composition. Similarly, educators need to be careful about dialects and/or cultural bias in selecting assessment tools that are appropriate for the students being assessed and in interpreting the results. For example, Briceño and Klein (2018) offer suggestions on formative assessments with specific suggestions for multilingual students.

   5. *Teachers need assistance in applying data to instructional decision making.* There is clear evidence that student performance improves when teachers use data to make instructional decisions. Thus, assessment

tools should be usable by the teachers who administer them, whether they are literacy specialists or classroom teachers. If teachers see these assessments as a burden, taking time away from the instructional program, and if they are not provided with the preparation they need to see the value of these measures, there will be little value in administering them. Too often, instruction in the classroom is activity or materials based; that is, teachers base their decisions about instruction on the selection that comes next in the book. One of the important roles of the literacy specialist is to help teachers make decisions about their instruction, informed by results of assessment data. This assessment process is critically intertwined with differentiation of literacy instruction (see Powell, Aker, & Mesmer, 2020). An example of how a literacy specialist worked with one teacher in reviewing assessment data is described below, using data presented in Figure 9.3 that lists scores of students in one second-grade classroom on several literacy assessment measures.

> Maria Hernandez, the literacy specialist, and Roberta Reed, the second-grade teacher, were reviewing the scores of some of Roberta's students on the initial classroom-level screening measures given at the beginning of the year. It was obvious to them that students were doing fairly well with basic sight words; almost all students scored 75% or better. Students were not performing as well on the pseudo-word test, with 11 of them getting less than 75% correct. Many students also were experiencing difficulty with fluent oral reading. The poor scores on the retelling were also of concern, and students had some difficulty responding to questions after reading. Based on the classroom-level assessments, Maria and Roberta identified two students (Sally and Henry) about whom they had serious concerns.
>
> After an extended problem-solving discussion, Maria and Roberta made the following decisions. First, all students in this second-grade class would benefit from activities that emphasized fluency practice, and Maria shared with Roberta various ways to facilitate this goal (e.g., repeated readings, choral reading). Maria suggested that she come into the classroom 4 days a week to work on decoding with the 11 students who seemed to have the most difficulty; she told Roberta that she would emphasize word building using letter tiles to help students apply what they knew about letter–sound matches to identifying new words. All lessons would include opportunities for reading connected text.
>
> Because of the low retelling score, both educators agreed that students did not seem to understand the task of retelling and that the entire group would benefit from lessons that helped them (1) understand the activity of retelling and why it helps them think about a story, and (2) develop strategies to help them with retelling (i.e., story structure or story mapping). They would also be given opportunities

Teacher name (last): _____ Grade 2 _____

Student name	Pseudo-word %	Sight word %	Fluency		Comprehension	
			Words read	Words correct	Retell n/55	Question n/8
Frank	60	89	52	44	7	3
Juan	55	93	90	86	6	6
Clyde	85	97	90	87	10	5
Melissa	45	93	102	98	13	5
Cindy	60	95	57	53	13	6
Sally	35	76	25	11	0	4
Bob	90	97	87	83	19	6
Jerome	90	98	143	143	11	8
Ralph	95	82	52	48	14	5
Gail	80	96	102	99	7	8
Celeste	20	95	57	52	11	4
Joseph	25	98	65	61	30	7
Tyrone	25	96	63	59	26	6
Henry	45	67	29	18	15	5
Mark	60	92	81	77	19	6
Julie	40	93	75	71	8	6

FIGURE 9.3. Example of a student data collection sheet, second grade, pretest.

to retell orally as well as in writing. Maria and Roberta agreed they needed to develop lessons that gave students opportunities to read more challenging and conceptually difficult text. Therefore, for the entire class, the two educators decided to address one of the second-grade CCSS standards on reading of informational text, that is, asking and answering questions to demonstrate understanding and referring to the text as a basis for their answers. Maria agreed to model a lesson, using the social studies text from that grade level.

Maria suggested some additional diagnostic testing of Sally and Henry to get a better understanding of their instructional needs. She agreed to administer an informal reading inventory to see how they responded to different genres of text at varying levels. She also thought it would be helpful to gather additional data on their decoding and writing skills. She suggested to Roberta it would be a good idea for the two of them to analyze the writing abilities of *all* the students within the next month. In fact, Maria had asked the second-grade team to bring samples of their student writing to a grade-level meeting to talk about what they could learn about the literacy instruction they were providing and how it might be improved. Maria and Roberta concluded their meeting by agreeing to meet in 2 weeks to talk about the success of their plans and to make adjustments, as needed.

This example provides a description of how one literacy specialist worked collaboratively with a classroom teacher in using test results to make instructional decisions. At the present time, especially with the RTI initiative, there is an emphasis on using data results to inform instruction. Often literacy specialists, as well as other specialized personnel, meet with teachers at specific grade levels to discuss results across the grade (e.g., to determine the number of students meeting standards or targets, as well as those who are not, and to discuss ways by which the teachers as a group can modify instruction to meet the needs at that grade level). In Rita's work with Reading First, teachers and administrators appreciated the way in which data helped to inform instruction (Zigmond & Bean, 2008). In teacher work areas, educators posted "data walls," showing results for students and changes in scores. We have reservations about such public posting of student scores and encourage administrators and teachers to recognize the problems inherent in such a display (e.g., embarrassment for individual students and teachers; tendency to overemphasize testing; possibility of negative, public comments about students; FERPA violations). Teachers and administrators can discuss the pros and cons of these public displays, so they do not have a negative effect on the school and its climate.

In some schools, teachers and literacy specialists develop charts indicating where students are in terms of performance so teachers can visually see the levels at which their students are performing and make some decisions about next steps. Figure 9.4 shows a summary sheet of the performance of students in three third-grade classrooms at midyear. A team of teachers and literacy specialists discussed the two measures—the STAR Reading Test and a fluency measure. The template provides a place where teachers and literacy specialists, meeting as a group, can set goals for the next quarter. Further, they can identify specific strategies to be taught or retaught, groupings, or educators responsible for instruction and with whom. Literacy specialists can develop a similar form for use in summarizing the decisions made to inform instructional decisions.

Progress Monitoring Form—Marigold School Grade Level: 3

Date of Meeting: Baseline   <u>1st Quarter</u>   2nd Quarter   3rd Quarter   End of Year

Attending the meeting:

Attendee	Position	Attendee	Position
Darrell	3rd-grade teacher	Thelma	Literacy specialist
Ava	3rd-grade teacher	Helena	Literacy specialist
Nina	3rd-grade teacher	Franklin	Principal

Performance indicators: Percentage of students at proficient level based on benchmark/standard:

	% At/above benchmark	% On watch (below benchmark)	% Intervention (below benchmark)	% Urgent intervention
STAR Reading	71% (44 students)	18% (11 students)	2% (1 student)	10% (6 students)
Fluency Measure	85% (53 students)		15% (9 students)	

Goals for the next quarter:

STAR Reading	Following eight students will move from on watch (below benchmark) to at/above benchmark: Ben, Brittany, Chad, Sara, Shauntee, Tyler, William, Zack Following three students will move from urgent intervention to intervention (below benchmark): Abby, Daniel, Dylan
Fluency	Following five students will move from below benchmark to at/above benchmark: Alosia, Chad, Jacob, Sara, Tyler

Strategies: Reinforce nonfiction text structures and other core reading skills (I/E time); reading buddies (with first graders); comprehension (focus on verifying responses in text; making inferences); vocabulary (synonyms and antonyms).

Groupings (pullout and in class): Add pullout group of six students (those in urgent intervention) (focus on vocabulary and comprehension).

FIGURE 9.4. Summary sheet of data analysis. Adapted from Acmetonia Primary School, Allegheny Valley School District, Pennsylvania.

6. *Opportunity for student self-assessment and reflection should be built into the program.* Although assessment and accountability are major concerns in schools today, unfortunately, there is less consideration given to the importance of *self*-assessment by the students. Nevertheless, there is strong support for involving students in the process of evaluating their own reading and writing (Afflerbach, 2016; Hansen, 1998; Tierney, Johnston, Moore, & Valencia, 2000). Such self-assessment is a hallmark of successful readers, enabling them to make decisions about their own learning. Moreover, involvement in self-assessment, as a means of developing independent learners, is strongly recommended in rigorous, high-level standards, such as the CCSS.

However, students need experiences to develop the ability to self-assess. The use of rubrics in classrooms can promote such self-evaluation. A rubric is a scoring guide, with criteria, for judging the relative quality of assessment products. For example, the NAEP (National Center for Education Statistics, 2005) has an oral reading fluency scale available to show a set of four fluency levels (see *https://nces.ed.gov/nationsreportcard/studies/ors/scale.aspx*). Such a rubric can be modified so students can self-assess their own oral reading or that of their peers. Teachers might develop a simple rubric asking students to self-evaluate their oral reading, for example, as follows:

> "Do I read at a speed that makes it easy for others to understand me [not too slow and not too fast]?"
> "Do I know most of the words in the story?"
> "Do I reread if something doesn't make sense?"
> "Do I read so that others enjoy listening to me?"

Students can use a simple 3-point scale to self-evaluate each of the elements (e.g., "I do a great job," "I'm okay most of the time," "I need to improve"). When students assess their own work, they become knowledgeable about the demands of the task and more comfortable with the notion of self-evaluation.

Teachers can also use portfolio assessment as a means of promoting ownership of work. Such assessment can begin in the early grades with the collection of student work, writing samples, reading attitude forms, and books read, and progress to more complicated portfolios created at the middle and high school levels.

7. Assessment systems should include more than testing. As mentioned, schools should have a well-designed comprehensive assessment system in place and that system should include more than data obtained from tests. Rita's teaching colleague used to say one key measure for assessing the quality of instruction in the classroom is "the number of students with smiles on their faces!" Kapinus (2008) discusses various topics about which data can be collected: attendance, parent involvement and perceptions about the school and its literacy program, safety of students, instructional schedule, and allotment of time for instruction and curriculum (p. 148). All of these factors need to be contextualized within the range of learners in a classroom and school (e.g., multilinguistic). Because teachers' views and beliefs greatly affect what they do and how they teach, obtaining perceptual information from them is especially useful. Other important areas are students' motivation to read, the number of books taken out from the library, and the environment that exists in the school as a whole and in classrooms. These data are useful indicators of whether a school is an effective place for learning—and of ways schools can improve their school reading programs. Often, literacy specialists are involved in developing questionnaires or surveys that can be completed by parents or by teachers to get a better sense of their views about the school's literacy program. For help in designing questionnaires, consult *Data Analysis for Continuous School Improvement* (Bernhardt, 2013).

THINK ABOUT THIS

How can a school collect data such as those described in Principle 7? What questions can school personnel ask about such topics as instructional schedule? Attitudes of teachers? How can educators use such data to improve instruction?

ISSUES IN ASSESSMENT

Who Should Be Involved in Developing the Assessment Plan?

Although assessment plans can be developed by an individual or a small group of administrators, it is best for a plan to be developed by a team or committee, including teachers from a range of grades and content areas, literacy specialists, department chairs, principals, and parent representatives. Such a team, led by an administrator knowledgeable about tests and assessments, can make decisions about important issues:

- Which assessments best match the curriculum in our schools, PreK–12?
- Which assessments does the state require?
- How can we get the best assessment information with the least amount of disruption to the instructional schedule?
- What professional learning is necessary if educators are to be able to administer, score (if necessary), and use the results?

Assessment decisions made in isolation, or at one level only, reduce the possibility of continuity across grade levels. Districts have difficulty using their assessments to make decisions when (1) they have changed them too frequently, (2) the measures are not comparable from one level to another, (3) the measures do not match the curricular/instructional goals, and/or (4) reliability, validity, and/or bias issues.

School personnel should be familiar with the district assessment tools and be able to discuss and communicate the results of such assessments to parents and other stakeholders in the community interested in the work of the school. The emphasis by the federal government (i.e., Race to the Top, ESSA) on assessment results and accountability makes it imperative that schools can explain not only *what* they are doing but *how well* they are doing!

How Are Assessment Results Reported?

Again, literacy specialists may find it necessary to assist in developing processes and procedures for how schools report assessment results. They themselves may also be responsible for such reporting. Different audiences are interested in these results, including teachers, students, district administration, parents, school board, and community members. The school district should have an established means of reporting students' scores to each teacher; such reports may be similar to the one in Figure 9.3. The literacy specialist should be available to assist the teacher in interpreting and using the results for instructional decision making. The literacy specialist may also assist the teachers in deciding how scores of individual students can best be reported and explained to parents or to students themselves. Building principals may need reports highlighting results for specific populations or areas: class, grade level, literacy component (e.g., reading comprehension, fluency). They may wish to have data disaggregated by ethnic group, socioeconomic, EL status, or special education eligibility. Again, the literacy specialist can work with the principal on interpreting the results of the literacy assessment and what they suggest about adjustments to curriculum or instruction. The literacy specialist and principal together may make presentations about test results to the entire faculty.

Reporting to parents is a key responsibility of the schools. Literacy specialists should, of course, be aware of how the school district reports literacy performance and what the specific scores mean: letter grades, effort scores, and grade-level reporting. In addition, they should be able to interpret those results to families, especially parents/guardians of readers experiencing difficulties. It is probable those parents/guardians may want to meet with the literacy specialist to discuss their children's scores. Test data should be reported to parents/guardians in a simple and clear manner, so they understand what the scores mean. Although not all literacy specialists will have the responsibility for presenting assessment results to the school board or community, including the media, some may. The district should be proactive in sharing assessment results, presenting not only results but recommendations about what the school is doing to improve students' learning.

What Are the Limitations of Standardized Tests?

Literacy specialists, because they frequently make use of standardized tests in their work, must be aware of the limitations of those tests, especially those that are high stakes or have the potential to label or affect students' lives in a detrimental manner (ILA, 2017c). The following limitations apply to the systematic school assessment system, in which literacy professionals have an important role.

First, a test is a *sample* of all questions that can be asked about a subject and, in addition, it is a *sample* of a student's performance at a single point in time. Therefore, although test publishers work to ensure that the items selected constitute a representative sample of important knowledge and skills, the fact remains that some students might have done better if a different sample of equally adequate questions had been used on the test. Furthermore, on any given day, an external factor such as illness or a disagreement with a family member may have affected a particular student's performance.

Second, changes in the schools' scores can be influenced by changes in student population. If a school is one whose population demonstrates high mobility or attrition, there can be significant differences in the population from one administration date to another. Some students may not have been in the school for more than 2 or 3 months. In fact, Kane and Staiger (in

Kober, 2002) estimated that more than 70% of the year-to-year variations in average test scores for a given school or grade could be attributed to external factors rather than educational factors.

Third, the ways by which scores are reported affect perceptions in terms of positive or negative outcomes. For example, look at the data in Figure 9.5 illustrating reading achievement proficiency at the third-grade level for two schools over a 3-year period. Which school do you think is doing better?

Pine School has more students reading at proficiency; most likely Pine School met the requirements for "adequate yearly progress" as required by federal legislation that year. However, if we look at change in performance of students, then we see greater growth or change in Oak School, where student performance improved from a low of 20.7% scoring at proficiency to 37.5% at the proficiency level in Year 3. Previously, NCLB considered only status or level of proficiency to determine whether schools were improving satisfactorily. At the present time, regulations changes have given states permission to use evidence of growth or change scores as a means of determining school improvement.

In addition to looking at the results in terms of change or status, those who interpret data can look at trends in a school. For example, in looking at only 2 years of growth for Oak School, we can be misled by the data, because in Year 2, 38% of the students were proficient and in Year 3, the proficiency rate was 37.5%; if we use only the previous year's results, we see no improvement, but if we analyze scores from Year 1 to Year 3, we see significant improvement. In other words, we must be careful when analyzing and interpreting assessment results. Results are arbitrary; that is, improvement depends on the approach used for analysis. Literacy specialists should be familiar with these limitations.

Literacy specialists who want to know more about high-stakes testing may wish to read the policy brief and position statement on high-stakes assessment (*Using High-Stakes Assessments for Grade Retention and Graduation Decisions* [IRA, 2014]; *The Roles of Standardized Reading Tests in Schools* [ILA, 2017c]).

	Year 1	Year 2	Year 3
Oak School	20.7%	38.0%	37.5%
Pine School	56.6%	57.0%	57.5%

FIGURE 9.5. Percentage of third graders scoring at the proficiency level.

ASSESSMENT AT THE MIDDLE OR HIGH SCHOOL LEVEL

This chapter provides key information for all literacy specialists, regardless of the level at which they work. Assessment is a reality at all levels; currently, the federal government requires that schools conduct an end-of-the-year assessment in grades 3–8 and at least once in high school. However, these tests provide for summative or outcome measures and are not necessarily helpful for making decisions about instruction. So, educators at the secondary level should develop or select formative measures to assist teachers in assessing literacy learning and making decisions to improve instruction for their students. In this section, we describe several key points for those working with adolescent learners.

First, given the diversity and range in achievement found among adolescent learners, assessment is an essential tool for learning more about their instructional and literacy needs. In the document "Assessments to Guide Adolescent Literacy Instruction," Torgeson and Miller (2009) discuss the importance of a comprehensive assessment plan for grades 4–12 for achieving the following goals: increase overall levels of proficiency; help students continue to progress so that they can achieve the more difficult, rigorous, standards in the middle and secondary schools; and assist students who are reading below grade level to increase their reading performance. A comprehensive plan must show evidence of outcomes, provide for progress monitoring enabling teachers to make instructional decisions, and identify students who need instructional interventions. Emphasizing the importance of self-assessment, Torgeson and Miller (2009) recommend providing students with opportunities to reflect on their learning, using rubrics they develop with their teachers.

One of the challenges at the middle and secondary levels is obtaining information about students' performance in the various content areas or disciplines, and how such information can be used by teachers to make instructional decisions (Gillis & Van Wig, 2015). As indicated in the IRA (2012) position statement on adolescent literacy, assessment of adolescents should be based on an inquiry framework that explores how learners become independent, collaborative thinkers and problem solvers. The best assessments give students opportunities to "make meaning from an idea in print and then represent their new understandings in a variety of modes (e.g., video, audio, graphical)" (IRA, 2012, p. 11). Further, the role of engagement is a critical component of both instruction and assessment for adolescent learners (ILA, 2019d; Ivey & Johnston, 2013). The manner in which the assessment task occurs (e.g., standardized test, self-selected literature assignment, writing project) is critical to understanding assessment results relative to student interest and engagement in the activity.

SUMMARY

Assessment is and will continue to be a topic generating much interest and concern in schools. New directions in assessing student growth, however, suggest assessment systems that are multidimensional, focusing on both what students learn and how they apply what they learn. Assessment is an important responsibility of the literacy specialist, not only for assessing the strengths and needs of individual students but also for making decisions about the performance of classes, schools, and the district as a whole. Assessment should be closely related to instruction, and there should be a sequential, comprehensive assessment system, PreK–12. In addition, various stakeholders, including teachers and community representatives, must be involved in making decisions about the assessment of literacy. Schools should use multiple assessment measures with established technical adequacy. Literacy specialists may have responsibility for working with teachers, administrators, and the community in interpreting and applying the results of assessment. They should be knowledgeable about the strengths as well as the limitations of all assessment measures, especially those used for high-stakes purposes.

ADDITIONAL READINGS

Afflerbach, P. (2016). Reading assessment: Looking ahead. *The Reading Teacher,* 69(4), 413–419.—In this article, Afflerbach focuses on key areas of formative assessment for reading and the effects of high-stakes testing on reading efforts.

Goatley, V. J., Dozier, C., & Puccioni, J. (2020). Using literacy assessments to improve student learning. In A. Swan Dagen & R. M. Bean (Eds.), *Best practices of literacy leaders: Keys to school improvement* (2nd ed., pp. 135–153). New York: Guilford Press.—This book chapter assists literacy leaders in how to use assessment to learn about students and support their instruction, to collaborate in data-based decision making for instructional improvement, and to use assessments to advocate for learners.

International Literacy Association. (2017c). *The roles of standardized reading tests in schools* (Literacy leadership brief). Newark, DE: Author.—This ILA brief gives an overview of standardized reading tests, including the role of these tests, limitations, accountability, and key areas for consideration.

● REFLECTIONS

What are the strengths and weaknesses of various assessment instruments with which you are familiar or that are used by your school or district?

274 THE LITERACY SPECIALIST

● ACTIVITIES

1. Interview a literacy specialist in a district about their role in assessment. What type of assessment tools are used? How does the literacy specialist work with teachers to use results in planning instruction?

2. Interview a literacy specialist or another school leader to discuss the district's PreK–12 assessment plan. What measures does the district use and for what purpose? How do the assessments differ across grade levels?

3. Review several assessment tools a district uses and discuss how they might be used for formative and/or summative assessment goals.

CHAPTER TEN

School, Community, and Family Partnerships

It takes a village to raise a child.
—AFRICAN PROVERB

KEY QUESTIONS

- In what ways can literacy specialists collaborate with families and community members to enhance student literacy learning?

- Drawing on the six types of parental involvement as described by Epstein et al. (2018), how might educators plan experiences that reflect their understanding of and appreciation for family cultural backgrounds?

- In developing an effective family–school collaborative program, what essential notions or guidelines need to be considered?

When teachers identify their greatest issue in teaching readers who are having difficulty, they often indicate the critical need to connect with families to provide additional support or attend to the child's needs. Teachers in the early grades notice the differences between students who come to kindergarten with school-based background knowledge/exposure essential for learning success, and those with few prior literacy and language experiences that support learning to read. Teachers in the upper grades have concerns about their students who do not complete their homework, rarely engage in their learning, and/or have poor attendance. Such issues require teachers to evaluate their own teaching to seek improvement in engagement and support networks. While these concerns reinforce a need to connect with families, an overarching principle is that of valuing what children *do* bring to the classroom, rather than focusing only on perceived issues.

Family involvement in schooling is critically important and is positively related to many factors, including test scores, student attendance,
and school completion rates (Morrison, Bachman, & Connor, 2005; Sheldon, 2007). We use the term *family involvement* to be inclusive of all children who live with many caretakers (grandparents, aunts or uncles, older
siblings, foster parents) rather than just one- or two-parent homes. Many
parents and family caretakers are involved in school-based activities: They
come to the initial "meet-the-teacher meetings" at the beginning of the
year, talk with their children about school experiences, assist them with
their homework, and work as partners with schools to make certain their
children are receiving a good education. In some cases, their children have
extensive experiences that give them a rich language and literacy background similar to the traditional expectations of academic discourse; they
have rich vocabularies and are familiar with the language of the classroom.

At the same time, there are students with parents whose linguistic,
economic, or social resources are different from the mainstream populations of certain schools, potentially limiting them from participating fully
in their children's education (Edwards, Paratore, & Sweeney, 2014). Moreover, too often, schools have not positioned themselves to understand and
use the *funds of knowledge* (e.g., knowledge, resources, and competencies)
these parents and their children bring to schools (Moll, 2000). Literacy
leaders play an important role in developing school communities that move
from a perception based on a deficit model to one that values students' cultural strengths and experiences. In other words, "Students bring assets into
the learning environment that should be valued and capitalized on in the
design of learning opportunities" (Milner, 2010, p. 15). Further, access to
literacy for all children can be a major impetus for eliminating roadblocks
and making the necessary changes to bridge in and out of school literacy
experiences (Au, 2011; Edwards, McMillon, & Turner, 2010).

In the past, some educators believed it was their job to teach and parents' to "parent." This viewpoint has changed; the education of the child is
one requiring the efforts of both family and school. When there is explicit
family involvement and support, students have a much better chance of
success in school (Edwards et al., 2010; Epstein et al., 2018; Morrison et
al., 2005). When families are involved in their children's schooling, children earn higher grades and test scores, and they stay in school longer. The
increased pressure on educators to account for levels of student achievement has generated support for even more family involvement. In its NCLB
legislation (U.S. Department of Education, 2002), the federal government
gave parents a range of options to pursue if their children were in unsuc-
cessful schools. Currently, some schools provide supplemental programs
for children with special needs, and parents/guardians have the choice of
transferring their children to better-performing public schools, including
public charter schools. Such policies require all schools and all teachers to

think about their involvement in the community in new and different ways. In Pam's case, the family and community partnerships are so important that she decided to focus on this area in her annual goals.

> In her annual goals for PL, Pam decided to focus on family and community partnerships with the school. She was particularly concerned about meeting the literacy needs of a growing EL student population. Her goals included analyzing the classroom text sets and read-alouds to understand how and where the books represented a range of diversity features, including characters, settings, and themes. Then, she wanted to collaborate with the local community center that students attended on evenings and weekends to increase access to books. Finally, she contacted the leaders of a free books program and held a book night at school during which families/students selected free books to take home prior to the summer vacation. Whew—the book analysis led to a series of meetings to find, read, and select new books for the school. Pam was excited to see increased representation of diversity in the classroom book sets, especially read-alouds, and student engagement with the content.

Epstein (2018; Epstein, Sanders, Sheldon, Simon, & Salinas, 2009), in a research-based framework, describes six types of involvement to improve school climate and student success:

1. Parenting: helping families establish home environments that support children's development as students and enable teachers to get to know the families.
2. Communicating: designing two-way connections and using effective forms of home–school communication about programs and children's growth.
3. Volunteering: recruiting, organizing, and providing opportunities for volunteers (including family members) to support student learning.
4. Learning at home: involving families in supporting their children's growth (e.g., helping with homework, supporting other school activities).
5. Decision making: including families in school decisions that impact students, including parent organizations.
6. Collaborating with the community: coordinating various activities among school, family, and community resources and services.

Although these six types of involvement help educators think about specific ways to involve parents, an overarching principle is for teachers to understand what students bring to the classroom that will help bridge home–school connections. Literacy specialists and their colleagues can serve as leaders in helping teachers to understand this principle and to implement many different efforts related to each of the six types of involvement (see *www.partnershipschools.org* for additional information).

INVOLVEMENT WITH EXTERNAL AGENCIES

There are many different agencies with which literacy specialists might work. Involvement with five important entities is discussed here: preschool providers, libraries, community- and faith-based organizations, universities and colleges, and volunteers and paraprofessionals in the schools.

Preschool Providers

The growing understanding that preschool education matters led to a national initiative by President Obama to provide universal early childhood education for children in the United States. In 2014, the federal government invited states to apply for development or expansion grants from the federal government through the Preschool Development Grant Initiative (*www2.ed.gov/programs/preschooldevelopmentgrants/index.html*). The focus of the grants was on building, developing, or expanding high-quality preschools for children from low- or moderate-income families. Five-year-olds who enter kindergartens come with a variety of experiences, many of them having attended a day care center, nursery, or preschool, including Head Start programs. Some arrive having learned school and learning behaviors, as well as literacy skills, enabling them to move comfortably into the kindergarten setting. Others struggle with literacy tasks and may not have had any preschool experience, or little exposure to literacy or school-like expectations. Research on the cognitive development of young children emphasizes the importance of high-quality early learning experiences. There is evidence of great variability in the quality of preschool experiences children receive, especially in preschool programs serving children from poor families (McGill-Franzen, Lanford, & Adams, 2002; Neuman, 2009; Snow et al., 1998). At the same time, the quality of child care programs has been identified as an important determinant of language acquisition in the form of preliteracy skills (Barnett, 1995; Barnett, Frede, Mobasher, & Mohr, 1987; Cannon et al., 2017; Phillips et al., 2017).

Below we describe three major approaches that can prepare young children for kindergarten and improve the preparation they receive in their day care or preschool setting. First, school districts can work collegially with preschool providers to establish understanding of what schools expect from entering kindergarteners, and learn more about the educational experiences provided in these preschool settings. Schools also need to know what preschool providers value and why their programs include various activities and experiences. Gathering this information can be accomplished in several ways: (1) Schools can share the list of standards or competencies for entering kindergarten; (2) preschool providers can share their curriculum; (3) teachers from the two sites can visit each other's classrooms to get a better understanding of students' experiences; and (4) teachers share information on the community and family practices that help bridge home/school connections. These activities can bridge the gap that often occurs between preschool and kindergarten educators and eliminate, or at least reduce, the blame game. Further, district leadership can acknowledge the importance of such transition activities and provide district-level support and resources.

Second, school districts can include preschool providers who educate students for that district in available PL activities. When school districts convene a PL session in which the speaker is addressing an issue relevant to the education of young children, invitations can be extended to preschool providers. It may not be possible for all preschool teachers to attend, but arrangements can be made at the preschools so teachers who attend the session can share the information with their colleagues.

Third, when opportunities for collaboration arise, seize them! At the present time, the interest in early learning is not only creating such opportunities, it is *demanding* them. Possible proposals for funding can be investigated and written, and community collaboration for such endeavors can be cultivated.

Literacy specialists can assume an important role in promoting each of these three approaches and are often the ones who can create opportunities for collaborative efforts. They can foster interaction between kindergarten and preschool teachers, especially in the discussion about literacy instruction. They may also be able to provide PL activities for preschool teachers. In Pennsylvania, as part of the Striving Readers grant, in some districts, literacy personnel traveled to specific preschools to provide job-embedded support for preschool teachers who may not have had extensive learning opportunities about literacy and language development. Given this increased focus on early childhood education, new opportunities are available for literacy specialists, especially those interested in literacy learning of young children.

Libraries

Literacy specialists can work collaboratively with school librarians to develop experiences for students that create excitement and enthusiasm for reading. In some states, all library specialist candidates in preparation programs complete literacy coursework as a required part of their program, setting up opportunities early in their career for collaboration with classroom teachers and literacy specialists. Within schools, the literacy specialist should be aware of resources available in the school library and assist the librarian in selecting print and nonprint materials that enhance students' motivation to read and promote learning across curricular areas (Thomas, 2018). The literacy specialist may collaborate with the librarian, identifying themes and topics addressed in the academic areas, and selecting books to enrich the curriculum. Further, librarians and literacy specialists can collaborate to continually update and expand library collections that reflect the diversity (e.g., cultural, race, abilities) of the school population and larger communities.

School librarians can also be involved in supporting the school's literacy program. Rita and her colleague (Bean & Eichelberger, 2007) evaluated a program in a local school district in which school librarians attended workshops led by district literacy coaches to increase their knowledge and understanding of the strategies and approaches used in the literacy program. These librarians were very positive about this experience, indicating they gained a better understanding of the language of literacy used by teachers and an awareness of how library resources and activities could reinforce what students were learning in their classrooms.

The community library is also a resource for the school. Most community libraries assign a staff member to interact with personnel from schools who are eager to participate in school–library collaborations. The community librarian may be able to purchase resources that relate to the curriculum emphasized in the school and help gather books for various theme units. The literacy specialist who takes the time to work with the community librarian is likely to find new ways to enhance student motivation to read. Some of the ways that schools and libraries can collaborate include the following:

- Librarians can come to school to read books to children and solicit membership in the community library. After reading a book, it can be left in the classroom for follow-up activities by the teacher.

- Students can visit the community library on a field trip; the librarian may lead the students through the various sections of the library, explaining the types of resources available, and offer children the opportunity to get a library card.

- School and library personnel can work together to develop a summer program for students. The school can promote the program and give recognition to students who complete the library program. Research findings indicate that there is a "summer slide" for children of poverty; that is, children from higher socioeconomic groups do not experience the summer learning loss experienced by those in lower socioeconomic groups (Alexander, Entwisle, & Olson, 2001; Allington & McGill-Franzen, 2018). Summer literacy programs can help to decrease this summer slide by providing children with books and opportunities to read.

• Literacy specialists can meet with community librarians to create programs benefiting readers at all levels. The literacy specialist can inform the librarian about special school initiatives (e.g., specific reading/writing programs or efforts that require specific books). Often, the librarian will then make certain to include those books, digital tools, and online resources in the library's collections.

• In a summer collaboration among a community library, local school district, and university, the community library hosted a University at Albany graduate-level university course where literacy specialist candidates taught middle school students. The library supported technology and text integration, while the setting reinforced to all stakeholders involved the importance of such collaborations (see Malavasic, 2019, for information on the instructional content).

During the past several years, a public library and school district in an urban setting collaborated to develop a special library program designed to promote reading in schools where there were large numbers of students experiencing difficulties. Funded by a local foundation, the teachers and librarians designed the program to: (1) stimulate motivation to read by exposing students to books about children from various cultures, including their own; and (2) enhance reading achievement by introducing and discussing various vocabulary words from those texts. Personnel from the library went to the third-grade classrooms twice a month to read and discuss a book with the children, and then left the book in the classroom. Evaluation of the program indicated students enjoyed listening to the book and often reread the book that had been read to them. Teachers felt the program enhanced students' reading interest, and they (the teachers) enjoyed learning about new trade books they could then use in their classroom work (Genest, 2014; Genest & Bean, 2007).

In another community, the library provides a monthly program for teens enrolled in life-skills classes at their high schools. During their 2-hour visit, these students are involved in activities to increase their information literacy and understanding of the library and its resources. Reference librarians provided technology support. The children's librarian indicated the importance of collaborating with teachers to design programs to reinforce life-skills classroom goals (Rita's personal communication with children's librarian, Whitehall Public Library, Pittsburgh, Pennsylvania, 2014).

Community- and Faith-Based Organizations

Not only do many communities, churches, community agencies, and organizations engage children and young adults in a variety of literacy events and activities associated with their mission, but some also provide after-school or summer programs for students. These programs provide a safe place for children and reinforce school learning by helping students with homework or providing tutoring and academic support. For example, a national Oasis Intergenerational Tutoring program pairs older adults with students who need additional help beyond the classroom. The adults must complete free training and pass background checks. In Pittsburgh, Pennsylvania, this initiative is associated with Literacy Pittsburgh, and provides free instruction in several districts with large numbers of students-at-risk.

Recent legislation has deemed faith-based organizations eligible to apply for approval to provide supplemental educational services to low-income students attending underachieving schools. Such services can provide assistance in literacy or math during a range of times, including before or after school, on weekends, or during the summer. For more information, McMillon (2016) offers 10 suggestions on how to get started in establishing literacy-focused community-based initiatives with schools and universities.

These organizations, whether faith- or community- or service-based, can support or extend the goals of the school and community. In order to help them achieve their collaborative goals, literacy specialists or other school personnel can get involved in several ways. First, they can help facilitate communication between the school and agencies offering services, so there is better awareness of additional supports available to students. Second, literacy specialists can volunteer to provide guidance about possible strategies or instruction that best support classroom practices. For example, if students in a school use a specific literacy program or curriculum, literacy specialists might suggest the community-based program use the supplemental books aligned with that program. Or, a check sheet might be devised for classroom teachers to send to the agency, indicating the needs of specific students (e.g., "J needs to practice his new sight words; I'm including them in this packet").

In addition, individuals who work with these organizations can be sources of information and wisdom for schools about a community and its resources. They may advocate for students if the family is not able to participate in more traditional parent/family involvement programs (Boutte & Johnson, 2014).

Service organizations often have literacy initiatives. For example, Rotary Clubs across the country often provide educational resources, such as dictionaries to students, and even teach them how to use them. The Lions Clubs International, the largest service organization in the world (*https://lionsclubs.org/en*), has a reading initiative—Reading Action

Program—focused on increasing literacy and access to learning resources; service projects and activities are organized to address specific needs within individual communities. In Rita's community, the Lions Club sponsored several well-attended events: a Book Walk, Book Bingo, Reading with Stars Night in which local officials read to students, and a community day activity in which children came to the library to read to the dogs! Literacy specialists who are proactive can look for ways to work with these organizations. Often, these organizations need the support of local school professionals to obtain access to classrooms or schools and to learn more about local literacy needs. Several organizations devoted to training therapy dogs also welcome access to schools. As a means of enhancing student motivation to read, literacy specialists develop programs in which trained dogs "listen" to students read (Lamkin, 2017). Lane and Zavada (2013) describe canine-assisted reading programs, and the website of Therapy Dogs International (*www.tdi-dog.org*) provides useful information.

Universities and Colleges

Many PreK–12 schools are located close enough to universities to be able to partner with them on projects that bring preservice teachers, graduate-level literacy candidates, volunteers, or faculty into their schools. Faculty involved with preservice education programs look for ways to form partnerships with schools in which there is quality, research-based instruction, and mentor teachers who are excellent role models. Many PreK–12 and university educators are eager to cooperate in different ways: teaching classes on-site and recruiting classroom teachers willing to participate, providing up-to-date resources and information to schools, and holding meetings in which there is in-depth discussion about what preservice students are learning and its congruence with the instruction occurring in the classrooms.

In recent years, universities and schools have been engaging in initiatives to increase the diversity of candidates in teacher preparation programs (e.g., Teacher Opportunity Corps–My Brother's Keeper federal program), which could potentially increase the diversity of the pipeline for literacy specialists, leading to a better representation of diverse student population and communities. Increasing the diversity of the teacher pool, however, is not enough. There must be a restructuring of the teacher education program so that critical issues related to diversity and social justice are embedded in the curriculum and instruction (Milner, 2012). Such congruence is shown to improve test scores, reduce discipline issues, and increase graduation rates (Carver-Thomas, 2018).

Many faculty members at universities and colleges also appreciate opportunities to participate in PL efforts of schools, or they are interested in conducting research that contributes to the understanding of how students learn to read and write. Although such partnerships need to be entered into thoughtfully so there is a clear understanding of the benefits for each partner, these ventures can be the catalyst for a win–win situation. In Chapter 5, we described the LEADERS project in which Rita worked with several school districts on a PL initiative. The outcome of the project included changes in classroom teacher practices and student achievement; in addition, university faculty learned a great deal about what works in schools, what is difficult to implement, and challenges to consider in efforts to improve the quality of literacy instruction.

Within preparation programs for literacy specialists, family engagement should be an integral component of the experience. Reflecting on her experience with the University at Albany literacy specialist practicum experiences, Dozier (2006) suggests that "insights gained from families bring forth the complexities of our learners and ensure that we think and act more broadly and deeply to bridge literacy, literacy instruction and literacy competencies beyond school walls" (p. 100). Each semester, the elementary practicum experience, taught at a local "high-needs" school, routinely draws 100% attendance from families for the final celebration event where children share their literacy projects. Family engagement readings and practices are integrated throughout the course, with graduate students talking with family members each week and encouraging collaboration.

For the past 30 years, graduate students in the reading specialist certification program at the University of Pittsburgh, Pennsylvania, have been recruited to serve as reading specialist interns; they are placed in a school site for an entire year to work with students needing reading support and with the teachers of those students; and at the same time these graduate students are enrolled in courses and applying what they are learning in their schools. This partnership has been a win–win for participants. It provides excellent and real experiences for the reading specialist candidates who come to class each week with new issues and ideas. It provides additional support for the readers in these schools, and it provides the classroom teachers and reading specialists in the schools with opportunities to work with teachers new to the profession (see Bean et al., 1999, for a more in-depth description of this initiative). This is only one example of how schools and colleges and universities can work together to promote effective literacy instruction for students.

Volunteers and Paraprofessionals in the Schools

Volunteers, of course, can come from many different sources: senior citizens, retired teachers, parents, grandparents, as well as college students. They can also come from the business sector or from service organizations. Currently, there is an emphasis on using volunteers or paraprofessionals to assist with instruction (e.g., listening to students read orally, reviewing sight words with them, or assisting them as they write). Such volunteer programs can be informal, with parents or tutors following the lead or suggestions of teachers to whom they have been assigned, or much more formal, with volunteers or paraprofessionals serving as tutors for children experiencing difficulties or for those students needing supplemental or Tier 2 instruction in school. The ILA Standards (2018a) indicate these "literacy partners" may have multiple roles for supporting the literacy development of students. For example, volunteers and paraprofessionals, with appropriate support from classroom teachers and literacy specialists, may tutor students to provide extra literacy support and enrichment for students. Regular support and communication between the teachers and volunteers are critical for successful programs.

Often, the literacy specialist is responsible for recruiting, training, and directing the work of paraprofessionals and volunteers in the school. One reading specialist in a school was responsible for directing the work of more than 17 tutors who worked with primary children in her building. She had a massive job of coordinating schedules, training these tutors, and then monitoring their work and the progress of students. Lapp, Fisher, Flood, and Frey (2003) described a tutoring program in which literacy specialists taught, monitored, and supported aides who provided one-to-one instruction to students experiencing reading difficulties. Both teaching and monitoring of their work are essential to ensure they are working effectively with students, and especially those who need additional support and intervention. In one Pennsylvania school, administrators recruited retired teachers to provide differentiated, supplemental instruction for all students in a lab setting. In this school, volunteers or paraprofessionals who had expertise as teachers were given more instructional responsibilities than less experienced individuals. In other words, although volunteers or paraprofessionals can be helpful, there is justifiable concern about using less qualified personnel to provide instruction for those who need the most help! The following guidelines may be helpful to those interested in initiating such programs in their schools.

1. *Provide adequate training for volunteers or paraprofessionals.* Wasik (1998) reported that in successful tutoring programs, literacy specialists (a) trained and provided feedback to volunteer tutors, and (b) wrote and supervised lessons. In other words, tutoring programs may not be successful if careful supervision of tutors is lacking. Indeed, an unsupervised program can result in wasted time and money. On the other hand, Baker, Gersten, and Keating (2000) described a volunteer tutoring program in which community volunteers were given brief training and a broad framework from which to plan. Students in the experimental group exhibited greater growth on several dimensions of reading, compared with students in the comparison group who received no tutoring. This study suggested that even minimally trained tutors can facilitate progress in readers

experiencing difficulties. The Baker and colleagues' study, and a later one by Fitzgerald (2001), indicated there is much we do not know about tutoring by volunteers. The caring relationship that develops between the volunteer and student may be a key element in motivating the child to do better in school. The gains, of course, may have been greater if tutors had received intensive training. However, in instances where fiscal or logistical restrictions limit the amount of training or supervision, leaders can still develop a tutoring program that can have a positive effect on students' attitudes toward reading and their reading performance.

The work–study portion of the America Reads Challenge Act of 1997 provided funding for college students who were eligible to become volunteer tutors in the schools. Many colleges and universities sent their students, often with little or no experiences with children or with literacy instruction, into schools or community agencies to tutor young children. They needed assistance in how to motivate and keep children engaged in learning. Bean, Turner, and Belski (2002) discussed lessons learned from implementing such a program, identifying issues to be addressed by university and school or community-based personnel. Many of these resources are valuable today as college tutors continue to be literacy volunteers through community engagement projects and preservice teaching experiences. In sum, a successful volunteer tutoring program requires leadership from a knowledgeable educator—often the literacy specialist—to provide preparation, and to monitor and evaluate the program.

THINK ABOUT THIS

What are your thoughts about minimally prepared tutors teaching students experiencing literacy difficulties? As a literacy specialist, how would you incorporate paraprofessionals or volunteers into your school?

2. *Help tutors understand the school culture, school procedures, and regulations.* Many volunteer tutors have little understanding or experience with schools other than the ones they attended, often years ago! Volunteers need to be given specific information about school rules and regulations, appropriate dress, and behavior. They need assistance in understanding how to communicate with classroom teachers and to have a clear understanding of the routines and rules of the classrooms (e.g., what to do if the child is not paying attention and distracting others). Tutors appreciate the time spent on these topics; anxiety and confusion are reduced and there is greater potential for a positive relationship between school personnel and tutors. The more tutors know about their students, the better they will be able to work effectively with them.

3. *Seek input from and provide feedback to classroom teachers.* Classroom teachers can provide useful information about students and

their reading needs. They can also provide information as to whether there are changes in the student's performance as the tutoring progresses. At the same time, the classroom teacher should be informed about the tutoring, its emphasis, and given feedback as to how the student is performing in the tutoring session. Teachers may be more receptive to the tutoring, which may pull students from classroom instruction, if they have input into the tutoring plan. Or if the tutoring takes place in the classroom, the classroom teacher needs to take a leadership role in how the volunteer works with students. Classroom teachers should have occasions to meet and talk with tutors; in fact, the literacy specialist may choose to work with the students while the classroom teacher meets for a brief time with tutors. Often, the classroom teachers can provide ideas to tutors about working with specific students.

4. *Monitor and evaluate the program.* The literacy specialist responsible for the tutoring program should monitor the work of each tutor and determine whether a student is making progress. If there is little or no progress, changes need to be made. The literacy specialist should have a system for evaluating the overall program. If the program is successful, great! But if the program is showing little in the way of results, there must be discussion about how it can be improved.

One of the criticisms of tutoring programs is that they are not aligned with the classroom instruction. This is a legitimate concern that should be addressed by those responsible for the tutoring program. In evaluating the program, the literacy specialist can develop and send questionnaires to teachers and parents to determine program effects. Student outcomes can also be investigated by using formal or informal assessment measures.

COLLABORATING WITH FAMILIES

Given the requirements in Title I regulations, many literacy specialists have a special role in promoting family involvement. They have to keep families apprised of the supplemental instruction received by students who have literacy difficulties and provide suggestions for how families can be helpful at home. Specialists may also be responsible for developing comprehensive family literacy programs for parents and caretakers who may need literacy instruction.

Awareness of the importance of family involvement has generated policies and procedures at all levels of government—federal, state, and local—and has affected school programs and practices. The following sections discuss various ways in which literacy specialists can work with parents and families to ensure greater literacy performance for children. First, consider these guidelines:

1. *School personnel must have an understanding of and appreciation for the families whose children they serve.* In today's schools, many teachers do not live in the communities they serve, and for that reason may lack an in-depth understanding of the culture and experiences of their students. Teachers may believe children are not learning because of their backgrounds or the lack of support from home. And although the educational task may be more difficult when children do not arrive at the school door with expected literacy experiences or skills, teachers with an understanding and appreciation of the talents and experiences that children *do* bring can be more effective in working with them. Some schools have asked teachers to conduct home visits; others schedule parent conferences in neighborhood agencies that are close to children's homes (especially necessary when children are bused to schools a far distance from their homes). The literacy specialist can serve as a catalyst for helping teachers gain knowledge and an understanding of and appreciation for students, their background, and their culture. As suggested by Boutte and Johnson (2014), helping teachers learn more about the culture of the families of their students provides an important bridge in establishing school–family relationships.

2. *Engage families in conversations to help them understand the school's academic and behavioral goals and expectations.* Although schools continue to communicate through written materials, others rely on phone networks and websites to communication with parents and families. Furthermore, social media is also a means of communication between schools and parents (Facebook, Twitter, blogs, etc.). Keep in mind that students and families have a range of access to the Internet and may have limited opportunities for these types of communication, with disparities in remote learning opportunities (Herold, 2020). It is important to establish the best means of communication for your local context.

3. *Create an environment that welcomes parents and families into the schools.* Too many parents, especially those who themselves were not successful in school, are not comfortable going into schools. Perhaps one of the first steps is for schools and parents to plan activities jointly. For example, ask parents to help develop the agendas for meetings or to make suggestions about the types of activities that might be held. Parents can make presentations to classes about their professions, serve as reader of the day or week, or as supervisors on field trips. In one school, the coordinator of a special reading project developed a program in which parents were responsible for reading a book and then presenting a craft or art activity to the children. The coordinator helped parents select the book and the activity, and the teacher assisted with the lesson and any management problems. Parents were delighted with the teaching experience and the added bonus of seeing their child in the classroom context. Children were excited their

mom or dad was going to teach (and other children often acknowledged, "Billy's mom is teaching today!"). At a celebration breakfast these parents talked about their increased appreciation for the teaching profession—and the teachers of their children! (Teaching is not as easy as they thought.)

In another school, the individual responsible for federal programs held several evening meetings a year to which students brought their families. These meetings were based on a theme: for example, teachers had read *Where the Wild Things Are* by Maurice Sendak (1988), and then each class constructed a large monster drawing to be hung in the school gym. Children and parents arrived at the gym in the early evening to construct masks, to listen to another reading of the book, and to sample light refreshments. The local bookstore sent a "monster" to walk around the gym and decide which of the classes' monsters was the very best. Attendance at these events ranged from 100 to 250 participants and included parents, children, and their siblings, grandparents, and interested relatives!

Results of a survey on family and school partnerships (National Center for Education Statistics, 1998) indicated parents are more likely to attend meetings if there is some possibility of interacting with their child's teachers. Parents can also serve on a school advisory team or participate in committees working to improve the school (e.g., a playground or after-school program planning committee).

4. *Family involvement should extend through the grades.* Research suggests that family involvement declines with each grade level, showing the most dramatic decrease at the point of transition into the middle grades (Billig, 2002). Nevertheless, opportunities to build parent involvement in the middle grades are available. Billig (2002) suggests that too often the communication during the middle and high school years tends to be one-way—from the school to the family—and recommends the following five guidelines for schools seeking to form strong partnerships with parents (pp. 43–45):

- Use the challenges of the middle school years to build parent involvement programs. Students at this age face more demanding academics and can be asked to assume more responsibility.
- Build on the need and value that adolescents place on strong relationships.
- Encourage parent and student participation in decision making. Parents and students can be involved in curriculum decisions (e.g., selection of textbooks).
- Prepare school faculty to work well with parents—how to communicate, report student progress, work with volunteers, and become involved with community partnerships.
- Keep families informed about what students are learning.

PRACTICAL IDEAS FOR INCREASING FAMILY INVOLVEMENT IN THE SCHOOLS

This section describes ideas and resources that may be helpful for increasing family involvement in the schools.

1. *Create a family involvement program that is systemic and an integral part of the school literacy program.* Too often, family involvement efforts are idiosyncratic; that is, they differ from teacher to teacher. Effective programs, however, require procedures for reflecting on what is being done and a systematic effort to involve parents/families in their children's educational process. This effort includes involving families/guardians in the decision making about the plan itself (i.e., What do families need and want?) and securing a long-term commitment to the plan on the part of teachers and parents alike. Sometimes it is necessary to educate teachers about how to work effectively with families; often, it means rethinking what family involvement entails in a specific school or community. In other words, teachers, administrators, and literacy specialists should decide as a group what means they will use to both communicate with and inform families and to learn from them about students. Such a plan may include ideas for formal events such as family workshops or conferences. It may include ideas for communicating with parents on a regular basis about the accomplishments of their children. The plan may also indicate who is responsible for the various activities (e.g., the literacy specialist will plan a meeting that provides suggestions for families on how they can help their children become better readers/writers, all teachers will send home a "positive" note to parents at least once a semester).

2. *Take every opportunity to communicate with families and use many different approaches to communication.* Effective teachers have always reinforced the positive. They send home notes/e-mail and text messages telling parents what their child has done well, reinforce a child's behavior with stickers or a certificate, or call parents to tell them about literacy successes. One kindergarten teacher created a photograph album of her class, with pictures and a caption dictated by the child. At the end of the year, this teacher held a kindergarten graduation at which she showed these photos to the attending parents. Each parent also received a copy of the album. The teachers, families, and students celebrated success together! This teacher routinely had high parent attendance at these school events. She also communicated on a weekly basis with families, posting a blog that told them what students had learned that week and how parents could reinforce the learning. Teachers often use technology to communicate with parents. Some teachers communicate via e-mail or text messages that provide designated time periods when parents can call to raise questions or address concerns.

In addition to the individual efforts of teachers, there should be a schoolwide systematic plan for communicating with families, K–12 about literacy information. Blogs, links, newsletters, YouTube videos, and e-mail blasts can be useful to families, especially if they include many practical ideas and demonstrations. Some schools send home a calendar over the summer suggesting daily or weekly literacy activities for children.

Literacy specialists can develop their own material to send home to families, or they can select from available material. For example, they can draw on professional organizations to provide a handout for families with tips about reading to their children. Specific suggestions can be found on websites such as the Keystone State Literacy Association "Families and Reading" (*https://ksla.wildapricot.org/Families-and-Reading*) or the Child Research and Study Center (*https://isaprofessionaldevelopment. org/parentbooklet.cfm*) site. Teachers can encourage families to use the community library to obtain books or suggest book titles their children might enjoy; the position statement on leisure reading (IRA, 2012–2013) lists many sources to identify books for children at all ages (e.g., Teachers' Choices Reading List: *www.literacyworldwide.org/get-resources/reading-lists/teachers-choices-reading-list*).

Literacy specialists can develop and hold workshops and meetings, increasing families' understanding of how important they are to the literacy learning of their children. They can share ideas about how to help children develop a love of reading and how to provide an environment that encourages reading. Parents can be given specific ideas about how to read effectively to their children and how to listen to their children read to them. Just as important, it is also a time for teachers to engage with and learn from families to bridge connections with home–community literacy practices.

3. *Provide PL experiences that improve teachers' ability to talk or confer with families.* Some suggestions for talking with families include:

- Be prepared. Have examples of student literacy activities easily at hand so that families can be shown what their child can and cannot do. As noted, it is important to talk about what the child *can* do and to emphasize the positive.
- Establish a friendly but professional atmosphere in the conference. It is preferable for the teacher or literacy specialist to avoid sitting behind his or her desk; a table is more welcoming and still provides the surface area for various materials and work samples.
- Talk only about the child and what he or she can do. Do not compare the child to other children in the classroom.
- Be a good listener. Educators learn so much more if they listen and seek information from families about their children (what they enjoy in school and at home, how they feel about school or specific subjects, what might motivate them to read, any health or emotional issues). Their comments will enhance teachers' understanding of children and parental expectations of them.
- Refrain from using school talk or jargon. Parents/families may

not be familiar with terms such as *phonemic* or *phonological awareness, fluency,* or *concepts about print.* It is best to *show* parents what is challenging their child.

SUMMARY

This chapter discussed the rationale for building partnerships with communities and families and described various ways in which literacy specialists can build relationships with community agencies, including preschool providers, universities, libraries, those who offer supplemental programs for students, and volunteers. In addition, we discussed the importance of family involvement and ways of enhancing that involvement in their children's education.

ADDITIONAL READINGS

Kim, S., & Song, K. H. (2019). Designing a community translanguaging space within a family literacy project. *The Reading Teacher, 73*(3), 267–279.—Kim and Song share an example of a multilingual literacy project that leverages families' funds of knowledge, with suggestions on designing and implementing family literacy projects in the community.

McMillon, G. M. T. (2016). School–university–community collaboration: Building bridges at the water's edge. *Journal of Adult and Adolescent Literacy, 60*(4), 375–381.—McMillon draws on her own experiences to then describe two community-based literacy initiatives, offering suggestions on how to create networks between schools and community, and ideas for getting started on such initiatives.

Peralta, C. (2019). Why are we still blaming the families in 2019? *The Reading Teacher, 72*(5), 670–674.—Peralta outlines key ideas about family engagement and draws on a project with teachers to help understand and expand on how to build knowledge about cultural and linguistic practices involving family engagement.

● REFLECTIONS

1. Why might some parents/families feel uncomfortable about meeting with a teacher? How could this discomfort be alleviated?

2. What activities and programs does your local library offer that enhance reading performance of students in the school? How can your school partner with the local library?

● **ACTIVITIES**

1. Develop a friendly newsletter for parents/families that provides them with ideas about how they can work effectively with their children. The newsletter can be one for parents/families of students in a specific age group (i.e., preschool, primary, intermediate, middle school, or secondary). Whenever possible, seek a translation into the home languages represented in your school and alternative ways to distribute the information, including an audio version or video to post on social media.

2. Using the guidelines in this chapter, practice holding a conference with a parent/ guardian, using one of the scenarios described below. Role-play in threes: one person is the family member, the other is the teacher or literacy specialist, and the third is the observer who provides feedback about the conference.

   Scenario 1: Maria. Maria's mom is concerned about her daughter's performance in school. She does not understand why Maria is receiving help from the literacy specialist. Maria is a fourth grader at an urban elementary school. She is coming to the literacy specialist because she is having difficulty in her social studies and science classes. She received all A's in reading and spelling in grades 1, 2, and 3, but this year she seems to be having trouble with her content subjects. She complains to her mom that she can read the words, but she does not know what they mean, and that when she gets to the end of a passage or chapter, she cannot remember anything she has read.

   Maria, an only child, has always lived with her mother and grandmother, who both work. Finances are limited, and Maria has not had many opportunities that might enrich her literacy background. Although her caregivers have taken her to the museum, the local zoo, and so on, Maria's mom notes time limitations due to her work schedule. While there are a few books in the home, the mother indicates that she would love to read to Maria, but she is tired at the end of the day, and somehow there never seems to be time. Maria has good health; she wears glasses (although she forgets them much of the time). She loves school and her teachers (except for the social studies teacher—who keeps asking her difficult questions). She also loves books—especially storybooks. She hates her content subjects, though, because "everything is just too hard" (or so she tells her mom). She has always received praise from her reading teachers for her excellent reading; she loves to read orally, and with expression. She cannot understand why she is unable to comprehend her new books in fourth grade.

   Scenario 2: Jayden. Jayden's parents have come for a consultation about Jayden's poor grades. They are eager to help him. Jayden is a ninth-grade student at a suburban high school. Jayden moved to this high school from a small rural school this past year. He had always been an average student in school. Now, he is getting D's and F's in courses such as American literature and history. He does fairly well in algebra and biology. He knows that he is a slow reader and often has difficulty figuring out the words. Once he identifies the words, he realizes that he does always know the meanings. Jayden does not read much, but when he does read, he chooses material about dog care (he has a Labrador retriever that he trains) or magazines dealing with the outdoors. He cannot remember reading a book that was not part of his school requirements. Jayden likes classes where he does not have to read much—and he hates to write. His teacher observed that his handwriting is slow and laborious. He does love working on the computer, though, and his parents have agreed to get one (he is really excited about that). Math is his favorite subject, and he likes science, too (especially biology).

Jayden is the oldest boy of four children (he has an older sister and younger twin brothers). All of his siblings are excellent readers, and Jayden realizes that he is the one who has the most difficulty in school. His parents try to help him with his schoolwork, but he does not like to bother them because of their other responsibilities. The family is very supportive of all the children. Jayden has decided to go out for the track team, and he knows that his family will attend all of the games, but he knows he will need to improve his grades to be eligible for the team.

Jayden had one serious illness in second grade, when he missed a great deal of school and was tutored at home for almost 3 months. Since that time, he has not had any difficulty with his health. He has always had difficulty with reading, especially after his return to school in second grade.

CHAPTER ELEVEN

Making Your Voice Matter
CONTRIBUTIONS TO THE PROFESSIONAL COMMUNITY

KEY QUESTIONS •

- In what ways can literacy professionals contribute their voices to school, district, and community audiences about literacy programs and practices?

- In what ways can externally funded grants have a positive effect on the school's literacy program? What is important to know about applying for a grant?

- How might literacy professionals contribute their voices to the field via presentations and writing?

Within any profession, the voices of experts contribute to a grow-ing understanding and interpretation of best practices. Within the literacy field, the specialists and coaches play a vital role in sharing their insights about student learning. There are several avenues for making your voice heard, such as presenting at a PL event, presenting at a local literacy council event or state conference, writing a blog or article, or seeking funding via a grant proposal. Professional contributions are critical components of the leadership role for literacy professionals.

For literacy professionals who are interested in contributing their ideas to the field, there are numerous ways to do so. First, consider joining a professional community that supports such opportunities. For example, many communities have local reading councils with regular meetings for members to discuss books, share ideas, and/or listen to presentations. The National Writing Project (NWP; *www.nwp.org*) has nearly 200 local sites across the United States. Affiliated with universities, NWP site directors and members support PL and leadership, including engaging educators and students in writing. Second, pick a literacy concept or practice that is critically important to you. You likely already have an interest in a particular literacy area and expertise on specific topics based on your graduate program experiences. Read extensively on the topic, including professional journals, research studies, and books. In the process, keep an open mind to develop support for your ideas, yet also challenge them in ways that may shift your views and perspectives. Be sure to write along the way as you gather information to support or challenge your ideas. Third, think through options for sharing your voice on this topic. For example, you might consider presenting what you learned at a local or state literacy council event. Or, you may submit a manuscript to a state literacy journal or teacher's sharing website. Regardless of what avenue you take, the best way to get started is to—get started! Read how Pam makes decisions about submitting a collaborative proposal to present at a local conference with her colleagues.

> Although Pam had attended the state literacy conference the last three years, she had never given a presentation. She realized sharing information on the summer book project (see Chapter 10) might be the perfect opportunity for a conference presentation. She could draw on her presentation at a PL workshop for the district, and the book list she created for her former graduate school colleagues who asked about specific books. Further, the upcoming conference theme would be focused on diverse learners and instructional ideas. Pam asked Hank and Jerome if they would like to join her in submitting a proposal to the conference, knowing their collaborative efforts for the project would be a key piece of information for the conference presentation too. She read the conference proposal guidelines carefully, asked the district literacy coordinator who regularly presented for feedback, and submitted the proposal. She was excited to see if the conference would accept the proposal!

In the next section, we use a detailed example of grant writing to illustrate a written document that many literacy specialists write at some point in their career. Keep in mind that some aspect of grant writing also applies to conference proposals and manuscript writing (e.g., developing a key great idea, goals/objectives, and a literature review).

WRITING A PROPOSAL TO SEEK GRANT FUNDING

One means of improving literacy instruction and practice is to seek funding to support new and innovative projects, or to try a new approach already established by research. Writing a grant proposal is a way for literacy professionals within schools or districts to obtain funding needed to advance literacy goals. Educators have many reasons to write grant proposals:

- The fifth-grade teachers want to apply for a mini-grant to support a special unit on diversity in which students conduct interviews and write oral histories of local citizens. Teachers want funding to purchase additional books for their classrooms and for digital voice recorders for note taking.
- The superintendent is excited about obtaining additional funds from the state to develop a summer school for third graders experiencing difficulty with writing.
- A literacy specialist has the responsibility for writing a Title I grant proposal to support funding for the literacy goals outlined in the district PL plan.
- A local foundation is offering funding to upgrade computers in the school, with the requirement that the proposal include information on how classroom teachers will integrate computers or tablets into classroom instruction.
- The literacy specialist wants to apply for funding from a professional organization to conduct an action research project about the effects of a student book club for adolescent boys on their literacy learning.

There are many different reasons for writing a proposal and many sources of local, state, and national funding. Even if you have never written a proposal or have some hesitations about your ability to write one, take that first step. Be sure to look for funding sources and grants that may be just right for you and your school district. Grant writing can become contagious! Moreover, grant writing is an opportunity to participate in meaningful PL.

In today's world, there are many opportunities for obtaining additional funds to support the efforts of schools. With the reduction in funds from local, state, and federal levels resulting in budget cuts for schools, grant monies provide resources to support great ideas for improving literacy instruction. Many small school districts do not have a designated grant writer, often leaving this activity to an administrator, specialist, or teachers. For example, the literacy specialists in schools may be required to write proposals to obtain Title I funds, special state funding, or foundation grants. Literacy specialists may also take the initiative and write a proposal because they see the possibility of improving the available reading texts with additional resources. There are many different types of proposals, and the requirements differ for each funder. For example, some research or governmental proposals often require lengthy submissions; some require a review of literature and research that supports the plan, while others may ask for a comprehensive needs analysis as well as other data supporting the request. In contrast, some proposal applications for obtaining materials or developing a special program may require only the rationale, the plan for use or implementation, and a budget. In fact, there are times when funding is a result of a positive relationship between you and the grant giver (a colleague of Rita's tells about receiving initial funding as a result of a conversation with a seatmate on an airplane). Generally, proposals have some characteristics in common.

GENERAL GUIDELINES FOR PROPOSAL WRITING

1. *A great idea!* Reviewers look for ideas that address an important issue, are creative, well developed, and meet the agency funding goal. No matter how well written or how elaborate a proposal is, without a great idea, it will probably not generate support from funding agencies. For example, if there is concern about the fact that primary students are regressing in their reading performance over the summer, coming up with a creative idea for motivating children and families to read over the summer may be the key to obtaining funds from a local foundation. Or, a secondary literacy specialist may want to purchase novels supporting a specific unit being taught in a content field (e.g., study of the Civil War in history class), choosing a funding source specifically for book purchases. Some school districts may want to develop a video to explain their literacy program to the community as a means of enhancing school–community relationships, thus seeking a grant from a community-based foundation.

Just as authors recognize the importance of writing about a topic well known to them, so, too, do great ideas for grants come from immersion in the idea being considered for funding. The content or ideas in a proposal should be based on the literacy specialist's expertise, interests, and knowledge of the field (i.e., what has been done and what has worked). Often these ideas come from discussions with colleagues, attendance at a conference, or from reading an article in a professional journal. At other times, ideas come from an identified need in the school (e.g., writing club involving parents, greater number of multicultural books in the school library, Saturday school for extended instruction, increased numbers of electronic tablets for middle school readers to increase literacy engagement).

2. *Work with others to develop the idea.* There are times when one individual will provide the impetus for moving forward and writing a grant; however, the best ideas generally occur when several individuals collaborate and talk about the idea and how it can be elaborated upon in a proposal. Moreover, most grants will require implementation at a grade or

school level. By working collaboratively with others, the grant writer can help to establish group ownership and excitement about the upcoming project. To the extent possible, form a team of individuals who can collaborate with you to think on the idea and what it means. You may do the majority of the writing, but including colleagues who are excited about the possibility of a new project is important during the writing process and even more important when the grant is funded. Individuals may not appreciate being told about a specific project at the time of its inception.

   3. *Locate a good match that addresses your needs.* Identifying district or school needs is a critical step (e.g., Should the focus of a grant be elementary? Secondary? Should it address the need to improve literacy instruction in the academic disciplines?). Once the need has been identified, start looking for grant sources. Funds may be available from federal, state, or local agencies; corporate foundations; or private foundations. A literacy specialist seeking funds to undertake a specific project must locate funders whose priorities match the proposed activities or initiative. The literacy specialist would not, for example, send a proposal for a PL project to a funding agency that indicates they are seeking proposals for summer programs for children. You would be wasting your time and their time! The goal is to locate a funding source that addresses your district needs.

   Several useful resources are available for those writing proposals to seek additional funds to support their efforts:

- *Creating Winning Grant Proposals: A Step-by-Step Guide* (Rothstein, 2019)
- Follett Learning Grants and Funding *(www.follettlearning.com/about-us/grants-and-funding)*
- Grants for Teachers (*www.grants4teachers.com*)
- "Teachers: Get the Grant" (Hennick, n.d.)
- *Grant Writing for Teachers and Administrators* (Sliger, 2009)
- The NEA Foundation Writing Tutorial (*www.neafoundation.org/for-educators/grant-resources/writing-tutorial*)

   Often, school administrators encourage literacy specialists to write proposals for state department of education grants that target monies to be allocated to districts. For example, a state may receive federal funds they can allocate to districts that submit successful applications. For a range of examples, see websites from California, Texas, and Tennessee:

- *www.cde.ca.gov/fg/fo*
- *https://tea.texas.gov/Finance_and_Grants/Grants/Applying_for_a_Grant*
- *www.tn.gov/education/finance-and-monitoring/school-improvement-grants.*

At times, a local foundation may encourage school districts to write a proposal for funding (e.g., support for additional after-school programming for students in a high-poverty school who need additional literacy support). Literacy specialists who have grant-writing responsibilities may find the *Creating Winning Grant Proposals: A Step-by-Step Guide* (Rothstein, 2019) a useful resource.

4. *Proposal should be well written.* This is, of course, easy to say but more difficult to do. Funders do not look favorably on proposals that have grammatical errors or are difficult to understand (e.g., procedures for implementation are not clear). The following tips may be helpful in thinking about this guideline:

- Use the terminology and organization suggested in the proposal application. If the application calls for a discussion of *objectives* followed by a plan *of implementation,* use those terms to identify those two sections of the proposal. If the application requires two specific types of evaluation (e.g., formative and summative), write the proposal to address those two dimensions. This is a place where creativity may count against the writer!
- Stay away from buzz words and avoid acronyms. Don't assume that reviewers understand educational language (e.g., CCSS, RTI). Explain what you mean by providing examples. Ask a friend who is not in education to read the proposal to help you identify confusing language.
- Follow the rules and address all questions. The submission should not have more than the required number of pages, it should arrive on or before the designated closing date, display the appropriate font size, and meet each requirement in the guidelines. The writer also needs to address the priorities mentioned in the proposal. If the funding is being offered for students who have been identified as living in high-poverty areas, receiving a proposal in which the population of students does not qualify as such will immediately disqualify it from consideration by the funding agency. Answer all questions asked in the application proposal. In a recent application, writers were asked to indicate how their project was aligned with the CCSS. For some proposals, the reviewing is done anonymously; thus, the writer's name and district should not be included in the application being submitted. Also, proposals being submitted will need signatures from the superintendent or another school official.

5. *Talk to funders.* It is appropriate to call and ask questions of those who want to fund proposals. After all, they have distributed a call for proposals, wanting to give funds to worthy recipients. Generally, they are

willing to answer questions about the proposal before the closing date. Grant writers should feel free to call or e-mail the funder to discuss their ideas or to raise questions about the proposal application itself. If there is a preproposal meeting scheduled for potential writers, it would be beneficial to attend those sessions. In one instance, Rita was able to collaborate with two educators from other universities in writing a PD proposal, because they had all attended the preproposal session and had an opportunity to sit and talk about their ideas.

6. *Solicit feedback.* Writing is a lonely task and, too often, writers think that what they have written is very clear! Soliciting feedback from a colleague is an excellent way to determine whether the content makes sense, whether there is enough detail, and whether there are any technical problems with the writing. The goal is to obtain constructive feedback based on a thoughtful, critical evaluation. Although it is not easy to have one's work criticized, we have found (most of the time) that reviewers can help you see where you have been unclear or where you can make some changes to strengthen the argument you are trying to make. Be willing to make your work public as a means of writing a strong proposal.

7. *Use effective formatting.* Although a great idea is very important, it can lose its luster in a poorly formatted presentation. A well-formatted proposal containing a great idea catches the eye and the mind of reviewers. Providing a table of contents and using section headings that guide the reader are important techniques to use. Likewise, use bold, italic, or underlining to highlight the important ideas. Graphics can help to clarify or embellish points made in the narrative text. Sometimes a figure or table can make your point stand out for the reviewer (e.g., table identifying the numbers of English learners in your school at each of the grade levels and their scores on a literacy assessment measure to illustrate the need for funding for a special program for these learners).

8. *Become familiar with the review criteria.* Proposal guidelines often include the criteria for proposal review (e.g., indicating the number of possible points awarded for each section). A smart proposal writer makes certain that each criterion is addressed and emphasizes the sections that are worth a significant number of points.

ELEMENTS OF A GRANT PROPOSAL

Most proposals require each of the elements or parts discussed below. When preparing to write a proposal, read all of the proposal guidelines, and then, after writing various sections, reread the guidelines again to determine whether each of the elements has been clearly addressed.

Goals and Objectives

All proposals require statements of goals or objectives for the potential project or program, even if some other elements may not be required in a specific proposal application. Some proposals require only broad goals (e.g., increase teachers' use of digital tools for teaching reading). In other applications, however, the writer must write objectives that indicate specifically what is going to change and by how much and when: "By the end of 5 years, we will improve the average comprehension performance of Title I students from 30 normal curve equivalents to 50."

Review of Literature

Depending on the funding source, the amount of funding offered, and the type of proposal (e.g., research) the funder may require a literature review. When there is a requirement for such a review, identify the relevant and current literature that (1) supports the need for the project you are proposing, and (2) summarizes current research on the proposed issue or project. For example, if a literacy specialist wants to develop a project for collaborating with preschool providers, a review of literature about the importance of early learning for young students and its impact on later reading achievement would be helpful to proposal reviewers. Such literature should include information about the need for additional knowledge in this area. Some funders do not require a literature review. However, you might use research to introduce your project and highlight its importance, given research evidence is an important component of any conceptual or practical literacy initiative.

Project Activities or Methods

In some proposal applications, there is a section titled "Design of the Project," "Project Activities," or "Methods." The general purpose is for writers to explain their ideas and plans. The activities or design must relate to the identified objectives or goals, and there must be clear evidence the plan will enable the school to reach those goals. Readers of the proposal should know exactly what will be done, when, and how. Examples are critical— let the readers know, by example, what will occur. Described below is an example of part of a Methods section:

> We plan to work with preschool providers in two ways. First, we will invite them to visit our kindergarten classrooms and then participate in a 2-hour discussion with the kindergarten teachers. Second, kindergarten teachers will visit classrooms in the preschool, and again, participate in a 2-hour discussion with preschool teachers. Our expectation is that participants will have

opportunities to address issues such as the following: What are the literacy expectations and standards in kindergarten and in what ways can preschool teachers prepare students for their kindergarten experience?; What experiences and activities are currently occurring in preschool programs, and how do they address the literacy needs of students?; How can each group of teachers be helpful to each other?

Creating a timeline for various activities is important not only to proposal reviewers, but also to the writer to identify exactly how and when each project or activity will be implemented. The timeline may be a required component of the grant proposal. Again, graphics or visuals can aid readers in understanding the plan of operation.

Personnel

Funders want to know who will work on the project and what skills and experiences they have that enable them to accomplish the planned work. So, for example, carefully describe the expertise of educators involved in the project, such as teaching experience, prior grant experience, professional activities (e.g., presentations, publications), consulting. Providing specifics about qualifications helps to assure funders that there is the expertise necessary to undertake the project. Likewise, the application may call for an iteration of the resources or capabilities of the organization or institution with which the writer is affiliated. What technology resources are available to assist in data analysis? Does the institution have an evaluation department to assess the success of the project? Are there other personnel who might be helpful with the project (e.g., director of curriculum, librarian)?

Evaluation

Almost all proposals call for some form of evaluation indicating how the writer will determine to what extent educators have accomplished the goals of the funded grant. Evaluation plans run the gamut from simple to complex. Some proposals require districts to agree to participate in specific evaluation activities, such as classroom observations and administration of specific assessment tests to be given at various times. The two types of evaluation that may be required—formative and summative—are described below.

Formative

Formative evaluation requires ongoing documentation of what occurs. This type of evaluation is often used to make midproject corrections or adjustments; in other words, to learn from what has transpired. Formative evaluation might include documentation logs of various meetings (i.e., when they occurred and who attended) and a summary of evaluation forms completed by attendees indicating their level of satisfaction with the meetings.

Summative

The summative evaluation provides the results, impact, or outcomes of the project; for example, the effects of the preschool–kindergarten project on participants (e.g., students, teachers, parents). The evaluation may also call for "deliverables"; a manual or listing of activities developed as a result of the project. Often, with summative evaluation, we think of effects as "changes" that have occurred. For example, a writer might propose the possibility of specific changes in teacher classroom practices. Likewise, various pretests and posttests can be administered to students to determine whether there are differences in reading performance or attitudes toward reading after the implementation of the project. In addition to documenting ongoing efforts, you might ask teachers and parents to respond to a final questionnaire, and use results of an assessment (e.g., reading tests) to determine the impact of a project.

Budget

All proposals require a budget outlining the requested amount of funds and how the project will use those funds. For example, a budget submission may be as simple as requesting $500 to purchase books, increasing a school's collection of literature written by and about people of different ethnicities. Or, the budget may be somewhat more complex, such as identifying costs for various activities (e.g., purchasing technology tools to facilitate virtual discussions among teachers, specialists, and coaches). Large proposals may require budgets including costs for personnel, supplies, materials, travel, and so on. In some instances, the writer must include indirect or overhead costs; that is, the amount the institution will charge for housing the grant. This item covers such necessities as lighting, office space, and computer accessibility. Generally, in a school context, the school district or institution has a specific amount or percentage identified. Sometimes the funding agency supplies a ceiling amount or indicates they do not pay overhead costs at all. Often this is the case with foundations. Finally, always note what the grant will and will not fund with grant monies (e.g., teacher salaries, refreshments). Some grants will ask that writers indicate how the district receiving the grant will contribute to its ongoing implementation (e.g., grant will provide monies for summer stipends for faculty attending workshops; district will provide cost of substitutes during the school year).

Dissemination Plan

Some proposals require that writers discuss how they will share the information they learn with others. Writers might indicate that they will present at conferences, submit a manuscript for publication, initiate PL workshops, or produce a deliverable to be distributed to various institutions and educators.

Continuation or Sustainability Plans

Although not always a required part of a proposal application, many funding agencies (especially foundations) ask for continuation plans because they are interested in the sustainability of various projects. Can they be assured that if they provide monies for a special project, such as a summer program, that the institution will then find a way to continue such an effort? Will grant activities be integrated into the curriculum or instruction? Often, funders are discouraged that projects are disbanded as soon as the funding is gone. Grants frequently require writers to discuss how they will sustain their literacy efforts.

Abstract

The all-important abstract, which is the beginning of the proposal submission, is best written after the rest of the proposal is complete. Only now is the writer ready to summarize, in a few lucid paragraphs, the exact plans. The abstract must catch the reader's eye (the value of a first impression) and identify the goals and activities of the proposed plan succinctly and clearly. It may also include an overview of the evaluation approaches.

SOURCES FOR FUNDING

Locating the right funding agency is important. Many different sources of funding can be investigated to determine whether various grant possibilities exist. Generally, the education department in the state posts announcements about various state or federal funding possibilities on its website; they may also list grants available from various foundations or corporations for specific issues (e.g., community projects, library work, family literacy). Newsletters and websites of various professional organizations are also excellent sources for obtaining information about support (e.g., Association for Supervision and Curriculum Development, ILA, National Council of Teachers of English). Local and national foundations often have calls for proposals on websites; foundation directories describing goals and purposes of these philanthropic organizations are also available. Some local foundations provide mini-grant opportunities for teachers. These grants generally provide smaller amounts of money ($1,000–$5,000), but they provide opportunities for teachers to generate unique and creative ideas to promote student learning. The ILA, for example, awards $5,000 for research on reading and writing (i.e., Elva Knight Research Grant).

One of the best ways to seek funding is to work collaboratively with another institution in the local area, such as a university, library, or community agency. Funding agencies look favorably upon such collaborative efforts because the unique contributions made by each partner strengthen a proposal. For example, a university can assist in the evaluation of a project designed by a school district. Or the school district and community library can work together to design a summer reading program for readers experiencing difficulties.

PROFESSIONAL DECISIONS

A chapter on professional contributions should not end on a negative note. However, the reality is that there are many literacy professionals seeking grant funding, manuscript acceptance, opportunities to present at a conference, and other professional activities. Receiving a rejection is not uncommon; we have both experienced it! If you receive a notice of acceptance or even a revise/resubmit, celebrate it!! If you receive a rejection note, remember that it can be very helpful. In some cases, reviews might help you realize that your major idea is new to you but not as new to others in the field— think about how you can read further to expand your ideas. Reviewers' comments can be used to rewrite and resubmit—either in a different funding cycle, or to another funding agency, conference, or publisher. Writing the grant proposal enables the writer to cultivate a relationship with the funding agency and learn expectations from the proposal scoring rubric to increase the potential for later success. Similarly, reading the reviews on a journal manuscript or conference proposal may give you specific ideas on how to revise the content. The second time around can be successful!

SUMMARY

This chapter provided an overview of how literacy professionals can share their voice in professional communities, using a grant proposal as a case example. Literacy professionals can make important contributions to the literacy field by sharing their knowledge through presentations, publications, and seeking funding to implement creative ideas.

ADDITIONAL READINGS

Jakob, E., Porter, A., Podos, J., Braun, B., Johnson, N., & Vessey, S. (2010, December). How to fail in grant writing. Retrieved from *http://chronicle.com/article/How-to-Fail-in-Grant-Writing/125620.*—A humorous collection of tips about what not to do when writing grant applications.

Rothstein, A. L. (2019). *Creating winning grant proposals: A step-by-step guide.* New York: Guilford Press.—A useful book that lays out each component of the grant proposal writing process, including a range of websites for funding and more information.

● REFLECTIONS

1. Drawing on your interests and those you share with colleagues, make a list of how your voice might make an important contribution to current issues in the literacy field.

2. What opportunities to become involved with proposal writing are available to you in your current position?

3. What grants has your school received, for what, and from what agencies? What have the evaluation requirements in those grants required of your school?

● ACTIVITIES

1. Go to your state's department of education website. Locate available grant possibilities to see what is being funded at the state level. Read one of the requests for proposals (RFPs) and compare its elements with those described in this chapter. Be prepared to discuss what you learned with colleagues.

2. Interview someone who writes proposals to get his or her ideas about what it takes to write a successful one. Be prepared to discuss what you learned in class or with your colleagues.

3. Consider a literacy concept or practice that is particularly important to you. What steps might you take to share your expertise and knowledge on the topic? Attend a local/state conference to see how other literacy professionals share information with colleagues.

4. Find mentor texts for the type of writing you wish to accomplish—successful grants, journal articles, website blogs, conference proposals, etc. Look carefully at the features of expectations for a particular document and consider joining a professional writing community to get started on your writing project.

CHAPTER TWELVE

The Literacy Specialist as Lifelong Learner
ADDRESSING CHANGES AND CHALLENGES

KEY QUESTIONS ● ● ● ● ● ● ● ● ● ● ● ● ● ● ● ● ● ●

● In what ways might literacy specialists continue their PL to remain knowledgeable of current changes and challenges?

● What might literacy specialists expect to learn within a literacy specialist certification program?

● When searching for a position, how can literacy specialists prepare for interviews?

Marshall McLuhan once remarked about the hazards of driving forward, looking through the rear-view mirror to illustrate the effects of past experience on current and future behavior (McLuhan & Fiore, 1967). This statement also applies to literacy specialists who have served students in schools in many ways throughout the years—as supervisors of literacy programs, remedial teachers, resource teachers, interventionists, or literacy coaches. After reading this book, it should be apparent that the roles of literacy professionals vary and are greatly influenced by the contexts in which they work. Further, the roles are changing constantly, with new knowledge about literacy, assessment, learning, and changes in student demographics and with politics and policies. Also, the role is defined by job descriptions, administrative preferences, school needs, funding, and the literacy specialists' own experiences and strengths.

308

Along with the different roles, there are also differences in titles: reading or literacy specialist, literacy or instructional coach, interventionist, facilitator, and literacy consultant, among others. Yet the underlying goal for literacy specialists remains one of promoting literacy achievement for *all* students, and especially for those who experience difficulty with reading or writing (ILA, 2018a, 2019a). Literacy professionals can accomplish this goal in several ways, from delivering instruction to students to working with teachers to improve classroom instruction to developing schoolwide literacy programs.

The chapters in this book addressed the many functions of literacy specialists and those they may be asked to assume in the future, as responsibilities and roles change. For example, many literacy specialists who previously worked with students only are currently serving as reading or literacy coaches in their schools. The greatest challenge for literacy specialists is to be prepared for changes that may occur. Indeed, change may be generated or initiated by specialists themselves, who see that they can affect student performance more effectively in new and different ways. Read about how Pam reflected on her first year and thought about next steps for her literacy role.

Although Pam was somewhat anxious about her upcoming meeting with the principal during which they were to discuss her yearly performance, she was also excited. Ms. Walker had always been positive in her interactions with Pam, and Pam appreciated the thoughtful insights the principal shared with her during their bimonthly meetings. As Pam walked away from the performance meeting, her excitement grew. Not only was Ms. Walker pleased with her work, she told Pam that she considered her to be an important leader in the school. Ms. Walker gave her specific feedback that supported Pam's efforts during this first year: Teachers felt that Pam worked as a partner, helping them to make improvements in their literacy instruction; she was fun to work with; had great ideas; and the teachers hoped that she would continue to work with them the following year. Ms. Walker asked Pam about her plans for ongoing learning. Where did she see herself in 5 years? That question gave Pam a lot to think about! She was pleased that she had signed up for a course during the summer— one that focused on increasing her knowledge about coaching and leadership. She knew she would be ready to attend that class—after a well-deserved vacation at the beach. She took a deep breath—what a wonderful year! Thank you students and teachers for making my first year a terrific experience.

PROFESSIONAL LEARNING FOR LITERACY SPECIALISTS

Professional learning for literacy specialists, as for teachers, occurs in many different ways (e.g., reading professional materials, either print or digital tools; formal participation in classes, both face-to-face and online courses; workshops held by the district or state; conferences and sessions of professional groups; networking with other literacy specialists or coaches; participating in blog discussions). When literacy specialists spearhead PL sessions for teachers, they learn a great deal by investigating, studying, and preparing presentations. In many schools, literacy specialists may also lead or participate in study groups in which they discuss a specific book pertinent to educational concerns or goals. Participation in groups in which teachers and literacy specialists discuss something they have read (e.g., ILA research briefs, Institute of Education Sciences [IES] practice guides, books) generates new ideas and expands knowledge of pertinent topics. Appendix D includes examples of websites we used throughout the book, many of which might be helpful for PL purposes.

Professional Organizations

Many literacy specialists choose to continue their formal education by taking classes at a university or attending professional meetings. We encourage literacy specialists to join, and become active in, one or more professional organizations to facilitate ongoing learning and sustained motivation. Or, a specialist may become a member of a local and state literacy association as well as the ILA (*www.literacyworldwide.org*) or the National Council of Teachers of English (NCTE; *www.ncte.org*), whose professional journals, websites, and other resources are invaluable to practicing literacy specialists. Other professional organizations to consider for membership, depending on grade level or school responsibilities may include:

- American Library Association (*www.ala.org*)
- Association for Supervision and Curriculum Development (*www. ascd.org*)
- Association of Literacy Educators (*www.aleronline.org*)
- International Society for Technology in Education (*www.iste.org*)
- Learning Forward (*www.learningforward.org*)
- Literacy Research Association (*www.literacyresearchassociation. org*)
- National Association for the Education of Young Children (*www. naeyc.org*)
- National Board for Professional Teaching Standards (*www.nbpts. org*)
- Association for Middle Level Education (*www.amle.org*)

Professional Reading

In addition to attending meetings of professional groups and PL activities in schools, literacy specialists can read professional journals and books as a means of keeping current, not only about literacy instruction and assessment but to understand the political and social climate in which they work. Given the amount of information available in print and electronically, literacy specialists must be able to evaluate the credibility of the information they are reading, especially when related to research findings. Figure 12.1, an infographic published by the IES, describes sources that might be considered credible (Regional Educational Laboratory Southeast, 2019).

Often, literature in a related area (e.g., leadership, school change) or even from another field (e.g., business, sociology) can provide a new way of thinking or looking at an educational issue. In addition, reports from the U.S. government or other agencies synthesizing research on various aspects of literacy provide important information about current trends or research emphases. Important sources of information for literacy specialists include the What Works Clearinghouse (*www.ies.ed.gov/ncee/wwc*) and the Center on Instruction (*www.centeroninstruction.org*). In each chapter in this book, we also identify key articles, resources, or research reports specific to the topic of that chapter. Other key reports that may be helpful to literacy specialists include:

- Practice guides found on the What Works Clearinghouse website (*www.ies.ed.gov/ncee/wwc*)
- Leadership and research briefs published by the ILA (*www.literacyworldwide.org*)
- *Report of the National Reading Panel* (National Institute of Child Health and Human Development, 2000)
- *Reading Next* (Biancarosa & Snow, 2004)
- *Adolescent Literacy* (Ippolito et al., 2012)
- *Developing Early Literacy: Report of the National Early Literacy Panel* (National Institute of Child Health and Human Development, 2010)
- *Report of the National Literacy Panel on Language Minority Children and Youth* (August & Shanahan, 2006)

Online resources provide much useful information to specialists for their own professional learning. The websites of each professional organization (ILA, NCTE) also make available position statements, articles, and reference lists useful to literacy specialists; in previous chapters, we cited many of the position statements of the ILA as sources of learning about various topics.

Sources of educational research

Decision-makers contend with information about educational interventions and programs claiming to be effective for improving students' learning. However, not all of those claims are supported by high-quality research. Decision-makers and practitioners need to be able to effectively review the research base.

MORE CREDIBLE

Academic books

BENEFITS
- In-depth and broad examination of a topic but with a focused view
- Include citations and bibliographies and many include original research

LIMITATIONS
- Less current; longer lag between an event, idea or discovery and a book's publication
- Intended for an academic or technical audience (e.g., researchers, academics, students, and professionals) and not for general readers

Academic journals

BENEFITS
- Narrowly focused topic
- Include citations and bibliographies
- Include original research critically evaluated by peers*

LIMITATIONS
- Usually offer a more current view than books but not as current as newspapers and magazines
- Intended for an academic or technical audience and not for general readers

LESS CREDIBLE

Newspapers, popular magazines, and television

BENEFITS
- Cover recent developments and events
- Intended for general audience without any particular expertise or advanced education

LIMITATIONS
- Limited coverage without much historical overview or context
- Rarely include citations and bibliographies; may refer to research studies, but do not contain original research

Popular press books

BENEFITS
- Offer more information regarding a specific topic
- More likely to include citations and bibliographies than newspapers, popular magazines,or television

LIMITATIONS
- Intent is often to entertain or inform in a broad, general sense
- Often do not contain original research
- Published by a commercial publisher

*What is peer review?

Peer review provides a measure of quality control, however, not all education journals are peer-reviewed. Many peer-reviewed articles include an abstract, literature review, methodology, results, conclusion, and references sections. They seldom contain advertisements and will sometimes include publication information such as date of initial submission, date for revisions, and final acceptance date.

Accessing research-based information

Google Scholar focuses on the scholarly literature available on the Internet and includes articles, theses, books, abstracts, government resources, professional societies, online repositories, and more.

The What Works Clearinghouse is a central and trusted source of scientific evidence for what works in education.

ERIC is an index of materials, many of which are free and peer-reviewed, that can help support the work of education policymakers.

Information in this infographic is supported by IES/NCEE's Regional Educational Laboratory Southeast at Florida State University (Contract ED-IES-17-C-0011) as resources and examples for the viewer's convenience. Their inclusion is not intended as an endorsement by the Regional Educational Laboratory Southeast or its funding source, the Institute of Education Sciences.

In addition, the instructional practices shown in this infographic are not intended to mandate, direct, or control a State's, local educational agency's, or school's specific instructional content, academic achievement system and assessments, curriculum, or program of instruction. State and local programs may use any instructional content, achievement system and assessments, curriculum, or program of instruction they wish.

REL
SOUTHEAST
Regional Educational Laboratory
at Florida State University

ies
NATIONAL CENTER FOR
EDUCATION EVALUATION
AND REGIONAL ASSISTANCE
Institute of Education Scien

FIGURE 12.1. Sources of educational research: IES infographic.

Literacy specialists and literacy coaches in the recent national study (Bean, Kern, et al., 2015) highlighted the importance of role-alike groups (e.g., network of coaches) as a means of learning. New coaches especially indicated that these networks provided an important source of learning; they were able to identify problems or issues and more experienced peers provided alternatives for next steps. Such groups may meet in face-to-face discussion settings, or in a range of digital opportunities, including Facebook groups, Twitter chats, and Zoom meetings. Groups of coaches, working in the same district, benefit if they have opportunities to talk about their challenges and to describe specific ways in which they can address them. Rita, working with coaches in one school district, found that most of the challenges for this group of coaches focused on improving their ability to work with teachers (e.g., supporting a novice teacher who had little understanding of a particular strategy, encouraging a teacher to become more engaged with her students). Not only did the group generate some solutions to these coaching dilemmas, but the coaches recognized that they were not alone in having to address these dilemmas.

Groups of literacy specialists can also meet on a regular basis to share resources and discuss ideas and challenges. In the Pittsburgh region, specialists from several districts meet in the early evening at one of their homes, on a monthly basis, to share ideas and a light meal. They appreciate the opportunities to socialize and to learn from each other. In many of their schools, they are the only specialist, and they appreciate talking with those who have similar positions.

The specialized literacy professionals whose vignettes appear in "Voices from the Field" are examples of educators who are lifelong learners. All have participated in formal education to obtain advanced degrees, all attend and present at various conferences and workshops, and all are readers who keep abreast of what is occurring in their field. Most of all, they are passionate about their profession and eager to learn all they can to improve instruction for the students in their schools.

LOCAL, STATE, AND FEDERAL GUIDELINES

Educators in today's schools face many challenging and complex political and social issues. Literacy specialists can advocate for students, literacy education, and for schools in which they work. To do so, they must keep current about the various school-related legislative actions and policies at local, state, and federal levels. As described in previous chapters, federal and state legislation has had a tremendous impact on schools. Recent policies have influenced selection of assessment tools, accountability for individual teachers and for schools, learning standards, and curriculum and instruction at all levels. Also, literacy specialists can work with their professional groups to bring important educational issues that affect literacy instruction and assessment to the attention of legislators (e.g., importance of support for preschool education, early literacy instruction, equity issues related to technology access, literacy coaching in schools). Moreover, because so many literacy specialists are funded with monies from Title I legislation, they need to be aware of the regulations of that program and how they affect literacy instruction in schools.

Rules and regulations in each state influence literacy curriculum, assessment, and instruction at all levels. The emphasis on standards, either the CCSS, or those approved by the state, creates a need for literacy specialists to be familiar with state standards so they can assist teacher colleagues in implementing an instructional program addressing those standards. Most states have websites containing resources and other information useful for developing professional development and for addressing policy initiatives.

As mentioned in Chapter 5, literacy specialists should share information with teachers with whom they work. In addition to the ideas described above, one helpful source that provides an update about many trends in education is the publication *Education Week* (*www.edweek.org*). A school subscription to that resource keeps educators aware of what is happening at the national level in the field of education and literacy specifically.

LIFELONG LEARNING: A NECESSITY FOR LITERACY SPECIALISTS

All those who work in schools must be lifelong learners; there is always something new to learn—new materials, new approaches, and new students! Given the many variables that affect the position of literacy specialist and the changes that may occur from year to year within a school—some prescribed by legislation or school needs, others from recommendations by literacy specialists themselves—literacy specialists must remain lifelong learners. The ideas below may be helpful in thinking about being a lifelong learner.

Set Learning Goals

Some specialists may want to involve families more actively in school programs or to work more closely with teachers of content; others may want to improve their knowledge of a specific topic (e.g., use of technology as a tool for improving literacy learning). Whatever the specific goal, the literacy specialist can identify activities to facilitate its achievement and set a deadline for accomplishment. Attending one or more conferences, reading several articles or books about the topic, and then meeting and sharing the information with teachers (e.g., possibly forming a study group) are examples of lifelong learning activities. Goals can be *personal* ones: For example, a literacy specialist may enroll in a program to obtain literacy coaching endorsement or attend the research conference at the national meeting of the ILA to stay abreast of current research efforts. Goals can also be ones related to school efforts or needs: For example, in one middle school, there may be an effort to enhance literacy instruction across the academic disciplines, or in a primary school, the goal may be to increase teachers' understanding of the best ways to instruct ELs. In these instances, literacy specialists may choose to identify PL activities that enable them to assist teachers and other professionals in the schools to achieve those goals. Summer is often a good time to read a new book about literacy, language, or learning. It is also an excellent time to join a book club (from within your district or including educators from other areas) to discuss a book with other educators interested in the same topic, perhaps while sitting around the pool, in another relaxed setting, or via video conferencing.

The beginning of the school year is a good time to set goals for your teaching in a specific school and is often a required component of the yearly annual evaluation process. Thinking about areas in which you have been successful, where you have had some difficulties, or perhaps "new" areas to explore (e.g., digital learning) may help you set goals for the school year. You may want to identify individuals who can help you with your goals and the resources needed to accomplish them. It may be useful to write these goals in a journal so you can review them throughout the year, or in a more systematic format to show others what you learned.

Be Prepared to Change or Modify Past or Current Practices

Perspectives and times change and so must we! One of the most difficult steps for all of us is to realize that we may have to give up familiar practices to make changes that will make us more effective in our roles. Literacy specialists who have always worked in a pullout setting may find it difficult to switch to working in the classroom. They may even grieve a little as they lose what they have always found to be a comfortable and rewarding approach to instruction. Grieving is fine, but it is important to *move on* and experience the rewards of the new and different. Research findings contribute to change, with new information and knowledge about literacy learning and assessment influencing how we organize schools and how we teach. Literacy specialists can serve as models for teachers who may also find it necessary to modify classroom practices when confronting notions that conflict with their present beliefs about teaching or learning. In Chapter 1, we wrote about the need to be nimble, that is, able to change practices or roles, given new situations or responsibilities. John F. Kennedy (1963) in an address in Frankfurt, Germany, made this statement: "Change is the law of life. And those who look only to the past or the present are certain to miss the future," reminding us of the inevitability of change.

Self-Recognition

All of us appreciate the rewards and recognition that come from others— the principal who commends your work with readers experiencing difficulties, the teacher who tells you that she was better able to facilitate class discussions because of the planning work that you and she did together, the mother who thanks you for the positive effect you have had on her child, or the student who leaves a note: "Mrs. Blake, you're the greatest." Similarly, literacy specialists need to pat themselves on the back for what they have accomplished regarding their own learning. After reading a professional book on assessment approaches for classroom teachers, it may be time to reward yourself for a job well done: a special dinner, a week without any professional reading (just a good mystery), going to the gym, or perhaps buying a new pair of shoes. Whatever works for you!

See Challenges as Opportunities

There will always be challenges and problems within the school setting that need the attention of the literacy specialist (e.g., working with a teacher who is hesitant to change, improving writing performance, planning a PL program for middle school content teachers, supporting teachers in leading effective remote learning activities). Viewing these demands or problems as opportunities for generating active thinking, group interaction, and the possibility of new and exciting ventures is a better approach than seeing them as burdens or obstacles. Large-scale efforts involving large numbers of people will produce disagreements and questions, but as indicated by Fullan, Bertani, and Quinn (2004), productive conflict is to be expected! Being receptive and listening to divergent ideas can be helpful in solving problems and moving the school in a positive direction (Berger, 2019).

Self-Reflection

Chapter 5 discusses the importance of teacher reflection to personal learning. Likewise, literacy specialists can take time to reflect on, and think about, what they have been doing, what they have learned, and what this learning means for future behavior. Recently, a teacher who had just completed a PL experience expressed this thought: "It's more than learning a lot of strategies. It's thinking in a different way." Her statement revealed that she was taking the time to reflect not only on her teaching methods—on what worked and what did not work—but also to consider the ways in which she approached teaching and learning. That reflection provided her with the impetus to seek new solutions to classroom problems. Taking the time for reflection means setting time aside, perhaps at the end of the day or the end of the week, to think about what happened and why, and the impact of that experience on future behavior. Some literacy specialists and coaches keep logs as a means of self-reflection; they can then look back and think about how they allocated their time, their responses to various events, and use these written records as a means of making positive changes. Figure 12.2 illustrates a partial log of one elementary literacy specialist.

For those working as literacy coaches at the elementary or secondary levels, a self-assessment rubric, titled *Adopting a Coaching Mindset,* can be found in Bean and Ippolito (2016). Those completing the rubric can score themselves as emerging, developing, or proficient and identify their own strengths and needs on 18 items categorized into seven domains.

By being a lifelong learner, the literacy specialist models for others in the school the behavior that is necessary for the school as an organization to change in order to become more effective. Leaders within a school provide the impetus for others to become lifelong learners.

BECOMING A LITERACY SPECIALIST

When we ask those who enter the literacy specialist certification program at our institutions why they have chosen to do so, they often tell us that they have become curious about students in their classrooms who have literacy difficulties and wonder how they can better help them to achieve. Some tell us that they feel unprepared to teach literacy, given the few courses with that emphasis in their teacher preparation programs. Some want to work especially with students experiencing reading or writing difficulties, whereas others are clear that they do not really want to leave the classroom; rather they want to become more proficient at teaching literacy and meeting the needs of all students in their classrooms. Others are eager to work with student experiencing literacy difficulties yet have no desire to work with classroom teachers; they are hesitant to step out of their comfort zone to work with other adults.

These are all good reasons for entering a literacy specialist preparation program. Most universities have well-developed programs that meet the standards required of their state and of the ILA (2018a). Such programs require students to become knowledgeable about the underlying theoretical bases for literacy development and acquisition, literacy assessment and instruction, and issues related to leadership and working with others. They usually require students to participate in practica or clinical experiences in which they demonstrate that they can fulfill the requirements of the

Harry

What I Did Today	Comments/Reflections
Morning Pullout class of five fourth graders (using informational text; focus on "during text" understandings and inferences).	Group works well together (good discussion and thinking). Science text on reptiles worked well because of student interest; get similar text specific to snakes (they were fascinated).
Met with sixth-grade teachers to discuss results of writing samples from their classes. What can we do to improve students' ability to summarize from their reading? Teachers felt need for some "input" and were very receptive to this.	I need to check my resources and get some material that they can read. The IES Practice Guide that I downloaded has four recommendations and some of them may be useful for our teachers. I'm going to consider discussing the recommendations and also sharing the strategies identified on pages 314 to 317 in that guide (Graham et al., 2012).
Worked in classroom of fifth-grade social studies teacher; how to introduce vocabulary and set a purpose (we co-taught this introduction).	Sam is excited about this; he wants me to continue working with him (wonder if he would be willing to do more with small group to get kids engaged). Will discuss with him and get his ideas; what are his goals for students (important!)?
Afternoon Planning for workshop on differentiation of instruction for all intermediate teachers.	Yikes! I need to focus on what my goals are. What do I want teachers to know and be able to do? What are they ready to do—next steps?
Meeting with principal to go over test results (which I discussed with sixth-grade teachers this morning).	She is concerned about writing test coming up in several months. Wants me to be sure to work with these sixth-grade teachers. (I need time—and they do too!) Asked her whether the workshop on differentiation should be postponed. Should we focus on writing? Too many directions for teachers. She agreed!

FIGURE 12.2. Partial log of a literacy specialist.

position. Most offer many practical experiences as an integral part of their programs, so that literacy specialist candidates become proficient in working both with students experiencing literacy difficulties and with teachers. As completion of the program draws near, candidates begin to think about applying for positions as a literacy specialist. They are curious about possible questions a school district may ask in an interview and how they can prepare for the application process. In Appendix E, we share questions that may be part of a job interview. Candidates for a literacy specialist position may wish to think about the questions and how they would answer them. Those in a literacy specialist certification program may role-play an interview in class, using some of the questions identified.

In addition to acquiring the knowledge and understanding needed to become a literacy specialist, another important attribute of any candidate for such a position is enthusiasm. School district personnel want to employ individuals who are excited and enthusiastic about becoming a literacy specialist and having the opportunity to make a difference for all the students in a school. Before an interview, candidates for positions may want to reread the notes that they have taken in their coursework. They may also want to read several articles that describe roles of literacy specialists.

In this book, we suggested additional readings at the end of each chapter, including some choices that provide more in-depth information about the role of literacy specialists. Several key articles that may be helpful include Galloway and Lesaux (2014), who summarize the research and describe the many roles of the literacy specialist; Bean and Kern (2018), who discuss the ILA 2017 Standards and the ways in which they influence the many roles of specialized literacy professionals; and L'Allier and colleagues' (2010) article, in which they discuss the coaching role of literacy specialists. Appendix F expands on activity suggestions with additional ideas for course and workshop instructors, including thinking through the roles and responsibilities of literacy specialists. Rereading the vignettes of the literacy specialists in this book and the case example of Pam may also provide candidates with a better idea of literacy specialists' roles and responsibilities. These literacy specialists in "Voices from the Field" exhibit passion and enthusiasm for their positions, regardless of challenges or problems.

SUMMARY

This chapter described ways in which literacy specialists can continue their learning and become lifelong learners, including the importance of familiarity with federal, state, and local legislation. We also discussed what literacy specialist candidates might expect in a preparation program and ideas for participating in a job interview for the literacy specialist position.

ADDITIONAL READINGS

Collet, V. (2018). *Breaking down the coaching barriers.* Retrieved from *https://blog.teachboost.com/breaking-down-the-coaching-barriers.*—In this blog, the author discusses ways of working effectively with teachers. She describes several ideas, including offering choice, being vulnerable, and performing acts of kindness. The notions in the blog can be useful for all specialists who work with teachers.

Crow, T. (2014). The pause that refreshes. *Learning Forward, 35*(3), 4.—In this brief editorial, Crow offers a suggestion on how to enhance PL and writing, including taking time to pause and reflect.

Ippolito, J., Bean, R. M., Kern, D., & Swan Dagen, A. (2019). Specialists, coaches, coordinators, oh my!: Looking back and looking forward on the roles and responsibilities of specialized literacy professionals. *Primer, 47*(2), 19–29.— The authors look back at the roles and responsibilities of reading specialists, and then look forward by discussing the ILA Standards (2018a) and their implications for the role of the literacy specialist. They also present information from a recent study describing perceptions of principals and specialized literacy professionals about the multiple aspects of the specialized literacy professional role.

● REFLECTIONS

1. Which type of learning—formal or informal—is most appealing to you, given where you are in your professional career? How can you take advantage of the opportunities that are available to you?

2. Think about the ideas suggested for those who are lifelong learners. Identify an area where you want to learn more, and develop a plan for doing so. Set a goal, develop a plan of action, set a deadline—and plan for a reward.

● ACTIVITIES

1. Organize a study group in which you and several others agree to read and discuss a specific article or book that addresses an issue or problem in your school or setting.

2. Participate in a role play of a job interview, using the questions in Appendix E.

APPENDIX A. Coaching Summary Sheet: The Observation Cycle

Teacher/Coach: _____ Grade/Subject Area: _____ Date: _____

PLANNING

Goals of lesson (What do you expect students to learn?):

Purpose of observation (What do you, teacher, hope to learn? What is the focus of the observation?):

What will students be doing? (What should I expect to see? What would you like me to look for?):

_____

ANALYSIS (Key points [related to goals set by teacher])—TO BE USED FOR DISCUSSION

_____

FOLLOW-UP   Date:
Teacher:

Coach:

_____

APPENDIX B. Observation Protocol for Content-Area Instruction

Teacher/Coach: _____   **Grade:** _____

Date: _____   **Start time:** _____   **End time:** _____

 # Students present: _____   **Content area:** _____

Lesson focus: _____

Materials: (Check all that apply)

☐ Textbook   Grouping: (Check all that apply)

☐ Board/Chart   ☐ Whole Class

☐ Computer   ☐ Small Group

☐ Worksheet   ☐ Pairs

☐ Student Work   ☐ Individual

☐ Other: _____

Protocol to be used as a guide. Scale to be completed after the observation has been completed.

Scale:	Great Extent	Some Extent	Minimal Extent	Not Observed
	(4)	(3)	(2)	(1)
Classroom Environment				
Materials supporting literacy are available *Books, visuals, print and nonprint materials about topic are evident*	☐	☐	☐	☐
Provides for social interaction *Areas for small-group/partner work*	☐	☐	☐	☐
Strategies for learning are displayed *Informative, positive strategies (e.g., why and how of summarizing)*	☐	☐	☐	☐

(continued)

Scale:	Great Extent	Some Extent	Minimal Extent	Not Observed
	(4)	(3)	(2)	(1)
Instruction				
<u>Before Reading</u>				
Sets purpose, makes connections, development of vocabulary	☐	☐	☐	☐
Small-group discussion	☐	☐	☐	☐
Engages in coaching/scaffolding, teacher models strategies	☐	☐	☐	☐
<u>During Reading</u>				
Think-alouds by teacher, connects to students' experiences, points out text features	☐	☐	☐	☐
Questioning that requires high-level thinking, engages in coaching/scaffolding	☐	☐	☐	☐
<u>After Reading</u>				
Small-group discussion or writing activities that require responding to text	☐	☐	☐	☐
Activities require high-level thinking	☐	☐	☐	☐
Opportunities for differentiation to meet student needs	☐	☐	☐	☐
Teacher monitors and supports student work	☐	☐	☐	☐

Scale:	Great Extent	Some Extent	Minimal Extent	Not Observed
	(4)	(3)	(2)	(1)
Classroom Climate/Engagement of Students				
High level of student participation *Students are actively engaged*	☐	☐	☐	☐
Positive learning environment *Interactions are respectful and supportive, encourages risk taking*	☐	☐	☐	☐
Students use strategies to learn *Evidence of students knowing when, how, and which strategies to use (e.g., note taking, summarizing)*	☐	☐	☐	☐
Students show evidence of being able to think about their own learning *Provide justification for thinking, evidence of being able to organize own learning*	☐	☐	☐	☐

Notes:

APPENDIX C. Sample Observation Form

Teacher's name: _____ **Grade level:** _____ **Date:** _____

Start time: _____ **End time:** _____ **Number of students:** _____

Focus of lesson: _____

Grouping: Whole class ____ **Small group** ____ **Individual** _____

Overall impressions of environment:

Teacher	Students	Observer Comments

APPENDIX D. Website Resources

PROFESSIONAL ORGANIZATIONS

- Alliance for Excellent Education: *www.all4ed.org*
- American Library Association: *www.ala.org*
- Association for Middle Level Education: *www.amle.org*
- Association for Supervision and Curriculum Development: *www.ascd.org*
- Association of Literacy Educators: *www.aleronline.org*
- International Society for Technology in Education: *www.iste.org*
- International Dyslexia Association: *https://dyslexiaida.org*
- International Literacy Association: *www.literacyworldwide.org*
- Learning Forward: *www.learningforward.org*
- Literacy Research Association: *www.literacyresearchassociation.org*
- National Association for the Education of Young Children: *www.naeyc.org*
- National Board for Professional Teaching Standards: *www.nbpts.org*
- National Council of Teachers of English: *www.ncte.org*
- National Writing Project: *www.nwp.org*

STATE AND FEDERAL GOVERNMENT RESOURCES

- Massachusetts Department of Education calibration videos: *www.doe.mass.edu/edeval/resources/calibration/videos.html*
- National Clearinghouse for English Language Acquisition: *www.ncela.ed.gov*
- NYSED New topics briefs: Linguistically diverse learners and the NYS Next Generation P–12 Learning Standards: *www.nysed.gov/bilingual-ed/linguistically-diverse-learners-and-nys-next-generation-p-12-learning-standards*
- NYSED Professional Learning Plan—Guidance Document: *www.nysed.gov/common/nysed/files/programs/postsecondary-services/plp-guidance.pdf*
- What Works Clearinghouse: *www.ies.ed.gov/ncee/wwc*
- What Works Clearinghouse (IES) Practice Guides: *https://ies.ed.gov/ncee/wwc/practiceguides*

CENTERS AND NETWORKS

- Center on Instruction: *www.centeroninstruction.org*
- Child Research and Study Center: *https://isaprofessionaldevelopment.org*
- Florida Center for Reading Research: *www.fcrr.org*
- International Society for Technology in Education Standards: *www.iste.org/standards*
- National Center for Adult Literacy and the International Literacy Institute: *www.literacy.org*

- National Center on Intensive Instruction: *https://intensiveintervention.org/audience/educators*
- National Center on Response to Intervention: *www.RTI4success.org*
- RTI Action Network: *www.RTInetwork.org*
- School, Family, Community Partnerships: *www.partnershipschools.org*
- School Reform Initiative: *www.schoolreforminitiative.org*

INSTRUCTIONAL RESOURCES

- International Literacy Association: Choices Reading Lists: *www.literacyworldwide.org/get-resources/reading-lists*
- Literacy Collaborative: *http://literacycollaborative.org*
- Phonological Awareness Literacy Screening: *https://pals.virginia.edu/public/rd-research.html*
- Reading Rockets: *www.readingrockets.org*
- ReadWriteThink: *www.readwritethink.org/classroom-resources*
- Remote Education Resource Center (University at Albany, State University of New York): *http://aatlased.org/remote-ed-getting-started*
- School Scheduling Associates: *www.schoolschedulingassociates.com*
- TextProject: *www.textproject.org*
- We Need Diverse Books: *https://diversebooks.org*

COACHING AND LEADERSHIP

- Association for Supervision and Curriculum Development: A Coach's Coach: *www.ascd.org/ascd-express/vol15/num06/a-coachs-coach.aspx*
- My Coaches' Couch by Vicki Collet: *https://vickicollet.com/my-coaches-couch*
- National Board for Professional Teaching Standards (2019). *ATLAS: Accomplished teaching, learning, and schools.* Retrieved from *www.nbpts.org/atlas*
- Pennsylvania Department of Education Coaching Course: *www.education.pa.gov/Teachers%20-%20Administrators/PA%20Inspired%20Leaders/Pages/PA-Coaching-Course.aspx*
- The Professional Institute for Instructional Coaching: *www.tpiic.org*
- TeachBoost Launch Pad: *https://blog.teachboost.com*

GRANT SUPPORT

- U.S. Department of Education, Preschool development grants: *www2.ed.gov/programs/preschooldevelopmentgrants/index.html*
- Follett Learning: Grants and funding: *www.follettlearning.com/about-us/grants-and-funding*

- National Education Association: Grant writing tutorial: *www.neafoundation.org/for-educators/grant-resources/writing-tutorial*
- Teacher Planet: Grants: *www.grants4teachers.com*
- Scholastic, Teachers: Get the grant: *www.scholastic.com/teachers/articles/teaching-content/teachers-get-grant*
- California Department of Education, Funding: *www.cde.ca.gov/fg/fo*
- Texas Education Agency, Applying for a grant: *https://tea.texas.gov/Finance_and_Grants/Grants/Applying_for_a_Grant*
- Tennessee Department of Education: School improvement grants: *www.tn.gov/education/finance-and-monitoring/school-improvement-grants.html*

APPENDIX E. Preparation for Job Interviews

Candidates for positions as literacy specialists often raise questions about how to prepare for job interviews. The questions identified below are some that may be asked by school personnel. Often, interviewers ask basic questions to get a sense of the experiences and education of candidates. In addition, they ask questions that elicit candidates' beliefs and perspectives about students, literacy teaching, and learning. These questions tend to be more difficult to answer because the interviewer probably has his or her own beliefs and values regarding each area. Be as honest and tactful as possible. The interviewer needs to know whether the literacy specialist is a "match" for the district. At the same time, the literacy specialist needs to determine whether the district is a place in which he or she will enjoy working.

BASIC QUESTIONS

1. Tell us about your past teaching experiences, especially those that prepare you for this position.

2. What certifications do you have? Where did you receive your literacy specialist certification? What were the strengths of the program?

QUESTIONS ELICITING KNOWLEDGE, BELIEFS, AND UNDERSTANDINGS

1. What are your beliefs about literacy instruction? Specifically (depending on position for which you are being considered), what are your beliefs about beginning literacy instruction? Phonics instruction? What are your beliefs about intermediate literacy instruction? Secondary literacy instruction?

2. How familiar are you with the standards in this state (CCSS or state standards)? What experiences have you had in learning about them, developing curriculum based on standards, and so on?

3. What assessment instruments have you had experience administering and interpreting? Talk about them and their possible uses. How familiar are you with (specific example), which we use in our district?

4. What do you think about teaching in pullout or in-class litreacy programs? Do you see advantages to one or the other? Why?

5. What do you think is important in working effectively with teachers whose students you will be teaching? Why? Describe ways you might collaborate with them.

6. In addition to teaching struggling readers, what other kinds of contributions can you make to the literacy program?

7. Have you had any experience in leading professional learning activities? If so, tell me about them?

8. What strengths (qualifications) do you think you would bring to this position? Why do you want this position?

9. What are your perspectives on the Science of Reading for literacy instruction?

QUESTIONS THE LITERACY SPECIALIST SHOULD ASK

The interview should also provide an opportunity for the literacy specialist to obtain information about the position. Interviewers often ask if the interviewee has any questions, so the candidate should go into the interview with several questions in mind. Broad categories of topics follow:

1. *Duties required:* What are the expectations of the position regarding teaching, assessment, and so on?
2. *Resources:* What materials and resources are available for teaching literacy?
3. *Opportunities for collaboration:* In what ways can I collaborate with teachers, parents, and community entities such as libraries, and so on?
4. *Professional opportunities:* Does the district encourage continuing education and provide opportunities for teachers to attend conferences?

The following guidelines might also be helpful in an interview:

1. *Listen carefully before answering any question.* Be certain you know what is being asked.
2. *Answer questions honestly.* If you do not know a specific answer, it is best to say so (or qualify your answer by saying that you are not certain, but to the best of your ability, you think . . .).
3. *Show enthusiasm and interest in the position.* Indicate why you want to work in that school or district, and why you believe you would be an excellent candidate for the job.

APPENDIX F. Ideas for Course or Workshop Instructors

In this section, we provide additional ideas for activities to use with a class or when leading PL sessions. We also suggest activities immediately after each chapter; these additional ideas may be useful to those wishing to expand on the chapter activities.

CHAPTER 1

1. Have participants work in small groups to brainstorm current issues and policies confronting educators, especially those involved with literacy instruction. Begin by talking briefly with them about important issues: for example, literacy across the curriculum, issues about how to assess student learning in literacy, or a potential state policy change. After participants identify the issues, share ideas across groups to look for commonalities and differences. You might keep this list to use for further group work later in the term, if desired.

2. Ask participants to read the latest issue of the annual survey "What's Hot, What's Not," generally found in *Literacy Today,* a publication of the ILA, and discuss whether they agree with experts in the field who have identified specific literacy topics as important or not.

3. Ask participants to download and read the most recent position statement on the roles of the literacy specialist from the website of the ILA (*www.literacy-worldwide.org*). Assign various sections to small groups of participants to read and identify important ideas. Discuss with the whole group.

CHAPTER 2

1. Ask participants to conduct a survey at a school in which they work or a school with which they are familiar to learn about its RTI approach to instruction, and how the school addresses the following:
   * Is there a core reading program for Tier 1 students, and if so, what is it?
   * What additional support do Tier 2 students receive (e.g., Who teaches them?)? What materials are used? How is Tier 2 time scheduled?
   * What additional support do Tier 3 students receive (e.g., Who teaches them?)? What materials are used? When do students receive Tier 3 instruction?
   * What successes does the school experience? What challenges does the school have in accomplishing RTI objectives?

2. Participants who are working at a middle or high school level can conduct a survey to determine how their school is implementing an RTI framework and how the school supports students who are experiencing difficulties with literacy. What problems does this school face in accomplishing its RTI objectives? Participants could discuss their findings in a class session, comparing results from various schools.

CHAPTER 3

Divide the class into three groups (primary, elementary/middle school, and secondary). Have each group read and discuss one of the sample schedules of literacy specialists in this chapter, using the questions in the "Think about This" sections. Have each group share the results of their discussion with the entire group.

CHAPTER 4

1. Ask participants to write a paper describing themselves as leaders: What do they see as their strengths, their limitations, and how might they change? What experiences have they had in their homes or education that have prepared them for a leadership role? Participants can save their papers until the conclusion of the course or workshops and reflect on what they had learned. For example, in what ways have they changed either their perspectives about leadership or their own leadership strengths or needs?

2. Have participants work on a T-chart in which they list attributes of an effective meeting and an ineffective meeting. This can be done individually or in small groups and then be shared with the entire group.

3. Divide the group into two smaller groups. Do a fishbowl activity in which those in one group role-play being a member of a group. The outer group members (sitting in a circle around the inner group) serve as observers, watching the other group as it goes through the role-playing experience. They then provide feedback to the group, responding to the following: What are some examples of active listening? Effective group behaviors (task behaviors, relationship behaviors)? Feedback from observers should be positive and encouraging. Below are examples of some possible role-playing scenarios:

    Scenario 1: A group of teachers has to decide how to reward students who achieve the goal of reading 25 books per year. They must decide what the reward will be and who will handle responsibility for deciding that students have met the goal. They will need to discuss how they will deal with the possibility that some students may not achieve this goal. There are issues that they must address in terms of whether they should provide an extrinsic reward for students who have met this goal.

    Scenario 2: A group of fourth-grade teachers has reviewed their assessment data and found that students' vocabulary scores are low. The principal has asked them to address two questions: What are the reasons for the low scores? How do they think they can improve student vocabulary learning? (Some of the teachers think that the students come from such poor backgrounds that vocabulary will always be low; others think that perhaps the textbooks don't provide enough rich vocabulary teaching.)

CHAPTER 5

1. Ask participants to use Figure 5.2 to assess the culture of the school in which they work or with which they are familiar. Have participants discuss the results of their assessment with others.

2. Ask participants to think about presentations they have heard and thought to be effective. Ask them to describe the ways in which the presenter kept them interested. Some ideas for discussion: How did the speaker begin the presentation? End the presentation? Was the audience involved and if so, how? In what ways did the presenter help the audience connect with the topic? Ask participants to generate a list of guidelines for making effective presentations.

CHAPTER 6

1. Form triads to discuss the activities in Figure 6.3. Have triads group the activities into one of three categories: low risk, medium risk, or high risk—in terms of what would be difficult for them to do—and then discuss what might be perceived as more "threatening" to teachers and more difficult for coaches to do. Discuss commonalities and differences in a large group.

2. Using interview questions developed by the group (see Chapter 6), ask each participant to meet with and interview a literacy coach. Group members should be encouraged to locate literacy coaches working at the preschool, elementary, or secondary levels. Share responses to these interviews. The group can also arrange for a conference call and interview a literacy coach by telephone.

3. Discuss this scenario in small groups and then share across groups:

   Your superintendent has told you that as a coach you are to spend your time with teachers who have low achievement scores and shouldn't spend any time with other teachers whose kids are doing well. You don't think this is the way to establish a relationship with teachers, believing that teachers will not want to work with you. They will realize that only those having problems work with the coach! What are some ways of addressing this? What actions can you take?

CHAPTER 7

1. Below are some coaching scenarios that can be used for discussion. Each addresses a situation at a different grade level. In small-group discussion, consider the following:

   - What are some ideas for working with the teacher?
   - What roadblocks might arise and how could you address them?

     Scenario 1: The kindergarten teacher asked the coach to observe her classroom. Although she has taught before (fourth grade), she has never taught kindergarten. She told the coach that she is having difficulties with classroom management. The coach observes and sees the following: The teacher is teaching a small group but has to stop frequently to reprimand students for their behavior: "J, get back in your seat," "S, stop hitting H," and so on. The students are not working in their centers (as they were told) but are wandering around the room. The coach and the teacher are now going to meet for a feedback session. How does the coach begin? What are some important points that need to be made?

Scenario 2: Although the students in this ninth-grade English classroom have "high" test scores, the teacher lectures most of the time and is not attempting to use the classroom discussion approaches that are part of the new literacy framework for use in content-area classrooms. She has indicated to other teachers and to the coach that she sees no need to do this because her students are "doing well." As the coach, you have been charged with helping teachers implement these new discussion techniques. What should and could you do?

Scenario 3: Josh, an experienced eighth-grade social studies teacher, was transferred to the elementary school where he was assigned to a third-grade classroom. He says, "I have never taught reading. All I know is that there are a number of students in my classroom who can't read the materials we use in reading class. I've been trying to use strategy instruction, but the kids are having trouble summarizing information." He has asked to meet with the coach to discuss this problem. The coach wants to get some idea of what Josh knows and believes about "teaching reading," and how he is actually facilitating the work of the students. What types of questioning might you use? What strategies might be helpful? What roadblocks might arise and how could you address them?

2. Assume that you have just been hired as a literacy coach for a school (you decide on the level). Write a letter you could send to teachers about you and your role. Share the letter with other participants in your workshop or class. Share the letters and compare similarities and differences.

CHAPTER 8

1. Ask participants to meet in small groups to discuss factors that positively or negatively affect change in their own schools. Have them think about the factors described in this chapter. Are any of these factors present in their schools? Others? Is the culture of their school one in which teachers would be receptive to change and why?

2. Ask participants to interview an administrator or school leader at a local school to discuss the reading program (K–12). Questions that might be asked include:
   - What is the process for decision making in curriculum development?
   - What materials or documents are available to explain the program?
   - What materials are used in the program to meet the needs of students of differing abilities and needs?
   - What PL is provided for teachers to help them implement the program?

3. Use the Internet to locate needs assessment documents and copies of comprehensive literacy plans from various states (if possible, from your own state). After reading Chapter 8 in this book, discuss the documents with peers and

compare their content to the recommendations in this book. How helpful would completing a needs assessment be for your school?

CHAPTER 9

1. Ask participants to identify and discuss specific assessment measures used at various levels. You may choose to group participants by level (e.g., primary, intermediate/middle school, high school). Share results of discussion with the entire group. Ask them to indicate purposes of the instruments: screening, diagnostic, progress monitoring, and outcome measures.

	Primary	Intermediate	Middle school	High school
Initial screening				
Diagnostic				
Progress monitoring				
Outcome				

2. Divide students into two groups. Ask one group to read the ILA (2017a) position statement on literacy assessment and the other group, the ILA (2017c) position statement on standardized reading tests. Ask each group to summarize what they learned and to discuss the difference in the perspectives of the two documents. Ask students to relate what they learned to the "reality" of their schools.

CHAPTER 10

1. Form small groups and then ask participants to discuss one of the following scenarios. Have them share with the entire group.

   Scenario 1: The parents of Natalie, a kindergarten child, ask for an appointment with the literacy specialist to talk about their child. They tell the literacy specialist that their child is reading chapter books, similar to those that a second- or third grader would read. She is now getting "homework" in kindergarten, which consists of activities such as the following: cut out pictures of things that start with the letter *B* and glue to a large sheet of paper; practice writing two new letters (*A* and *I*); and practice writing your name (which Natalie has been doing since she was age 3). Her parents indicate that this homework has not been very exciting and it's hard to get her interested. She would rather spend time reading independently or working on the computer, playing with video games requiring reading. Her parents are concerned Natalie will find school boring. Should they be considering options (e.g., a private school, skipping a grade)? They are seeking help from the literacy specialist.

   Scenario 2: The literacy specialists in one district recognize their student population is changing and they now have a large number of students from many different countries in their schools. They would like to take advantage of this cultural diversity; in addition, they would like to help all families understand the value of "culturally responsive" instruction. They are meeting to discuss whether they should pull together some material that would be "parent friendly" to address this topic, hold some workshops, have an ethnic fair, and so on. How should teachers be involved? Is this something that should be done only at the elementary level, or at higher levels, too?

2. Ask participants to interview the school librarian to determine in what ways she or he collaborates with teachers in the schools. Providing related materials? Coordinating instruction with the content teachers? How aware is the librarian about the literacy program in the school? Are there opportunities to collaborate with teachers? What does the librarian think should be done to improve the ways in which he or she works with teachers to improve instruction?

CHAPTER 11

Have students write a proposal that addresses the following mini-grant opportunity. This could be an individual assignment or could be done in small groups. Opportunity to share the finished product can be provided.

A local foundation is willing to provide $500 to classroom teachers who wish to implement a creative project for their classroom to enhance the reading performance of their students. The proposal should include the following elements: goals and objectives, plan of activities, timeline, personnel, evaluation, and budget (describe the funds you will need and how they will be used).

CHAPTER 12

1. Use a fishbowl activity to role-play a candidate applying for a literacy specialist position. Two participants should volunteer to be in the fishbowl: one who is the candidate for a literacy specialist or literacy coach position; and the other, the interviewer (perhaps a principal or curriculum director). The outer group (sitting in a circle around the two participants who have agreed to role-play an interview situation) observes and then provides feedback about the interview to the participants.

2. Ask participants to go to a website of a professional organization and have them identify and share with others the possible opportunities for PL that are available on that site.

3. Assign one of the vignettes in this book to a small group of class members. Ask them to read the vignette carefully, thinking about how the writer exemplifies lifelong learning. Discuss similarities and differences in how each literacy professional functions in their school and the challenges they face. Ask each individual in the group to write one sentence stating what they learned from their reading of the vignette and then share that sentence with the entire group. Ask each group to share with the entire class what they learned about the role of the literacy specialist from the vignette.

References

Achieve & Society for Human Resource Management. (2012). *The future of the U.S. workforce: A survey of hiring practices across industries.* Retrieved from *www.achieve.org/files/Achieve-SHRM-Survey.pdf.*

Affinito, S. (2018). *Literacy coaching: Transforming teaching and learning with digital tools and technology.* Portsmouth, NH: Heinemann.

Afflerbach, P. (2016). Reading assessment: Looking ahead. *The Reading Teacher, 69*(4), 413–419.

Afflerbach, P. (2017). *Understanding and using reading assessment, K–12* (3rd ed.). Alexandra, VA: Association for Supervision and Curriculum Development, International Literacy Association.

Aguilar, E. (2016). *The art of coaching teams: Building resilient communities that transform schools.* Hoboken, NJ: Wiley.

Alexander, K. L., Entwisle, D. R., & Olson, L. S. (2001). Schools, achievement, and inequality: A seasonal perspective. *Educational Evaluation and Policy Analysis, 23*(2), 171–191.

Allington, R. L. (1986). Policy constraints and effective compensatory reading instruction: A review. In J. Hoffman (Ed.), *Effective teaching of reading: Research and practice* (pp. 261–289). Newark, DE: International Reading Association.

Allington, R. L. (2006). *What really matters for struggling readers: Designing research-based programs.* New York: Pearson.

Allington, R. L. (2013). The six traits of effective elementary literacy instruction. Retrieved from *www.readingrockets.org/article/six-ts-effective-elementary-literacy-instruction.*

Allington, R. L., & McGill-Franzen, A. (1989). School response to reading failure: Instruction for Chapter 1 and special education students in grades 2, 4, and 8. *Elementary School Journal, 89,* 529–542.

Allington, R., & McGill-Franzen, A. (2018). *Summer reading: Closing the rich/poor reading achievement gap* (2nd ed.). New York: Teachers College Press.

Allington, R. L., & Shake, M. C. (1986). Remedial reading: Achieving curricular congruence in classroom and clinic. *The Reading Teacher, 39*(7), 648–654.

America Reads Challenge Act of 1997, H.R. 1516 (105th Congress). Available at *www.congress.gov/bill/105th-congress/house-bill/1516?s=1&r=96.*

American Recovery and Reinvestment Act of 2009, Public Law No. 111-5, 2009.

Anders, P. L., & Clift, R. T. (2012). Adolescent language, literacy and learning: Implications for a schoolwide literacy program. In R. M. Bean & A. Swan Dagen (Eds.), *Best practices of literacy leaders: Keys to school improvement* (pp. 162–183). New York: Guilford Press.

Annenberg Foundation. (2017). Reading and writing in the disciplines. Retrieved from *https://learner.org/series/reading-writing-in-the-disciplines.*

Au, K. H. (2011). *Literacy achievement and diversity: Keys to success for students, teachers and schools.* New York: Teachers College Press.

August D., & Shanahan, T. (2006). *Report of the National Literacy Panel on language minority children and youth.* Philadelphia: Erlbaum.

Baker, S., Gersten, R., & Keating, T. (2000). When less may be more: A 2-year longitudinal evaluation of a volunteer tutoring program requiring minimal training. *Reading Research Quarterly, 35*(4), 494–519.

Banks, J. (2003). Teaching literacy for social justice and global citizenship. *Language Arts, 81*(1), 18–19.

Barnett, W. S. (1995). Long-term effects of early childhood programs on cognitive and school outcomes. *The Future of Children, 5*(3), 25–50.

Barnett, W. S., Frede, E. C., Mobasher, H., & Mohr, P. (1987). The efficacy of public preschool programs and the relationship of program quality to efficacy. *Educational Evaluation and Policy Analysis, 10*(1), 37–49.

Barth, R. S. (2013). The time is ripe (again). *Educational Leadership, 71*(2), 10–16.

Bean, R. M. (2001). The reading coach: Professional development and literacy leadership in the school. In T. Rasinski (Ed.), *Rebuilding the foundation: Effective reading instruction for 21st century literacy* (pp. 315–336). Bloomington IN: Solution Tree Press.

Bean, R. M. (2004). Promoting effective literacy instruction: The challenge for literacy coaches. *The California Reader, 37*(3), 58–63.

Bean, R. M. (2008). Developing an effective reading program. In S. B. Wepner & D. S. Strickland (Eds.), *The administration and supervision of reading programs* (4th ed., pp. 11–29). New York: Teachers College Press.

Bean, R. M. (2009). *The reading specialist: Leadership for the classroom, school, and community* (2nd ed.). New York: Guilford Press.

Bean, R. M. (2011). The reading coach: Professional development and literacy leadership in the school. In T. Rasinski (Ed.), *Rebuilding the foundation: Effective reading instruction for 21st century literacy* (pp. 315–336). Bloomington, IN: Solution Tree Press.

Bean, R. M. (2014). Developing a comprehensive reading plan (PreK–grade 12). In S. B. Wepner, D. S. Strickland, & D. J. Quatroche (Eds.), *The administration and supervision of reading programs* (5th ed., pp. 11–29). New York: Teachers College Press.

Bean, R. M. (2020). The reading/literacy specialist: Still a multifaceted role. In A. Swan Dagen & R. M. Bean (Eds.), *Best practices of literacy leaders: Keys to school improvement* (2nd ed., pp. 44–68). New York: Guilford Press.

Bean, R. M., Belcastro, B., Jackson, V., Vandermolen, J., & Zigmond, N. (2008, December). *Literacy coaching in reading: The blind men and the elephant.* Paper presented at the National Reading Conference, Orlando, FL.

Bean, R. M., Cassidy, J., Grumet, J. V., Shelton, D., & Wallis, S. R. (2002). What do reading specialists do?: Results from a national survey. *The Reading Teacher, 55*(8), 2–10.

Bean, R. M., Cooley, W., Eichelberger, R. T., Lazar, M., & Zigmond, N. (1991). In-class or pullout: Effects of setting on the remedial reading program. *Journal of Reading Behavior, 23*(4), 445–464.

Bean, R. M., & DeFord, D. (n.d.). *Do's and don'ts for literacy coaches: Advice from the field.* Denver, CO: Literacy Coaching Clearinghouse.

Bean, R. M., Dole, J. A., Nelson, K. L., Belcastro, E., & Zigmond, N. (2015). The sustainability of a national reading reform initiative in two states. *Reading and Writing Quarterly: Overcoming Learning Difficulties, 31*(1), 30–55.

Bean, R. M., Draper, J. A., Hall, V., Vandermolen, J., & Zigmond, N. (2010). Coaches and coaching in Reading First schools: A reality check. *The Elementary School Journal, 111*(1), 87–114.

Bean, R. M., & Eichelberger, R. T. (2007). *Evaluation of improving literacy through school libraries grant.* Unpublished technical report.

Bean, R. M., Fulmer, D., & Zigmond, N. (2009). *Reading First Observation Checklist and Rating Scale.* Unpublished instrument, University of Pittsburgh, Pittsburgh, PA.

Bean, R. M., Grumet, J. V., & Bulazo, J. (1999). Learning from each other: Collaboration between classroom teachers and reading specialist interns. *Reading Research and Instruction, 38*(4), 273–287.

Bean, R. M., & Ippolito, J. (2016). *Cultivating coaching mindsets: An action guide for literacy leaders.* Blairsville, PA: Learning Sciences International.

Bean, R. M., & Kern, D. (2018). Multiple roles of specialized literacy professionals: The ILA 2017 Standards. *The Reading Teacher, 71*(5), 615–621.

Bean, R. M., Kern, D., Goatley, V., Ortlieb, E., Shettel, J., Calo, K., . . . Cassidy, J. (2015). Specialized literacy professionals as literacy leaders: Results of a national survey. *Literacy Research and Instruction, 54*(2), 83–114.

Bean, R. M., & Lillenstein, J. (2012). Response to intervention and the changing roles of schoolwide personnel. *The Reading Teacher, 65*(7), 491–501.

Bean, R. M., & Morewood, A. (2007). Best practices in professional development for improving literacy instruction. In L. Gambrell, L. M. Morrow, & M. C. Pressley (Eds.), *Best practices in literacy instruction* (3rd ed., pp. 373–394). New York: Guilford Press.

Bean, R. M., Swan, A. L., & Knaub, R. (2003). Reading specialists in schools with exemplary reading programs: Functional, versatile, and prepared. *The Reading Teacher, 56*(5), 446–455.

Bean, R. M., Swan Dagen, A., Ippolito, J., & Kern, D. (2018). Principals' perspectives on the roles of specialized literacy professionals. *Elementary School Journal, 119*(2), 327–350.

Bean, R. M., Trovato, C. A., & Hamilton, R. (1995). Focus on Chapter 1 reading programs: Views of reading specialists, classroom teachers, and principals. *Reading Research and Instruction, 34*(3), 204–221.

Bean, R. M., Turner, G. H., & Belski, K. (2002). Implementing a successful

America Reads Challenge tutoring program: Lessons learned. In P. E. Linder, M. B. Sampson, J. Dugan, & B. Brancato (Eds.), *24th yearbook of the College Reading Association* (pp. 169–187). Easton, PA: College Reading Association.

Bean, R. M., & Wilson, R. M. (1981). *Effecting change in school reading programs: The resource role.* Newark, DE: International Reading Association.

Beck, I. L., & Beck, M. E. (2013). *Making sense of phonics* (2nd ed.). New York: Guilford Press.

Beck, I. L., & McKeown, M. G. (2001). Text-talk: Capturing the benefits of read-aloud experiences for young children. *The Reading Teacher, 55,* 10–20.

Beck, I. L., & McKeown, M. (2006). *Improving comprehension with Questioning the Author: A fresh and expanded view of a powerful approach.* New York: Scholastic.

Beers, K. (2003). *When kids can't read, what teachers can do: A guide for teachers.* Portsmouth, NH: Heinemann.

Berger, J. G. (2012). *Changing on the job: Developing leaders for a complex world.* Redwood City, CA: Stanford University Press.

Berger, J. G. (2019). *Unlocking leadership mind traps: How to thrive in complexity.* Stanford, CA: Stanford University Press.

Bernhardt, V. L. (2013). *Data analysis for continuous school improvement* (3rd ed.). New York: Routledge.

Beschorner, B., & Woodward, L. (2019). Long-term planning for technology in literacy instruction. *The Reading Teacher, 73*(3), 325–337.

Biancarosa, G., Bryk, A., & Dexter, E. (2010). Assessing the value-added effects of literacy collaborative professional development on student learning. *The Elementary School Journal, 111,* 7–34.

Biancarosa, G., & Snow, C. E. (2004). *Reading next: A vision for action and research in middle and high school literacy: A report to Carnegie Corporation of New York.* Washington, DC: Alliance for Excellent Education. Retrieved from *www.carnegie.org/publications/reading-next*.

Bildner, P. (2015). *Marvelous Cornelius: Hurricane Katrina and the spirit of New Orleans.* San Francisco: Chronicle Books.

Billig, S. H. (2002). Involving middle-graders' parents. *Education Digest, 67*(7), 42–45.

Blachowicz, C. L. Z., Buhle, R., Ogle, D., Frost, S., Correa, A., & Kinner, J. D. (2010). Hit the ground running: Ten ideas for preparing and supporting urban literacy coaches. *The Reading Teacher, 63*(5), 348–359.

Blanchard, K., Bowles, S., Carew, D., & Parise-Carew, E. (2001). *High five: The magic of working together.* New York: HarperCollins.

Bond, N., & Hargreaves, A. (2014). *The power of teacher leaders: Their roles, influence, and impact.* New York: Routledge.

Borman, G. D., & D'Agostine, J. V. (2001). Title 1 and student achievement: A quantitative synthesis. In G. D. Borman, S. C. Stringfield, & R. E. Slavin (Eds.), *Title I compensatory education at the crossroads* (pp. 25–58). Mahwah, NJ: Erlbaum.

Boutte, G. S., & Johnson, G. J. (2014). Community and family involvement in urban schools. In H. R. Milner & K. Lomotey (Eds.), *Handbook of urban education* (pp. 167–187). New York: Routledge.

Breidenstein, A., Fahey, K., Glickman, C., & Hensley, F. (2012). *Leading for powerful learning: A guide for instructional leaders.* New York: Teachers College Press.

Briceño, A., & Klein, A. F. (2018). A second lens on formative reading assessment with multilingual students. *The Reading Teacher, 72*(5), 611–621.

Briggs, D. A., & Coulter, F. C. (1977). The reading specialist. In W. Otto, N. A. Peters, & C. W. Peters (Eds.), *Reading problems: A multidisciplinary perspective* (pp. 215–236). Reading, MA: Addison-Wesley.

Brock, C., Goatley, V., Raphael, T., Trost-Shahata, E., & Weber, K. (2014). *Teaching disciplinary literacy, K–6: Reading, writing and talk as tools.* New York: Teachers College Press.

Brozo, W. G., & Gaskins, C. (2009). Engaging texts and literacy practices for adolescent boys. In K. D. Wood & W. E. Blanton (Eds.), *Literacy instruction for adolescents: Research-based practice* (pp. 170–186). New York: Guilford Press.

Bryk, A. S., Gomez, L. M., Grunow, A., & LeMahieu, P. G. (2015). *Learning to improve: How America's schools can get better at getting better.* Cambridge, MA: Harvard Education Press.

Bryk, A. S., Sebring, P. B., Allensworth, F. E., Luppescu, S., & Easton, J. Q. (2010). *Organizing schools for improvement: Lessons from Chicago.* Chicago: University of Chicago Press.

Buehl, D. (2011). *Developing readers in the academic disciplines.* Newark, DE: International Reading Association.

Buly, M., & Valencia, S. (2002). Below the bar: Profiles of students who fail state reading assessments. *Educational Evaluation and Policy Analysis, 24*(3), 219–239.

Camburn, E., Rowan, B., & Taylor, J. (2003). Distributed leadership in schools: The case of elementary schools adopting comprehensive school reform models. *Educational Evaluation and Policy Analysis, 25*(4), 347–373.

Canady, R. L., & Rettig, M. (1995). The power of innovative scheduling. *Educational Leadership, 53*(3), 4–10.

Canady, R. L., & Rettig, M. (2008). *Elementary school scheduling: Enhancing instruction for student achievement.* Larchmont, NY: Eye on Education.

Cannon, J. S., Kilburn, M. S., Karoly, L. A., Mattox, T., Muchow, A. N., & Buenaventura, M. (2017). *Investing early: Taking stock of outcomes and economic returns from early childhood programs.* Santa Monica, CA: RAND Corporation. Retrieved from *www.rand.org/pubs/research_reports/RR1993.html.*

Carnegie Council on Advancing Adolescent Literacy. (2010). *Time to act: An agenda for advancing adolescent literacy for college and career success.* New York: Carnegie Corporation of New York.

Carroll, J., Raphael, T., & Au, K. (2011). *QAR comprehension lessons: Grades 6–8.* New York: Scholastic.

Carroll, K. (2007). *Conversations with coaches: Their roles in Pennsylvania Reading First schools.* Unpublished doctoral dissertation, University of Pittsburgh, PA.

Carver-Thomas, D. (2018). *Diversifying the teaching profession: How to recruit and retain teachers of color.* Palo Alto, CA: Learning Policy Institute.

Cassidy, J., & Cassidy, D. (2009, February/March). What's hot for 2009: National Reading Panel influence wanes in 13th annual survey. *Reading Today, 26*(4), 1, 8, 9.

Castek, J., & Gwinn, C. B. (2012). Technology in the literacy program. In R. M. Bean & A. Swan Dagen (Eds.), *Best practices of literacy leaders: Keys to school improvement* (pp. 295–316). New York: Guilford Press.

Center for American Progress and the Education Trust. (2011). *Essential elements of teacher policy in ESEA: Effectiveness, fairness, and evaluation.* Washington, DC: Author.

Clay, M. (1985). *The early detection of reading difficulties* (3rd ed.). Portsmouth, NH: Heinemann.

Clay, M. (2019). *An observation survey of early literacy achievement* (4th ed.). Portsmouth, NH: Heinemann.

Coburn, C. E., & Woulfin, S. L. (2012). Reading coaches and the relationship between policy and practice. *Reading Research Quarterly, 47*(1), 5–30.

Cochran-Smith M. (2010). Toward a theory of teacher education for social justice. In A. Hargreaves, A. Lieberman, M. Fullan, & D. Hopkins (Eds.), *Second international handbook of educational change* (pp. 445–467). New York: Springer.

Coiro, J. (2005). Every teacher a Miss Rumphius: Empowering teachers with effective professional development. In R. Karchmer, M. Mallette, J. Kara-Soteriou, & D. J. Leu, Jr. (Eds.), *Innovative approaches to literacy education: Using the Internet to support new literacies* (pp. 199–219). Newark, DE: International Reading Association.

Collet, V. S. (2017). Lesson study in a turnaround school: Local knowledge as a pressure-balanced valve for improved instruction. *Teachers College Record, 119*(6), 1–58.

Collet, V. (2018, April 3). Breaking down the coaching barriers. Retrieved from *https://blog.teachboost.com/breaking-down-the-coaching-barriers.*

Collins, J. (2001). *Good to great.* New York: HarperCollins.

Collins, J. (2019). *Turning the flywheel: A monograph to accompany* Good to Great. New York: Harper Business.

Comber, B. (2015). Critical literacy and social justice. *Journal of Adolescent and Adult Literacy, 58*(5), 362–367.

Common Sense Media. (2017). Common Sense Census 2017: Media use by kids age zero to eight. Retrieved from *www.commonsensemedia.org/research/the-common-sense-census-media-use-by-kids-age-zero-to-eight-2017.*

Common Sense Media. (2019). Common Sense Census 2019: Media use by tweens and teens. Retrieved from *www.commonsensemedia.org/sites/default/files/uploads/research/2019-census-8-to-18-key-findings-updated.pdf.*

Connor, C. M., & Morrison, F. J. (2004). Beyond the reading wars: Exploring the effects of child instruction on growth in early reading. *Scientific Study of Reading, 8*(4), 305–336.

Costa, A. L., & Garmston, R. J. (2002). *Cognitive coaching: A foundation for Renaissance schools* (2nd ed.). Norwood, MA: Christopher-Gordon.

Covey, S. R. (1989). *The 7 habits of highly effective people.* New York: Simon & Schuster.

Covey, S. R. (2004). *The 8th habit: From effectiveness to greatness.* New York: Free Press.

Crow, T. (2014). The pause that refreshes. *Learning Forward, 35*(3), 4.

Crowther, F., Ferguson, M., & Hann, L. (2008). *Developing teacher leaders: How teacher leadership enhances school success* (2nd ed.). Thousand Oaks, CA: Corwin Press.

Cunningham, P. M., & Hall, D. P. (1994). *Making words*. Torrance, CA: Good Apple.

Curtis, R. (2013). *Finding a new way: Leveraging teacher leadership to meet unprecedented demands*. Washington, DC: Aspen Institute.

Darling-Hammond, L. (2013). Inequality and school resources: What it will take to close the opportunity gap. In P. L. Carter & K. G. Weiner (Eds.), *Closing the opportunity gap: What America must do to give every child an even chance* (pp. 1–10). New York: Oxford University Press.

Darling-Hammond, L. (2014–2015, Winter). Want to close the achievement gap?: Close the teaching gap. *American Educator, 38*(4), 14–18.

Darling-Hammond, L., Hyler, M. E., & Gardner, M. (2017). *Effective teacher professional development*. Palo Alto, CA: Learning Policy Institute.

Darling-Hammond, L., Wei, R. C., Andree, A., Richardson, N., & Orphanos, S. (2009). *Professional learning in the learning profession: A status report on teacher development in the United States and abroad*. Oxford, OH: National Staff Development Council.

Desimone, L. M., Porter, A. C., Garet, M. S., Yoon, K. S., & Birman, B. F. (2002). Effects of professional development on teachers' instruction: Results from a three-year longitudinal study. *Educational Evaluation and Policy Analysis, 24*(2), 81–112.

Deussen, T., Coskie, T, Robinson, L., & Autio, E. (2007). *"Coach" can mean many things: Five categories of literacy coaches in Reading First* (REL 2007-No. 005, U.S. Department of Education). Washington, DC: National Center for Education Statistics. Retrieved from *https://ies.ed.gov/ncee/edlabs/regions/northwest/pdf/REL_2007005_sum.pdf.*

Dobbs, C. L., Ippolito, J., & Charner-Laird, M. (2017). *Investigating disciplinary literacy: A framework for collaborative professional learning*. Cambridge, MA: Harvard Education Press.

Dozier, C. L. (2006). *Responsive literacy coaching: Tools for creating and sustaining purposeful change*. Portland, ME: Stenhouse.

Duffy, G. G. (2014). *Explaining reading: A resource for explicit teaching of the Common Core Standards* (3rd ed.). New York: Guilford Press.

Duffy, H. (2009). *Meeting the needs of significantly struggling learners in high school: A look at approaches to tiered intervention*. Washington, DC: National High School Center.

Duke, N. (2014). *Inside information: Developing powerful readers and writers of informational text through project-based instruction*. New York: Scholastic.

Dysarz, K., & Dabrowski, J. (2016). Checking in update: More assignments from real classrooms. Retrieved from *https://edtrust.org/resource/checking-in-update-more-assignments-from-real-classrooms.*

Edelsky, C. (2006). *With literacy and justice for all: Rethinking the social in language and education* (3rd ed.). New York: Routledge.

Edwards, P. A., McMillon, G. M. T., & Turner, J. D. (2010). *Change is gonna come: Transforming education for African American students*. New York: Teachers College Press.

Edwards, P. A., Paratore, J. R., & Sweeney, J. S. (2014). Working with parents and the community. In S. B. Wepner, D. S. Strickland, & D. J. Quatroche (Eds.), *The administration and supervision of reading programs* (5th ed., pp. 214–222). New York: Teachers College Press.

Eidman-Aadahl, E. (2019). Getting better at getting better: Lessons from the national writing project. *Journal of Adolescent and Adult Literacy, 3*(63), 342–346.

Elbaum, B., Vaughn, S., Hughes, M. T., & Moody, S. W. (2000). How effective are one-to-one tutoring programs in reading for elementary students at risk for reading failure?: A meta-analysis of the intervention research. *Journal of Educational Psychology, 92*(4), 605–619.

Elementary and Secondary Education Act of 1965. Public Law No. 89-10, 29 Stat. 27.

Elish-Piper, L., & L'Allier, S. K. (2011). Examining the relationship between literacy coaching and student reading gains in grades K–3. *The Elementary School Journal, 112*(1), 83–106.

Elish-Piper, L., & L'Allier, S. K. (2014). *The Common Core coaching book: Strategies to help teachers address the K–5 ELA standards.* New York: Guilford Press.

Elish-Piper, L., L'Allier, S. K., Manderino, M., & DiDomenico, P. (2016). *Collaborative coaching for disciplinary literacy: Strategies to support teachers in grades 6–12.* New York: Guilford Press.

Elliott, J. G., & Grigorenko, E. L. (2014). *The dyslexia debate.* New York: Cambridge University Press.

Epstein, J. L., Sanders, M. G., Sheldon, S., Simon, B. S., & Salinas, K. C. (2009). *School, family, and community partnerships: Your handbook for action* (3rd ed.). Thousand Oaks, CA: Corwin Press.

Epstein, J. L., Sanders, M. G., Sheldon, S., Simon, B. S., Salinas, K. C., Jansorn, N. R., . . . Williams, K. J. (2018). *School, family, and community partnerships: Your handbook for action* (4th ed.). Thousand Oaks, CA: Corwin Press.

Erdmann, A., & Metzger, M. (2014). Discussion in practice: Sharing our learning curve. In J. Ippolito, J. F. Lawrence, & C. Zaller (Eds.), *Adolescent literacy in the era of the common core* (pp. 103–115). Cambridge, MA: Harvard Education Press.

Fisher, D., Frey, N., & Hattie, J. (2016). *Visible learning for literacy: Implementing the practices that work best to accelerate student learning.* Thousand Oaks, CA: Corwin Press.

Fisher, D., Frey, N., & Lapp, D. (2016). *Text complexity: Stretching readers with texts and tasks* (2nd ed.). Thousand Oaks, CA: Corwin Press.

Fitzgerald, J. (2001). Can minimally trained college student volunteers help young at-risk children to read better? *Reading Research Quarterly, 36*(1), 28–47.

Fixsen, D. L., Naoom, S. F., Blasé, K. A., Friedman, R. M., & Wallace, F. (2006). *Implementation research: A synthesis of the literature* (FMHI Publication No. 231). Tampa: University of South Florida, Louis de la Parte Florida Mental Health Institute, National Implementation Research Network.

Foorman, B., Beyler, N., Borradaile, K., Coyne, M., Denton, C. A., Dimino, J., . . . Wissel, S. (2016). *Foundational skills to support reading for understanding in kindergarten through 3rd grade* (NCEE 2016-4008). Washington, DC:

National Center for Education Evaluation and Regional Assistance, Institute of Education Sciences, U.S. Department of Education. Retrieved from *https://ies.ed.gov/ncee/wwc/PracticeGuide/21.*

Foorman, B. R., Smith, K. G., & Kosanovich, M. L. (2017). *Rubric for evaluating reading/language arts instructional materials for kindergarten to grade 5* (REL 2017-2019). Washington, DC: U.S. Department of Education Institute of Education Sciences, National Center for Education Evaluation and Regional Assistance, Regional Educational Laboratory Southeast. Retrieved from *https://ies.ed.gov/ncee/edlabs/projects/project.asp?projectID=4506.*

Foorman, B. R., & Torgeson, J. (2001). Critical elements of classroom and small-group instruction promote reading success in all children. *Learning Disabilities Research and Practice, 16*(4), 203–212.

Fountas, I. C., & Pinnell, G. S. (2006). *Teaching for comprehending and fluency K–8: Thinking, talking, and writing about reading.* Portsmouth, NH: Heinemann.

Fountas, I. C., & Pinnell, G. S. (2018). Every child, every classroom, every day: From vision to action in literacy learning. *The Reading Teacher, 72*(1), 7–19.

Friend, M., & Cook, L. (2000). *Interactions: Collaboration skills for school professionals.* New York: Longman.

Friend, M., & Cook, L. (2016). *Interactions: Collaboration skills for school professionals* (8th ed.). New York: Pearson.

Friend, M., Cook, L., Hurley-Chamberlain, D., & Shamberger, C. (2010) Co-teaching: An illustration of the complexity of collaboration in Special Education. *Journal of Educational and Psychological Consultation, 20,* 9–27.

Frost, S., & Bean, R. M. (2006, September 27). *Qualifications for literacy coaches: Achieving the gold standard.* Denver, CO: Literacy Coaching Clearinghouse.

Fuchs, L., & Vaughn, S. (2012). Responsiveness-to-Intervention: A decade later. *Journal of Learning Disabilities, 45*(3), 195–203.

Fullan, M. (2001a). *Leading in a culture of change.* San Francisco: Jossey-Bass

Fullan, M. (2001b). *The new meaning of educational change* (3rd ed.). New York: Teachers College Press.

Fullan, M. (2002). The change leader. *Educational Leadership, 59*(8), 16–21.

Fullan, M. (2011). Choosing the wrong drivers for whole system reform. Retrieved from *http://michaelfullan.ca/wp-content/uploads/2016/06/13396088160.pdf.*

Fullan, M. (2020). *Leading in a culture of change* (2nd ed.). San Francisco: Jossey-Bass.

Fullan, M., Bertani, A., & Quinn, J. (2004). New lessons for districtwide reform. *Educational Leadership, 61*(7), 42–46.

Fullan, M., & Hargreaves, A. (1996). *What's worth fighting for in your school?* New York: Teachers College Press.

Fullan, M., & Quinn, J. (2016). *Coherence: The right drivers in action for schools, districts, and systems.* Thousand Oaks, CA: Corwin Press.

Gabriel, R. (2018). Preparing literacy professionals: The case of dyslexia. *Journal of Literacy Research, 50*(2), 262–270.

Gabriel, R., & Woulfin, S. (2017). *Making teacher evaluation work: A guide for literacy teachers and leaders.* Portsmouth, NH: Heinemann.

Galloway, E. P., & Lesaux, N. K. (2014). Leader, teacher, diagnostician, colleague, and change agent: A synthesis of the research on the role of the reading specialist in this era of RTI-based literacy reform. *The Reading Teacher, 67*(7), 517–526.

Gelzheiser, L. M., Scanlon, D. M., Hallgren-Flynn, L., & Connors, M. (2019). *Comprehensive reading intervention in grades 3–8: Fostering word learning, comprehension, and motivation.* New York: Guilford Press.

Genest, M. T. (2014). Reading is a BLAST!: Inside an innovative literacy collaboration between public schools and the public library. *Reading Horizons, 53*(1), 4.

Genest, M., & Bean, R. M. (2007). *Bringing libraries and schools together (BLAST): A collaborative program between Carnegie Library of Pittsburgh and the Pittsburgh Public School District (year 5).* Unpublished technical report.

Gersten, R., Compton, D., Connor, C. M., Dimino, J., Santoro, L., Linan-Thompson, S., & Tilly, W. D. (2009). *Assisting students struggling with reading: Response to intervention (RTI) and multi-tier intervention for reading in the primary grades. A practice guide* (NCEE 2009-4045). Washington, DC: National Center for Education Evaluation and Regional Assistance, Institute of Education Sciences, U.S. Department of Education. Retrieved from *ies.ed.gov/ncee/wwc/PracticeGuide/3.*

Gerwitz, C. (2019). Which states were using PARCC or Smarter Balance in 2016–17? *Education Week, 36*(21). Retrieved from *www.edweek.org/ew/section/multimedia/which-states-were-using-parcc-or-smarter.html.*

Gillis, V., & Van Wig, A. (2015). Disciplinary literacy assessment: A neglected responsibility. *Journal of Adolescent and Adult Literacy, 58*(6), 455–460.

Goatley, V. J. (2009). Thinking together: Creating and sustaining professional learning communities. In C. A. Lassonde & S. E. Israel (Eds.), *Teacher collaboration for professional learning: Facilitating study, research, and inquiry communities* (pp. 143–144). San Francisco: Jossey-Bass.

Goatley, V. J. (2013). Critical voices: Complexities in literacy leadership. In C. Lassonde (Ed.), *The literacy leaders' handbook: Best practices for developing professional learning communities* (pp. 16–17). New York: Pearson.

Goatley, V. J., Dozier, C. L., & Puccioni, J. (2020). Using literacy assessments to improve student learning. In A. Swan Dagen & R. M. Bean (Eds.), *Best practices of literacy leaders: Keys to school improvement* (2nd ed., pp. 135–153). New York: Guilford Press.

Goddard, R., Goddard, Y., Kim, E. S., & Miller, R. (2015). A theoretical and empirical analysis of the roles of instructional leadership, teacher collaboration, and collective efficacy beliefs in support of student learning. *American Journal of Education, 121*(4), 501–530.

Graham, S., Bollinger, A., Booth Olson, C., D'Aoust, C., MacArthur, C., McCutchen, D., & Olinghouse, N. (2012). *Teaching elementary school students to be effective writers: A practice guide* (NCEE 2012-4058). Washington, DC: National Center for Education Evaluation and Regional Assistance, Institute of Education Sciences, U.S. Department of Education. Retrieved from *https://ies.ed.gov/ncee/wwc/Docs/PracticeGuide/WWC_Elem_Writing_PG_Dec182018.pdf.*

Grierson, A. L., & Woloshyn, V. E. (2013). Walking the talk: Supporting teachers' growth with differentiated professional learning. *Professional Development in Education, 39*(3), 401–419.

Guskey, T. R. (1986). Staff development and the process of teacher change. *Educational Researcher, 15*(5), 5–12.

Guskey, T. R. (2000). *Evaluating professional development.* Thousand Oaks, CA: Corwin Press.

Hall, B. (2004, Fall). Literacy coaches: An evolving role. *Carnegie Reporter, 3*(1), 10–19.

Hansen, J. (1998). *When learners evaluate.* Portsmouth, NH: Heinemann.

Hanushek, E. A. (1992). The trade-off between child quantity and quality. *Journal of Political Economy, 100*(91), 84–117.

Harari, O. (2002). *The leadership secrets of Colin Powell.* New York: McGraw-Hill.

Hedges Company. (n.d.). Four listening moves to get the best ideas. Retrieved from *thehedgescompany.com/four-listening-moves-tp-get-the-best-ideas.*

Hennick, C. (n.d.). Teachers: Get the grant. *Scholastic Teacher Magazine.* Retrieved from *www.scholastic.com/teachers/articles/teaching-content/teachers-get-grant.*

Henwood, G. F. (1999–2000). A new role for the reading specialist: Contributing toward a high school's collaborative educational culture. *Journal of Adolescent and Adult Literacy, 43*(4), 316–325.

Herold, B. (2020, April 29). The disparities in remote learning under coronavirus (in charts). *Education Week, 39*(30), 12–13.

Hersey, P., & Blanchard, K. (1977). *Management of organizational behavior: Utilizing human resources* (3rd ed.). Englewood Cliffs, NJ: Prentice-Hall.

Hicks, T., Sailors, M., & International Literacy Association. (2018). *Democratizing professional growth with teachers: From development to learning* (Literacy leadership brief). Newark, DE: International Literacy Association.

Hinchman, K., & Sheridan-Thomas, J. (Eds.). (2014). *Best practices in adolescent literacy instruction* (2nd ed.). New York: Guilford Press.

Hitlan, G. (2018). Internet/broadband fact sheet. Retrieved from *www.pewinternet.org/fact-sheet/internet-broadband.*

Hoffman, A. R., & Jenkins, J. (2002). Exploring reading specialists' collaborative interactions with school psychologists: Problems and possibilities. *Education, 122*(4), 751–758.

Hord, S. M. (2004). *Learning together: Leading together.* New York: Teachers College Press.

Houghton Mifflin Harcourt. (2019). *READ 180.* New York: Author. Retrieved from *www.hmhco.com/programs/read-180-universal.*

Hutchison, A., Beschorner, B., & Schmidt-Crawford, D. (2012). Exploring the use of the iPad for literacy learning. *The Reading Teacher, 66*(1), 15–23.

Individuals with Disabilities Education Improvement Act of 2004. (2004). Public Law No. 108-446, 118 Stat. 2647.

International Dyslexia Association. (2016). *IDA urges ILA to review and clarify key points in dyslexia research advisory.* Baltimore, MD: Author.

International Literacy Association. (2016a). *Every Student Succeeds Act* (Advocacy toolkit). Newark, DE: Author.

International Literacy Association. (2016b). *Research brief: Dyslexia.* Newark, DE: Author.

International Literacy Association. (2016c). *Research advisory addendum dyslexia: Response to the International Dyslexia Association.* Newark, DE: Author.

International Literacy Association. (2017a). *Literacy assessment: What everyone needs to know* (Literacy leadership brief). Newark, DE: Author.

International Literacy Association. (2017b). *Overcoming the digital divide: Four critical steps* (Research brief). Newark, DE: Author.

International Literacy Association. (2017c). *The roles of standardized reading tests in schools* (Literacy leadership brief). Newark, DE: Author.

International Literacy Association. (2018a). *Standards for the preparation of literacy professionals 2017.* Newark, DE: Author.

International Literacy Association. (2018b). *What effective Pre-K literacy instruction looks like* (Literacy leadership brief). Newark, DE: Author.

International Literacy Association. (2019a). *Children experiencing reading difficulties: What we know and what we can do* (Literacy leadership brief). Newark, DE: Author.

International Literacy Association. (2019b). *Children's rights to excellent literacy instruction* (Position statement). Newark, DE: Author.

International Literacy Association. (2019c). *Digital resources in early childhood literacy development* (Position statement and research brief). Newark, DE: Author.

International Literacy Association. (2019d). *Engagement and adolescent literacy* (Position statement and research brief). Newark, DE: Author.

International Literacy Association. (2019e). *Meeting the challenges of early literacy phonics instruction* (Literacy leadership brief). Newark, DE: Author.

International Reading Association. (1968). *Guidelines for reading specialists.* Newark, DE: Author.

International Reading Association. (1999). *Adolescent literacy: A position statement.* Newark, DE: Author.

International Reading Association. (2000). *Teaching all children to read: The roles of the reading specialist.* Newark, DE: Author.

International Reading Association. (2004). *The role and qualifications of the reading coach in the United States.* Newark, DE: Author.

International Reading Association. (2006). *Standards for middle and high school literacy coaches.* Newark, DE: Author.

International Reading Association. (2010). *Response to intervention: A position statement.* Newark, DE: Author.

International Reading Association. (2012). *Adolescent literacy: A position statement of the International Reading Association.* Newark, DE: Author.

International Reading Association. (2012–2013). *Leisure reading: A position statement.* Newark, DE: Author.

International Reading Association. (2014). *Using high stakes assessment for grade retention and graduation decisions.* Newark, DE: Author.

Ippolito, J. (2010). Three ways that literacy coaches balance responsive and directive relationships with teachers. *Elementary School Journal, 111*(1), 164–190.

Ippolito, J. (2013). Professional learning as the key to linking content and literacy instruction. In J. Ippolito, J. F. Lawrence, & C. Zaller (Eds.), *Adolescent literacy in the era of the common core: From research into practice* (pp. 215–234). Cambridge, MA: Harvard Education Press.

Ippolito, J., & Bean, R. M. (2018). *Unpacking coaching mindsets: Collaboration between principals and coaches.* West Palm Beach, FL: Learning Sciences International.

Ippolito, J., & Bean, R. M. (2019). A principal's guide to supporting instructional coaching. *Educational Leadership, 77*(3), 69–73.

Ippolito, J., Bean, R. M., Kern, D., & Swan Dagen, A. (2019). Specialists, coaches, coordinators, oh my!: Looking back and looking forward on the roles and responsibilities of specialized literacy professionals. *Primer, 47*(2), 19–29.

Ippolito, J., Dobbs, C., & Charner-Laird, M. (2019). *Disciplinary literacy: Inquiry and instruction.* West Palm Beach, FL: Learning Sciences International.

Ippolito, J., Dobbs, C. L., & Charner-Laird, M. (2020). Middle and high school literacy programs: Attending to both instructional and organizational challenges. In A. Swan Dagen & R. M. Bean (Eds.), *Best practices of literacy leaders: Keys to school improvement* (2nd ed., pp. 187–208). New York: Guilford Press.

Ippolito, J., Lawrence, J. F., & Zaller, C. (Eds.). (2013). *Adolescent literacy in the era of the common core: From research into practice.* Cambridge, MA: Harvard Education Press.

Ippolito, J., & Lieberman, J. (2012). Reading specialists and literacy coaches in secondary schools. In R. M. Bean & A. Swan Dagen (Eds.), *Best practices of literacy leaders: Keys to school improvement* (pp. 63–85). New York: Guilford Press.

Ippolito, J., Steele, J. L., & Samson, J. F. (2012). Introduction: Why adolescent literacy matters now. In J. Ippolito, J. L. Steele, & J. F. Samson (Eds.), *Adolescent literacy* (pp. 1–5). Cambridge, MA: Harvard Education Review.

Ivey, G., & Johnston, P. J. (2013). Engagement with young adult literature: Outcomes and processes. *Reading Research Quarterly, 48*(3), 255–275.

Jacobs, H. (2004). *Getting results with curriculum mapping.* Alexandria, VA: Association for Supervision and Curriculum Development.

Jakob, E., Porter, A., Podos, J., Braun, B., Johnson, N., & Vessey, S. (2010, December). How to fail in grant writing. Retrieved from *http://chronicle.com/article/How-to-Fail-in-Grant-Writing/125620.*

Jaquith, A., Mindich, D., Wei, R. C., & Darling-Hammond, L. (2010). *Teacher professional learning in the U.S.: Case studies of state policies and strategies.* Dallas, TX: National Staff Development Council.

Johnson, D. W., & Johnson, F. P. (2013). *Joining together: Group theory and group skills* (11th ed.). Boston: Pearson Education.

Johnston, P. H. (2010). *RTI in literacy: Responsive and comprehensive.* Newark, DE: International Reading Association.

Jolles, R. L. (2001). *How to run seminars and workshops* (2nd ed.). New York: Wiley.

Joyce, B., & Calhoun, E. (2010). *Models of professional development: A celebration of educators.* Thousand Oaks, CA: Corwin Press.

Joyce, B., & Showers, B. (1995). *Student achievement through staff development: Fundamentals of school renewal.* White Plains, NY: Longman.

Joyce, B., & Showers, B. (2002). *Student achievement through staff development* (3rd ed.). Alexandria, VA: Association for Supervision and Curriculum Development.

Kaminski, R., & Good, R. (2011). DIBELS Next. Retrieved from *www.voyagersopris.com/assessment/acadience-reading/overview.*

Kaner, S., Lind, L., Toldi, C., Fisk, S., & Berger, D. (1996). *Facilitator's guide to participatory decision-making.* Gabriola Island, BC, Canada: New Society.

Kapinus, B. A. (2008). Assessment of reading programs. In S. A. Wepner & D. Strickland (Eds.), *The administration and supervision of reading programs* (4th ed., pp. 144–156). New York: Teachers College Press.

Kelly, B., & Caprino, K. (2016, February 9). Teaching tips: Five tips for collaboration. *Literacy Daily.* Retrieved from *www.literacyworldwide.org/blog/literacy-daily/2016/02/09/five-tips-for-collaboration.*

Kennedy, J. F. (1963) Address in the Assembly Hall at the Paulskirche in Frankfurt (266), June 25, 1963. Retrieved from *www.jfklibrary.org/learn/about-jfk/life-of-john-f-kennedy/john-f-kennedy-quotations.*

Kervin, L., & Mantei, J. (2016). Assessing emergent readers' knowledge about online reading. *The Reading Teacher, 69*(6), 647–651.

Killion, J., Harrison C., Colton, A., Bryan, C., Delehant, A., & Cooke, D. (2016). *A systemic approach to elevating teacher leadership.* Oxford, OH: Learning Forward.

Kim, S., & Song, K. H. (2019). Designing a community translanguaging space within a family literacy project. *The Reading Teacher, 73*(3), 267–279.

Kise, J. A. (2006). *Differentiated coaching: A framework for helping teachers change.* Thousand Oaks, CA: Corwin Press.

Klingner, J. K., Vaughn, S., & Boardman, A. (2015). *Teaching reading comprehension to students with learning difficulties* (2nd ed). New York: Guilford Press.

Knaub, R. (2002). *The nature and impact of collaboration between reading specialists and classroom teachers in pullout and in-class reading programs.* Unpublished doctoral dissertation, University of Pittsburgh, Pittsburgh, PA.

Knight, J. (2007). *Instructional coaching: A partnership approach to improving instruction.* Thousand Oaks, CA: Corwin Press.

Kober, N. (2002, November). What tests can and cannot tell us. *The Forum, 2,* 1–16.

Kraft, M. A., Blazar, D., & Hogan, D. (2018). The effect of teacher coaching on instruction and achievement: A meta-analysis of the causal evidence. *Review of Educational Research, 88,* 1–42.

Kragler, S., Martin, L. E., & Sylvester, R. (2014). Lessons learned: What our history and research tell us about teachers' professional learning. In L. E. Martin, S. Kragler, D. J. Quatroche, & K. L. Bauserman (Eds.), *Handbook of professional development in education* (pp. 483–505). New York: Guilford Press.

Kucan, L., & Palinscar, A. M. (2013). *Comprehension Instruction through text-based discussion.* Newark, DE: International Literacy Association.

L'Allier, S., Elish-Piper, L., & Bean, R. M. (2010). What matters for elementary literacy coaching: Guiding principles for instructional improvement and student achievement. *The Reading Teacher, 63*(7), 544–554.

Lamkin, D. (2017). Fostering literacy learning with three middle school special-education students using therapy dogs as reading partners (doctoral dissertation). Retrieved from *www.worldcat.org/title/fostering-literacy-learning-with-three-middle-school-special-education-students-using-therapy-dogs-as-reading-partners/oclc/1027968673.*

Lane, H., & Zavada, S. W. (2013). When reading gets ruff: Canine-assisted reading programs. *The Reading Teacher, 7*(2), 87–95.

Lane, S. (2010). *Performance assessment: The state of the art.* Stanford, CA: Stanford University, Stanford Center for Opportunity Policy in Education.

Langer, J. A. (2001). Beating the odds: Teaching middle and high school students to read and write well. *American Educational Research Journal, 38*(4), 837–880.

Lapp, D., Fisher, D., Flood, J., & Frey, N. (2003). Dual role of the urban reading specialist. *Journal of Staff Development, 24*(2), 33–36.

Leana, C. R., & Pil, F. K. (2006). Social capital and organizational performance: Evidence from urban public schools. *Organization Science, 17*(3), 353–366.

Leana, C. R., & Pil, F. K. (2017). Social capital: An untapped resource for educational improvement. In E. Quintero (Ed.), *Teaching in context: How social aspects of schools and school systems shape teachers' development and effectiveness* (pp. 113–130). Cambridge, MA: Harvard University Press.

Learning Forward. (2011). *Standards for professional learning.* Oxford, OH: Author.

Leighton, C. M., Ford-Connors, E., Robertson, D. A., Wyatt, J., Wagner, C. J., Proctor, C. P., & Paratore, J. R. (2018). "Let's FaceTime tonight": Using digital tools to enhance coaching. *The Reading Teacher, 72*(1), 39–49.

Lieberman, A., & Miller, L. (2008). *Teachers in professional communities: Improving teaching and learning.* New York: Teachers College Press.

Lieberman, A., & Miller, L. (2014). Teachers as professionals: Evolving definitions of staff development. In L. E. Martin, S. Kragler, D. J. Quatroche, & K. L. Bauserman (Eds.), *Handbook of professional development in education: Successful models and practices, PreK–12* (pp. 3–21). New York: Guilford Press.

Lipson, M. Y., & Wixson, K. K. (2010). *Successful approaches to RTI: Collaborative practices for improving K–12 literacy.* Newark, DE: International Literacy Association.

Lipson, M. Y., & Wixson, K. K. (2012). *Assessment of reading and writing difficulties: An interactive approach* (5th ed.). New York: Pearson.

Little, J. W. (1993). Teachers' professional development in a climate of education reform. *Educational Evaluation and Policy Analysis, 15,* 129–151.

Lortie, D. C. (1975). *Schoolteacher: A sociological study.* Chicago: University of Chicago Press.

Lyons, C. A., & Pinnell, G. S. (2001). *Systems for change in literacy education: A guide to professional development.* Portsmouth, NH: Heinemann.

Malavasic, J. (2019). *Collaborative learning communities in middle school literacy education: Increasing student engagement with authentic literacy.* New York: Routledge.

Mangin, M. M., & Dunsmore, K. (2015) How the framing of instructional coaching as a level for systemic or individual reform influences the enactment of coaching. *Education Administration Quarterly, 51*(2), 179–213.

Manset-Williamson, G., & Nelson, J. M. (2005). Balanced strategic reading instruction for upper-elementary and middle school students with reading disabilities: A comparative study of two approaches. *Learning Disability Quarterly, 28*(1), 59–74.

Mason, P. M., & Ippolito, J. (2009). What is the role of the reading specialist in promoting adolescent literacy? In J. Lewis (Ed.), *Essential questions in adolescent literacy: Teachers and researchers describe what works in classrooms* (pp. 312–336). New York: Guilford Press.

Massachusetts Department of Elementary and Secondary Education. (n.d.). Classroom instruction videos and sample observation and feedback calibration activities. Retrieved from *www.doe.mass.edu/edeval/resources/calibration/videos.html*.

Matsumura, L. C., Garnier, H. E., & Spybrook, J. (2013). Literacy coaching to improve student reading achievement: A multi-level mediation model. *Learning and Instruction, 25*, 35–48.

Matsumura, L. C., Sartoris, M., DiPrima Bickel, D., & Garnier, H. E. (2009). Leadership for literacy coaching: The principal's role in launching a new coaching program. *Educational Administration Quarterly, 45*(5), 655–693.

McDonald, J. P., Mohr, N., Dichter, A., & McDonald, E. C. (2007). *The power of protocols: An educator's guide to better practice* (2nd ed.). New York: Teachers College Press.

McGill-Franzen, A., Lanford, C., & Adams, E. (2002). Learning to be literate: A comparison of five urban early childhood programs. *Journal of Educational Psychology, 94*(3), 443–464.

McKenna, M. C., & Walpole, S. (2008). *The literacy coaching challenge: Models and methods for grades K–8*. New York: Guilford Press.

McLuhan, M., & Fiore, Q. (1967). *The medium is the message: An inventory of effects*. New York: Penguin.

McMillon, G. M. T. (2016). School–university–community collaboration: Building bridges at the water's edge. *Journal of Adult and Adolescent Literacy, 60*(4), 375–381.

McTighe, J., & Wiggins, G. (2012). From Common Core standards to curriculum: Five big ideas. Retrieved from *http://grantwiggins.files.wordpress.com/2012/09/mctighe_wiggins_final_common_core_standards.pdf*.

McVee, M. B., & Dickson, B. A. (2002). Creating a rubric to examine literacy software for the primary grades. *The Reading Teacher, 55*(7), 635–639.

Mesmer, E. M., & Mesmer, H. E. (2009). Response to intervention (RTI): What teachers of reading need to know. *The Reading Teacher, 62*(4), 280–290.

Mesmer, H. A. (2019). *Letter lessons and first words: Phonics foundations that work*. Portsmouth, NH: Heinemann.

Mesmer, H. A. E., Mesmer, E., & Jones, J. (2014). *Reading intervention in the primary grades: A common-sense guide to RTI*. New York: Guilford Press.

Messina, L. (2013). Disciplinary literacy in practice: The disciplinary literacy network as a vehicle for strengthening instruction across content areas. In J. Ippolito, J. F. Lawrence, & C. Zaller (Eds.), *Adolescent literacy in the era of the Common Core: From research into practice* (pp. 37–60). Cambridge, MA: Harvard Education Press.

Michaels, S., O'Connor, S., Hall, M. W., & Resnick, L. B. (2010). *Accountable talk® sourcebook: For classroom conversation that works*. Pittsburgh, PA: Institute for Learning, University of Pittsburgh.

Miller, S., & Miller, P. A. (1997). *Core communication: Skills and processes*. Evergreen, CO: Interpersonal Communications Programs.

Milner, H. R. (2010). *Start when you are, but don't stay there: Understanding diversity, opportunity gaps, and teaching in today's classrooms*. Cambridge, MA: Harvard Education Press.

Moje, E. (2007). Developing socially just subject-matter instruction: A review of the literacy on disciplinary literacy teaching. *Review of Research in Education, 31,* 1–44.

Moje, E. B. (2008). Foregrounding the disciplines in secondary literacy teaching and learning: A call for change. *Journal of Adolescent and Adult Literacy, 52*(2), 96–107.

Moll, L. (2000). The diversity of schooling: A cultural–historical approach. In M. Reyes & J. Halcon (Eds.), *The best for our children: Critical perspectives on literacy for Latino students* (pp. 29–47). New York: Teachers College Press.

Molner, M. (2019, November 27). Some K–12 leaders are beating CEOs at "Greatness" game. *Education Week, 39*(14), 10. Retrieved from *www.edweek.org/ew/articles/2019/11/13/how-some-k-12-leaders-are-beating-businesses.html*.

Morris, D. (2014). *Diagnosis and correction of reading problems* (2nd ed.). New York: Guilford Press.

Morrison, F. J., Bachman, H. J., & Connor, C. M. (2005). *Improving literacy in America: Guidelines from research*. New Haven, CT: Yale University Press.

Nater, S., & Gallimore, R. (2006). *You haven't taught until they have learned: John Wooden's teaching principles and practices*. Morgantown, WV: Fitness Information Technology.

National Board for Professional Teaching Standards. (2019). ATLAS: Accomplished teaching, learning, and schools. Retrieved from *www.nbpts.org/atlas*.

National Center for Education Statistics. (1998). *Parent involvement in children's education: Efforts by public elementary schools*. Washington, DC: Author.

National Center for Education Statistics. (2005). NAEP Oral Reading Fluency Scale, grade 4. Retrieved from *https://nces.ed.gov/nationsreportcard/studies/ors/scale.aspx*.

National Center on Time and Learning. (2014). *Time for teachers: Leveraging expanded time to strengthen instruction and empower teachers*. Boston: Author.

National Governors Association Center for Best Practices & Council of Chief State School Officers. (2010). *Common Core Standardsfor English language arts and literacy in history/social studies, science, and technical subjects*. Washington, DC: Authors.

National Institute of Child Health and Human Development. (2000). *Report of the National Reading Panel. Teaching children to read: An evidence-based assessment of the scientific research literature on reading and its implications for reading instruction* (NIH Publication No. 00-4769). Washington, DC: U.S. Government Printing Office. Retrieved from *www.nichd.nih.gov/publications/pubs/nrp/Pages/smallbook.aspx*.

National Institute of Child Health and Human Development. (2010). *Developing early literacy: Report of the National Early Literacy Panel*. Washington, DC: U.S. Government Printing Office.

National Staff Development Council. (2001). *Standards for staff development.* Oxford, OH: Author.

Nation's Report Card. (2019). *Results from the 2019 Mathematics and Reading Assessments.* Washington, DC: U.S. Department of Education, Institute of Education Sciences, National Center for Education Statistics, National Assessment of Educational Progress (NAEP). Retrieved from *https://nces.ed.gov/nationsreportcard.*

Neuman, S. B. (2009). *Changing the odds for children at risk: Seven essential principles of educational programs that break the cycle of poverty.* New York: Teachers College Press.

New York State Education Department. (2017). New topic brief series: Linguistically diverse learners and the NYS Next Generation P–12 Learning Standards. Retrieved from *www.nysed.gov/bilingual-ed/news/new-topic-brief-series-linguistically-diverse-learners-and-nys-next-generation-p.*

No Child Left Behind Act of 2001, Public Law No. 107-110, 1-1076, 115 Stat. 1425-2094.

O'Connor, R. E. (2014). *Teaching word recognition: Effective strategies for students with learning difficulties.* New York: Guilford Press.

O'Connor, R. E., Bell, K. M., Harty, K., Larkin, K. R., Sackor, S. M., & Zigmond, N. (2002). Teaching reading to poor readers in the intermediate grades: A comparison of text difficulty. *Journal of Educational Psychology, 94*(3), 474–485.

Ogle, D. (1986). K-W-L: A teaching model that develops active reading of expository text. *The Reading Teacher, 39*(6), 564–572.

Ogle, D., & Fogelberg, E. (2001). Expanding collaborative roles of reading specialists: Developing an intermediate reading support team. In V. Risko & K. Bromley (Eds.), *Collaboration for diverse learners: Viewpoints and practices* (pp. 152–167). Newark, DE: International Reading Association.

O'Shell, D. (2019). Using video to showcase great teaching. *Educational Leadership, 77*(3), 50–52.

Parker, S. (2012). *Lead simply: How to create that special team of people.* Richmond, VA: Give More Media.

Parrott, L., III. (1996). *High-maintenance relationships: How to handle impossible people.* Carol Stream, IL: Tyndale House.

Patel, L. (2018). Immigrant populations and sanctuary schools. *Journal of Literacy Research, 50*(4), 524–529.

Pennsylvania Department of Education. (2014). Pennsylvania comprehensive literacy: Local literacy needs assessment. Retrieved from *http://static.pdesas.org/content/documents/Pennsylvania%20Comprehensive%20Literacy%20Needs%20Assessment%20RevisedFinal3_1.2015.pdf.*

Peralta, C. (2019). Why are we still blaming the families in 2019? *The Reading Teacher, 72*(5), 670–674.

Phillips, D. A., Lipsey, M. W., Dodge, K. A., Haskins, R., Bassok, D., Burchinal, M. R., . . . Weiland, C. (2017, April 20). *The current state of scientific knowledge on pre-Kindergarten effects.* Washington, DC: Brookings Institution and the Duke Center for Child and Family Policy. Retrieved from *www.brookings.edu/wp-content/uploads/2017/04/duke_prekstudy_final_4-4-17_hires.pdf.*

Pikulski, J. (1994). Preventing reading failure: A review of five effective programs. *The Reading Teacher, 48*(1), 30–39.

Pletcher, B. C., Hudson, A. K., John, L., & Scott, A. (2019). Coaching on borrowed time: Balancing the roles of the literacy professional. *The Reading Teacher, 72*(6), 689–699.

Powell, J. J., Aker, L., & Mesmer, H. A. (2020). Differentiated literacy instruction. In A. Swan Dagen & R. M. Bean (Eds.), *Best practices of literacy leaders: Keys to school improvement* (2nd ed., pp. 209–230). New York: Guilford Press.

Prensky, M. (2012). *From digital natives to digital wisdom: Hopeful essays for 21st century learning.* Thousand Oaks: CA: Corwin Press.

Quatroche, D. J., Bean, R. M., & Hamilton, R. L. (2001). The role of the reading specialist: A review of research. *The Reading Teacher, 55*(3), 282–294.

Raphael, T. (1982). Question-answering strategies for children. *The Reading Teacher, 36*(2), 86–90.

Reed, D. K., Wexler, J., & Vaughn, S. (2012). *RTI for reading at the secondary level: Recommendations for literacy practices and remaining questions.* New York: Guilford Press.

Regional Educational Laboratory Southeast. (2019). Infographic: Sources of educational research. Retrieved from *https://ies.ed.gov/ncee/edlabs/infographics/pdf/REL_SE_Sources_of_Educational_Research.pdf.*

Rettig, M. D., & Canady, M. L. (2013). *Scheduling strategies for middle schools.* New York: Routledge.

Richardson, J. (2009). *The next step in guided reading: Focused assessments and targeted lessons for helping every student become a better reader.* New York: Scholastic.

Richardson, J. (2016). *The guided reading teachers' companion: Prompts, discussion starters and teaching points.* New York: Scholastic.

Rickert, D. (2017). Learning stations in secondary ELA classrooms. Retrieved from *http://davidrickert.com/2017/06/06/learning-stations-secondary-ela-classrooms.*

Risko, V., & Vogt, M. E. (2016). *Professional learning in action: An inquiry approach for teachers of literacy.* New York: Teachers College Press.

Rivkin, S. G., Hanushek, E. A., & Kain, J. F. (2005). Teachers, schools and academic achievement. *Econometrica, 3*(2), 417–458.

Robb, L. (2014). *Vocabulary is comprehension, grades 4–8.* Thousand Oaks, CA: Corwin Press.

Robbins, P. (1991). *How to implement a peer coaching program.* Washington, DC: Association for Supervision and Curriculum Development.

Rohlwing, R. L., & Spelman, M. (2014). Characteristics of adult learning: Implications for the design and implementation of professional development programs. In L. E. Martin, S. Kragler, D. J. Quatroche, & K. L. Bauserman (Eds.), *Handbook of professional development in education: Successful models and practices, PreK–12* (pp. 231–245). New York: Guilford Press.

Rothstein, A. L. (2019). *Creating winning grant proposals: A step-by-step guide.* New York: Guilford Press.

Sackor, S. (2001). *Three-to-one tutoring: Strategies to enhance the reading comprehension of poor intermediate readers.* Unpublished doctoral dissertation, University of Pittsburgh, Pittsburgh, PA.

Sailors, M., & Price, L. (2015). Support for the Improvement of Practices through Intensive Coaching (SIPIC): A model of coaching for improving reading instruction and reading achievement. *Teaching and Teacher Education, 45,* 115–127.

Salas, R. (2017). Disrupting equilibrium: Working for equity and social justice in education for English Learners. *International Journal of Multicultural Education, 19*(1), 7–23.

Salas, R. (2019, March 29). What all educators should know: The laws that provide undocumented, unaccompanied minors the right to an education in the United States (Commentary). *Teachers College Record.* Retrieved from *www.tcrecord.org/Content.asp?ContentId=22709.*

Salinger, T., Zmach, C., Thomsen, K., & Lefsky, E. (2008, December). *Examining the impact of adolescent literacy interventions.* Paper presented at the National Reading Conference, Orlando, FL.

Samuels, C. A. (2009). High schools try out RTI. *Education Week, 28*(19), 20–22.

Samuels, C. A. (2016). What are multitiered systems of supports? *Education Week, 36*(15), 8–9.

Scanlon, D. M., Anderson, K. L., & Sweeney, J. M. (2017). *Early intervention for reading difficulties: The interactive strategies approach* (2nd ed.). New York: Guilford Press.

Scanlon, D. M., Goatley, V., & Spring, K. (2020). Literacy leadership in special education. In A. Swan Dagen & R. M. Bean (Eds.), *Best practices of literacy leaders: Keys to school improvement* (2nd ed., pp. 281–303). New York: Guilford Press.

Sendak, M. (1988). *Where the wild things are.* New York: Harper & Row.

Shaler Area Education Association. (1986). Where have all the children gone? *Scanner, 13*(2), 3.

Shanahan, T., & Shanahan, C. (2012a). Teaching disciplinary literacy to adolescents: Rethinking content-area literacy. In J. Ippolito, J. I. Steele, & J. F. Samson (Eds.), *Adolescent literacy* (pp. 40–59). Cambridge, MA: Harvard Education Press.

Shanahan, T., & Shanahan, C. (2012b). What is disciplinary literacy and why does it matter? *Topics in Language Disorders, 32*(1), 7–18.

Shaywitz, S. (2003). *Overcoming dyslexia: A new and complete science-based program for reading problems at any level.* New York: Knopf.

Shearer, B. A., Carr, D. A., & Vogt. M. (2018). *Reading specialists and literacy coaches in the real world.* Long Grove, IL: Waveland Press.

Sheldon, S. B. (2007). Improving student attendance with school, family, and community partnerships. *Journal of Educational Research, 100*(5), 267–275.

Skiffington, S., Washburn, S., & Elliott, K. (2011). Instructional coaching: Helping preschool teachers reach their full potential. *Young Children, 66*(3), 12–19.

Slavin, R. E. (1987). Making Chapter 1 make a difference. *Phi Delta Kappan, 69*(2), 110–119.

Slavin, R. E., Madden, N. A., Dolan, L. J., & Wasik, B. A. (1996). *Every child, every school: Success for all.* Thousand Oaks, CA: Corwin Press.

Sliger, B. (2009). *Grant writing for teachers and administrators.* Durham, CT: Strategic Book Group.

Smoker, M. (2011). *Focus: Elevating the essentials to radically improve student learning.* Alexandria, VA: Association for Supervision and Curriculum Development.

Smoker, M. (2018). *Focus: Elevating the essentials to radically improve students learning* (2nd ed.). Alexandria, VA: Association for Supervision and Curriculum Development.

Snow, C., Burns, M. S., & Griffin, P. (Eds.). (1998). *Preventing reading difficulties in young children.* Washington, DC: National Research Council.

Sparks, D., & Loucks-Horsley, S. (1990). Models of self-development. In R. Houston (Ed.), *Handbook of research on teacher education* (pp. 234–250). New York: Macmillan.

Spear-Swerling, L. (2019). Structured literacy and typical literacy practices: Understanding differences to create instructional opportunities. *Teaching Exceptional Children, 51*(3), 202–211.

Spillane, J. P. (2005). Distributed leadership. *Educational Forum, 69*(2), 143–150.

Spillane, J. P. (2015). Leadership and learning: Conceptualizing relations between school administrative practice and instructional practice. *Societies, 5,* 277–294.

Stanier, M. B. (2016). *The coaching habit: Say less, ask more and change the way you lead forever.* Toronto, ON, Canada: Box of Crayons Press.

Stauffer, R. G. (1967). Change, BUT—. *The Reading Teacher, 20*(6), 474–499.

Steinbacher-Reed, C., & Powers, E. (2011/2012). Coaching without a coach. *Educational Leadership, 69*(4), 68–72.

Stigler, J. W., & Hiebert, J. (1999). *The teaching gap: Best ideas from the world's teachers for improving education in the classroom.* New York: Free Press.

Supovitz, J., Sirinides, P., & May, H. (2010). How principals and peers influence teaching and learning. *Educational Administration Quarterly, 46*(1), 31–56.

Swan Dagen, A., & Bean, R. M. (2007). Providing professional development to improve literacy achievement: Tinkering or transforming? *Pennsylvania Reads, 8*(1), 27–40.

Swan Dagen, A., & Bean, R. M. (2014). High-quality, research-based professional development: An essential for enhancing high-quality teaching. In L. E. Martin, S. Kragler, D. J. Quatroche, & K. I. Bauserman (Eds.), *Handbook of professional development in education: Successful models and practices, PreK–12* (pp. 42–63). New York: Guilford Press.

Swan Dagen, A., & Bean, R. M. (2020). Schools as places of learning: The powerful role of literacy leaders. In A. Swan Dagen & R. M. Bean (Eds.), *Best practices of literacy leaders: Keys to school improvement* (2nd ed., pp. 411–434). New York: Guilford Press.

Sweeney, D. (2010). *Student-centered coaching: A guide for K–8 coaches and principals.* Thousand Oaks, CA: Corwin Press.

Taylor, B. M., Pearson, P. D., & Rodriguez, M. C. (2005). The CIERA school change framework: An evidence-based approach to professional development and school reading improvement. *Reading Research Quarterly, 40*(1), 40–69.

Taylor, B. M., Pressley, M., & Pearson, P. D. (2002). Research-supported characteristics of teachers and schools that promote reading achievement. In B. M. Taylor & M. Pearson (Eds.), *Teaching reading: Effective schools, accomplished teachers* (pp. 361–374). Mahwah, NJ: Erlbaum.

Teemant, A. (2014). A mixed-methods investigation of instructional coaching for teachers of diverse learners. *Urban Education, 49,* 574–604.

Thibodeau, G. M. (2008). A content literacy collaborative study group: High school teachers take charge of their professional learning. *Journal of Adolescent and Adult Literacy, 52*(1), 54–84.

Thomas, K. L. (2018). Building literacy environments to motivate African American boys to read. *The Reading Teacher, 72*(6), 761–765.

Tierney, R. J., Johnston, P., Moore, D. W., & Valencia, S. W. (2000). Snippets: How will literacy be assessed in the next millennium? *Reading Research Quarterly, 35*(4), 244–250.

Toll, C. A. (2005). *The literacy coach's survival guide: Essential questions and practical answers*. Newark, DE: International Reading Association.

Toll, C. A. (2006). *Lenses on literacy coaching: Conceptualizations, functions, and outcomes*. Norwood, MA: Christopher-Gordon.

Toll, C. A. (2018). *Educational coaching: A partnership for problem solving*. Alexandria, VA: Association for Supervision and Curriculum Development.

Torgeson, J. K., & Miller, D. H. (2009). *Assessments to guide adolescent literacy instruction*. Portsmouth, NH: RMC Research Corporation, Center on Instruction.

Tschannen-Moran, B., & Tschannen-Moran, M. (2011). The coach and the evaluator. *Educational Leadership, 69*(2), 10–16.

United States Agency for International Development. (2014, February). *The power of coaching: Improving early grade reading instruction in developing countries*. Washington, DC: Author. Retrieved from *http://pdf.usaid.gov/pdf_docs/pa00jv67.pdf.*

University of Texas at Austin. (2005). Introduction to the 3-tier reading model (4th ed.). Retrieved from *https://buildingrti.utexas.org/sites/default/files/booklets/Intro3TierModel_4ed.pdf.*

U.S. Department of Education. (2002). *No Child Left Behind: A desktop reference*. Washington, DC: Office of Elementary and Secondary Education. Retrieved from *www.ed.gov/admins/lead/account/nclbreference/page_pg5.html#i-b1.*

U.S. Department of Education. (2015). *Every Student Succeeds Act: ESSA consolidated state plans*. Washington, DC: Author. Retrieved from *www2.ed.gov/policy/elsec/leg/essa/index.html.*

U.S. Department of Education, IES/National Center for Education Statistics. (2018, April). *English language learners in public schools*. Washington DC: Author. Retrieved from *https://nces.ed.gov/programs/coe/indicator_cgf.asp.*

U.S. Department of Education, National Center for Educational Statistics. (2019a, February). Status and trends in the education of racial and ethnic groups: Indicator 6 elementary and secondary enrollment. Retrieved from *https://nces.ed.gov/programs/raceindicators/indicator_rbb.asp.*

U.S. Department of Education, National Center for Educational Statistics. (2019b, May). Characteristics of children's families. Retrieved from *https://nces.ed.gov/programs/coe/indicator_cce.asp.*

USAFacts. (2020, April). More than 9 million children lack Internet access at home for online learning. Retrieved from *https://usafacts.org/articles/internet-access-students-at-home.*

Vescio, V., Ross, D., & Adams, A. (2008). A review of research on the impact of professional learning communities on teaching practice and student learning. *Teaching and Teacher Education, 24*(1), 80–91.

Walp, T. P., & Walmsley, S. A. (1989). Instructional and philosophical congruence: Neglected aspects of coordination. *The Reading Teacher, 42*(6), 364–368.

Walpole, S., & Beauchat, K. A. (2008, June 2). *Facilitating teacher study groups.* Denver, CO: Literacy Coaching Clearinghouse.

Walpole, S., & McKenna, M. (2017). *How to plan differentiated reading instruction: Resources for grades K–3* (2nd ed.). New York: Guilford Press.

Walpole, S., & Vitale, M. N. (2020). PreK–12 literacy programs: Moving from curriculum to collaboration to collective efficacy. In A. Swan Dagen & R. M. Bean (Eds.), *Best practices of literacy leaders: Keys to school improvement* (2nd ed., pp. 113–132). New York: Guilford Press.

Wanless, S. B., Patton, C. S., Rimm-Kaufman, S. E., & Deutsch, N. L. (2013). Setting-level influences on implementation of the responsive classroom approach. *Prevention Science, 14*(1), 40–51.

Wasik, B. A. (1998). Volunteer tutoring programs in reading: A review. *Reading Research Quarterly, 33,* 266–292.

Wasik, B. A., & Slavin, R. E. (1993). Preventing early reading failure with one-to-one tutoring: A review of five programs. *Reading Research Quarterly, 28*(2), 178–200.

Wei, R. C., Darling-Hammond, L., & Adamson, F. (2010). *Professional development in the United States: Trends and challenges.* Dallas, TX: National Staff Development Council.

Wilcox, K. C., Lawson, H. A., & Angelis, J. (2017). *Innovation in odds-beating schools: Exemplars for getting better at getting better.* Lanham, MD: Rowman & Littlefield.

Williams, S. S., & Williams, J. W. (2014). Workplace wisdom: What educators can learn from the business world. *Journal of Staff Development, 35*(3), 10–12, 14–20.

Williamson, D. (May, 2018). Why leadership today is like playing jazz. Retrieved from *www.theglobeandmail.com/report-on-business/careers/leadership-lab/why-leadership-today-is-like-playing-jazz/article15222682.*

Willink, J. (2019). *Leadership strategy and tactics.* New York: St. Martin's Press.

Willis, A. I. (2019). Race, response to intervention, and reading research. *Journal of Literacy Research, 5*(4), 394–419.

Wilson, B. A. (1996). *Wilson reading system.* Millbury, MA: Wilson Language Training.

Wixson, K. K., & Dutro, E. (1999). Standards for primary-grade reading: An analysis of state frameworks. *Elementary School Journal, 100*(2), 89–110.

Wood, D. (2007). Teachers' learning communities: Catalyst for change or a new infrastructure for the status quo? *Teachers College Record, 109*(3), 699–739.

Worthy, J., Svrcek, N., Daly-Lesch, A., & Tily, S. (2018). "We know for a fact": Dyslexia interventionists and the power of authoritative discourse. *Journal of Literacy Research, 50*(3), 359–382.

Zigmond, N., & Bean, R. M. (2008). *External evaluation of Reading First in Pennsylvania.* Annual report, University of Pittsburgh, Pittsburgh, PA.

Zygouris-Coe, V., Yao, Y., Tao, Y., Hahs-Vaugh, D., & Baumbach, D. (2004). Qualitative evaluation of facilitator's contributions to online professional development. Retrieved from *eric.ed.gov/fulltext/ED485072.pdf.*

Index

Note. *f* or *t* following a page number indicates a figure or a table.